Contents

Characteristics of and Strategies for Teaching Students with Mild Disabilities

Martin Henley
Westfield State College

Roberta S. Ramsey
Albany State College

Robert Algozzine
University of North Carolina

Allyn and Bacon
Boston • London • Toronto • Sydney • Tokyo • Singapore

Series Editor: Ray Short
Series Editorial Assistant: Christine Shaw
Production Administrator: Susan McIntyre
Editorial-Production Service: Ruttle, Shaw and Wetherill, Inc.
Manufacturing Buyer: Louise Richardson
Cover Administrator: Suzanne Harbison

Copyright © 1993 by Allyn & Bacon
A Division of Simon & Schuster, Inc.
160 Gould Street
Needham Heights, Massachusetts 02194

Library of Congress Cataloging-in-Publication Data

Henley, Martin. 1943–
    Characteristics of and strategies for teaching students with mild
disabilities/Martin Henley, Roberta S. Ramsey, Robert Algozzine.
        p.   cm.
    Includes bibliographical references and indexes.
    ISBN 0-205-145752
    1. Learning disabled—United States. 2. Mainstreaming in
education—United States. 3. Behavior modification—United States.
I. Ramsey, Roberta S.   II. Algozzine, Robert.   III. Title.
LC4705.H46 1993
371.9—dc20   92-28682
                                                                   CIP

Printed in the United States of America

10 9 8 7 6 5 4 3 2 1   97 96 95 94 93 92

For our children—Margaret, Bobby, Kathryn, Michael, Randy, and Carl

Preface

This book is written for undergraduate and graduate students who are being trained to teach students with behavior disorders, mild mental retardation, and learning disabilities. These mild disabilities impede students' school performance so that special education services are necessary. Due to the mild nature of their learning problems, most of these students spend the major portion of their days in regular classrooms. This means that the responsibility for educating students with mild disabilities is shared by general and special educators; thus, this book is intended for future teachers in both general and special education.

This type of book is long overdue. No other text on the market provides an in-depth description and analysis of issues relating to the education of students with mild disabilities. Our purpose is to provide, in a single volume, a comprehensive overview of educational practices that influence the identification, placement, and teaching of these students who constitute the largest subgroup of students with special needs. Approximately 2.5 million school-aged children receive special education services because they have been identified as having either a learning disability, a behavior disorder, or mild mental retardation. By all accounts, the incidence of these school-based learning problems continues to increase each year.

The book contains three major parts. The first part addresses the foundations of special education for students with mild disabilities. Chapter 1 outlines the roots of special education; compares general and special education; and describes the purpose of special education, eligibility and placement procedures, and types of special education programs.

Presently there is much discussion in professional circles about the use and misuse of labels to categorize students so they can receive special education services. Chapter 2, an overview of learners with mild disabilities, explains how these students are more similar than different. It outlines noncategorical and categorical approaches. Chapter 2 describes common causes of mild disabilities, discusses shared characteristics of these students, and outlines procedures for referring, evaluating and placing students in special education programs.

The second part of this book provides an in-depth analysis of each category of mild disabilities: mild mental retardation, behavior disorders, and learning disabilities. Each chapter includes historical origins, definitional concerns, prevalence estimates, causes, and functional abilities in academic achievement, cognition, language, social adaptation, and mental processing. Although the emphasis is on noncategorical educational programming, this information explains how typologies of disabilities influence identification procedures, placement decisions, educational intervention, and research practices. Categorical typologies are particularly useful in establishing the existence of a mild disability.

Part III discusses mainstreaming, learning and teaching, behavior management, and partnerships with parents. This part approaches teaching students with mild disabilities from a noncategorical perspective, based on the premise that quality instruction works for all students regardless of labels used to secure special education services. Each chapter explains research-based educational interventions that are useful in both regular and special education classrooms. This section describes various mainstreaming programs and guidelines for implementing them. We analyze the Regular Education Initiative and discuss recommendations for enhancing collaboration between special and regular educators.

The chapter on learning and teaching examines the experience of schooling and highlights learner traits, classroom organization, and strategies for teaching students with mild disabilities. The chapter on behavior management provides novice teachers with an array of effective regular and special education classroom management practices. Emphasis is on teacher actions that prevent discipline problems and on such classroom management practices as behavior modification, life space interviewing, and prosocial curriculums. The final chapter describes the importance of parent-school cooperation. It discusses model programs and gives an overview of issues that surface when a family discovers that their child has a mild disability.

Advance organizers state competencies that students will acquire from each chapter. Tables, figures, and examples illustrate information throughout. In this textbook we have attempted to achieve a writing style that is readable without sacrificing content. Many issues relating to the education of students with mild disabilities require thoughtful analysis. As in most educational issues, the "right" answer is elusive. Our goal is to present an honest and straightforward picture of the issues that confront teachers and parents as they strive to educate students with mild disabilities.

We owe sincere thanks to our families, who supported our months of research and writing. We also are grateful to our undergraduate and graduate students who, in their quest for knowledge, have pushed us to expand our awareness. Answering their questions and providing the information they needed to be the best possible teachers of students with mild disabilities helped to establish the content and organization of this book.

We are grateful to the many professionals who cared enough about our work to review manuscripts and provide helpful suggestions. Our reviewers, Dr. Andrew Brulle, Northern Illinois University, and Dr. Mark Posluszney, SUNY Buffalo, provided many valuable insights and suggestions. Colleagues were no less helpful. Special recognition is owed to the expertise shared by Dr. Judy Smith-Davis, editor of *Counterpoint*, Dr. Bill Wolking, University of Florida, and Dr. Robert Martin, Westfield State College. Two graduate assistants—Robin Morse and Sharon Underwood—worked many long hours to help complete our manuscript.

When three collaborative writers use different word processing systems every imaginable glitch becomes a reality. Without the patient help of Ken Haar and Rich Emmings from the Westfield State College Computer Center, our manuscript could never have taken shape. We especially owe our appreciation to that outstanding educator Rudy Hebert, assistant professor of computer science, Westfield State College, Division of Continuing Education. More than once, his electronic wizardry saved entire chapters from disappearing into the void of the blank screen.

We are grateful to Lois Creech, our artist from Albany, Georgia, who added a touch of humor to our otherwise serious topic. The continued support of special education practitioners Kathie Rigsby, Larry Aultman, and Jim Whiting of the Dougherty County Public Schools in Albany, Georgia, was appreciated and provided needed motivation when the going was rough.

Our editor, Ray Short, never lost faith in this project. His support and understanding braced us against the many difficulties we encountered in organizing, writing, and editing this text. Finally we want to thank JoEllen Caffrey, editorial assistant, for her warm words of encouragement. Her cheerful countenance was a constant reminder that yes, indeed, this book could be completed.

Chapter 1

Foundations of Special Education for Students with Mild Disabilities

Advance Organizer

When you complete this chapter you will be able to:

1. Explain the historical roots of general and special education.
2. Discuss how the diversity of the school population influences educational policy.
3. Describe how perspectives on handicappism influence opportunities for individuals with disabilities.
4. Indicate significant legislation and judicial decisions that have advanced the rights of individuals with disabilities.
5. Describe who is eligible for special education services.
6. Describe students with mild disabilities.
7. Compare the advantages and disadvantages of labeling students by placing them in categories of disabilities.
8. Identify key components of the Individuals with Disabilities Education Act.
9. Explain the purpose and elements of an individual education program.
10. Explain least restrictive environment and how this mandate influences types of special education placements.
11. Compare general and special education.

This book is for people who teach students with behavior disorders, learning disabilities, or mild mental retardation. As you learn about these students, you will undoubtedly have questions about them. For example, early in the semester our students ask such questions as: What is a learning disability? What does behavior disordered mean? What causes mild mental retardation? Why are students with these conditions called 'mildly disabled'? Why do they receive special education and how can I effectively teach students with mild disabilities?

Within this book you will find the answers to these questions and more. You will discover commonalities among students with mild disabilities and differences between these students and students without disabilities. A chapter on mainstreaming will provide ideas for teaching students with mild disabilities in the regular classroom. Chapters on learning and teaching and on behavior management give practical guidelines for classroom instruction and discipline. One of the most overlooked aspects of teaching is parent involvement. Our chapter on working with families offers suggestions for increasing cooperation between home and school. Each chapter is based on current research and written in a style we hope you will find "user friendly."

In chapter one, the foundations of special education for students with mild disabilities, we will address questions such as: What is special education? Why is special education necessary? Who receives special education services? Before we answer these questions, we want to introduce you to some students.

Jake, Mary, Phillip

Jake always seems to be one step behind the other students in his seventh-grade class. Despite the slowness that is a part of Jake's performance and social development, his teacher enjoys having him in class. Because Jake is talkative with a good sense of humor, many of his schoolmates enjoy helping him. Jake's teacher likes teaching him because he responds favorably to efforts to help him develop new skills. Jake's classroom performance is similar to students with mild mental retardation.

Jake's class contains a mixture of students who are easy to teach and students who are hard to teach. Mary is one of the difficult kids. When she was younger she was diagnosed as "hyperactive," and she was put on medication to control her behavior. She comes from a home where both parents work hard to maintain a comfortable lifestyle. There is a lot of pressure put on Mary to succeed. Both of her parents are upwardly mobile professionals who have little time for parenting. Mary does not trust adults and often takes her anger out on her classmates. When she is not physically disrupting the classroom, Mary is socially withdrawn, isolated, and unhappy. Mary's teacher believes she has a behavior disorder and emotional problems.

Phillip is also difficult to teach—not because of what he does, but because of what he does not do. Phillip does not read or write as well as his seventh-grade classmates. He has never done well in reading, but his scores on ability tests and tests of achievement in other areas (e.g., mathematics) have always been average when compared to his peers. Now that Phillip is in junior high school, his difficulties are particularly troublesome. He is expected to read and complete homework assignments in English, history, science, psychology, and economics. Phillip appears to have a learning disability. Each of these students, Jake, Mary, and Phillip, are difficult to teach. They are at-risk of failing in school, and they are potential school dropouts. Jake, Mary, and Phillip have mild disabilities that are interfering with their progress in the regular classroom.

Every classroom contains students like Jake, Mary, and Phillip. Helping students with learning problems is part of the motivation that stimulates many to become teachers. As one experienced teacher put it, "Some teachers like the underdog." The purpose of special education is to help students like Jake, Mary, and Phillip achieve success in school. Special educators and regular classroom teachers want to see all students stay in school, graduate, and succeed in life; but because of differences between the two systems of education, we sometimes work at cross-purposes. When special and regular educators communicate and share responsibility for educating students with special needs, everybody benefits.

The Roots of Special Education

Origins of the United States' national education system date from the colonial days. Early schools educated a select, limited segment of the population—white, male children of upper class families (Smith, Price, & Marsh, 1986). Before 1815, schools serving this small proportion of school-aged youth were primarily church sponsored.

Public support of schools by local taxation began during the first half of the nineteenth century. Children previously excluded from schooling—middle class, poor, female, or culturally different—were included. During the mid-nineteenth century, states began enacting compulsory education laws (i.e., Rhode Island in 1840, Massachusetts in 1852). A change in the values and economic thinking of our society was reflected by this Common School Movement.

These early common schools educated students of all ages in the same classroom. In the one-room schoolhouse, students of different ages, different abilities, and different backgrounds learned side by side. Horace Mann, the architect of public education, believed universal education was the great equalizer. Cremin (1961) characterized this early vision.

Mann's school would be common, not as a school for the common people—for example, the nineteenth-century Prussian Volksschule—*but rather as a school common to all people. It would be open to all, provided by the state and the local community as part of the birthright of every child. It would be for rich and poor alike, not only free but as good as any private institution. It would be nonsectarian, receiving children of all creeds, classes, and backgrounds. (p.10)*

Mann's humanitarian ideal began to take hold, and by 1860 a majority of the states established public school systems. Throughout this period of rapid growth,

Mann advised that instruction be adapted to meet the needs of children who differed in temperament, ability, and interests.

As the United States grew, the one-room schoolhouse was replaced by graded elementary, middle, and high schools. Explicit academic requirements were established for each grade level of the common public school. Students were taught a specific curriculum, and that curriculum was organized into graded units. Educators believed grouping students by age would make the task of teaching easier (Sarason & Doris, 1979; Ysseldyke & Algozzine, 1982). Achievement was determined by how well children learned the predetermined, graded curriculum. This curriculum-centered characteristic of the new schools made it difficult for many children to keep pace (Smith, Price, & Marsh, 1986; Ysseldyke & Algozzine, 1984).

Immigration and compulsory school attendance broadened the school-aged population to a larger, more variant membership. With the influx of immigrants during the early twentieth century, cultural and ethnic differences in students created a mismatch between teacher expectations and student performance. Some children adapted to school and learned; others dropped out. Many children worked in factories; others took to the streets. Few of the absent students were missed. Little concern was shown for children with disabilities and what we now refer to as at-risk youth.

The influence of social reformers, such as Jane Addams, encouraged some cities to establish alternative instructional programs for "special cases." The superintendent of the Baltimore schools wrote, "Before the attendance laws were effectively enforced there were as many of these special cases in the community as there is now; few of them, however, remained long enough in school to attract serious attention or to hinder the instruction of the more tractable and capable" (Van Sickle, 1908–1909, 102). Early public educational programs offered two choices. Students either received and profited from instruction in lock-step, curriculum-centered classes, or they were placed in a special class. Many administrators believed that these first special education programs were proper preparation for institutionalization. In a speech to the National Education Association, E.R. Johnstone stated that the special education class "must become a clearing-house."

> *To it will be sent the slightly blind and partially deaf, but also incorrigibles, the mental deficients, and the cripples. . . . The only thing to do is to give them the best of care and training possible. Keep them in the special classes until they become too old for further care in school, and then they must be sent to the institutions for safety (Johnstone, 1908, 1115).*

A few early special programs were set up for children with specific disabilities such as deafness or blindness. However, many early public school special classes were repositories for diverse youngsters who did not fit into the regular classroom. In 1899, Elizabeth Farrell described students in her first special education class in New York City.

> *The first class was made up of the odds and ends of a large school. There were the over-age children, the so-called naughty children, and the dull, and stupid children. They were taken from any and every school grade. The ages ranged from eight to sixteen years. They were the children who could not get along in school. They were typical of a large number of children who even today are forced directly or indirectly out of school; they were the children who were interested in street life; many of them earned a good deal of money in one way or another. While some of them had been in trouble with the police, as a class they could not be characterized as criminal. They had varied interests but the school, as they found it, had little or nothing for them . (Farrell, 1908, 297)*

From the first decades of the twentieth century until the mid-1970s, students who were different—the odds and ends—were either ignored, placed in isolated special classes, or transferred to state institutions. In Pennsylvania, for instance, legislation provided for the exclusion of specific children from school. Children evaluated as uneducable because of below-average IQ scores were assigned to the Department of Public Welfare for training in state-run institutions. Most notable about the process of classifying and rejecting students who didn't fit the standard public school curriculum was the lack of due process in educational decisions.

Diversity in the Schools

In 1970, the Task Force of Children Out of School studied the Boston Public School System. The Task Force report—*The Way We Go to School: The Exclusion of Children in Boston*—found over ten thousand students excluded from public school classrooms because they didn't match school standards for the normal student. Patricia Reilly, age sixteen, was told to leave school because she was pregnant. Kathy Fitzgerald, age nine, was excluded from public school because she had a seizure disorder (i.e., epilepsy). Richard, eleven years old, was placed in a special class for the retarded because he was emotionally disturbed, and no other program was available. These children were denied the right to an appropriate education because they did not fit into the system. In 1974, Congress estimated that over a million school-aged youngsters were denied a proper education in America's schools because they were different in some way.

How could a nation based on equal opportunity for all its citizens support such discriminatory practices towards children? The answer is found in attitudes towards people who are different. Prejudice, like creeping shadows, can take many forms. The public school system mirrors our society. Schools reflect the attitudes and prejudices of teachers, administrators, and parents. Students who are different often have special needs, and those special needs have been used as a rationale to exclude them from the mainstream of life in American schools.

Education once intended for a small, elite sector of the population is now mandated for all children. During the past century, the curriculum-centered format of public schools has remained static while the needs of students have changed significantly. School dropouts, discipline problems, low achievement, and increased referrals to special education are a concern to educators and the public at large. Diversity of students, simply defined as the condition of being different, is at odds with a system of education that requires conformity and assimilation of an unyielding curriculum.

Smith-Davis (1989) identified some important events and acts of legislation that increased diversity in United States' education. The *Brown v. Topeka Board of Education* decision in 1954 radically altered the national school population. This landmark case, acted upon by the U.S. Supreme Court, decreed that segregated but equal school facilities for black and white school children were discriminatory and unconstitutional. *Brown v. Topeka Board of Education* reversed a prior decision rendered in *Plessy v. Ferguson* in 1894 that made separate schools based on racial lines legal.

The Civil Rights Act of 1964 gave support to advocates who pushed for the inclusion of students with disabling conditions in public schools (Smith-Davis, 1989a, b; Smith, Price & Marsh, 1986; Ysseldyke & Algozzine, 1990). Mainstreaming, a term used to promote the integration of school-aged youth with disabilities into classrooms with nondisabled peers, followed on the heels of successful efforts to deinstitutionalize programs for adults and children with disabilities. Placement of youth and adults with moderate and severe disabilities within community settings dramatized their capability to live normal lives. These changes diversified the student population in the nation's schools and emphasized the need for schools to accommodate children with special learning needs (Ysseldyke, Algozzine, & Thurlow, 1992). Yet public school practices towards students with disabilities have been slow to come. For instance, the steady increase each year in youngsters identified as mildly disabled and placed in special programs is testimony to the intractability of a system of education that, when unsuccessful, looks first to blame the student.

Handicappism

Advocates for individuals with disabilities use the word "handicappism" to refer to the perception that a person is incompetent because of a physical or psychological impairment. When asked about their most difficult adjustments, adults with disabilities invariably comment about dealing with the prejudices of the population. For example, friends and neighbors may refer to Elise Jones, who has a visual impairment, as "poor, blind Elise!" Condescending remarks about individuals with disabilities may be masked as sympathy, but the message is a clear illustration of handicappism. Elise's visual impairment is only a part of her individuality, not the sum total of what Elise is as a person.

Sooner or later, most of us will experience a disability. Old age, injuries, or illness are inescapable aspects of the human condition. While the idea that at some point in your life you will be disabled might seem remote, the simple truth is we are not talking about infrequent or isolated cases. The number of United States' citizens with disabilities is equal to the combined population of New York City, Los Angeles, Chicago, and Miami.

Despite the hurdles of handicappism, examples of magnificent accomplishments by individuals with disabilities abound. Stephen W. Hawking is incapacitated by motor neuron disease. He cannot walk, dress, or feed himself. He is confined to a wheelchair, and he is unable to verbally communicate the most elementary idea. Yet in 1974, Stephen W. Hawking was invested as a fellow in the Royal Society, one of the oldest and most prestigious scholarly societies. Hawking is a brilliant physicist. He is the preeminent expert on black holes in space, and his book, *A Brief History of Time* (1988), topped the *New York Times* best seller list.

Persons with disabilities are individuals first and disabled second. The label is not the person. Franklin D. Roosevelt guided the United States through the Second World War from the vantage point of a wheelchair. Einstein was considered too slow to attend school with his peers. Nelson Rockefeller and Thomas Edison had learning disabilities. These extraordinary people were not limited by their disabilities. Throughout this book, we highlight the individual first and the disability second by our phrasing "student with a disability." We do this because language shapes thought. Our persistent theme is that students with mild disabilities are more like their peers than different. This is the most important lesson you can learn from reading this book. Your language, your expectations, and your actions when you teach students with mild disabilities will determine their success or failure. Remember a disability is a problem that can be overcome; don't handicap your students by limiting your expectations for their personal growth.

Litigation

Prior to the early 1970s, handicappism, the notion that individuals with disabilities were severely limited in their ability to learn, was the predominant educational perspective. Most notable about this view was the lack of due process afforded students as educators either excluded them from school or placed them in dead-end special classes. Due process is a constitutional right guaranteed by the Fourteenth Amendment. During the 1970s, concern about the legal rights of students with special needs spurred several significant class action suits that challenged due process procedures in school evaluation and placement practices. A class action suit is litigation on behalf of a class or group of individuals. For example, when a small group of students who were classed as mentally retarded won a class action suit, all other students with mental retardation within the court's jurisdiction benefitted.

In *Diana v. California State Board of Education* (1970), the issue of Mexican-American student overrepresentation in special classes for the mildly retarded

---

HIGHLIGHT 1–1 Francis

Francis enjoyed going out to eat with his friends. However, he often encountered difficulties because few restaurants were accessible to his wheelchair. Curbs, narrow doors, stairs, and small public restrooms were all obstacles for Francis. One evening Francis and his friends were ordering dinner. When the waitress came to Francis, she asked one of his friends, "What would he like to eat?" The waitress assumed that because Francis was in a wheelchair he was incapable of ordering his own dinner! Just as physical obstacles handicapped Francis's ability to live a normal life, so did stereotypes by well-meaning but thoughtless people. A disability may be born, but society handicaps.

---

was addressed. The plaintiffs were nine children who came from homes where Spanish was the primary language. The class action suit alleged that Mexican-American students had been improperly categorized as mildly retarded on the basis of invalid IQ testing. In a consent agreement, the opposing parties agreed that school children should be tested in their native language. This case laid the groundwork for future lawsuits based on cultural bias in educational evaluations.

The following year, 1971, fourteen families sued the State of Pennsylvania on the basis that their children with mental retardation were denied equal access to a public education. This case, *Pennsylvania Association for Retarded Children (PARC) v. Commonwealth of Pennsylvania* was prompted by the state policy of denying a public education to youngsters with mental retardation. During the legal proceedings, parents described their futile attempts to fight a system that arbitrarily and callously excluded their children from school.

Nancy Beth Bowman was expelled from kindergarten because she wasn't toilet trained. The 15-year-old daughter of Leonard Kalish was never allowed to enroll in school. It cost him $40,000 to have her educated in private schools. The parents of David Tupi said their son was expelled from school without notice. One morning the school bus just stopped coming to pick him up. The three-judge panel, in a consent decree, ruled that the state could not predetermine educability. In their decision the judges stated that Pennsylvania must:

1. Admit all children with mental retardation into public school.
2. Place students with mental retardation in regular classrooms when possible.
3. Make all school records accessible to parents.
4. Provide preschool programs for children with mental retardation when such programs were available to nondisabled children.
5. Precede all placement decisions with a hearing to allow parental participation and consent.

The PARC decision emphasized the due process rights of parents to review and challenge placement decisions regarding their children.

In *Mills v. the Board of Education of the District of Columbia* (1972), litigants challenged the exclusion of children identified as mentally retarded, emotionally disturbed, learning disabled, visually impaired, hearing impaired, and physically disabled from Washington, D.C. schools. As in the PARC case, Mills demonstrated the unconstitutionality of school exclusion procedures. Both the PARC and Mills "right to education" cases highlighted the right of students with disabilities to due process in educational decisions.

By 1973 thirty-one similar court cases comprised a groundswell of political activism on behalf of students with disabilities (Taylor & Searl, 1987). It was clear to Congress that schools could no longer be allowed to violate the Fourteenth Amendment rights of students with disabilities. The Fourteenth Amendment states that "no state shall make or enforce any law which shall abridge the privileges or immunities of citizens of the United States; nor shall any state deprive any person of life, liberty, or property without due process of law."

The Education for All Handicapped Children Act (P.L. 94-142)
The culmination of many years of struggle on behalf of children with disabilities occurred on November 29, 1975, when President Ford signed into law Public Law 94-142, The Education for All Handicapped Children Act. This landmark federal legislation mandates a free and appropriate education for all students with disabilities aged three to twenty-one. The Education for All Handicapped Children Act has been called the "first compulsory special education law," and much of what happens in special education classes today is a direct response to the provisions embodied in it (Ysseldyke & Algozzine, 1984). The Education for All Handicapped Children Act, recently reaffirmed by the passage of the Individuals with Disabilities Education Act, provides students and their families with specific rights.

By law, school personnel must prepare an **individualized education program** for every student enrolled in a formal special education program. This means that teachers must have clearly documented plans for how instructional time in special education will be used. A written document, the individual education plan (IEP), specifies long-range goals and short-term objectives for the student, the kinds of services to be provided, the personnel who will deliver the services, and a plan for evaluating the student's progress.

By law, students with disabilities and their families are entitled to **protection in evaluation** activities that are part of the educational experience. This means that students cannot be placed in special programs in an arbitrary and capricious manner. Students with disabilities and their families are entitled to a multidisciplinary evaluation. Each evaluation must be a team effort comprising the expertise of any school professional who can help decipher the needs of a student with a disability. Occupational therapists, school psychologists, special education teachers, regular classroom teachers and speech clinicians are a sample of professionals that contribute to a multidisciplinary evaluation. The evaluation methods used to make educational decisions must be appropriate for use with students with disabilities, and they must be made in an unbiased fashion (e.g., without regard to ethnic, cultural, or racial characteristics).

By law, students with disabilities and their families are guaranteed rights of **due process**. This means that these students and their families have the same Fourteenth Amendment rights enjoyed by all citizens. School personnel cannot change the educational placement of students with disabilities without the informed consent (e.g., written permission) of the students' parents or guardians. Parents are also entitled to independent assessments and impartial hearings when decisions about their children are being made.

By law, students with disabilities must be educated in the **least restrictive environment**. This means that students with disabilities should be educated to the maximum extent feasible with nondisabled students. Students with disabilities receive special education in a variety of settings. Some are enrolled full-time in general education classes and receive only indirect services from special education personnel. Many students with mild disabilities are pulled out of their general education classes daily to go to resource rooms for special education services. Still others are enrolled in self-contained special education classes but, to the maximum extent possible, attend general education classes for part of the school day for certain kinds of instruction. For example, a student might be enrolled in a special class but attend a general education class for instruction in math, music, art, or physical education. Table 1–1 lists key provisions of the Education for All Handicapped Children Act.

TABLE 1–1   Major Provisions of Public Law 94-142

Due Process Provisions

Right to examine all pupil records
Right to independent assessment of pupil
Right to written notice of any program change
Right to impartial hearing on any school decisions

Protection in Evaluation Provisions (PEP)

Right to individual assessment before placement
Right to assessment with appropriate instruments
Right to unbiased assessment and team decisions

Individualized Education Program (IEP) Provisions

Right to written statement of present functioning
Right to written statement of goals and objectives
Right to written statement of services expected
Right to written statement of expected time frame
Right to written statement of annual monitoring

Least Restrictive Environment (LRE) Provisions

Right to education as much like normal as possible

In addition to the Education for All Handicapped Children Act, other significant federal legislation promotes the rights and services for individuals with disabilities. The Education for All Handicapped Children Amendments (EHA), enacted in 1983 and 1986, provided added services to extended age groups (Lipsky & Gartner, 1989; Ysseldyke & Algozzine, 1990). Public Law 98-199 (1983) gave emphasis to parental education, and preschool, secondary, and postsecondary programs for disabled children and youth. Public Law 99-457 (1986) included financial incentives for states to educate children three to five years old by the 1990-1991 school year and established incentive grants to promote programs serving infants with disabilities (birth to two years of age). The mandate for a free, appropriate public education for adults with disabilities is also paralleled in the Vocational Rehabilitation Act of 1973 (P.L. 93-112). Section 504 of this act made it illegal for institutions or organizations that receive federal funds to discriminate against citizens with disabilities.

In 1990 Congress passed the Americans with Disabilities Act. This law gives civil rights protection to individuals of all ages with disabilities in public services, transportation, private sector employment, public accommodations, and communications. The Americans with Disabilities Act (ADA) is modeled after Section 504 of the Rehabilitation Act of 1973. The Americans with Disabilities Act is sweeping in its authority and might rightly be called the civil rights act for persons with disabilities (Council for Exceptional Children, 1990). In the future, every sort of public accommodation and commercial facility from automatic teller machines to football bleachers will be accessible to individuals with disabilities.

In 1990 Congress amended the Education for All Handicapped Act in several significant ways. The act was renamed the Individuals with Disabilities Education Act (IDEA (Public Law 101–476)). The name change reflects the need to emphasize the person first and the disability second. Amendments in IDEA include an expansion of related services such as therapeutic recreation, social work services, and rehabilitation counseling. Transition services are mandated to be written into individual education plans (IEPs). Transition services begin at age sixteen (fourteen when appropriate). These services coordinate rehabilitative services, for example supported employment and independent living, beyond the school years. The purchase or leasing of customized equipment to support educational services (e.g., computers, wheelchairs, adaptive equipment) is also authorized by this federal law. Students with autism and traumatic brain injury are added to the list of populations provided special education in the Individuals with Disabilities Education Act.

By now it should be clear that legal mandates to educate and provide services to individuals with disabilities have been the driving force to provide equal opportunities for all school-aged children. The Individuals with Disabilities Education Act is continually being reviewed in state and federal courts. For example, overrepresentation of African-American students in special classes and the use of IQ tests to identify minorities as mildly retarded have been scrutinized by federal courts. Such key provisions of P.L. 94-142 as "appropriate education" and "nondiscriminatory assessment" have also spurred important judicial decisions. There is no end to this refinement of the Individuals with Disabilities Education Act. Table 1–2 lists some court cases that have influenced the delivery of special education services to students with mild disabilities.

Special education is a complex alternative for providing instruction to students who fail to profit in general education classes. Students with special needs are served in a variety of special education settings, and they receive differing

TABLE 1–2 Significant Judicial Decisions Since Passage of P.L. 94–142
Focus on Students with Mild Disabilities

1975 -*Issac Lira et al.* v. *The Board of Education of New York et al.* Nondiscriminatory assessment procedures must be used when placing minority students with emotional problems in special education programs.

1976 -*Frederich L.* v. *Thomas.* (Philadelphia) Class action suit that reaffirmed the right of students with learning disabilities to have appropriate education programs.

1979 -*Larry P.* v. *Riles.* (California) Intelligence tests banned in California when assessing African-American students as mildly retarded. Disproportionate numbers of African-American students were placed in special classes for the mildly retarded.

1981 -*Luke S. and Hans S.* v. *Nixe et al.* (Louisiana) Prereferral interventions, curriculum-based assessment, and direct classroom interventions were mandated for students with mild disabilities.

1982 -*Board of Education of the Henrick Hudson School System* v. *Rowley.* This Supreme Court decision clarified "appropriate" education by determining that the intent of P. L. 94-142 is to open the doors of public schools to students with disabilities, not to provide opportunities for students to reach maximum potential. Due process procedures to determine an appropriate education were reaffirmed by the Court.

1984 -*Smith* v. *Robinson.* Supreme Court decision that restricted the ability of students and their families to recover legal fees incurred in due process hearings. This decision was negated in 1986 when Congress passed the Handicapped Children's Protection Act which restored the courts' authority to award legal fees to parents who succeed in lawsuits or administrative hearings.

1984 -*Marshall et al.* v. *Georgia.* Judge Edenfiel ruled that the overrepresentation of African-Americans in special classes was not discriminatory. In his view, lower socioeconomic conditions rather than discriminatory assessment and placement practices was the reason African-American students were placed in programs for the mild mentally retarded. This was the first court case that highlighted the need to include a measure of adaptive behavior within the classroom as part of the criteria for determining mild mental retardation.

1985 -*Burlington* v. *Department of Education, Massachusetts.* The Supreme Court found that parents had the right to public school reimbursement of private school tuition if the public school program rejected by parents was inappropriate.

1988 -*Honig* v. *Doe.* Supreme Court decreed that school systems may not unilaterally exclude children with disabilities from the classroom for dangerous or disruptive behavior that is a symptom of their disability. Any programmatic changes because of behavior disturbances must follow due process procedures outlined in P. L. 94-142. In drastic situations the school can suspend a student for up to ten days.

amounts of special education assistance. Two kinds of services are available. Direct services are provided by working with students to correct or compensate for the problems that have caused them to fall behind in school. Indirect services are provided by special education personnel to others who are working with students in their general or special education classes, for example consultation services. Appendix A describes a chronology of educational services provided youngsters with disabilities since the eighteenth century.

Who Receives Special Education?

In most countries, people who are disabled are entitled to special services. During the past twenty years, the politics of disabilities have undergone considerable study (Lipsky & Gartner, 1989). Activists and academicians have insisted that disabilities (the biological conditions) be conceptually untangled from the social ramifications (the handicaps) experienced with the condition. A person with a disability usually has a problem either temporary or permanent that requires special devices (e.g., wheelchairs, prostheses) or specialized instruction.

In the United States, school-aged children who are disabled are entitled to a free, appropriate public education. It is illegal to discriminate against individuals with disabilities. This means that an individual cannot be denied an education or a job because of a disability. When thinking about who receives special education, remember that special education is a subsystem of general education. Special education is mandated to provide services to students who have been identified as disabled and who are unable to progress effectively in the regular classroom as a result of that disability. It is important to note that the presence of a disability alone is not sufficient reason to initiate special education services. Special education is warranted only after all attempts to help a youngster within the confines of the regular classroom have proven ineffective.

In the first textbook dealing with the "education of exceptional children," Horn (1924) observed that mental, temperamental, and physical differences were the basis for some students needing special education. Today, most states organize their special education departments along similar categorical lines. A category is a descriptor or label assigned to a group of students. Although the names of the categories vary slightly from state to state, special education is generally provided for children within each of the following categories:

1. Students with visual impairments or blindness.
2. Students with hearing impairments or deafness.
3. Students with deafness and blindness.
4. Students with physical or other health impairments.
5. Students with multiple disabilities.
6. Students with language or communication impairments.
7. Students with learning disabilities.
8. Students with behavior disorders or serious emotional disturbances.
9. Students with mental retardation.

Students with special talents are not disabled; consequently, they do not receive federally mandated special education, although your state or local school system might subsidize a special education program for gifted students and talented students.

Physical Reasons for Needing Special Education

Special learning needs in areas of physical abilities (e.g., seeing, hearing, moving) are the basis for several categories of students with special needs. Most of us take normal vision and hearing for granted. The expression "20/20 vision" is used to describe normal visual functioning. Vision is measured by having people read letters or discriminate objects at a distance of twenty feet. The task is not difficult for most people. There are people, however, who must stand closer to see what others see easily from twenty feet away. These differences in visual functioning are the basis of deciding if a student is blind or visually impaired. There are also people who cannot hear at a louder volume what we hear easily. Between normal hearing and deafness are various degrees of hearing loss, and it is differences in these degrees of hearing that are the basis for another category of exceptional students (i.e., deaf or hearing impaired).

How different do vision or hearing have to be before a person is considered blind or deaf? Even with correction (e.g., glasses), a person who must be twenty feet from a target that a person with normal vision can see at two hundred feet or more is considered blind. People with corrected vision better than 20/200 but not better than 20/70 are considered *visually impaired*. Ability to hear is measured along two scales: intensity and frequency. Intensity or loudness is measured in decibels (dB), and frequency or pitch is measured in hertz (cycles per second). Moores defines deaf and hard of hearing in terms of the effects on hearing loss:

> *A deaf person is one whose hearing is disabled to an extent (usually 70 dB or greater) that precludes the understanding of speech through the ear alone, without or with the use of a hearing aid. A hard of hearing person is one whose hearing is disabled to an extent (usually 35–69 dB) that makes difficult but does not preclude, the understanding of speech through the ear alone, without or with a hearing aid. (Moores, 1987, 9)*

For practical purposes, deafness means the absence of hearing in both ears; people with deafness have great difficulty hearing conversational speech without the assistance of a hearing aid. People with hearing impairments experience significant difficulty in hearing.

There are other disabling conditions that are of a physical nature. For example, *arthritis* is a measurable inflammation of a joint that limits movement. *Cerebral palsy* is impaired motor function due to brain damage; it produces difficulties in motor control that are observable in movement of large and small muscle groups. *Seizure disorder* (i.e., epilepsy) is also a brain disorder that results in measurable convulsive episodes and periods of unconsciousness. Other health impairments include severe orthopedic problems that adversely affect educational performance and limit strength, vitality, or alertness. Special education may be provided to people with physical differences caused by congenital anomalies (for example, spina bifida) as well as other general health problems (for example, heart disease, asthma, diabetes).

Cognitive Reasons for Needing Special Education

Differences in intellectual performance or mental abilities are the basis for identifying a special need. To be considered mentally retarded, an individual must demonstrate subaverage intellectual functioning and delayed social development. Intelligence tests are frequently used to determine if an individual's intellectual performance is below that of peers. Students with scores from 75–50 on an intelligence test fall within the mild range of mental retardation. Students with more complex forms of mental retardation are often categorized as moderately, severely, or profoundly disabled. Besides the differences in severity linked to IQ scores, students with moderate to profound mental retardation usually have communication and health problems. We refer to these students as having clinical mental retardation because they have serious physical and medical complications that are identified by a physician at birth or soon afterwards (e.g., fetal alcohol syndrome, Down syndrome).

These students demonstrate deficits in adaptive behavior (i.e., social development). There is no formal definition of adaptive behavior, but the term generally refers to the way in which an individual functions in his or her community. As with intelligence tests, adaptive behavior evaluations are based on age group comparisons. Formalized inventories of functional abilities (such as dressing oneself, using the telephone, or independently moving about the neighborhood) help educational evaluators determine adaptive behavior. Any determination of mental retardation must include a measure of intelligence and a measure of adaptive behavior skills (Robinson & Robinson, 1976). No student should be identified as mentally retarded solely on the basis of an intelligence test. Just as there are students with low intelligence test scores, there also are students whose intellectual performance is above that of their classmates. Historically, giftedness was determined by high IQ test scores. This approach is no longer favored by many educators because intelligence tests sample too narrow a range of abilities. Creativity, musical talent, leadership skills, and problem-solving abilities are a sample of talents not measurable through intelligence testing. More recently, experts in the field of giftedness recommend a multidimensional approach to establishing criteria for identification of students with special gifts or talents. According to Renzulli, Reis, and Smith (1981), in order to be identified as gifted, students should demonstrate:

1. High ability including measured intelligence evaluation.
2. Creativity in the development and implementation of innovative ideas.
3. High task commitment—perseverance or diligence.

Four groups of students are underrepresented in gifted education programs: culturally different, female, disabled, and underachievers (Patton, Kauffman, Blackbourn, & Brown, 1991).

How different do measures of intelligence have to be before an individual is considered mentally retarded or gifted? Differences in scores on intelligence tests and measures of adaptive behavior are evaluated in the same way as differences in scores on hearing, vision, or physical performance tests. Standards for normal intelligence and adaptive behavior are set by testing large groups of individuals. Professionals then set criteria for retardation or giftedness that are based on differences from mean intelligence or adaptive behavior ratings. For example, the common standard for normal performance is a score of 90–110 on an intelligence test; scores below 75 or above 130 are considered reflective of mental retardation or giftedness. It is important to remember that special education services for students identified as gifted are not mandated by federal legislation. Figure 1–1 traces the normal curve distribution of IQ scores used to determine degrees of mental retardation and giftedness.

Academic Reasons for Needing Special Education

With the categories of mental retardation and gifted, it is assumed that the individual's performance on achievement tests will be consistent with the performance on intelligence tests. This means that if a student obtains a high score on an intelligence test, high performance on an achievement test also is expected. If students perform poorly on intelligence tests, it is expected that their

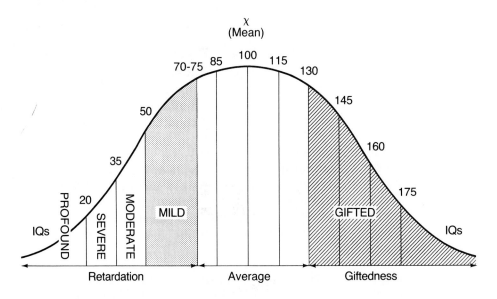

FIGURE 1–1 Normal Curve Distribution of IQ Scores

achievement test scores also will be low. There are students whose performance on achievement tests is not consistent with their performance on intelligence tests. When the difference between ability (e.g., intelligence test performance) and achievement (e.g., reading, math) is significant, the student may be identified as learning disabled.

How different do scores on ability tests and scores on achievement tests have to be before a student is classified as learning disabled? While officials of the federal government have provided guidelines for use in identifying students with learning disabilities, no specific criteria have been provided for judging when discrepancies between ability and achievement are severe enough to call a student learning disabled. Criteria differ from state to state for determining the identification of a learning disability.

Students are considered eligible for special education if they meet guidelines spelled out in state regulations. Due to a lack of consistent criteria between and within states, it is likely that many students are misplaced in special education programs for students with learning disabilities. Students with learning disabilities comprise the largest subgroup of students with mild disabilities.

Communication Reasons for Needing Special Education

Just as there are differences in reading, writing, and mathematical skills of students, there are also differences in the ways students speak and express themselves. Some people speak clearly, pronouncing each part of their speech exactly as it should be said. Others speak quickly, making it difficult for others to understand them. Some children use speech as a means of making their desires, feelings, and opinions known. Others are less adept at verbalizing personal needs. There are accepted ages at which children are expected to demonstrate use of various forms of communication. For example, most children understand about one-thousand words, combine their words into simple sentences, and understand concepts related to language (e.g., on, off, later) by the time they are 2 years old. By the age of 7, children are expected to use culturally acceptable grammar when speaking; language at this age is much like that used by family and friends. Differences in language and communication skills are measured by performance on tests and classroom observations of students interacting. Differences in language development and communication skills are commonly observed in children of all ages. When these differences adversely affect educational performance, the individual may be entitled to special services provided for students with language impairments.

How different does language have to be before a student is considered language impaired? Many students in this category receive special services for problems such as lisping, stuttering, and word pronunciation problems (e.g., they say "wabit" instead of "rabbit," "pasketti" instead of "spaghetti," or "bud" for "bird"); some of these students have voice tones that are too low, too high, nasal, too harsh, or too hoarse. There are no absolute standards for determining when an individual's speech is "too" nasal or "too" harsh or when it will adversely affect educational performance. When speech mannerisms cause difficulties for the listener, a student may be referred for speech therapy. Some teachers are better than others at understanding differences in the language produced by their students. Similarly, the context in which speech occurs influences the judgments made about it. Recent government figures indicate that there are more students in this category than in any other except learning disabilities. This is probably not surprising for a category based on differences in speech clarity or tone.

Behavioral/Emotional Reasons for Needing Special Education

While standards for normal intellectual performance have evolved within the educational system, standards for how students should act in school and society also have evolved. Standards for normal behavior are based more on what is judged acceptable in a specific setting than on judgments about how an individual performs on a test. Demonstrating intellectual performance that is sufficiently above or below normal is the basis for being identified as gifted or mentally retarded. Demonstrating unacceptable behavior in school is the basis for being identified as behaviorally disordered.

Just how different does behavior have to be before a student is considered behaviorally disordered or emotionally disturbed? Based on what you have learned about the other conditions of special education, your answer may be behavior that is significantly different from the behavior of their peers. You are right, but you will have trouble explaining behavioral differences. There are no numerical standards for normal behavior. There are no tests to measure the normality of behavior. Classroom observations by teachers carry the most weight in identifying students with behavior disorders. Defining behavior disorders is like defining beauty; the activity is very subjective. What is acceptable behavior for one classroom may not be acceptable in another. What is acceptable behavior for one teacher is not necessarily acceptable for another.

How Many Students Receive Special Education?

As of 1989 nearly 4.5 million students received special education services in public school or private settings (U.S. Department of Education, 1990). In thinking about the number of students involved, consider that it is about the same as the total full-time undergraduate enrollment in all United States colleges and universities. The number of students who receive special education exceeds the total population of thirty-two different states and is about the same as the total combined population of North Dakota, South Dakota, Montana, Nevada, Idaho, and Wyoming.

There has been a steady increase in the number of students receiving special education. During the eleven-year period from 1977 to 1989, the number of students with disabilities rose from 3,708,913 to 4,587,370; in that span 878,457 students were added to special education enrollments (Table 1–3).

The increase in number of students enrolled in special education classes coincided with the growth in general education attendance. Other reasons for the steady rise of students identified as requiring special education include:

1. The availability of pull-out (resource room programs) for hard-to-teach students.
2. Upward swing in the poverty rate, resulting in more children coming to school with health, psychological, and intellectual difficulties.
3. More culturally and linguistically different students attending public schools.
4. Dramatic increase in numbers of students identified as having a learning disability.

This growth has increased the need for certified special education teachers. For example, using a conservative average of fifteen students for each special class teacher, an average of 4,759 new teachers were needed each year from 1977 to 1989. The growth of special education services also has caused problems. For example, school personnel have to decide how to pay for the increasing numbers of students. Since the cost of educating students with special needs may come at the expense of educating students in general education, school personnel face

TABLE 1–3 Numbers of Students with Disabilities Aged Three to Twenty-One

Year	Total Number of Students	Number of New Students	Rate of Increase (%)
1977	3,708,913		
1978	3,777,286	68,373	1.84
1979	3,919,073	141,787	3.75
1980	4,036,219	117,146	2.99
1981	4,177,689	141,470	3.51
1982	4,233,282	55,593	1.33
1983	4,298,327	65,045	1.54
1984	4,341,399	43,072	1.00
1985	4,362,968	21,569	0.50
1986	4,370,244	7,276	0.17
1987	4,421,601	51,357	1.18
1988	4,494,280	72,679	1.64
1989	4,587,370	93,090	2.07
Average Annual Increase:		73,205 or	1.79

U.S. Department of Education, 1990

hard choices when allocating funds. The growth of special education is directly attributed to passage of the federal special education law (P.L. 94-142) that mandates a "free and appropriate public education" for all students with disabling conditions.

Most school districts organize their special education programs along categorical lines. For example, your local school district may have a supervisor who is responsible for types of disabilities (e.g., emotionally disturbed, learning disabled) recognized in your state. Your local school district also probably has special classes set aside for different categories of special education students served in your state. Some states (e.g., New Jersey) are moving toward noncategorical organization. Only two states (Massachusetts and South Dakota) do not use categories as the basis for organizing their special education systems (Garret & Brazil, 1989). Up to 1991, Massachusetts education regulations, for example, used the generic term "child with special needs" to refer to all students who require special education regardless of their type of disability.

Students with Mild Disabilities

Students with mild disabilities are those typically categorized as learning disabled, mild mentally retarded, or behavior disordered. Students with language or communication impairments is another large category of students with mild special needs; however, because their difficulties are treated by speech clinicians rather than teachers, we have not included information about them in this book.

The term mildly disabled is not used to imply that these students do not have serious learning problems or that their problems are less important than those of other students. We think the term has come to be used for this group of students because many of their characteristics overlap, and they can be educated in regular classrooms.

According to the definition included in the Education for All Handicapped Children Act (1975) and reaffirmed in the Individuals with Disabilities Education Act (1990), students with learning disabilities exhibit a disorder in one or more of the basic psychological processes involved in understanding or using spoken or written language. These may be manifested in disorders of listening, thinking, talking, reading, writing, spelling, or arithmetic. Learning disabilities include conditions which have historically been referred to as perceptual handicaps, brain injury, minimal brain dysfunction, dyslexia, and developmental aphasia. They do not include learning problems which are due primarily to visual, hearing, or motor handicaps, to mental retardation, emotional handicaps, or environmental disadvantages.

Students with mild mental retardation are those with impaired intellectual and adaptive behaviors and whose development reflects a reduced rate of learning. If a student's IQ score is 75–50, and the student's socialization skills are uniformly below age expectations, an evaluation of mild mental retardation is likely. In some school systems, students with mild mental retardation are categorized as educably mentally retarded (EMR). We will avoid that term throughout this text because it implies a predetermined level of ability—educable. The deviousness of language used to describe students with mental retardation becomes more evident when students with moderate mental retardation are categorized as trainable (TMR), and students with severe mental retardation are categorized as custodial (CMR).

Students with behavior disorders are those who exhibit persistent and consistent behavioral problems that disrupt their own or others' learning. Sometimes these students are referred to as emotionally disturbed. The term "behavior disordered" is more descriptive of this population of students. Using the term "emotionally disturbed" implies that we know *why* the student is unable to adapt to classroom routines—he or she has an emotional or psychological problem. In fact, this is often not the case. Many students are referred for special education because they are impulsive, distractible, or hyperactive. These behaviors can be caused by any number of factors that have no connection with a student's emotional development. Neurological factors, diet, allergies, delayed development, and ineffective teaching are some explanations for students' inability to control their behavior in a classroom.

We recognize, however, that many students with behavior disorders do, in fact, have emotional problems. There is a great deal of overlap among students identified as behavior disordered and emotionally disturbed. Even if the primary cause of a student's behavior problems is diet or allergies, the reaction of others to the disruptive behavior can affect that student's emotional development. Moreover, a student may have an emotional problem and demonstrate no overt behavior disorders. This is a particularly acute problem with adolescents who may be withdrawn or depressed but mask their emotional distress with good grades. We will go into more detail about this overlap between behavior disorders and emotional disturbances in Chapter 4.

Students classified as learning disabled, mild mentally retarded, or behavior disordered account for more than two-thirds of all students with disabilities (U.S. Department of Education, 1990), and they share many characteristics (Hallahan & Kauffman, 1977). For example, students with learning disabilities often have problems with reading comprehension, language development, interpersonal relations, and classroom behavioral control (Lerner, 1988). These same characteristics are common in teacher descriptions of students called mild mentally retarded and behavior disordered (Coleman, 1986; Kauffman, 1984; Robinson & Robinson, 1982).

If you have observed that these characteristics also can be found in students who do not receive special education services, you are correct. It is a thin and sometimes arbitrary line that separates students with mild disabilities from other students. Many classroom problems are interactional: the result of a mismatch between teaching and learning style. The behavior, expectations, and attitude of the regular classroom teacher often is a key component in determining if a student is referred and evaluated as having a mild disability. For example, some characteristics of learning disabilities, such as dyslexia (i.e., an impairment in reading ability), are neurologically based; other characteristics, such as distractibility, can be based on teacher perception of student performance. A student with dyslexia will be dyslexic in every classroom; on the other hand, a student identified as distractible and hyperactive in one teacher's classroom may have no difficulty attending in another classroom. How can this happen? Some teachers are more adept at engaging students in their schoolwork than others. In special education, we have learned never to underestimate the power of good teaching to "cure" a mild disability.

Whether or not it helps students with mild disabilities to be categorized as mild mentally retarded, learning disabled, or behavior disordered is controversial. Over the years, each of these three subgroups of mild disabilities have been separated by distinct identification criteria, different teaching methods, teacher certificates linked to a single disability, and different special education placements. Each category is represented by separate professional organizations and advocacy groups. The American Association for Mental Retardation and the Association for Citizens with Learning Disabilities are two examples of category-specific organizations. Researchers develop expertise within a single category of mild disabilities and report their findings in journals that specialize in mental retardation, learning disabilities, or behavior disorders.

Yet students who are placed in different categories of mild disabilities share many common traits. Lack of interest in school and low motivation are two traits displayed by many youngsters categorized as having a mild disability. It is also clear that instructional practices proven effective for students in one category of mild disabilities can be useful with students within another category. Such instructional strategies as peer tutoring, whole language, and cooperative learning can help students learn regardless of how their mild disability is categorized.

There are advantages and disadvantages to classifying students by specific categories of mild disabilities. Special educators sometimes use the term "labeling" to describe this categorization process. Is it a good idea to label students? We will present the facts about both sides of this issue. Ultimately you will need to make your own professional decision about labeling students with such terms as mildly retarded, learning disabled, and behavior disordered. Whether or not to place a student into a mild disability category is an issue you will be faced with throughout your career as a teacher.

Labeling

Students identified as having problems in school either will meet eligibility criteria for special education services or will be unofficially labeled with such negative adjectives as "lazy," "unmotivated," "slow learner," or "behavior problem." In the latter case, neither the teacher nor the student will get help. The student will remain in general education and most likely continue to fail in school. There is an increased probability that the student will eventually drop out of school.

In most states, a student is identified as requiring special education when school evaluation data matches the student with a specific disability category that is outlined by state education regulations. This labeling process assumes that assigning a student a categorical name implies knowledge about the characteristics of the student's learning problem. This categorical approach to providing help has been roundly criticized by many educators who claim that labeling a student does more harm than good. Even when students are not labeled by evaluation, the placement process is often synonymous with labeling. In Massachusetts, for example, students are labeled with the generic title "student with special needs," but they are often placed in programs that clearly communicate the child's disability. For instance, students who receive special services because of behavior problems may be placed in "pupil adjustment classes" or classes for "emotionally disturbed." What students are called determines what services they receive and where they will receive them. Because this de facto categorization or labeling process alters the school experience of many students, professionals have researched and described the advantages and disadvantages of labeling.

Advantages of Labeling

The advantages of labeling were more obvious in the formative years of special education (mid-1940s to early 1970s) than they are now. For instance, without the category of learning disabilities, advocates for these children would have had no rallying point to promote educational programs. Imagine how ineffective scientists would be in raising money for cancer research if we had no name for it. The advantages of labeling can be summarized as follows:

1. Federal and local funding of special education programs are based on categories of disabilities.
2. Labeling enables professionals to communicate with one another because each categorical label conveys a general idea about learning characteristics.
3. The human mind requires "mental hooks" to think about problems. If present categorical labels were abolished, a new set of descriptors would evolve to take their place. There is ample evidence of this in the evolution of the term mildly retarded, which you will read more about in Chapter 3.
4. Labeling the disability spotlights the problem for the general public. Labeling can spark social concern and aid advocacy efforts.
5. Labeling may make the nondisabled majority more tolerant of the disabled minority. In other words, the actions of a child identified as having mental retardation might be tolerated, whereas the behavior of a nondisabled child would be criticized.
6. Labeling has led to the development of sophisticated teaching methods, assessment approaches, and behavioral interventions that are useful for teachers of all students (Hallahan & Kauffman, 1982).

Disadvantages of Labeling

Because of the Individuals with Disabilities Education Act, children with disabilities have made significant gains in public schools. These advances have been accompanied by problems inherent in officially designating someone abnormal. Make no mistake about it—these labels stick. Once a child is categorized as mildly retarded, behavior disordered or learning disabled, that information will be forwarded to every new teacher in the child's cumulative folder. Along with the label comes the stigma of being deficient. For this reason alone, assigning a student to a category for special education purposes is a fateful step that should not be taken unless all other options have proven unsuccessful. The disadvantages of labeling are summarized as follows:

1. Labels shape teacher expectations. Imagine what your reaction would be if the principal informed you that the new student in your class is mild mentally retarded. Studies on teacher expectations have demonstrated that what teachers believe about student capability is directly related to student achievement.

2. All children have some troubling behaviors. Labels can exaggerate a student's actions in the eyes of a teacher. A teacher may overreact to behavior of a labeled child that would be tolerated in another.

3. Labels send a clear message—the learning problem is with the student. Labels tend to obscure the essence of teaching and learning as a two-way street. Some students placed in a mild disability category have nothing wrong with them. They are the unfortunate recipients of ineffective schooling.

4. Labels perpetuate the notion that students with mild disabilities are qualitatively different from other children. This is not true. Students with mild disabilities go through the same developmental stages as their peers, although sometimes at a slower rate.

5. Teachers may confuse the student with the label. Labels reflect categories of disabilities. Categories are abstract, not real, concepts that are general enough to incorporate many different individuals. Almost two million school children are identified as learning disabled, but as individuals, each is a unique human being. When a student is placed in a category, a teacher who knows some of the characteristics of a category may ascribe all known characteristics to each labeled child. This is stereotyping. Stereotypes handicap students when teachers rationalize low achievement by citing characteristics of the label. An example is the teacher who explains away a teaching-learning problem by stating, "We can't really expect Mary to remember too much math because she is mildly retarded."

6. Students cannot receive special education services until they are labeled. In many instances, the intervention comes too late. The need to label students before help arrives undermines a preventive approach to mild learning problems.

7. Diagnostic labels are unreliable. Educational evaluation is filled with quirks. States use different descriptive criteria for the same categories; many evaluation instruments have questionable validity and reliability; specific labels go through trends (for example, at one time learning disabilities was a white, middle class affliction, while African-American students were overrepresented in the mild mental retardation category).
8. Labels often put the blame (and the guilt) for a student's learning problems squarely on the parents' shoulders. In many cases, this is unjustified because students may be mislabeled or teachers may not fully understand the many different causes of mild disabilities.

Focus on What to Teach Students

The purpose of the Education for All Handicapped Children Act and more recently the Individuals with Disabilities Education Act is to ensure that all students with special needs receive a free and appropriate education. Congress did not define what it meant by the term "appropriate." The legislators recognized that there is no one instructional approach that is best. Instead they viewed "appropriate" as a process rather than a product. Whether or not a program is appropriate is based on the ability of the school system and parents to work out a mutually acceptable individualized education program.

Individual Education Program

An individualized education program (IEP) must be written for each student receiving special education. Special education includes many services related to classroom instruction such as transportation, occupational therapy, counseling, and adaptive equipment. Assessed instructional needs of each student determine the areas for which an IEP is developed. Each IEP must contain the following components:

1. The student's present level of academic functioning.
2. A statement of annual goals or anticipated attainments.
3. Short-term objectives that lead to the stated goals.
4. Specific educational services to be provided and a list of professional providers.
5. Evaluation criteria and timelines for determining whether or not objectives have been met.
6. Projected dates for beginning services and their anticipated duration.
7. The extent to which a student will participate in regular and special education programs. (Ramsey, 1988)

Each school district may develop its own IEP format as long as the required information is included. The IEP must be developed within a meeting by participants stipulated by legislation. These persons include:

1. A representative of the local education agency (LEA), other than the student's teacher, who can provide or supervise special education provisions.
2. The student's teacher (the LEA may specify whether regular or special educators or both).
3. The student's parents or guardians.
4. The student when appropriate (i.e., at a specific age set by state regulations).
5. Other persons requested by the parents to provide support or advocacy.
6. For a student evaluated for the first time, a person knowledgeable about evaluation procedures.

The IEP must be reviewed and revised at least once a year.

In the case of students with mild disabilities, the IEP is usually determined by the portion of the regular school curriculum with which a student is having difficulty. A student with a learning disability might have an IEP that emphasizes reading and mathematics. A student with a behavior disorder would have an IEP that emphasizes self-control and adjustment to classroom routines. An adolescent with mild mental retardation might have an IEP that describes vocational goals and objectives.

Focus on Where to Teach Students

When Congress passed the Education for All Handicapped Children Act in 1975, the media hailed it as the mainstreaming law. This caused considerable concern among teachers and administrators who feared mainstreaming would lead to dumping students with disabilities into the regular classrooms. Newspeople inadvertently misled the public. The term "mainstreaming" is not mentioned in the law. Congress believed that students with disabilities should be educated with nondisabled students whenever feasible. The law states that students should be educated in the least restrictive environment. The intent of the least restrictive environment mandate is to assure that students are not segregated because they are disabled and to give them every opportunity to have a normal school experience. More restrictive settings, such as self-contained special classes and residential programs, should only be utilized when a student's needs are so complex that he or she would not receive an appropriate education in a less restrictive environment. Evelyn Deno's *Cascade of Services* (Figure 1–2) provides a visual representation of the relationship between least and most restrictive settings. Level I is least restrictive. Each succeeding level establishes more distance between special and regular education services.

It is the responsibility of each school system to provide a continuum of educational services ranging from least to most restrictive. We will briefly describe the types of special education services you could expect a school system to provide.

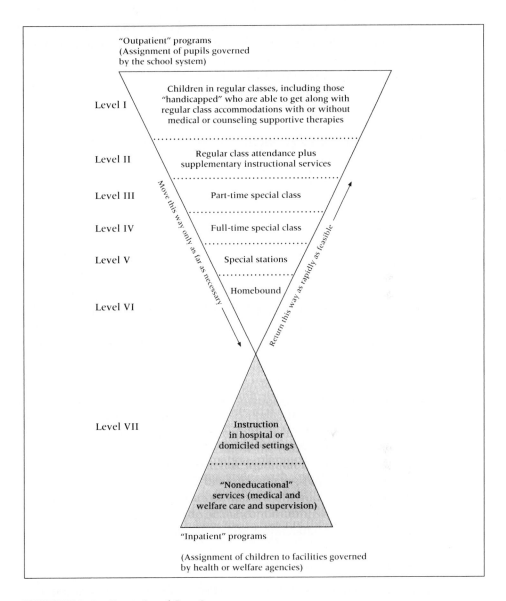

FIGURE 1–2 Cascade of Services.

From: "Special Education as Developmental Capitol" by E. Deno, *Exceptional Children*, 1970, 37, 229-237. © 1970 by the Council for Exceptional Children. Reprinted with permission.

Regular Classroom Placement (Level I, Level II)

Regular placement with supportive services (e.g., materials, consultation, team teaching) is the least restrictive environment in the hierarchy of services. If a student spends no more than 21 percent of the school day outside the regular classroom receiving special instruction, the federal government defines the placement as a regular classroom. Students with learning disabilities usually spend most of their day in the regular classroom. Speech clinicians, social workers, special education teachers, and school psychologists may consult with the regular classroom teacher on student needs and progress.

Resource Room Placement (Level III)

Resource rooms are commonly referred to as pull-out programs. The resource room is a special education classroom located within the student's school. A youngster goes to the resource room on a scheduled basis to receive tutorial help from a special education teacher. Students may spend from 10 to 60 percent of their school day in a resource room. Typically, resource room teachers teach fundamental skills and/or tutor students in the academic subjects that were the source of the referral. It is the resource room teacher's job to take a lead role in the development and implementation of IEPs for students placed in this setting. The majority of students who receive resource room help remain in the regular classroom for most of their school day. In 1989, 68 percent of all students with special needs received special education services in a combination of resource room and regular classroom placements (U.S. Department of Education, 1990).

Special Class Placement (Level IV)

Special classes are self-contained programs located in a public school system. They are sometimes called segregated programs because only students with disabilities are enrolled. Students are usually grouped in special classes by categories of disability. The special class is the most criticized of special education placements when it is used for students with mild disabilities. While students with learning disabilities are not usually placed in special classes, students with mild mental retardation and behavior disorders are sometimes placed in these programs. Placement rates for special classes have remained around 25 percent of the total special education population since 1975.

Special Day School Placement (Level V)

Alternative high school programs, special education early childhood programs, and private day programs are examples of special day school placements. Students are transported to these special education programs at the school system's expense. Public school systems sometimes contract with private vendors to provide special education services for students with low-incidence disabilities such as autism or multiple disabilities. In addition to the disadvantages inherent in segregation, students who attend special day school programs may spend lengthy amounts of time being transported from home to program and back home again. In 1989, 5.6 percent of students with special needs were educated in separate day facilities (U.S. Department of Education, 1990).

Residential Programs (Level VII)

When a student requires intensive, around-the-clock treatment, residential programs are an option. Residential placements are expensive, however, and can cost a school system over $50,000 a year to send one student to a residential facility for a year. One program for students with severe disabilities in Providence, Rhode Island, presently costs in excess of $135,000 a year. Ironically, the funding mechanisms in some states actually create incentives for such restrictive placements by providing reimbursements that increase in proportion to time in a special education program.

Blackman reported that in Illinois "it frequently costs a school district less money to send a child to a private day, often a residential school, than educating the child within the school district" (Blackman, 1989, 461). Illinois has set aside money to fully reimburse school districts for room and board costs incurred as a result of residential placements. Despite the additional expense, residential placements cannot match the quality of public school special education programs. Private school teachers are often uncertified or inexperienced. They work longer hours (usually through the summer) and for less pay than public school teachers. Union representation, a sine qua non of public school life, is virtually nonexistent in private, residential facilities. In 1989, less than 1 percent of students with special needs were placed in residential programs (U. S. Department of Education, 1990).

Homebound/Hospital Programs (Level VI)

Students who are ill or require intensive medical services are educated by itinerant teachers at home. Some hospitals have their own special education programs. Only a small percentage, less than 1 percent, of all special needs learners are restricted to home or hospital care (U. S. Department of Education, 1990). With the passage of P.L. 99-457 in 1986, incentives were created to develop individualized family service plans for infants and toddlers with disabilities at home. Thus, we can expect to see the number of students served in this placement to climb over the next decade. P.L. 99–457 (Handicapped Infant and Toddler Program, Part H) amended the Education for All Handicapped Children Act to extend special education services to pre-schoolers in 1991–1992.

Correction Facilities (Level VII)

More than 450,000 adolescents are incarcerated in correctional facilities across the country each year (Margolis, 1988). Many of these young people are from minorities and uneducated. If a special need is identified, an incarcerated youth up to age twenty-one has the same right to special education services as students in the public school system. Nelson, Rutherford, and Wolford in their book *Special Education in the Criminal Justice System* (1987) suggest that this population is underserved and that there may be a higher prevalence of mild disabilities among prisoners than the general population. Within the past few years, some special educators have argued that an adjudication of delinquency (i.e., socially maladjusted) may be a disability in itself (Benson, Edwards, Rosell, & White, 1986). Correctional facilities include prisons, jails, and detention centers. DiGangi, Perryman, and Rutherford (1990) reported 42 percent of offenders in a state juvenile facility required special education.

Focus on How to Teach Students with Mild Disabilities

Schools can no longer ignore individual and unique instructional needs of pupils (Lipsky & Gartner, 1989). The laws and court decisions which mandate an appropriate educational program for youth with disabilities are equally beneficial for regular education students. Working separately, general and special educators have developed instructional approaches that can benefit students both with and without disabilities. By working together, general and special educators can improve the education of all students. Some special educators have proposed a merger of general and special education. They believe that the splintering of educational services in schools has diminished efforts to help difficult-to-teach students (Stainback, Stainback, & Forest, 1989). If the ideal is the establishment of an appropriate education for students with disabilities, can this be accomplished in the general education classroom with collaborative efforts of general and special educators? The movement known as the Regular Education Initiative has addressed this concern and is discussed in more detail in Chapter 6.

Smith-Davis put the onus of educational change on general education when she stated: "The only impediment to greater access to the [educational] mainstream by students with disabilities and other types of variance is the capacity of general education to respond with effective instruction to the diversity of needs, learning styles, and other characteristics of students who are not typical" (Smith-Davis, 1989a, 2). Both general and regular educators are aware that we are in a state of transition as we conceive best strategies for helping students with mild disabilities. Therefore, the future focus may well shift from where (setting) and why (rights) students are placed in special education to a focus on how to educate successfully those students who are difficult to teach. Smith-Davis (1989a) foresees the following factors under consideration during the upcoming years: (1) curriculum, (2) instruction, (3) methods, (4) materials, (5) options, (6) alternatives, and (7) instructional roles and relationships. In order to understand how these factors can make a difference in the realm of general education, it is necessary to understand the current status of the field.

Comparing General Education and Special Education

Because general education has traditionally represented conformity to fixed, sequential curriculum, pupils with differences have been squeezed out of the system (Smith-Davis, 1989a). Many of these youth have ended up in special education, not so much to meet unique individual needs but because special education is one of the few services available to help children who are unable to meet the requirements of general education (Sarason & Doris, 1979; Ysseldyke & Algozzine, 1982). Some of these children are not truly disabled, but in need of instructional remediation. This practice neglects preventive efforts to solve classroom problems. Often, the only way a teacher can get help for a student (or for herself) is to refer the youngster for special education evaluation. This scenario casts general and special educators in roles that make preventive collaboration difficult to achieve.

There are many differences between the two systems of general and special education. A comparative overview of the two systems is shown in Table 1–4. Basically, special education is adaptive to individual needs of students. Concepts

TABLE 1–4 Comparisons between General and Special Education

General Education	Special Education
Curriculum addresses group	Curriculum addresses individual
Standardizes curricula	Tailors curricula
Assumes a standardized approach to instruction	Assumes an adaptive approach to instruction
Instruction emanates from a global view of student readiness and progress	Instruction emanates from individual assessment, diagnosis, prescription
Maintains larger class sizes; has larger pupil-teacher ratio	Maintains smaller class sizes; has smaller pupil-teacher ratio
Uses basal materials and texts; uses standard materials and texts	Uses specialized materials and texts; uses modified materials and texts
Teaches to the norm	Teaches to varying learning styles and levels
Emphasizes grades	Emphasizes meeting instructional objectives
Adheres to the learning pace of the average student	Adheres to the learning pace of individual students
Seeks help for students with academic and behavioral deviations	Specializes in students with academic and behavioral deviations
Is responsible for curriculum achievement	Is responsible for solving learning problems and helping difficult-to-teach students
Focuses on content, especially at the secondary level	Focuses on methods and student skills
Is similar to medical "general practitioner"	Is similar to the "specialist" in medicine
Emphasizes student adaptation to classroom routines	Emphasizes student learning how to control behavior
Does not stress early intervention	Stresses intervention at infancy or preschool age
Minimal focus on postschool transition	Significant focus on postschool transition
Involves parents peripherally	Involves parents centrally
Refers to related services	Incorporates related services

Source: Smith-Davis, J. 1989a.

such as individualization, specialization, heterogeneity, and life-long learning are among those that drive practices in special education. On the other hand, regular education is group-oriented, global, norm-referenced, and presents standardized curriculum.

Since 1975, special education has grown as a subsystem of general education. This growth has tended to accentuate differences between the two systems. Students have received special services, but not without cost. The stigma of being identified as deficient, along with a loss of regular classroom instructional time, has pushed students with mild disabilities further down the ladder of school success. If general and special educators can find ways to work together, the combination of knowledge and expertise will benefit all students. The following chapters will focus on the unique characteristics of students with mild disabilities. Using this knowledge as a base, we will describe in ensuing chapters those strategies that can help general and special educators work more closely to assist students with mild disabilities reach their fullest potential.

Summary

Special education serves students with disabilities. Students with mild disabilities comprise the majority of students in special education programs. These students have problems and characteristics that make success in school difficult without special assistance. Students with a severe discrepancy between their intellectual ability and their performance in school are called learning disabled. Students with subaverage performance on intelligence tests and adaptive behavior problems are called mild mentally retarded. Students with social and emotional problems that inhibit learning are called behavior disordered. These three groups of students are often referred to as mildly disabled because their problems are basically educational in nature. Many of their special learning needs and characteristics overlap. Public schools began providing special education services to all students with mild disabilities in 1975 when it became clear that some were not profiting from the educational menu of experiences provided in regular public school classes. Today, more than two-thirds of the students served in special education programs are classified as learning disabled, mild mentally retarded or emotionally disordered.

Early special education programs were sometimes isolated special classes, or custodial placements that left much to be desired in terms of good instruction and sound educational practices. With the advent of Public Law 94-142, the Education For All Handicapped Children Act, and its subsequent supplements and amendments, special educators focused on providing appropriate education for students with mild disabilities. As a result of this monumental legislation, students who receive special services are entitled to education that is as much like normal as possible. Cooperation between general and special educators is the best strategy for ensuring the success of educational interventions for students with mild disabilities.

Chapter *2*

Overview of Students with Mild Disabilities

Advance Organizer

When you complete this chapter, you will be able to:

1. Compare categorical and noncategorical perspectives of students with mild disabilities.
2. Discuss general cross categorical characteristics of students with mild disabilities.
3. Make comparisons about students with mild versus severe learning and behavioral disabilities.
4. Discuss organic and environmental causes of mild learning and behavioral disabilities.
5. Describe special populations at-risk of educational and school failure.
6. Discuss social programs for students at-risk.
7. Explain the due process procedures that must be followed when making decisions about who will receive services in special education.
8. Identify student behaviors required for success in the regular classroom.
9. Discuss common learning and behavioral characteristics of students with mild disabilities.
10. Identify strategies for modifying classroom instruction.

In Chapter 1, students with mild disabilities were identified as those who are served in special education in the categories of learning disabilities, mild mental retardation, or behavioral disorders. These students are referred to as having a mild disability because many of their special learning needs and characteristics go undetected until they begin formalized schooling, and they are compared to peers. The majority are enrolled full-time within regular education classrooms or receive special services in a resource room one to several periods a day. Whether you are a general or special education teacher, you will have these students in your classroom.

Tale of Three Students: Vignettes

Joe's third-grade teacher reported that Joe's academic abilities were significantly delayed. In reading, Joe had difficulty blending letter sounds and recalling content from reading and listening. Mathematics was also a problem for Joe, although he experienced some success with basic facts. He did have, however, difficulty mastering reasoning and problem-solving skills. His teacher estimated that he was two to three years behind his classmates in academics. Joe's teacher also reported that Joe had poor social skills. Working cooperatively with classmates and controlling impulses were two areas in which Joe experienced difficulty. His teacher stated that Joe's "immaturity" and social withdrawal were a source of frustration to her. His IQ was sixty-nine. Joe has been identified as a student with mild mental retardation.

Jack was in constant trouble because he did not turn in assignments or complete work in class. His fifth-grade teacher reported that his academic performance suffered due to his incomplete work. Jack was a constant source of frustration to his teacher and family. Although she tried to handle most discipline problems herself, his teacher sent Jack to the principal's office an average of three times per week. His teacher described Jack as "sullen and hostile." When he was in these moods, he talked out in class, refused to work, and became disruptive. Jack had been involved in several fights in school and on the bus; one was enough to get him suspended from school. Jack was identified as a student with a behavior disorder.

Lou was eight years old. His IQ was 110. His teacher reported that Lou had average intelligence and a good understanding of spoken language. He was extremely verbal and often engaged in long conversations on a variety of topics; however, Lou's performance in spelling and written language was comparable to students who were three years younger than he. He was unable to reproduce letters legibly. Although he readily recognized each letter of the alphabet, he had difficulty both remembering what the letters looked like and executing the motor patterns necessary to form each letter. When Lou was given a set of letters to copy, his written product was often illegible. Lou's fine motor coordination and memory difficulties extended into the area of arithmetic. He understood mathematical concepts but had difficulty reproducing numbers and remembering basic facts. His academic performance in math was approximately two years below his peers. Lou has been identified as a student with learning disability. *(Myles & Simpson, 1989)*

Each of these students exhibited learning and behavior problems that indicated the presence of a mild disability. Joe's intelligence test score, his performance in academics, and his social skills were significantly behind expectations for his age. Jack's primary difficulties were behavioral. His social and emotional problems interfered with his learning. Lou's classroom problems stemmed from specific impairments in visual memory and fine motor coordination. These specific developmental problems contributed to the discrepancy between his potential as measured by his average IQ and his lackluster academic achievement.

Joe, who was identified as having mild mental retardation, remained in his regular classroom. Twice a week the special education teacher consulted with Joe's teacher. This team approach produced positive results, and Joe's classroom performance improved. Joe is mainstreamed, and, in special education terminology, he is receiving services in the least restrictive environment.

Jack was identified as having a behavior disorder, and he was placed in a self-contained classroom. In this placement, Jack is attending school with seven other students who have been identified as having behavioral or emotional problems. His special education teacher was trained to work specifically with students who are emotionally disturbed. This segregated program is one of the most restrictive settings in which a special education student can be placed. Once students are assigned to self-contained special education programs, it is hard for them to get back into a regular classroom on a full-time basis.

Lou, who was identified as having a learning disability, was placed in a resource room for two periods every day. In the resource room he received one-on-one instruction from a special education teacher. His progress is steady, and he will soon return full-time to the regular classroom.

These students are different in some characteristics, and, therefore, they were assigned to different categories of mild disabilities (i.e., mildly retarded, behavior disordered, learning disabled). Some might say they were given different labels. As was discussed in Chapter 1, the historical approach in special education has been to separate students into categories that reflect their primary impairment or disability. Out of this categorization practice has grown a proliferation of teacher training programs, research studies, and instructional practices all geared to the characteristics of students identified as having a specific type of mild disability. For example, multisensory programs were developed for students with learning disabilities. Students with mild mental retardation were often taught a watered down version of the basic school curriculum, and behavior modification programs were commonly designed to change the behavior of students with behavior disorders. Throughout this text, we will explain how students with learning disabilities, mild mental retardation, and behavior disorders are both different and alike in their learning needs and in the ways that professionals view them.

Recently, educators are emphasizing similarities among the three mild learning disorders. Lilly (1979), for instance, points out that all students have common functional needs related to their development and schooling. He views students with mild disabilities as not that much different from their regular classroom peers. The "effective schools" research has identified teaching practices that help many different types of students including hard-to-teach pupils and those with mild disabilities (Bickel & Bickel, 1986). Orderly classrooms, systematic monitoring of student performance, and an emphasis on basic skills characterize "effective schools" that have documented higher math and reading achievement. As you will discover, understanding the needs of students with mild disabilities means keeping an open mind and remaining flexible in your opinions. In most states, students must meet specific criteria for a disability in order to recieve special education services, but the ensuing categorization or labeling of students does not mean that they are all the same in their learning needs. Every student is an individual with different wants, needs, and interests. Educators must be cautious when generalizing knowledge about "types" of disabilities to individual cases.

Noncategorical Identification of Students with Mild Disabilities

Special education labors under the weight of two contradictory beliefs. The first is that each student is unique in his or her individual learning needs. That is why all students are required by law to have an individual education program. The second belief is that there are homogeneous groups of mild disabilities that can be described, classified, and remediated. This typology assumption led to the formulation and separation of mild mental retardation, behavior disorders, and learning disabilities into distinct categories of learning disorders. We can see the results of this bipolar perspective in the debate over whether students with mild special needs are best served in special education or general education programs. If special education is selected, the debate switches to the most appropriate type of special education program.

Leaders in the field have proposed noncategorical and cross-categorical placement options for students with mild disabilities. Noncategorical refers to generic or broad-based special education programs, and cross-categorical means that no specific label need be placed upon a youngster who can profit from part-time special education resource room services. The majority of cross-categorical instruction would occur in the regular classroom.

Reynolds and Balow (1971) give the following reasons for revolting against categorical terms like "retarded," "disturbed," and "handicapped" to identify students with mild disabilities.

1. The tendency to stereotype or to ascribe characteristics of the group to individuals is prejudicial to interests of the labeled individuals.
2. The stigmatizing effect of labeling a person may lead to scapegoating.
3. Teachers may develop negative expectations towards pupils carrying specific labels.

Through the years, certain characteristics have been attributed to the various special education categories. Table 2–1 shows the generally accepted categorical descriptions of students with mild disabilities. In reality, these generalized

TABLE 2–1   Generally Accepted Categorical Descriptions of Students with Mild Disabilities

	Mildly Retarded	Emotionally Disturbed (ED) Behavioral Disordered (BD)	Learning Disabled
Cognitive	Subaverage intellectually Eligibility criteria/2 SDs below the mean (50-75 IQ); often demonstrate short memory span, difficulty transferring learning, inability to project beyond the present situation, poor reasoning skills, poor abstract thinking, attention deficits	Average to low-average intelligence scores; behavior interfaces with test scores	Average or above intellectually Mental processing dysfunctions affect thinking and learning abilities
Academic	Delayed academically Demonstrates expectancy of failure, has slow learning rate, repeats unsuccessful strategies or behaviors, does not attempt new tasks	Behavior interfaces with school achievement Weak, average, or superior academic performance	Have processing deficits Lack generalization skills, demonstrate learned helplessness, work slowly on tasks, may or may not have developed coping skills
Adaptive	Eligibility criteria specifies poor adaptive skills Hyperactive, low tolerance/frustration, easily fatigued, moral judgment comparable to mental age Delayed community-family adaptive skills	Discipline problem May have anxiety, fears, physical pain May be unhappy or depressed	Learn to compensate for deficiencies Dependency needs Outer-directed
Social	Socially and emotionally immature Unfavorable self-concept Lacking in self-esteem Susceptible to peer influences	Poor peer relations Disruptive behavior/conduct problems May be shy/withdrawn or aggressive Disturbing behavior demonstrated in various settings Often elicit emotional responses in others	Lack social insightfulness Poor self-esteem Susceptible to peer influences Often feel inferior but want acceptance
Perceptual-Motor	Delayed developmental skills affect perception and motor abilities	Intact perceptual and motor skills generally	Impaired perceptual and motor abilities Eye-hand coordination problems Awkward May lack orientation skills
Language	Speech/language delayed or deficient Poor social communication	Spoken content problems (e.g., profane, argumentative, disrespectful language)	Receptive, integrative, and expressive language difficulties Deficient processing abilities Poor social communication
General Characteristics	Manifest problems adapting to the environment Lag behind in most academic areas Perform best in physical/motoric skills	Display behavior that is persistent and incompatible with cultural norms to a significant extent May have concomitant academic deficits	Manifest specific learning problems in one or two academic areas May have concomitant negative behavioral manifestations

Note: These characteristics have historically been attributed to each category. Individual students' profiles will vary considerably.

characteristics are not descriptive of any individual with the disability (e.g., mild mental retardation, learning disabilities, behavior disorders). They are generalized characteristics which are representative of many individuals identified as having a mild intellectual, learning, or behavioral disability.

There seems to be utility in categorizing students with developmental disabilities (e.g., autism) because at the more severe level, learning and behavioral characteristics, etiological roots, and instructional approaches are more readily identifiable. But at the mild level, there is overlap between learning and behavioral characteristics of students.

Gallagher (1972) presents a paradox. He contends that there is a price that must be paid when we label a student mildly disabled, but without the label, we will never know what would have happened to the individual in the absence of special education services. Of course, placement may or may not lead to effective treatment. Another thought expressed by Gallagher that finds truth in contemporary practices is that special education placement may occur as an "exclusionary process masquerading as a remedial process." There are those regular classroom teachers who refer their most troublesome cases to special education and ask that they be given no further responsibility for these youngsters.

Domains of functioning for any child during school include cognitive, academic, adaptive, social, and language skills. Table 2–1 identifies functioning characteristics of students with mild disabilities across the three high prevalence categories of mild retardation, emotional disturbance, and learning disabilities. The categorical view of students with mild disabilities begins to unravel when researchers investigate what happens after special education placement.

Hallahan and Kauffman (1982) state that categorically differentiated instruction matched to characteristics is largely nonexistent. The authors give an example:

> *Anyone, who happens to look in on each of three special classes or resource rooms for mildly disturbed, mildly retarded, or learning disabled children is not likely to see very different teaching techniques being used. . . . The appropriate teaching strategies and the materials used are very nearly the same for each of the three areas. (Hallahan & Kauffman, 1982, 435)*

Similarly, Ysseldyke, Algozzine, Shinn, and McGue (1982) suggest that a child diagnosed as having a learning disability may *not* require instructional treatment different from that of youngsters with diagnoses of mild mental retardation or behavior disorders. They also state that many students without disabilities can benefit from specialized instruction designed for students with mild disabilities.

Miller and Davis (1982) suggest ways in which alterations of present categorical arrangements could occur. They recommend: (1) redefining existing exceptionality categories, (2) creating novel structures in which existing categories could be expanded or limited, or (3) establishing a category-free approach. Most advocates of a noncategorical approach have not suggested that *all* classification systems be rejected because without classification systems, it is difficult to distinguish students with mild learning disorders from hard-to-teach, unmotivated, or underachieving students. In order to receive special education services a student should have an identifiable disability.

Massachusetts is one state that has instituted a noncategorical approach to identifying students with special needs. The result has been rampant referrals and the highest percentage of students with special needs in the nation (U.S. Department of Education., 1990). During the mid 1980s in some urban areas, over 20 percent of the entire Massachusetts school population received special education. The challenge for educators is to accurately identify students with mild disabilities and ensure students are placed in programs that enhance rather than stifle learning.

Cross Categorical Generalities about Students with Mild Disabilities

Some generalities can be made about students with mild learning disorders—who they are and who they are not.

Students with mild mental retardation, learning disabilities, and behavior disorders are the largest subgroup of students receiving special education services.

In 1989, 6.7 percent of school-aged students aged 3 to 21 were served in special education programs. The total number served for 1989 was 4,587,370 students. Students with learning disabilities (1,973,291) comprised the single largest category. Estimates of incidence of students with mild mental retardation and students with behavior disorders are more difficult to calculate because these students are not differentiated from moderately to seriously retarded or seriously emotionally disturbed students in federal reports. Approximately three-quarters (390,000) of the total 1989 student population of 522,864 for mental retardation fell in the mild range. Any count of students with behavior disorders is complicated by inconsistency in state definitions and wide variance in placement procedures for this population. Using regular public school placements as a criteria to separate behavior disordered students from more severely disturbed students who are placed in residential facilities or separate schools, we estimate that in 1989 approximately 270,000 students had behavior disorders. We also estimate the number of students identified as having a mild disability is approximately 75 percent of all students who receive special education services.

Student counts are taken annually in each state across the nation, and these data are reported to the Department of Education as FTE (Full Time Equivalency) statements. Since the first report in 1976, disabled students nationwide have been reported to be approximately 11 percent of the total school population.

Students with mild disabilities are served during the school-aged years.
Mild disabilities are often unrecognizable before entering and after exiting school. The physical appearance of these students is like that of students without disabilities. There are no differences in facial features or body dimensions. Students with mild disabilities are, in almost all respects, normal children who have encountered serious learning problems. They often remain unidentified until entry into public school and mesh into the mainstream of society upon leaving school. Acquaintances and employers usually don't make a connection between social and work difficulties and the fact that at one time, an individual received special education services. After all, most people exhibit some minor skill deficits in particular situations and under certain circumstances.

The categories mild retardation, behavior disordered,
and learning disabled are unreliable.
Education is not precise in pinpointing students with mild disabilities. Consider a scenario where measles would be identified by different criteria in various states. A sick child traveling cross-country would be diagnosed as sick in one state and healthy in the next. Despite the difference in diagnosis, the child would still be ill.

This is the problem with mild disabilities. Because there is no national criteria, some students are accurately diagnosed while others are misevaluated as false positives or false negatives. This means some students are incorrectly identified as having a mild disability, and some students who have a mild disability are overlooked.

Unreliable evaluations are complicated by the diversity of behaviors that are subsumed under the category learning disabled. Everybody has trouble in school at one time or another. As James Ysseldyke, an authority on special education assessment practices, has pointed out, at one time or another eighty percent of all American schoolchildren could be identified as having a learning disability!

Similar troublesome problems are observed across these categories when we must determine which mild disability category fits a student. An analogy could be that of a preschool child attempting to put geometric shapes into the right holes of a container. When the particular objects do not fit into any of the holes, he just pounds on them or pushes harder to make them go in. Perhaps a hypothetical student with mild disabilities is like a square shape. We try to shove him or her into the circle representative of mild mental retardation, or, seeing at least two straight sides, we try to push him or her into the triangle representative of learning disabilities. If that does not work, then we try the behavior rectangle because, even though it does not have all sides equal, it does have four sides like a square. The child may not have the exact dimensions of the category, but he or she is similar enough to all three that we figure if we just try hard enough, we can make a fit with one of them.

This analogy is much like the example given by Blackman in his assessment of "negative school labels." Recently on the television news program *60 Minutes,* a local sheriff was being questioned about the probable guilt of a particular fugi-

tive (the accused allegedly had been observed in a criminal act by several people). Said the sheriff: "Hey, man, if it looks like a duck, flies like a duck, flaps like
a duck, eats like a duck, walks like a duck, tends to like the company of other
ducks. . . hey, I think you got yourself a duck!" (Blackman, 1989, 460)

***Students with mild disabilities are those who are most likely to be placed in the
regular classroom with resource services.***
Collaboration between general and special education teachers is necessary.
Educational services must be delivered in all assigned classes. For these students,
the issue is not so much mainstreaming as it is concern for the effectiveness of the
education they are receiving in both special and regular classrooms.

In an earlier study by Glavin, Quay, Annesley, and Werry (1971), students
with mild behavior disorders were randomly assigned to either a resource
program with regular class placement or regular class placement solely. Those
receiving resource room services gained significantly in reading and math
achievement. Two recent studies similarly support the effectiveness of the

"Oh dear, some of these kids don't **fit** into the categories."
"No problem— —we'll just stuff 'em in."

FIGURE 2–1   School Category Machine.

Illustration by Lois Creech.

resource room as an instructional site. In 1988, Marston compared the reading improvement shown by pupils with mild disabilities in the regular classroom and in the resource room through curriculum-based assessment measures. The subjects in his study made more improvement in the resource room than in the regular classroom. Fuchs and Fuchs (1986) used a statistical technique known as meta-analysis in their study which reviewed earlier research. These researchers found that when individualized instruction and curriculum-based assessment techniques were used, special education students did well in special education classes.

For every study that presents a dismal portrayal of students with mild learning disorders in special classes, there is a contradictory study that demonstrates gains through resource room or special classroom placement. Educators are attempting to refocus this murky picture by shifting the viewfinder from *where* students are educated to *what* teaching methods work best. In subsequent chapters, you will find that many strategies that work well with students in general education are just as useful for teaching students with mild learning disorders. Good teaching is a constant that cuts across both special and general education.

The concern about quality and benefits of special education services has more recently surfaced in the Regular Education Initiative (REI) literature. The REI provoked a controversy in special education concerning whether students with mild disabilities should be taught solely in the regular classroom. Presently, most students with mild disabilities receive special education services through pull-out resource room instruction. With the proposed changes, the special education teacher might team teach in the regular classroom or serve as a consultant to general education teachers of students with mild disabilities, who would remain full time in their regular classrooms. Supporters of the REI believe that the federal mandates, which legislate an appropriate education in the least restrictive environment, are not being realized in the case of significant numbers of students with mild learning and behavior disabilities.

Causes of Mild Disabilities

Causes for mild disabilities can primarily be subdivided into two major categories: organic (biological) and environmental (Figure 2–2).

Under the category of organic, we will discuss pre- , peri- , and postnatal factors, genetic factors, biochemical factors, and maturational lag. These are contributors that originate within the body (i.e., endogenous). We include under environmental reasons for mild learning and behavior disabilities discussions about factors relating to poverty, nutrition, toxins, language differences, sensory deprivation, emotional problems, and inadequate education. Although some environmental factors (e.g., toxins) cause organic dysfunction, the point of origin is outside the body (i.e., exogenous).

FIGURE 2-2 Common Cause of Mild Disabilities

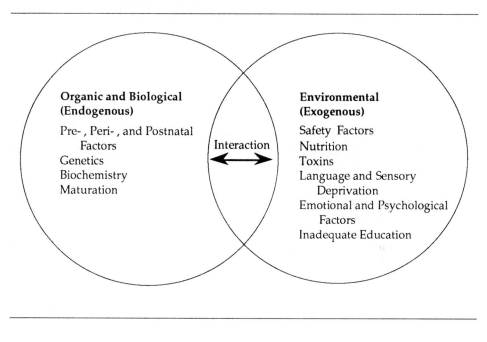

Mild *verses* Severe

The more severe the disability, the earlier the problem can be identified. In fact, it is not unusual for a parent of a child with mental retardation to learn of this at birth. The appearance of the infant may differ from that of normal babies, with enlarged head circumference, tell-tale facial features, or inadequate response to visual or auditory stimuli. Several medical tests are now in use with expectant mothers to provide information about possible abnormalities in their unborn fetus. These include ultrasound scans (the recording of tissue densities by sound waves), amniocentesis (examination of amniotic fluid and culturing of fetal cells), chorionic villus biopsy (examination of fetal cells in placental tissue), fetoscopy (the surgical placement of an endoscope into the uterus), and blood analysis (analyses of embryonic cells that migrate from the fetus in the mother's bloodstream).

As mentioned earlier, mild learning and behavior difficulties are usually not discovered until children enter school because, in classrooms, teachers are able to detect intellectual and behavioral problems that can go unnoticed in less formal settings. The schedule and routines of classroom life serve as a backdrop to compare children's ability to cope with various academic and social demands. Such mild learning problems as distractibility or delayed social development become apparent when students are unable to sit for variable periods of time or follow prescribed classroom routines.

As a teacher of students who have learning or behavioral difficulties, you may never know for sure the origin of their learning problems. Attention deficit disorder with hyperactivity (ADD-H), for example, has been attributed primarily to minimal brain dysfunction; but allergies, inordinate junk food consumption, developmental lag, emotional problems, and lead poisoning can also cause attention difficulties and hyperactivity. For individual students, the cause may be any one of the above agents or a combination.

Fortunately, educational intervention is not contingent on identifying and curing the cause of a problem. Educational intervention begins with the identification of a student's strengths and weaknesses in thinking, behaving, concentrating, using language, and functioning in other areas. Once an educational assessment profile of an individual student is compiled, teachers can select any one of numerous educational strategies to enhance learning. No one plan works for all students even though their functional problem may be the same. For example, one student who is identified as hyperactive may respond to a behavior modification program that uses positive reinforcement to extend the student's ability to concentrate. Another student with hyperactivity may flourish in a classroom that provides indirect instructional methods such as learning centers and peer tutoring.

An informed understanding of causal agents can prove beneficial in the identification of students who are at-risk for developing learning or behavioral difficulties. For example, students who live near toxic waste discharge run a high risk of developing a mild disability. Better knowledge about etiology provides educational programs with information to prevent learning problems. For instance, Head Start preschool programs are aimed at ameliorating the effects of poverty, such as inadequate nutrition and lead poisoning.

Determination of causes can also:

- Provide a better understanding of the child for family members and educators.
- Provide justification for government policies to prevent disabilities.
- Enable better communication among various human service agencies.
- Suggest a particular treatment approach (e.g., diet instead of behavior modification).
- Provide information that may facilitate referrals outside the educational system.
- Enable more accurate prognosis. (Smith, Price, & Marsh, 1986, 58)

Organic Causes

Pre- , Peri- , and Postnatal Factors

Mild learning, intellectual, and behavioral problems may be the result of prenatal, perinatal, and postnatal problems. Learning problems have been traced to the following prenatal conditions:

- Maternal endocrine disorders (e.g., hypothyroidism, diabetes)
- Maternal-fetal blood type incompatibilities (i.e., Rh factor)
- Maternal age, reproductive readiness, and efficiency
- Maternal cigarette smoking
- Maternal drug and alcohol abuse
- Rubella
- Radiation exposure
- Anoxia
- Accidents (Pasamanick & Knoblock, 1973)

Maternal health, diet, and lifestyle are important factors that affect fetal developmental deficits. Recently, educators have become alarmed at the increasing number of children who are born with disabilities as the result of maternal cocaine addiction. The appeal of crack, a cheap, smokable form of cocaine, has tragically increased the number of children afflicted with learning disorders. Although crack passes through the mother's system in a few days, it remains in the uterus for eighteen to twenty days. Cocaine restricts the oxygen supply to the infant by constricting blood vessels in the placenta. Neurological damage, respiratory ailments, social-emotional disturbances, and physical impairments are possible effects of crack usage on the newborn infants. Extreme hyperactivity, irritability, unresponsiveness, learning disabilities, and mental retardation are some of the problems educators are encountering in children born to crack users.

Infants born of mothers who have consumed alcohol during pregnancy may develop fetal alcohol syndrome. This disability is characterized by mental retardation and other serious learning problems. Prenatal and postnatal growth deficiencies are present in approximately 50 percent of babies born to mothers classified as severely and chronically alcoholic, with an unknown number of babies affected by a lesser degree of alcohol abuse during pregnancy and nursing (Smith, Price, & Marsh, 1986; Umbreit & Ostrow, 1980). *Abstinence from alcohol consumption during pregnancy is recommended by many obstetricians, as the amount which can be consumed without ill effects currently is unknown.*

Researchers have attributed various pre- and post-natal factors to mild disabilities. Maternal malnutrition can harm the development of the fetus's central nervous system and modify the growth and biochemical maturation of the brain (Hallahan & Cruickshank, 1973; Silver, 1989). Secondary cigarette smoke and substance abuse by nursing mothers have been reported as cumulative, postnatal toxins (Silver, 1989; Smith-Davis, 1989a, b).

Genetics
There is some evidence that dyslexia, a type of learning disability that impairs a student's ability to read, occurs in family lineages. Schizophrenia, a severe emotional disturbance, also appears to have, in some instances, a genetic component. Some forms of mental retardation leave unmistakable genetic tracers. Riley-Day syndrome is an inherited form of mental retardation that occurs principally

among people of Jewish backgrounds. Marfan's syndrome is a rare, inherited disorder that causes visual impairments and mild mental retardation.

Until recently, the best way to determine a genetic factor in learning disorders was to count cases in a particular family or in a specific ethnic group. This approach is relatively clear-cut when tracking medically obvious developmental disabilities such as Riley-Day syndrome. The presence of such anomalies as small stature, spinal curvature, insensitivity to pain, and behavior problems allow for construction of a clinical profile that is both observable and measurable. Because students with mild learning disorders are normal in appearance and have no obvious medical complications, conclusions about the relative importance of genetic factors are tentative. The history of mild mental retardation, in particular, is replete with assertions and counterassertions about genetic versus environmental factors. You will read more about this "nature-nurture" debate in Chapter 3.

As neuroscientists and geneticists become more adept at chromosome and gene identification, they will unravel the mystery of why some individuals develop learning disabilities and other mild learning disorders. In the meantime, the code word is caution when making assertions about an individual's innate, inherited characteristics. When any disorder appears with regularity in different generations of the same family, environmental influence cannot be dismissed as a causal factor. Home life, readiness for school, adequacy of teaching, motivation, and attitude toward learning are the deciding factors in a large number of cases of students with mild learning disorders.

Biochemistry
Despite its durability, the human body is a delicately balanced organism. The way our body functions depends on how well approximately 100,000 different chemicals work together. In order for the body and mind to function in unison, these chemicals must mesh in rhythmic patterns that assure optimum performance of all body organs. An imbalance in one area, such as glucose metabolism, will adversely affect mood, perception, and thinking. In the flurry of educational evaluations that precede a determination of special education services, physiological reasons for a learning problem are often overlooked. Alan C. Levin, Director of the New York Institute for Child Development, reported that 75 percent of the students referred for learning or behavior problems had a physical or biochemical problem that contributed to their difficulties (Brickland, 1976). Vitamin deficiencies, allergic reactions, and abnormal mineral levels (e.g., iron deficiency) are just a sample of biochemical explanations for why students fail to develop normal learning and socialization skills.

It is also possible that many behaviors that are considered disturbing in school are stress related. Hans Seyle (1975) defines stress as the nonspecific response of the body to a demand. By this he means that regardless of the type of stressor experienced, the biochemical reactions of the body are the same. The student who views reading as a threatening activity or who perceives the teacher as hostile may instinctively resort to a flight or fight response. Withdrawal, apathy, resentment, moodiness and anger are nonverbal responses to stress that are common both inside and outside the classroom. The ability of the teacher to identify physical signs of a youngster in distress (e.g., eyes with dilated pupils or increased muscle tone of the body) is important because many students do not have the verbal facility to describe feelings like panic, tension, and anxiety. Students with behavior disorders, in particular, are apt to act these feelings out rather than communicate them verbally.

Educators, both general and special, have been reluctant to accept biochemical explanations for learning problems. There are two reasons for their indisposition. First, possible biochemical causes for learning problems are difficult to track down. Hair analysis, for example, can pinpoint mineral deficiencies, but the procedure requires expertise that is outside the range of most family physicians. The oral glucose tolerance test can evaluate hypoglycemia (low blood sugar), but it requires six hours of medical attention and frequent blood samples. The cost, time, and complications of these evaluation procedures are discouraging. Second, educators, in general, simply do not accept biochemical explanations for learning problems because the evidence is largely anecdotal. For example, while Feingold's (1974) and Crook's (1980) research on how specific foods can cause allergic reactions and learning problems caught on with parents, educators remained unimpressed. School menus, which weekly offer school children large doses of preservative-laden and chemically-treated foods, graphically illustrate a lack of concern about biochemical contributors to learning problems.

Maturation
While it is common knowledge that children physically develop at different rates, parents and educators sometimes overlook the fact that children's nervous systems follow the same idiosyncratic pattern as height and weight. Differences in development are not uniformly equal. Small children in a classroom may have quick reflexes, while larger children may lag behind others in the ability to coordinate movement. This developmental lag is normal and eventually, as the students' nervous systems mature, they will be on an equal physical footing with others in the class. Developmental delay is more serious with some children, presumably because there is an irregularity in the physical development of their nervous system.

Developmental delay is a characteristic of mental retardation. Moreover, Bender (1968) and de Hirsch (1965) suggest a relationship between the immaturity evident in some youth with learning disabilities and a lag in the maturation of some central nervous system components. Immaturity also can be an individual trait and, given time, corrected on its own.

Much is being written about developmental lag and mild learning and behavior disorders in relationship to recent brain research. Within the brain, some reasoning abilities are localized in specific areas. For instance, in most individuals the language center of the brain is in the left frontal and temporal lobe of the neocortex. A slight anomaly to a small area of the brain can be responsible for problems in such abstract skills as calculating and reading. Often these problems are detectable only in a formal learning environment, such as a classroom.

Hynd and Hynd contend that developmental anomalies exist in all brains. Not all brains develop in the same way (e g., time stages, growth sections, and so on), and not all parts of the brain develop uniformly within a single individual. These researchers contend:

> *While it is easy for psychologists and educators to conceive of separate distributions for IQ, reading achievement, math achievement, personality, and so on, it seems almost impossible for these same professionals to conceive of a separate distribution of neurological development. It is almost as if an assumption is made that everyone was born with a perfect unblemished cerebral cortex. (Hynd & Hynd, 1984; 491)*

This statement has several implications. First, rather than assuming that students with mild disabilities have organic deficits, consider the possibility of developmental lag that, given time, can "catch up." Second, educational modifications can stimulate development in school children while maturation proceeds. Third, if all brains are "blemished" in some fashion, learning disabilities may be contextual. In school the context is verbal skills. Thus students with language-based learning disabilities stand out, while students with deficits in musical or artistic abilities would be overlooked.

Environmental Causes

Environmental factors can enhance a child's learning potential or retard progress. The most rapid developmental growth in physiological, intellectual, emotional, motor, and linguistic functioning domains occurs during preschool years.

Safety Factors

Physical safety is necessary for healthy growth and development of any child. A complicated delivery, early injury, illness, or falls and accidents can be traumatic and show their effects as the child develops learning readiness. Harmful events can occur even under well-supervised medical and familial conditions. Nevertheless, accidents frequently occur during times of inadequate supervision at home, on the playground, and even in school.

Nutrition

Adequate nutrition of mothers prior to pregnancy, during pregnancy, and of children during growing years is necessary for normal development (Peterson, 1987; Smith & Patton, 1989; Smith-Davis, 1989). Nutrition can affect learning potential and has been identified as a contributing factor in mild mental retardation, learning disabilities, and some forms of disturbed behavior (Smith et al., 1986). Nutritional intake has been studied extensively and has contributed to the enactment of federal programs such as Head Start, the Woman, Infant, and Children Program (WIC), Home Start, subsidized school lunches and breakfasts, along with grant approvals for parent education programs.

Many different children are at risk of learning problems as a result of poor nutrition. Poor children, children of teenagers, migrant children, and children in rural areas are most likely to develop learning and behavior problems as the result of poor nutrition. Some of the symptoms of a lack of a proper diet are listlessness, irritability, fatigue, and inability to concentrate. While poor nutrition slows metabolism and restricts the functioning of the central nervous system, the effects are reversible. The most prevalent nutritional disorder in the United States today is iron deficiency. Mothers of iron deficient children tend to be younger, less educated, poor, and depressed. Iron deficient children have short attention spans and behavior problems. Drinking cow's milk rather than mother's milk or formula can harm infants. Uneducated families who are unable to afford formula sometimes feed their infants cow's milk or sweetened beverages such as carbonated colas.

Feingold (1976) proposed the elimination of food additives and natural substances called salicylates by adherence to a special diet called the Kaiser-Permanente (KP) Diet. Though unproven in curbing hyperactivity and learning disabilities in controlled studies, parents and teachers have attested to beneficial effects from use of the elimination diet with children with learning and behavior problems (Mayron, 1979). Allergies, which come about as abnormal responses to substances within the environment (e.g., food, chemicals, inhalants, dust, mold, selective foliage), have been associated with learning and behavior problems. It is estimated that 60 to 80 percent of this nation's population has suffered an allergic reaction to food at some time during their lives (Mayron, 1979). Cott (1974) supported megavitamin therapy (i.e., massive use of vitamins to eliminate deficiencies associated with learning and behavior problems); however, success in using large doses of vitamins to treat learning and behavior problems has not been substantiated in independent studies (Silver, 1975). Other dietary deficiencies correlated with learning and behavior disorders include deficiencies in protein, zinc, magnesium, and calcium (Mayron, 1978).

The cumulative aspect of nutritional effects is most aptly illustrated and summarized by Crook (1980):

> *If you don't use the right kind of fuel in your automobile, it won't run properly. It may sputter, jump, jerk, and knock. Similarly, the poor performance of the inattentive, overactive child is often caused by improper "fuel": too much sugar and other junk food and insufficient amounts of essential nutrients, including complex carbohydrates, essential fatty acids, vitamins, and minerals.*

The impact of maternal substance abuse, malnutrition during pregnancy, and poor medical care of mother and child is discussed under prenatal, perinatal, and postnatal delivery factors.

Toxins

Environmental pollution is a contributory source for mild disabling conditions. Toxins found in the environment that have a strong likelihood for causing

causing intellectual, learning, and behavioral problems include hydrocarbon from coal, petroleum, and natural gas (Mayron, 1978); lead (e.g., paint, plaster, automobile exhausts) (Smith & Patton, 1989); and mercury (factory contaminated

FIGURE 2–3   Cars and Kids Don't Run on Bad Fuel.

Illustration by Lois Creech.

waterways) (Peterson, 1987). Contamination from toxic waste sites and landfills that burn lead batteries contribute to learning problems as well. A follow-up study of 425 children treated for lead poisoning in the Chicago inner-city area reported 39 percent with neurological damage, 54 percent with recurrent seizures, 38 percent with mental retardation, and 13 percent with cerebral palsy (Wallace, 1972). Oil and chemical spills continue to be studied for negative effects upon development and learning.

While high doses of radiation are known to be deadly, effects from low-level radiation are not so easily determined. Pregnant mothers, however, are advised to avoid unnecessary dental, chest, and other body X-rays because of possible damage to the developing fetus. Electromagnetic radiation in radio frequency wavelengths have been implicated as a possible cause of hyperactivity and underachievement (Mayron, 1979). And, though not well understood, evidence has linked radiation from fluorescent lights and televisions to learning and behavior problems (Smith, Price, & Marsh, 1986). In addition, the pollution of our air, soil, and water has resulted in the contamination of many foods. Animal products are especially apt to contain insecticides and other toxic substances. These toxic substances may place a further burden on a child's developing immune and nervous systems.

Language and Sensory Deprivation

Intellectual learning and behavioral development is retarded by the absence of sensory, linguistic, and cognitive stimulation. Children learn through interaction within their environment (Piaget, 1952). During infant and preschool years, overlooked health problems such as ear infections can hinder involvement in activities that are important to the development of academic readiness. Regular trips to the pediatrician or family physician are necessary to detect subtle hearing and visual difficulties. Unfortunately, many poor or uneducated parents are unable to provide preventive health attention for their children.

Children can develop verbal language problems when adequate models are unavailable to them during early years when speech is forming (Smith & Patton, 1989). Deficits occur in homes where there is language deprivation. For example, if a primary caregiver does not initiate speech or respond to a youngster's speech efforts, the child's language will suffer. A blaring television prevents active language interaction and makes discrimination of unique sounds impossible. Sometimes bilingual confusion exists. Adverse effects in the academic setting may be countered in classrooms where respect for diverse language forms (e.g., bilingual, Afro-American and Anglo-Saxon derivatives) is shown, while instruction continues in standard English (Bryen, 1982).

Emotional and Psychological Factors

Many children with mild learning, intellectual, and emotional disorders exhibit lack of self-esteem, insecurity, low frustration tolerance, and impulsive behavior. Home life that at an early age is unstable, abusive, or psychologically stressful, contributes to poor emotional and social development of the young. Furthermore, some children are slow to respond to maternal bonding and nurturing. Sometimes these children will not allow themselves to be comforted during stressful times.

Mary Ainsworth (1978) studied infant–mother bonding at twelve months of age. Ainsworth found that infants respond differently to their mothers. In an experiment called the "strange situation," Ainsworth analyzed infant reaction when the mother left them in an observation room. Securely attached infants cried when the mother left and greeted the returning mother with pleasure. Avoidant infants gave the impression of independence and did not seem to be affected by mother leaving or returning. Insecurely attached infants clung to mother and cried profusely when mother left. However, upon return of the mother, avoidant infants resisted all attempts to be soothed and would angrily arch away from mother's comforting embrace.

The infant behavior influenced the mother's response. Attached mothers were more responsive to feeding signals and crying of infants. These mothers readily returned smiles. Mothers of avoidant and insecurely attached infants were unresponsive or rejecting. Without intervention, these attachment patterns persisted. Insecure and avoidant infants often become problem children. At age two, they tend to lack self-reliance and show little enthusiasm for problem solving. From three to five, they have poor peer relations and little resilience. At six, insecure and avoidant children are apathetic and unmotivated. Ainsworth has found that teachers tend to treat securely attached children in age-appropriate ways. Teachers tend to excuse and infantilize insecurely attached children. With avoidant children, teachers are controlling.

Ainsworth's research is valuable because it highlights the interactional aspect of social-emotional growth. Significant adults in a child's life, whether they are parents or teachers, help mold a youngster's personality by the way they respond to his or her behavior. A teacher who ignores a child because "she just wants attention" or gets angry at a child who is "immature" is unwittingly contributing to the development of the offensive behaviors. Child abuse, inconsistent nurturing, neglect, and poverty all play a role in contributing to avoidant and insecure children. The effect of an early unnurturing or depriving living environment may result in youth who lack motivation for learning and are unconcerned about others. Further unacceptance may be shown by teachers who have a differing value system coupled with intolerance for youth who are disturbing in the classroom.

Inadequate Education

Negative expectations for students with mild learning and behavior problems are handicapping factors in the classroom (Algozzine & Stroller, 1981). Poor instructional programming, disorganized teaching practices, and low expectations for educational outcomes of children with mild disabling conditions contribute to learning difficulties. Hallahan and Kauffman (1982) include the following teacher behaviors as contributors to school failure: insensitivity to individuality, requirement of conformity to rules and routines, inappropriate and inconsistent disciplinary practices, reinforcement of inappropriate behaviors, and emphasis upon student inadequacies.

Insufficient development of prerequisite readiness skills occur both in home and school environments. The absence of intellectually stimulating experiences and lack of exposure to materials that will be used in school contribute to academic delay (Smith & Patton, 1989). Lack of readiness for school coupled with desultory teaching in school almost guarantees school failure.

Special Population at Risk

Infants, Toddlers, Preschoolers

The most vulnerable at-risk population is infants, toddlers, and preschoolers born under precarious circumstances. (Smith-Davis, 1989a, b). This is shown in Table 2–2.

A large number of young children will have mild disabilities or other related problems indicative of school failure. Many will qualify for special education services, while others will not meet specific classification criteria. Support for early prevention and intervention programs have never been more crucial. Smith-Davis (1989a) suggests that the following programs receive recognition for their potential for offsetting school failure for the at risk youth populations:

TABLE 2–2   Facts about Infants and Preschoolers at Risk

- More than 43,000 infants weigh less than three and one-half pounds at birth.
- Low birth weight and prematurity are associated with multiple risks, including mental retardation and physical disability.
- Teenaged mothers are likely to bear low-birth-weight babies with disabilities.
- Between 100,000 and 150,000 babies are born each year with defects which will lead to some degree of mental retardation.
- At least 1,500 to 2,000 infants are born each year with fetal alcohol syndrome resulting from heavy drinking by the mother during pregnancy.
- For each child with an identified fetal alcohol syndrome, there are several others who have been affected by alcohol during pregnancy but lack the physical characteristics (i.e., small head, facial bone maldevelopment, drooping eyelids) required for diagnosis at birth.
- Infants and toddlers aged three and under account for thirty percent of the 800,000 reported cases of child abuse each year. Of all children born in 1983, forty-five percent will have parents who divorce, and fifty-nine percent will live at some time in a single-parent home.

Source: Smith-Davis, 1989a.

- Development of new preschool programs.
- Implementation of preschool programs for students identified as disabled, contained in Public Law 99–457, Part H.
- Expansion of existing Head Start programs.
- Training of professional and support personnel for these programs.

Schools alone cannot counter the social problems that debilitate children. The community must also take responsibility for offsetting school failure by the creation of special programs (Smith-Davis, 1989a, b). The formation of school–business partnerships is one example of how this can be accomplished. Through these partnerships, many problems affecting society in general can be addressed. Concerns can be targeted jointly by schools and businesses in the community. An example is a preschool center on the campus of Albany State College in Albany, Georgia. The center is supported by grant funding obtained by the Albany Association of Retarded Citizens, sponsorships of local businesses, and an arrangement by which there is no cost for housing the program in the college facilities.

School-Aged Youth

Students at risk is a generic term that describes a range of problems of school-aged youth. Low achievement, retention in grade, truancy, and behavior problems are indicators that a student may be at risk of school failure. Approximately 15 percent of all high school students leave school before their graduation date. In 1985, 4.3 million students between 16 and 24 dropped out of school (Hahn, 1987). School dropouts are clearly at risk of failure in life outside of school. Almost one-fourth of 17-year-olds in school do not have the literacy skills to read a popular magazine (National Assessment of Educational Progress, 1985). Clearly these students are at risk. Frymier and Gansneder believe that a student is at risk when failure is likely to occur—either in school or in life.

> For example, if a student fails a course in school and is retained in grade, or drops out of school, that student is at risk. Likewise, if a child uses drugs, has been physically or sexually abused, or has contemplated or attempted suicide, that child is also at-risk. Failure—in school or in life—is evidence that a youngster is at-risk (Frymier & Gansneder, 1989, 142).

After infants, the most vulnerable at-risk population is adolescents. This is due to the escalating number of secondary level students dropping out of school. Smith-Davis (1989a) offers the following facts:

1. Approximately 14 percent of Caucasian students, 25 percent of African-American students, and more than 50 percent of Hispanic students drop out before completing high school.
2. Teenage dropouts produce the highest rate of babies born out of wedlock.

3. Among the special education population, those with mild disabilities and capable of being mainstreamed are at the greatest risk of dropping out.
4. In a U. S. Department of Education study, dropout rates for students with disabilities ranged from a low of about 19 percent for students with orthopedic handicaps to a high of about 37 percent for students with learning disabilities.

Whether or not a youth is at-risk is a function of the family and community as much as school factors. Problems linked to family and society include drug abuse, deficient school readiness skills, emotional problems, absenteeism, and family turmoil. Retention, low achievement, behavior problems, and absenteeism are school variables that are characteristic of students at risk. A Phi Delta Kappa (1989) study on at-risk students asked teachers if they thought it was possible to help students with out-of-school problems. More than 60 percent of the teachers said that they could not help students with family discord, crime, or alcohol abuse. Over 90 percent of the teachers felt that parents rather than teachers should be responsible for helping students cope with their out-of-school problems. These teachers' perceptions of their minimal role in assisting at-riskstudents highlight the difficulties faced by these young people. If most of their problems originate in the home and community and their teachers feel their role does not include assistance with out-of-school problems, to whom can at-risk students turn for help?

School Programs

School efforts to help at-risk students have focused almost exclusively on children and youth from low socioeconomic backgrounds. The term *compensatory education* is used to describe federal programs that are targeted for disadvantaged children who are at risk of academic failure.

HIGHLIGHT 2–1

Jerome is sixteen years old. He has barely scraped through school. His reading and calculating skills are on par with those of an average ten year old. Each year his teachers promote him hoping that their successor will have more luck in teaching Jerome. Jerome's poor academic skills are counterbalanced by his leadership ability. The other students look up to him because he is tough and kind. In the inner-city school Jerome attends, this a charismatic combination. When Jerome leaves school at the end of the day, he walks home through a maze of drug dealers, winos, and storefronts girded with iron gates. His mother would like to move Jerome and his two sisters to a nicer neighborhood, but her salary as a fast food restaurant worker barely provides the family with rent and food money. Jerome is street-wise, and lately he has begun to make extra money by selling crack. All his teachers agree that Jerome is a good kid, who, with a few opportunities, could be a success; but, in educational jargon, he is a functional illiterate. Jerome is at risk of graduating from high school unable to read a newspaper.

Chapter 1 of the Education Consolidation and Improvement Act (1981) and Head Start are federal programs aimed at helping at-risk poor students. Between 1984 and 1985, Chapter 1 (formerly Title I of the Elementary and Secondary Education Act, 1965) provided remedial services to almost 5 million school children (Guttman & Henderson, 1987). It is the largest federal education program with an annual budget in excess of 4 billion dollars. Almost every school system in the country (over 90 percent) receives Chapter 1 funds. The major portion of Chapter 1 funds go to elementary schools. Chapter 1 guidelines provide latitude in terms of program development. Chapter 1 funds are given to schools based on numbers of low income students, but within each school receiving the funds, the money is used to service students according to educational need, rather than income level. The majority of students receiving Chapter 1 services are not poor. Remedial education is provided through Chapter 1 pull-out programs, in-class tutoring, early childhood programs, self-contained remedial classes and schoolwide projects for all the students (Slavin, Karweit, & Madden, 1989).

Head Start provides preschool education for low income children (Peterson, 1989). Head Start programs began in 1965 as a national effort to offset at-risk factors associated with poverty. Eligible children can begin at age three toattend half-day programs that are home- or center-based. Head Start center-based programs operate out of church basements, storefronts, or public schools. In the home-based programs, Head Start teachers visit the children's homes and work with their parents to help develop school readiness skills. One of the advantages of the Head Start program is its emphasis on other aspects of a child's life besides education. Parent training, nutrition assessment, and health screening help ensure that Head Start children are provided with some of the basic necessities required for normal development.

School programs for at-risk students are generally based on the assumption that grouping students for intensive remediation will help solve their academic problems. When a student is identified as at risk of academic failure, the

---

HIGHLIGHT 2–2

Luvia is fifteen years old and pregnant. She moved with her family from Mexico when she was seven years old. They settled in a small southwestern town with a large Mexican-American population. Her father was lured to the area by the hope of employment and adequate inexpensive housing. Instead, they found sleazy tenements and unemployment. A year after their arrival, Luvia's mother returned to Puerto Rico with her younger brother and sister. Luvia lives with her father, who is absent from their apartment more than he's home. Luvia works hard at school, but her grades are consistently poor. She started out in a bilingual program where she was taught for two years by an uncertified teacher. By the time she worked her way into a regular classroom, Luvia was far behind her agemates in basic skills. She was retained in sixth grade, and since that time has been truant from school frequently. Most of her time is spent with her friends on the streets. Luvia is at risk of dropping out of school.

educational response has often been to place the student in a special education program rather than a compensatory education program. For instance, since the passage of the Individuals with Disabilities Education Act, the number of learning-disabled students identified by the schools has increased beyond all reasonable expectations. However, as Slavin points out, labeling students mildly disabled is no guarantee that their learning problems will be remediated.

> *This increase (in learning disabled students) represents the entry into the special education system of low achievers who would not have been served in special education in the past. In other words, special education has assumed a substantial burden in trying to meet the needs of students at-risk of school failure. Yet research comparing students with mild handicaps in special education to similar students left in regular classrooms finds few if any benefits for this expensive service. (Slavin, 1989, 15)*

The Challenge to Schools

The better response to at-risk students is to identify effective teaching practices from all sectors (general, compensatory, and special education) and use these methods with all students receiving education in the mainstream (for example, cooperative learning based on planned student groupings, and peer tutoring work with students who are accelerated, average, at-risk, and have mild disabilities). Effective teaching methods need to be shared among general educators, compensatory educators, and special educators. Unsuccessful teachers need to be retrained in effective teaching practices. Teachers must be willing to work with a broad spectrum of students, including those identified as at-risk or with a mild disability.

Perhaps the most difficult challenge is to convince teachers that their responsibilities to youth do not end at the schoolhouse door. Most of the problems of at-risk students begin in the home and community. Teachers who make home visits and who value parental participation in school activities are capable of understanding the needs of at-risk students more clearly than teachers who have little interest in their students' lives outside of school. You will read more about family/teacher cooperation in Chapter 9.

Due Process Procedures

A series of mandated steps must occur before a student can be delivered services in any special education category (Figure 2–4). They must be addressed in sequence, and specific procedures by which each must be carried out are outlined in IDEA. More specifically, these steps are referred to as due process procedures because they are required before a student is declared eligible for special education. How these procedures are carried out is governed by law.

A nationwide survey was conducted by Ramsey and Algozzine in 1989 to find out what states consider important for teachers to know on their state's teacher competency test in special education. Officials of each of the 48 reporting states confirmed that knowledge of student due process procedures was a necessity (Ramsey & Algozzine, 1991; Ramsey, Algozzine, & Smith, 1990; Ramsey, Algozzine, & Stephens, 1989). Due process procedures include: identification of learning problem, prereferral intervention, referral, evaluation, eligibility, classification, and placement.

Identification of Learning Problems

The following is a description of a typical chain of events outlined in Figure 2–4. Identification of a student's learning problem occurs when comparisons are made within the general population about a student's academic or behavioral characteristics. Teachers hold expectations for student behaviors, and those who

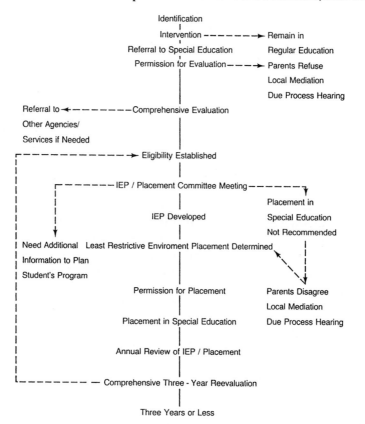

FIGURE 2–4 Due Process Procedures.

From: Georgia Department of Education.

exhibit actions that differ are singled out. Student achievement tests are given to determine grade level progression in most states. Salend and Lutz (1984) identified student behaviors required for success in the regular classroom. These behaviors are grouped into the following major areas of concern:

1. Interact positively with other students.
   Work well with others.
   Respect feelings of others.
   Play cooperatively.
   Share materials and property.
   Avoid fights.
   Refrain from stealing.
2. Follow class rules.
   Remain quiet while others are talking.
   Use appropriate language.
   Tell the truth.
   Keep hands and feet to self.
   Use time wisely.
3. Display proper work habits.
   Follow directions.
   Seek assistance when appropriate.
   Initiate assignments independently.
   Attend to task.
   Persist at difficult tasks.
   Attend regularly.
   Have materials ready.

Students with mild disabilities are identifiable by academic and social behaviors that deviate from those of their classmates; however, these students are not always so obvious. Imagine a continuum of children working on an assigned worksheet. On the far left side of the continuum, students are working on task, appearing to be concentrating on what they are doing, and are busily writing answers on a worksheet. As you look a bit further toward the center, you can see that these students are working on task, concentrating, and recording answers about 50 percent of the time. Now, as you move past the center toward the right of the continuum, notice that students are off task, staring into space, or jesting with each other while they ignore worksheets on their desks.

Students at the far right end of the continuum are displaying disturbing academic and social behaviors at a high rate, duration, or intensity; these students are easily identified by their non-conforming behaviors. It would make things simpler if a certain portion of the continuum could be designated as representative of the characteristics and traits of students who are special education candidates. Unfortunately, identification of students with mild disabilities is not this simple. Imagine that some of the students at the left side of the continuum appear to be working appropriately, but closer inspection shows no rhyme or reason for the answers they are writing. Others appear to be working on task, but are drawing doodles on their worksheets.

These students often fall further and further behind. Their learning problems are not as noticeable, and they are tolerated by the teacher. Students like these are often told to pay attention, listen, and try harder. Because they have no obvious disability, they are mistaken for being lazy or apathetic. These children are at risk because if they are not identified as deviating from the norm in their learning styles, they are likely to fall increasingly further behind age-mates in school.

Intervention

Once a student is identified as being at risk academically or socially, remedial interventions are attempted within the regular classroom. Federal legislation requires that sincere efforts be made to help the child learn in the regular classroom. The concept of regular education intervention is based on a redistribution of the resources of special education toward more immediate problem solving in general education (Pugach & Johnson, 1989). This preventive approach to learning problems is discussed in more detail in Chapters 6 and 8.

In some states, school-based teams of educators are formed to solve learning and behavior problems in the regular classroom. These informal problem solving teams have a variety of names that include concepts of support (school support teams, student support teams), assistance (teacher assistance teams, school assistance teams, or building assistance teams), and appraisal (school appraisal teams) (Pugach & Johnson, 1989).

Regardless of what the teams are called, their purpose is similar. Chalfant, Pysh, and Moultrie (1979) state that teacher assistance teams are created to make professional suggestions about curricular alternatives and instructional modifications. These teams may be composed of a variety of participants, including regular education teachers, building administrator, guidance counselor, special education teacher, and the student's parent(s). The team composition varies based on the type of referral, the needs of the student, the availability of educational personnel and state requirements (Georgia Department of Education, 1986).

Modifications are tried in an attempt to accommodate the student in the regular classroom. Modifications are based on the presumption that learning problems can occur because of a mismatch between teaching and learning style. Students have different learning styles. While one student might benefit from phonics instruction, another student could be baffled by the system of blending sounds to make words. The second student might excel at a reading approach that emphasizes children's literature rather than phonics-oriented basal readers. Effective instruction recognizes differences in how students learn. The strategies for modifying regular classroom instruction shown in Table 2–3 are effective with students at risk, students with mild disabilities, and students without learning problems.

Implementation and results of any intervention that is tailored to meet the unique needs of a student should be documented. Anecdotal records, test results, and samples of work help team members assess progress during regularly scheduled meetings. Thus, appropriate changes within the classroom environment and teaching approaches are attempted prior to or in lieu of special education referral. At this time, focus remains on what can be done in the regular classroom to assist the student. Special education labels are not considered—only modifications that might help the student to progress in the regular classroom (Georgia Department of Education, 1986).

Referral to Special Education

Referral is the process through which a teacher, a parent, or some other person formally requests an evaluation of a student to determine eligibility for special education services. Ramsey (1988) lists six factors which may influence a decision to refer. The factors are: (1) student characteristics, such as the abilities, behaviors, or skills that students exhibit (or the lack of them); (2) individual differences among teachers in their beliefs, expectations, or skill in dealing with specific kinds of problems; (3) expectations for special education assistance with a student who is exhibiting academic or behavioral learning problems; (4) availability of specific special education programs; (5) parents' demand for referral or oppo-

TABLE 2–3 Strategies for Modifying Classroom Instruction

Strategy 1	Provide active learning experiences to teach concepts. Student motivation is increased when students can manipulate, weigh, measure, read, or write using materials and skills that relate to their daily lives.
Strategy 2	Provide ample opportunities for guided practice of new skills. Frequent feedback on performance is essential to overcome student feelings of inadequacy. Peer tutoring and cooperative projects provide nonthreatening practice opportunities. Individual student conferences, curriculum-based tests, and small group discussions are three useful methods for checking progress.
Strategy 3	Provide multisensory learning experiences. Students with learning problems sometimes have sensory processing difficulties; for instance, an auditory discrimination problem may cause misunderstanding about teacher expectations. Lessons and directions that include visual, auditory, tactile, and kinesthetic modes are preferable to a single sensory approach.
Strategy 4	Present information in a manner that is relevant to the student. Particular attention to this strategy is needed when there is a cultural or economic gap between the lives of teachers and students. Relate instruction to a youngster's daily experience and interests.
Strategy 5	Provide students with concrete illustrations of their progress. Students with learning problems need frequent reinforcement for their efforts. Charts, graphs, and checksheets provide tangible markers of student achievement.

sition to referral; and (6) institutional factors which may facilitate or constrain teachers in making referral decisions.

Fewer students are referred when school districts have complex procedures for referral, lengthy paperwork is required, special education classes are filled to capacity, psychological assessments are backlogged for months, or building principals and other site administrators do not fully recognize the importance of special education services.

It is important that referral procedures be clearly understood and coordinated among all school personnel. All educators need to be able to identify characteristics typically exhibited by special-needs students. Also, the restrictiveness of special service settings must be known and the appropriateness of each clearly understood. The more restrictive special education programs tend to group students with similar disabilities for instruction. Last, the specialized services afforded through equipment, materials, teaching approaches, and specific teacher–student ratios should also be clearly understood.

Student Evaluation and Eligibility

If instructional modifications in the regular classroom have not proven successful, a student may be referred for multidisciplinary evaluation. The evaluation is comprehensive and includes norm- and criterion-referenced tests (e.g., IQ and diagnostic tests), curriculum-based assessment, systematic teacher observations (e.g., behavior frequency checklist), samples of student work, and parent interviews. The results of the evaluation are twofold: to determine eligibility for special education services and to identify a student's strengths and weaknesses in order to plan an individual education program.

Eligibility is based on criteria defined in federal law or state regulations. Identification of a mild disability occurs in many states when a student evaluation meets established eligibility criteria for learning disabled, mild mentally retarded, or behavior disordered. As mentioned previously, there is variation in state eligibility criteria.

Evaluation by a multidisciplinary team is the means by which eligibility criteria is determined. A variety of professionals including a speech-language pathologist, school psychologist, special education teacher, and guidance counselor can be involved in the multidisciplinary evaluation. The wording in federal law is very explicit about the manner in which evaluations must be conducted, and about the existence of due process procedures that protect against bias and discrimination. According to Ramsey, provisions stated in the law include:

1. The testing of children in their native or primary language unless it is clearly not feasible to do so.
2. The use of evaluation procedures selected and administered to prevent cultural or ethnic discrimination.
3. The use of assessment tools validated for the purpose for which they are being used (e.g., achievement levels, IQ scores, adaptive skills).

4. Assessment by a multidisciplinary team utilizing several pieces of information to formulate a placement decision. (Ramsey, 1988, 61)

Furthermore, parental involvement must occur in the development of the child's educational program. According to the law, parents *must:*

1. Be notified before initial evaluation or any change in placement by a written notice in their primary language describing the proposed school action, the reasons for it, and the available educational opportunities.
2. Consent, in writing, before the child is initially evaluated.

Parents *may:*

3. Request an independent educational evaluation if they feel the school's evaluation is inappropriate.
4. Request an evaluation at public expense if a due process hearing decision is that the public agency's evaluation was inappropriate.
5. Participate on the committee that considers the evaluation, placement, and programming of the student.

All students referred for evaluation for special education should have on file the results of a relatively current vision and hearing screening. This will determine the adequacy of sensory acuity and ensure that learning problems are not due to a vision and/or hearing problem.

Evaluation methods correspond with criteria for special education disabilities. For example, a multidisciplinary evaluation for a student being evaluated for mild mental retardation would include the individual's intellectual functioning, adaptive behavior, and achievement levels. Other tests are based on developmental characteristics exhibited (e.g., social, language, and motor).

A student evaluated for learning disabilities is given reading, math, and/or spelling achievement tests, an intelligence test to confirm average or above average cognitive capabilities, and tests of written and oral language ability. Classroom observations and samples of student work (such as impaired reading ability or impaired writing ability) also provide valuable indicators of possible learning disabilities.

Eligibility for services in behavior disorders requires documented evidence of social deficiencies or learning deficits that are not due to intellectual, sensory, or physical conditions. Therefore, any student undergoing multidisciplinary evaluation for this categorical service is usually given an intelligence test, diagnostic achievement tests, and social and/or adaptive inventories. Results of behavior frequency lists, direct observations, and anecdotal records collected over an extended period of time often accompany test results.

Additional information frequently used when making decisions about a child's eligibility for special education include:

• Developmental history
• Past academic performance

- Medical history or records
- Neurological reports
- Classroom observations
- Speech and language evaluations
- Personality assessment
- Discipline reports
- Home visits
- Parent interviews
- Samples of student work

If considered eligible for special education services, the child's disability should be documented in a written report stating specific reasons for the decision.

Three year reevaluations of a student's progress are required by law and serve the purpose of determining the growth and changing needs of the student. During the reevaluation, continued eligibility for services in special education must be assessed using a range of evaluation tools similar to those used during the initial evaluation. All relevant information about the student is considered when making a decision about continued eligibility.

Placement for Special Education Services

By law, placement in a special education class must be the student's least restrictive environment. Special education delivery services occur at a variety of levels, some more restrictive than others. The least restrictive environment in the hierarchy of services is the regular classroom—students with mild disabilities are usually served in an environment as similar to this as possible.

Students with mild disabilities may be placed in resource rooms for one or several periods a day. The regular classroom remains the primary placement for the majority of the school day. This decision is made by a multidisciplinary team *after* eligibility and classification is determined. In fact, even before a placement decision can be made, the multidisciplinary team must develop an individualized education plan (IEP) with goals and objectives tailored to meet individual needs. The placement site at which the child's goals and objectives can best be met is considered to be his or her "least restrictive environment."

Common Characteristics of Students with Mild Disabilities

Learning and behavioral characteristics of children differ as they progress through developmental stages. Students whose characteristics substantially deviate from those of the normal population may be in need of special services. As was noted, if learning problems are of a mild, correctable type, the regular teacher with assistance is capable of intervening and ameliorating these conditions. The students' needs may be of a behavioral, academic, or social nature.

Students whose characteristics deviate from the norm are typically classified in the mild disability category that has defined criteria corresponding with identified traits. The fact that students have behavioral traits that are not part of the original classification parameters may be overlooked. In reality, individual students within a defined category may be more similar than different. Educators should keep in mind that all children who exhibit mild disabling characteristics do not fit neatly into a specified slot.

Overlapping of academic and behavioral characteristics is found particularly among the high prevalence categories serving students with mild disabilities (e.g., learning disabilities, mild mental retardation, behavior disorders). Students in these categories often share a variety of traits and behaviors that cut across characteristics associated with each. There is both variance within the categories and overlap between the categories. This phenomenon has led to cross-categorical and interrelated service delivery for the mildly disabled in many states.

Common characteristics of students with mild disabilities are listed in clusters in Table 2–4. These clusters contain characteristics representative of psychological, educational, and social behaviors, in particular.

For example, the psychological cluster is characterized by items which make reference to the fact that the disability is difficult to detect. Typically, a mild disability remains undetected until the child begins school. The condition surfaces when learning demands are placed upon the individual and the person is unable to produce accordingly. The physical appearance of the student is the same as that of students in full-time regular education, and the cause of the mild disability is usually unknown. A poor self-concept often results.

As we said, the problem first becomes apparent in the educational setting. Thus characteristics reflective of educational behaviors are fairly common. The child is a low achiever and exhibits an obvious lack of interest in schoolwork. The preference for concrete rather than abstract lessons reflects his or her need for better understanding of what is being taught. These students respond better to active rather than passive learning tasks. Teachers often observe weak listening skills and limited verbal and/or writing skills. These students may be distractible. Unfortunately, teachers sometimes overlook talents and abilities that many of these students possess. These students are often self-conscious and prefer to receive special help in the regular classroom. They require modifications in classroom instruction in order for learning to occur. Due to the difficulties these students experience in school, they often have a higher dropout rate than regular education students.

Socially, students with mild disabilities sometimes experience friction when interacting with others, and demonstrate problem behaviors in the classroom. They show a need for adult approval and are often stereotyped by others. During school years most function better outside of school than in school; however, following school years, many experience difficulties finding and maintaining employment.

TABLE 2–4 Common Characteristics of Students with Mild Disabilities

The following characteristics will vary from one student to another but are generally the same across the categories of mild mental retardation, behavior disorders, and learning disabilities. They are clustered under psychological, educational, and social characteristics.

Psychological Characteristics

- Mild disability undetected until beginning school years
- Cause of mild disability is difficult to detect
- Physical appearance the same as students in full-time regular education
- Poor self-concept

Educational Characteristics

- Lack of interest in school work
- Prefer concrete rather than abstract lessons
- Weak listening skills
- Low achievement
- Limited verbal and/or writing skills
- Right hemisphere preference in learning activities
- Respond better to active rather than passive learning tasks
- Have areas of talent or ability that are overlooked by teachers
- Prefer to receive special help in regular classroom
- Higher dropout rate than regular education students
- Achieve in accordance with teacher expectations
- Require modifications in classroom instruction
- Distractible

Social Characteristics

- Experience friction when interacting with others
- Function better outside of school than in school
- Need adult approval
- Have difficulties finding and maintaining employment after school
- Stereotyped by others
- Behavior problems exhibited

Summary

Students with mild disabilities addressed in this book are those who receive services in special education for learning disabilities, behavior disorders, and mild mental retardation. As a regular classroom teacher, or as a special education teacher or consultant, you work with these children and youth every day. If you are or will be a regular classroom teacher, these are the students who you teach most of the day but who go to the special education resource room for one to several periods each day. If you are, or are training to be, a special education teacher, these are the students who either appear at your classroom door at a regularly scheduled time each day, or they are those to whom you provide services in the regular classroom. You may teach them on the elementary level in an academic content area like mathematics, reading, or spelling, while simultaneously integrating social skills training into their scholastic studies. If you are a special teacher of secondary level students, you may also teach prevocational or life career skills, along with content in subject areas like history, geometry, English, and so on.

Regardless of the category in which they are receiving services, these students have similar learning needs. In fact, unless you are informed about each one's specific exceptionality classification, you may not know whether a particular student is labeled mild mentally retarded, learning disabled, or behavior disordered. Because of this, states now deliver services under noncategorical and cross-categorical systems. Students with mild disabilities are generally more alike than different.

Generalities can be made about mild disabilities. First, students with mild mental retardation, learning disabilities, and behavior disorders are the largest subgroup of students receiving special education services. In fact, the total group of students with mild mental retardation, behavior disorders, and learning disabilities comprise about half of the total special education population. Second, they are served primarily during their school-aged years. Mild disabilities are often unrecognized before and after school years. Third, the categories for mild mental retardation, behavior disorders, and learning disabilities are unreliable. No nationally accepted criteria exist. While many students with mild disabilities receive special education services, there are some who are incorrectly identified as having a mild disability and others who have a mild disability are overlooked. Last, students with mild disabilities are most likely to be placed in the regular classroom and in resource services. Effective collaboration between general and special education teachers is vital.

Causes for mild disabilities can primarily be subdivided into two major categories: organic (biological) and environmental. The organic category includes prenatal, perinatal, and postnatal factors, genetic factors, biochemical factors, and maturational lag. Environmental reasons address factors relating to poverty, nutrition, toxins, safety, language differences, sensory deprivation, emotional problems, and inadequate education. In most cases, it is difficult to trace mild disabilities to their origins, and mild learning and behavior difficulties usually remain undetected until children enter school.

Particularly vulnerable populations of at-risk students are identified: infants, preschoolers, and adolescents. Existing and new programs can offset school failure. The inability of some students to keep up and make successful progress within our educational system results in an increased number of school dropouts on the secondary level. Failure in school and failure in life is highly predictable.

More effective teaching practices need to be directed toward at-risk students throughout their school careers. More effective collaboration needs to occur between general education, compensatory education, and special education. Likewise, these same efforts must be made among educators and other professionals, parents, and community service personnel.

A series of mandated steps must occur before a student can be delivered services in special education. The full sequence of procedural steps includes: identification of learning problem, intervention, referral, evaluation, eligibility, classification, and placement. Identification is made from comparisons of academic and behavioral characteristics with those of age-mates. Interventions are modifications that are tried to help the child learn in the regular classroom. The special education referral process is initiated when the student is unable to progress satisfactorily following interventions in the regular classroom. An evaluation is conducted by a multidisciplinary team. If the student meets criteria set forth by the law, or other governing regulations, he or she is determined eligible and assigned to a special education category or service. An individual education plan (IEP) is developed and the student is placed in a special education class that the multidisciplinary team agrees is the individual's least restrictive environment.

Chapter *3*

Students with Mild Mental Retardation

Advance Organizer

When you complete this chapter, you will be able to:

1. Discuss the nature–nurture controversy.
2. Explain the contribution of IQ testing to social and educational practices for individuals identified as mildly retarded.
3. List organic and environmental causes of mild mental retardation.
4. Explain how poverty contributes to mild mental retardation.
5. Define mental retardation.
6. Describe the role of adaptive behavior in determining mild mental retardation.
7. Explain the relationship between identification criteria and prevalence of mild retardation.
8. Relate the cognitive theory of Jean Piaget to assessment and teaching of students with mild mental retardation.
9. Describe specific educational programs for students identified as mildly retarded.
10. Discuss educational strategies to increase language skills of students with mild retardation.
11. Explain the connection between perception and learning.
12. Describe and critique methods of assessing mental processing skills.
13. Discuss the relationship between social and intellectual development.
14. Describe the "new" mildly retarded population.

Larry was nine years old. Each day he boarded a yellow school bus for a half-hour journey to George Washington Elementary School. When he arrived at school, he walked past a series of cheery, primary-grade classrooms and entered a small classroom at the end of the hall. In this, the special EMR class (educable mentally retarded), Larry struggled with reading and arithmetic. He had difficulty sitting still and attending to lessons. Because of his distractibility, he was a constant discipline problem. Despite these negatives, Larry's schooling provided him with a safe and secure routine for five hours a day.

After school, Larry returned to another world—one of disorganized squalor in a "welfare hotel." Larry, his mother, and two-year-old sister shared a single room in the rundown tenement, which was also inhabited by drug addicts and prostitutes. Hunger, anxiety, and depression were a way of life for Larry in this bleak world, where even a trip down the hall to the communal bathroom was a hazardous journey. Larry never knew his father. His mother tried to make do on their welfare check, but it barely provided enough money to pay the month's rent. She tried several times to find a full-time job, but she was handicapped by her lack of formal schooling.

Larry was one of many children who strained the resources of the city social and educational services. His teacher described him as "depressed" and "apathetic." "Even when he smiles," she reported, "his eyes are sad." Larry was evaluated as a student with mild mental retardation soon after he began school at George Washington Elementary School six months ago. Larry's chaotic and insecure life made the prognosis bleak. His teacher felt that school could offer Larry an orderly environment, a nutritious lunch, and emotional stability. "I don't know if Larry will ever learn to read," she admitted, "he has been in three different schools in the past two years, and I doubt if he will be here much longer." This teacher's remarks underscore how unfavorable social conditions can over-whelm the best educational intentions.

In 1989, 522,864 students with mental retardation participated in special education programs throughout the country (U.S. Department of Education, 1990). Most of these students, approximately 75 percent, are students with mild mental retardation. The majority are poor. While many students with mild mental retardation are white, minorities, especially African-Americans, are overrepresented. Students with mild mental retardation may be placed in self-contained special classes for the educably mentally retarded (EMR), where they have few opportunities to mingle and learn alongside their nondisabled peers.

Because of their lack of success in school, students with mild retardation lose confidence in their ability to learn. Motivation is a persistent problem for teachers. Although individual students differ significantly, generally students with mild mental retardation exhibit problems in academics and social adjustment. Such specific disabilities as distractibility, weak verbal skills, and speech disorders are common to this population. In appearance, these students are normal. Most are not identified as having a mild disability until they enter school and begin to fall behind their age-mates in learning. After they leave school, these young people merge with the general population. In the mainstream of society, they usually leave the label "mentally retarded" behind them.

Moderate to Severe Mental Retardation

It is important to discriminate between mild mental retardation and other, more severe types of mental retardation. One demarcation point is IQ score. An IQ range from 75-50 indicates mild mental retardation. As IQ scores move below 50, the degree of mental retardation is more severe. For the most part, students who score 50 or below on IQ tests are clearly disabled. Unlike students with mild mental retardation, students with IQs below 50 usually demonstrate observable physical and behavioral anomalies. Educators usually use the continuum moderate to severe mental retardation when discussing students with IQs below 50. When their disability is organic in nature, students with IQ scores below 50 may be described by physicians as having clinical mental retardation.

Children with clinical mental retardation are identified at birth or soon after because of obvious physical anomalies such as hydrocephalus (i.e., pressure on the brain from cerebrospinal fluid) or spina bifida (i.e., a defect in the bony arch of the vertebra protecting the spinal cord). Students with clinical mental retardation usually have multiple disabilities, for example, communication and health impairments. While students with mild mental retardation are developmentally delayed, clinically mentally retarded students are developmentally disabled. This means that their condition is chronic, and they often require lifelong rehabilitation services in such areas of functioning as independent living, employment, or mobility. Clinical mental retardation cuts across all socioeconomic levels. Prevention is the most effective strategy to reduce the incidence of clinical mental retardation in children. Genetic counseling and amniocentesis are methods for preventing clinical mental retardation.

Despite the permanent nature of their disability, students with clinical mental retardation are capable of learning and becoming useful members of society. In the past, educators placed preconceived limits on the ability of students with clinical mental retardation. For example, students with moderate (IQ 50-35) mental retardation were referred to as "trainable." Because of preconceived labels, students with clinical mental retardation were institutionalized or placed in dead-end self-contained special classes. These limits became self-fulfilling prophecies. Bereft of normal childhood experiences and maintained in caretaking facilities, children with clinical mental retardation stagnated. The deinstitutionalization movement of the 1970s combined with the passage of the Education For All Handicapped Children Act increased their opportunities for normal learning experiences. With early intervention and well-coordinated human services, the prospects for students with clinical mental retardation have dramatically improved over the last twenty years. Some students with clinical mental retardation, as a result of environmental stimulation, may achieve a score in the mildrange (75–50) on an IQ test. Table 3–1 contrasts students with mild mental retardation and students with clinical mental retardation.

TABLE 3–1   Comparison of Mild and Clinical Mental Retardation

Mild Mental Retardation	Clinical Mental Retardation
Primary cause is environmental	Primary cause is biological
Normal physical appearance	Physical anomalies
Subtle health complications	Obvious health complications
Identified after beginning school	Identified at birth or soon afterwards
IQ range 75-50	IQ range 50 and below
Developmentally delayed	Developmentally disabled
After school, able to merge into the general population	Disability is chronic and requires life-long rehabilitative services
Higher prevalence among poor with African-Americans overrepresented	Cuts across all socioeconomic and ethnic groups
Subject to misidentification	Demonstrates clearcut medical diagnostic criteria
Not recognized as a disability in all countries	Universally recognized as a disability

Nature–Nurture Controversy

Since the nineteenth century, researchers have disagreed about the causes of mild mental retardation. Some believed mild mental retardation was familial, an inborn trait passed from one generation to the next—this is the nature perspective. Other researchers took the position that individuals with mild mental retardation were born biologically normal, and their intellectual development was impaired by inadequate environmental stimulation—this is the nurture point of view. Often the debate has produced more heat than light, particularly when IQ scores of different ethnic groups have been compared, and questions about racial superiority or inferiority took center stage.

In 1969, Arthur Jensen made the following statement in the *Harvard Educational Review*:

> *We are left with various lines of evidence, no one of which is definitive alone, but which, viewed all together, make it a not unreasonable hypothesis that genetic factors are strongly implicated in the average Negro–white intelligence difference. The preponderance of the evidence is, in my opinion, less consistent with a strictly environmental hypothesis than with a genetic hypothesis, which, of course, does not exclude the influence of environment or its interaction with genetic factors (Jensen, 1969, 82).*

Jensen went on to suggest that compensatory education programs for African-Americans would not alleviate school failure because such programs could not offset biological causes of low intelligence. Jensen's article set off a firestorm of criticism. Jensen was branded a racist, and he was hounded by political activists wherever he made public appearances.

Jensen's argument was based on two scientific facts as he understood them. One was that African-Americans as a group scored lower on IQ tests than whites. Jensen assumed that IQ tests provide an accurate assessment of intelligence and that differences in IQ are not related to differences in culture. Second, Jensen was influenced by studies of twins raised separately after birth. These studies reported that different environments had little effect on IQ scores, thereby eliminating environment as a significant contributor to intelligence. Because he believed that IQ was primarily biological in nature, Jensen attributed low IQ to genetically inferior intelligence. He believed that approximately 80 percent of intelligence was determined by heredity (Fancher, 1985).

Jensen relied heavily on the research of Cyril Burt to support his position. Cyril Burt was born in London in 1883. As a young man, Burt was interested in both juvenile delinquency and mental retardation. These interests aroused his curiosity about the relative influence of heredity and environment on deviant behavior. His studies of twins, raised in separate environments, were the foundation of his reputation as an academician and scholar. In his seminal paper, "The Genetic Determination of Differences in Intelligence: A Study of Twins Reared Together and Apart" (1966), Burt reported that he had traced the life histories of fifty-three pairs of twins raised apart. When tested, their IQ correlations were .874. This meant to Burt and the followers of his research that genetics made up 87% of intelligence, while environment contributed a meager 13% to intelligence. Burt's research tipped the scales of the nature–nurture disagreement towards the biological interpretation.

Although politically and morally distasteful to some, it appeared that Jensen's proposition that intelligence was biologically determined was based on solid footing—Cyril Burt's twin research. Leon Kamin, a Harvard psychologist, decided to take a closer look at Burt's research. For many years, Burt frustrated social scientists by closely guarding his data and turning away specific requests for further elaboration on his twin subjects. Kamin, although a psychologist by training, was a whiz at statistical analysis. As he reviewed Burt's 1966 article, which demonstrated minimal environmental effect on separated twins, Kamin became suspicious.

> *I think it is true to say that within ten minutes of starting to read Burt, I knew in my gut that something was so fishy here that it just had to be fake. He anticipates every possible objection to the hereditarian case, and comes out with a definitive empirical rebuttal to the objection. The work was so incredibly patly perfect and beyond cavil, and beyond challenge, that I just couldn't believe it.*

My experience of the messy nature of the real world was such that I just could not believe that what this guy was writing was true.

At the same time there was a kind of vagueness and ambiguity, and under-description and underrepresentation of method and detail. He didn't even name the IQ test used, no case histories, no information about the sex composition of the samples, or the times they were tested. So I was profoundly suspicious at once, and then started to read other Burt articles. (Fancher, 1985, 207)

Kamin's probing into the data on twins research revealed many inconsistencies that made Burt's conclusions suspect. A few years later, in 1976, Oliver Gillie, a medical correspondent for the London *Sunday Times,* discovered the associates Burt claimed helped carry out his research did not exist. Cyril Burt was branded a fraud. In one of the greatest scientific scandals of the century, the hereditarian view that intelligence was primarily biological in nature was dealt a severe blow.

Careful scientific scrutiny was able to accomplish in a rational manner what many people failed to do in an emotional way—demonstrate that Burt's and Jensen's genetic interpretation on differing IQ levels for African-Americans and whites was based on inaccurate data. However, Jensen's observation about differences in IQ levels was accurate—in general Caucasians do score higher on IQ tests than African-Americans. What are we to make of this discrepancy if genetics is not the solution? The answer is found in the urban ghettos and backward rural communities that one out of every five American children call home. Most students with mild mental retardation come from poor families and disadvantaged environments. When these students take IQ tests, they are unprepared to do well because many of the questions assume a shared United States middle-class, cultural experience.

The book is not closed on the nurture–nature debate. There is too much empirical evidence of child prodigies and extraordinarily talented individuals to dismiss the notion that biology is a factor in the development of intelligence. The nature point of view has been muddled in the past by the tendency of researchers to focus on the heritability of intelligence, thus obscuring the question about how much intelligence may be influenced by random biological factors. We see evidence of this random selection of inborn talent all around us. How do we explain the performance of a Michael Jordan on the basketball court or a Itzhak Perlman in a concert hall without marveling at their inborn talent?

The difference between discussions about entertainers and intelligence is that judgments about the former can be agreed upon by many without argument. Perlman and Jordan may not be up to par every performance, but few would disagree with the evaluation that they exceed their peers in their chosen professions. Intelligence is a different matter. Binet called intelligence good judgment. Piaget called it the ability to adapt. School officials often call it an IQ score. More than anything else, it is the IQ test that has fueled and misdirected the nature–nurture debate during the past century.

Intelligence and IQ

In 1968, Lloyd Dunn was president of the Council for Exceptional Children, the nation's largest professional special education organization. During a speech at the Council's annual conference, Dunn urged educators to reevaluate their view on students with mild mental retardation. He criticized special education placements that tracked students into dead-end special education programs. Dunn characterized students with mild retardation as children of poverty who were denied equal access to educational opportunity in regular classrooms. He called for the elimination of self-contained special education classes for students identified as mildly retarded. Dunn stated that the label "mildly retarded" was used by educators to explain away the school's inability to educate African-Americans, native American Indians, Mexicans, Puerto Ricans, and other nonstandard-English-speaking students. Dunn was particularly forthright in his condemnation of the use of intelligence testing to categorize these hard-to-teach students.

> *Again the purpose has been to find out what is wrong with the child in order to label him and thus make him eligible for special education services. In large measure this has resulted in digging the educational graves of many racial and/or economically disadvantaged children by using the WISC or Binet IQ score to justify the label "mentally retarded." This term then becomes a destructive, self-fulfilling prophecy. (Dunn, 1969, 9)*

Dunn's speech alerted educators to the need to reexamine practices for diagnosing and educating students with mild retardation. The use of IQ tests to label students with mild retardation and the educational practices that follow are so closely knit that an understanding of one is virtually impossible without knowledge about the other (Zucker & Polloway, 1987).

Alfred Binet

In 1904, Alfred Binet and his colleague, Theodore Simon, were asked by Paris school officials to help identify students in need of special education. Binet was a fervent believer in the power of education, and he agreed to the project because he saw an opportunity to improve school services for slow learners. Previously, Binet had attempted to measure intelligence in school children by following the accepted "objective" method of calculating head size with a tape measure. He soon found that the pseudoscience of "craniometry" could not provide information to accurately select students who needed special education. The differences he found in head sizes of students designated by teachers as the smartest or dullest was insignificant.

When presented with the task of screening large numbers of Paris school children for mental retardation, Binet changed tactics and decided to follow the practical strategy of presenting youngsters with problems in abstract reasoning.

He tested students on a variety of tasks including counting money, classification, and choosing "pretty" faces drawn on cards. Binet's procedure was empirical; that is, he did not start from a theory of intelligence, rather he experimented with an array of tasks until he was satisfied that he could derive a "mental level" that would indicate a child's potential for school achievement. Because of the high priority schools placed on verbal skills, items on Binet's original test emphasized language-based cognitive skills. This accent on language skills as a primary indicator of intelligence still persists in IQ tests today.

Binet did not speculate about the meaning of his intelligence test beyond its ability to screen students for special education. And his success did not blind him to the limitations of his work. He designed his scale for a specific reason—to screen children whose poor performance indicated a need for special education. He did not believe his test should be used to measure the intelligence of normal children, nor did he believe a low score indicated a permanent intellectual deficiency. Just the contrary, Binet was a firm believer in the educability of slow learners and throughout his career he opposed the conclusion that his scale identified inborn and unchangeable traits of general intelligence.

Intelligence Tests in the United States

The turn of the century in this country was a time of rapid cultural and social change. Vast numbers of immigrants provided industry with cheap labor. As slums, teeming with thousands of poor immigrants, sprang up in major cities, social reform became a national necessity. While educators tried to cope with students who were different, some United States psychologists focused their attention on the relationship between intelligence and social status. In Vineland, New Jersey, Henry Goddard founded an institute to investigate the connection between heredity and intelligence. After a visit to Paris in 1907, Goddard imported Binet's intelligence scale and used it to classify the residents with mental retardation at the Vineland Training School into categories of mental deficiency. To the already existing groups of "idiot" and "imbecile," he added a new term, "moron," to describe the highest functioning level of mental retardation. It was the moron or "feebleminded" group that became the centerpiece of Goddard's research.

In 1912, Goddard set out to detect feebleminded immigrants. He selected Ellis Island as his research site. Goddard intended to use the intelligence test to detect feebleminded immigrants who would, he believed, upon entry into this country, spread pauperism and crime. Each day thousands of immigrants poured through the massive disembarkation building in New York harbor. Goddard sent two of his female associates to test immigrants as they passed through customs. Candidates for testing were selected by visual inspection. Goddard believed that an individual's posture, facial characteristics, and dress provided clues about mental ability.

Using this nonrandom selection procedure, Goddard's female associates administered intelligence tests to twenty-two Hungarians, thirty-five Jews, fifty

Italians, and forty-five Russians. When the scores were tabulated Goddard found that 83 percent of Jews, 80 percent of Hungarians, 79 percent of Italians, and 87 percent of Russians were feebleminded! He dismissed language as an explanation because the Jews had been tested by a Yiddish-speaking psychologist, and their scores were as low as the other groups. Goddard did not consider testing conditions a contributing factor, rather he concluded that immigrants from southeastern Europe were genetically inferior (Gould, 1981).

Goddard's views on the genetic character of "feeblemindedness" was reinforced by his infamous Kalikak Study (1912). Goddard claimed to have traced the offspring of a Revolutionary War soldier, Martin Kalikak, to an impoverished community located in the Pine Barrens of New Jersey. He claimed that these uneducated and dirt poor residents of this isolated area were the descendants of a sexual liaison between Kalikak and a "tavern wench." Goddard compared the intellectual abilities and economic lives of the Pine Barren residents with the legitimate descendents from Kalikak's marriage. The legitimate Kalikak clan produced lawyers, business professionals, and doctors. The illegitimate Pine Barren descendents were characterized as sexually immoral, alcoholics, and mentally retarded. Goddard's "research" provided powerful arguments for the heritability of mild mental retardation. Recently, Goddard's study has been "thoroughly discredited" because he failed to consider environmental factors (Taylor & Searl, Jr., 1987). Stephen Jay Gould (1981) discovered that the photographs displayed in Goddard's research had been retouched to give the Pine Barren residents a sinister and dimwitted look.

Other psychologists, including Lewis Terman, continued Goddard's work with intelligence testing and came to the same conclusions about the heritability of feeblemindedness in such poor, ethnic groups as Mexicans, Spanish-Indians, and African-Americans. After the publication of his "Stanford-Binet Intelligence Test," Terman made his ultimate claim for the role of intelligence testing and social engineering.

> . . . in the near future intelligence tests will bring tens of thousands of these high grade defectives under the surveillance and protection of society. This will ultimately result in curtailing the reproduction of feeblemindedness and in the elimination of an enormous amount of crime, pauperism, and industrial inefficiency. It is hardly necessary to emphasize that the high grade cases, of the type now so frequently overlooked, are precisely the ones whose guardianship it is most important for the State to assume. (Kamin, 1977, 47)

Politicians gave Terman's notion of guardianship a macabre twist by initiating a number of state sterilization laws. In 1907, the Indiana legislature passed a law that allowed the state to sterilize prisoners and orphans. Beginning with the preamble, "Whereas heredity plays a most important part in the transmission of crime, idiocy, and imbecility . . ." this, the first of many state sterilization laws, was passed amid high hopes of controlling the spread of mental retardation.

It was the "high grade defectives" or the feebleminded, identified through intelligence tests, that were the primary targets for sterilization. Iowa, in a 1911 sterilization law, listed criminals, rapists, idiots, feebleminded, imbeciles, lunatics, drunkards, drug fiends, epileptics, syphilitics, moral and sexual perverts as primary targets for sterilization. Any adult who was institutionalized or any child who became a ward of the state was a potential candidate for sterilization. From 1907 to 1972, thousands of "social misfits" in state institutions throughout the country were sterilized in the name of social reform (Houts, 1977; Taylor & Searl, 1987).

By the 1930s Binet's procedure for measuring intelligence was fully Americanized and in the process distorted. Instead of a measure of school potential to identify students for special education, the United States IQ test was used as an "objective" measure of innate intelligence. Binet's concept of environmental stimulation to increase intelligence was turned inside out as low IQ became synonymous with intractable dullness.

Between 1928–1929, 65,000 intelligence tests were administered in Los Angeles elementary schools. Youngsters whose scores ranged from 50–75 were placed in special classes for the "educable feebleminded" (Hendrick & MacMillan, 1987). As the use of IQ tests became common practice nationwide, immigrant and minority children were placed in segregated special classes at a higher rate than their middle-class, white peers. The tenacity with which educators cling to the IQ test as a measure of intelligence and identification of students with mild mental retardation is remarkable. When pressed, most scholars admit that IQ tests don't measure intelligence. There is no correlation, for instance, between an individual's IQ and success in life after school. But the IQ test still serves the purpose for which it was originally intended by Binet. Intelligence test scores are reasonably good predictors of school achievement, and, for this reason, until a better method is developed, IQ remains the most frequently used standard for identifying students with mild mental retardation.

Definitional Concerns

Since the mid-sixties there has been a decline of interest among researchers in students with mild retardation (Epstein et al., 1989; MacMillan, 1989). One of the reasons for the neglect of this population is that the numbers of students in this category have steadily decreased since 1977, and researchers have taken up such new interests as learning disabilities and the education of the severely disabled. Furthermore, because of variability in state identification criteria, it has become more difficult for researchers to determine who is mildly retarded and who is not. As a result, information about such fundamental issues as prevalence of students with mild retardation, learning characteristics of students with mild retardation, and successful educational programming for these students is inadequate. Simply put, the problem is this—how can we determine what school programs work best for students with mild mental retardation if we don't have a consistent procedure to discriminate mildly retarded students from non-retarded, low achievers?

Identification of Mild Retardation

The definition of mental retardation, published in the 1977 Federal Register, was the most widely accepted description of students with mental retardation. The Federal description was based on the 1973 American Association on Mental Deficiency (AAMD) definition which stated:

> *Mental retardation means significant subaverage general intellectual functioning existing concurrently with deficits in adaptive behavior and manifested during the developmental period, which adversely affects a child's educational performance (Grossman, 1973).*

Prior to the 1973 definition, many psychologists (including the early researchers on feeblemindedness) used an IQ score of 85 or below as the cutoff point for mild retardation. The 1973 criteria operationalized "significant" intellectual ability by lowering the IQ cutoff point from one to two standard deviations below the mean. The AAMD lowered the IQ cutoff point from 85 to 70 in order to eliminate borderline, underachieving students from the category of mild mental retardation.

Reliance on IQ scores alone can lead to an inaccurate diagnosis of mild retardation. Imagine a first grader called outside his classroom one morning. Standing in the hall, briefcase in hand, is a stranger. The child is introduced to Dr. Jones who would like to "play some games." Dr. Jones leads the youngster into a small, unfamiliar office, and the questions begin. "How many miles is it from New York to Paris?" "What is missing from this picture?" "Repeat the following digits backwards."

Is it possible that the unfamiliar surroundings and the test can produce stress in a child that will affect test performance? Fuchs and Fuchs (1989) investigated the relationship between tester familiarity in minority versus white students' IQ test results. They reviewed and analyzed fourteen previous studies that compared Caucasian and minority performance with familiar and unfamiliar examiners. Caucasian students performed uniformly on IQ tests conducted by familiar and unfamiliar examiners. African-American and Hispanic children scored significantly lower when the tester was a stranger. The Fuchs findings said nothing about the test itself. Rather, they pointed out that when a minority youngster is brought into an unfamiliar testing situation, the IQ score may not be a true representation of the youngster's ability. Given the fact that many minority students are identified as mildly retarded, it appears that more attention should be given to testing conditions.

Adaptive Behavior

The 1973 definition of mental retardation also included, for the first time, a direct reference to "adaptive behavior" as a key component of mild mental retardation. Adaptive behavior refers to the degree to which an individual demonstrates age appropriate behavior outside of school. Included among criteria for adaptive behavior are independent functioning, self care, and social skills within the community. By focusing the clinician's attention on a youngster's adaptive behavior skills outside of school, the AAMD hoped to establish comprehensive guidelines that would prevent children from being mislabeled mildly retarded solely on the basis of their performance on an intelligence test.

The need to ascertain a youngster's adaptive behavior outside of school before making an educational diagnosis of mild mental retardation was highlighted by the research of Jane Mercer (1973). In an eight-year study in Riverside, California, Mercer found that the schools were the chief labelers of students as mildly retarded. As might be expected, the majority of these youngsters were poor. When Mercer examined the classification of students by race, she found a disproportionate number of Mexican-Americans and African-Americans placed in special classes for the mildly retarded. Mercer used the term "six-hour retarded child" to describe the subjects of her research. At home and in the community the "six-hour retarded child" was considered normal; in school the same youngster was considered retarded. Why the discrepancy? Mercer concluded that the schools failed to take a youngster's adaptive functioning outside of school into account. In Mercer's judgment, the lack of attention to socialization skills outside of school resulted in the mislabeling of many minority students as mildly retarded. Mercer's research highlighted the need to take adaptive behavior into account before making a diagnosis of mild mental retardation.

The definition of mental retardation includes subaverage intellectual functioning associated with impairments in adaptive behavior. *No student with mild mental retardation should be identified without sufficient documentation of deficits in adaptive behavior.* Reschly (1989) recommended the Comprehensive Test of Adaptive Behavior (CTAB), the Vineland Adaptive Behavior Scales, and the Scales of Independent Behavior (SIB) as best choices for getting a standardized analysis of a student's adaptive behavior abilities. The CTAB is criterion-referenced, thus the results are useful for individual education programs.

Adaptive behavior refers to the ability to be independent and socially responsible (Reschly, 1989). This means that students with mild mental retardation require a curriculum that teaches socialization skills. Such adaptive behavior skills as independent functioning (e.g., self-help, safety, travel, consumer, communication, and leisure); social functioning (e.g., interpersonal relationships, sharing, expressing feelings, recognition of other's feelings, and situational appropriateness); and occupational functioning (e.g., responsibility, specific work skills, and cooperation) should be included in a student's individual education program.

TABLE 3–2   Levels of Mental Retardation by IQ

Mental retardation refers to significantly subaverage general intellectual functioning resulting in or associated with concurrent impairments in adaptive behavior and manifested during the developmental period, birth to age 18 (Grossman, 1983).

IQ Measure of Retardation

Mild (EMR)	50 to 70–75	(depending on the reliability of test)
Moderate	35 to 50	
Severe and profound	Below 35	

Grossman, 1983

In 1983, the AAMD (since renamed the AAMR—American Association of Mental Retardation) extended the cutoff score for mild retardation to 75, depending on the reliability of the intelligence test used. Table 3-2 matches the Grossman (1983) IQ score range to degrees of severity of mental retardation. In reversing its decision about cutoff scores set in 1973 for mild mental retardation, the AAMR responded to concerns that students with special needs were being overlooked when they scored above 70 on IQ tests.

Changes in IQ guidelines were followed by debate over the meaning of adaptive behavior. Some researchers pointed out that adaptive behavior assessment should include such in-school behavior as functional academic skills (Reschly, 1989; Zucker & Polloway, 1987). This was a departure from past adaptive behavior measurement practices. In the seventies, primarily as a result of Mercer's research on the "six-hour retarded child," adaptive behavior assessment focused exclusively on out-of-school socialization skills.

In a study of students classified as mildly retarded in Pueblo, Colorado, Talley (1979) found that when the Adaptive Behavior Inventory for Children developed by Mercer was used to measure adaptive behavior, 85 percent of referred students with IQs below 70 were decertified as having mild retardation. This massive declassification raised questions about whether or not the best interests of students were served by denying them special education services. For example, one research study that tracked decertified students found that their level of achievement was several grade levels below their peers in the regular classroom (Meyers, MacMillan, & Yoshida, 1975).

A renewed interest in assessment, as related to the quality of educational programming for students with mental retardation, was spearheaded by the National Academy of Science. In an Academy panel report, Heller (1982) and his associates emphasized the need for a valid assessment of a student's functional educational needs. Intelligence tests were criticized because they provide insufficient information for classroom instruction. The National Academy of Science took the position that quality of educational intervention, rather than disabling condition, should be the focus of future assessment methods. Lambert summarized key elements of the report.

1. *Assessment specialists should demonstrate that the measures employed validly assess the functional needs of the child for which there are effective instructional interventions.*
2. *Placement teams should demonstrate that a differential label (e.g., mild mental retardation) is related to a distinctive prescription for educational practices and that the prescribed practices are likely to lead to improved outcomes.*
3. *Special education and evaluation staffs should demonstrate that high quality effective special instruction is being provided. (Lambert, 1988, 300)*

Differences in criteria for identifying students with mild retardation is an important issue. Assessment methods influence prevalence figures, availability of programming, and descriptions of learner characteristics. In the final analysis, it is the quality of education, not the label (i.e., mildly retarded, learning disabled, behavior disordered) that determines school failure or success for students with mild disabilities.

Prevalence of Students with Mild Mental Retardation

During the 1989 school year 4,587,370 students received remedial and special education services. Eleven percent of these students were identified as mentally retarded. The number of students identified as mentally retarded declined from 820,290 in 1977 to 522,864 in 1989 (U.S. Department of Education, 1990). This was a decrease by 37 percent of students identified as mentally retarded in twelve years. One explanation for the decrease of students identified as mentally retarded is that the tightening of eligibility requirements (i.e., lowering the cutoff score from 85 to 70) and the inclusion of a measure of adaptive behavior made it more difficult for a youngster to be identified as having mild mental retardation. This would account for the decrease in numbers of identified students if all states followed the AAMR guidelines, but they do not.

In a survey of state guidelines for identification of mental retardation, Frankenburger (1984) found that the majority of states do not adhere to the AAMR criteria. For instance, Frankenburger found, fifteen of the forty-five reporting states set no criteria for IQ cutoff. Of the thirty states that specified IQ criteria, only fifteen followed the 1973 AAMR guideline of two standard deviations below the mean (i.e., 70–50) as the cutoff point for mild retardation. Thirty states used some measure of adaptive behavior, yet only nine specified specific criteria for determining what adaptive behavior means. Four states indicated that a youngster's academic achievement should be considered in determining mental retardation. A follow-up study of state guidelines by Utley, Lowitzer, and Baumeister found that many states (44 percent) substituted other terms, such as "learning impaired" and "individuals with exceptional needs," for mental retardation. The researchers also found differences in IQ criteria and definitions of adaptive behavior. They summarized their findings by stating,

> *Inconsistencies exist not only with respect to the terminology and definitions applied, but also with respect to eligibility criteria and categorization of children identified as mentally retarded. There appears to be considerable disagreement about who is mentally retarded, what eligibility criteria should be used, and what systems of classification are most functional in the delivery of instructional services. (Utley, Lowitzer, & Baumeister, 1987, 40)*

The variability with which states determine the presence of mild retardation means it is conceivable that a youngster would be considered to have a mild disability in one state and nondisabled in another. Prevalence figures reported by the individual states confirm this hypothesis. In 1987 three states reported 30,000 or more students with mental retardation, while eleven states reported less than 2,000 students identified as mentally retarded and receiving special education services (Jordan, 1989). Differences in state populations could explain some of these discrepancies, but not all. For example, Ohio identified 43,740 students as having mental retardation in 1987, while California, the most populous state, identified 26,733 students.

The Search for the Student behind the Label

From 1977 to 1989, the rate of students with special needs identified as mentally retarded decreased from 26 percent to 11 percent of the total special education population. As the number of students identified as having mild retardation declined, the number of students identified as having a learning disability more than doubled. In 1976–77, 797,266 students were identified as learning disabled. Ten years later, 1,926,097 youngsters with learning disabilities received special education and remedial services (Jordan, 1989). It may be that many youngsters who would have been identified as mildly retarded in the mid-seventies were diagnosed as learning disabled during the mid-eighties (Polloway & Smith, 1983).

Professionals might prefer to classify students as learning disabled rather than mildly retarded because the term learning disabled carries less stigma. As a result, it has more appeal to parents who would prefer not to have their children branded mentally retarded. Also, learning disabled students spend most of their school day in the regular classroom, while over 50 percent of students with mild mental retardation are placed in self-contained special classes (MacMillan & Borthwick, 1980; Polloway et al., 1986). Once a student is placed in a special class, chances for a return to the regular classroom diminish. Therefore, a strategy for increasing a student's participation in the regular classroom placement is to opt for the label learning disabled.

Another explanation for the declining number of students with mild retardation is that many disadvantaged children now reside in an educational "no man's land" (MacMillan, 1989). These "marginal learners" are ineligible for special education services because their IQs are too high (over 75) for identification as mildly retarded and too low (under 90) for identification as learning disabled. Many educational evaluators look for a discrepancy between IQ and school achievement to determine if a learning disability exists. This means that a student with "borderline" IQ score of 85 to 76 would not meet any criteria for special education. For instance, Forness (1985) found that in California 82.7 was the lowest average IQ that would qualify a student for services as learning disabled.

As stated in Chapter 2, "Overview of Students with Mild Disabilities," many marginal learners would qualify for Chapter 1 compensatory education programs. Chapter 1 funds are targeted specifically for underachieving, disadvantaged learners who do not meet criteria for special education. However, success in Chapter 1 programs is limited to underachieving students who make rapid improvements and soon move out of Chapter 1 programs. The weaker students tend to make little progress and continue to receive Chapter 1 services year after year (Ralph, 1989). These unsuccessful Chapter 1 students may be some of the "missing" students with mild retardation who began to disappear from special education rolls soon after the 1973 AAMR revision of the criteria to identify students with mental retardation.

Finally, students with mild mental retardation are usually poor youngsters who don't receive adequate preparation for their beginning school years. This is precisely the population that is targeted by Head Start programs. Head Start is a federal compensatory program for children aged three to five. It provides a combination of educational, social, and health services for underprivileged children. The purpose of the Head Start program is to increase the intellectual and socioemotional development of poor preschool children. Recent Head Start evaluations have concluded that Head Start was successful in meeting many of its goals. Researchers found an improvement in grade retention and decrease in special education placements for disadvantaged youth who participated in Head Start prior to beginning public school (Lazar & Darlington, 1982; McKey et al., 1985). The apparent successes of Head Start could account for some of the downward change in number of students identified with mild retardation after beginning school.

Organic Causes of Mild Mental Retardation

Mild mental retardation can be caused by organic impairments in the developing child or a lack of adequate environmental stimulation. Among the poor, inadequate health care and lack of environmental stimulation often combine to cause mild mental retardation. As noted earlier, researchers have also attempted to document hereditary causes of mild mental retardation, but that explanation is still unproven.

Drugs

From the moment of conception, a child is vulnerable to toxins and infections that can stunt normal development. A pregnant mother's health is a crucial determiner of a healthy child. Whatever a pregnant woman puts into her body will eventually be absorbed into fetal tissue. Alcohol and cocaine are especially toxic to the fetus. Even small amounts of these drugs pose a threat to the fetal nervous system, especially during the first trimester of pregnancy.

Drug abuse cuts across all socioeconomic levels and poses an immediate threat to the nervous system of an unborn child. Because drug abusers neglect their bodies in general, the fragile nervous system of the fetus may be jeopardized by malnutrition, iron deficiency, or anoxia. Newborn infants of drug abusers often are addicted to whatever drug the mother was using. The National Institute on Alcohol Abuse and Alcoholism estimated that 1,500 of three million newborns annually will be born with fetal alcohol syndrome (FAS). Thousands of other children will have some of the characteristics of FAS including prenatal and postnatal growth deficiencies, mental retardation, and fine-motor impairments. Low birthweight (i.e., less than 5.5 pounds) can lead to a variety of health problems, including mild retardation. Teenage pregnancies and inadequate prenatal care, for instance smoking, can cause low birth weight.

Infections

Several forms of congenital mild retardation are caused by maternal infection. Rubella is a disorder resulting from the mother being infected with German measles. Retardation of the child can range from mild to severe. Toxoplasmosis is caused by a protozoan infection of a pregnant woman. The protozoa is sometimes found in cat litter. Toxoplasmosis can cause mild to severe mental retardation, along with a variety of health problems. Cytomegalic inclusion disease is caused by a viral infection. The child's intelligence can range from normal to severe retardation. Cytomegalic inclusion disease can cause visual and hearing problems. Microcephaly often accompanies this disease. Kernicterus is a form of neonatal brain damage that is caused by the destruction of fetal red blood cells in utero. The principal cause of kernicterus is Rh incompatibility, but drugs, infections, and enzyme abnormalities have also been identified as etiological factors. While mild mental retardation is sometimes present, such other symptoms as disturbed speech articulation and athetoid cerebral palsy can lead to a misdiagnosis of mild retardation in an individual with normal intelligence. Children who run high fevers for an extended period of time are also at risk of permanent brain damage that can result in mild mental retardation.

Genetics

In the past, many pediatricians and educators assumed that children with inherited mental retardation disorders were moderately to severely retarded. While this may sometimes be true, it is a mistake to assume that mental retardation exists at any level—mild, moderate, severe, or profound. Inherited disorders are genetic in origin. Some are found in specific ethnic groups. For example, Riley-Day syndrome occurs principally within Semitic groups. Autonomic nervous system function is impaired, and children are usually small with poor coordination. Emotional problems are common, but intelligence can range from above normal to moderate mental retardation.

Down syndrome is caused by a chromosome imbalance resulting in three number 21 chromosomes instead of two. Mental retardation can range from mild to severe. Down syndrome is one of the most common forms of organic mental retardation. Since the recent institution of preschool special education programs, children with Down syndrome have demonstrated an increased ability to learn and participate in age appropriate activities. Some Down syndrome children score in the normal range on IQ tests. Second only to Down syndrome as a inherited form of mental retardation is fragile X or Martin-Bell syndrome. Only recently identified as a genetic form of clinical mental retardation, fragile X syndrome occurs in 1 of 1,000 males; however, many cases may go undiagnosed. This sex linked disorder occurs in males four times as often as females. The name "fragile X" is derived from a break in the long arm of the X chromosome. Characteristics of fragile X syndrome may include delayed language development, hyperactivity, a long narrow face, and prominent ears. Other forms of organic, inherited mental retardation in which children may fall into the mild category include Prader-Willi syndrome, Marfan's syndrome, oral facial digital syndrome (OFD, Type I), and Klinefelter's syndrome. Each of these organic forms of mild mental retardation is complex in its educational, medical, and psychological symptoms. Seizures, behavior disorders, metabolic problems, organ dysfunctions, motor problems, speech disorders, and emotional disturbance can combine in any number of ways in specific individuals (Lemeshow, 1982).

The greatest difficulty for many children with congenital and inherited mental retardation disorders is overcoming the handicap of their physical appearance. Children with Down syndrome, for instance, are sometimes placed in self-contained special classes simply based on the fact that they look "retarded." Limited expectations for success, along with isolation from nondisabled peers, can become a self-fulfilling prophecy of failure for these youngsters. Adolescence, with its emphasis on being attractive and popular, can be a particularly painful period. The aphorism, "Nature disables but society handicaps," aptly describes the constant struggle of these children for acceptance by their nondisabled peers.

Environmental Causes of Mild Retardation

The majority of students with mild retardation are poor and have no observable organic impairments. Poverty contributes to mild mental retardation by limiting access to experiences that lay the foundation for educational achievement and good health. Consequently, mild mental retardation is as much a social dilemma as an educational problem.

Toxins

Lead and other heavy metals, like mercury, poison children through inhalation, ingestion, and skin contact. The toxin is absorbed by central nervous system tissue where it can cause a variety of learning problems. Lead poisoning causes irritability, listlessness, clumsiness, and distractibility. Verbal and attending skills are most vulnerable to lead's toxic effects. A child can get lead poisoning by drinking from water pipes that are soldered with lead. Lead is found in plaster and paint. Children are exposed to lead from carbon monoxide exhaust in automobiles and factory emissions. Half of the estimated 16,000 children who are treated for lead poisoning each year develop mental retardation (Moore & Moore, 1977).

While all children are exposed to lead in some form, poor children are most susceptible to lead poisoning. Old, dilapidated buildings and houses are often covered with lead paint. Major highways, circling over inner-city ghettos, spew hydrocarbons into the air. Eventually the lead soaks into the soil, which remains contaminated for decades. Children playing in yards or playgrounds near highways and factories are at risk of lead poisoning. Youngsters in both urban and rural areas sniff gasoline and cleaning fluid to get high. A study of gasoline sniffing among Canadian Indians revealed that half the children suffered from tetraethyl lead poisoning (Remy et al., 1978).

Diet

A proper diet is necessary for normal growth and development. Nutrition is most important during fetal, neonatal, and early life when body cells are dividing, organs are forming, and developmental reflexes are beginning. Lack of proper nutrition in early development can contribute to growth retardation, intellectual delay, and behavior disorders. Winick (1976) found that undernutrition is a widespread problem in the United States, particularly among low-income African-Americans, native American Indians, and Spanish-Americans. While research has not proven that malnourishment alone causes mild mental retardation, it is evident from studies of Third World children that there is a significant relationship between proper nutrition and normal development (Edgerton, 1979).

Environmental Deprivation

The cultural gap between the lives of poor children and the white middle class standards of school puts these youngsters at a disadvantage. This is particularly true in the case of minorities, especially non-English speaking students. A study of students with mild retardation in New Jersey reported overrepresentation of minorities in special education programs (Brady, Manni, & Winikur, 1983). A national survey of special education found African-American children were identified as mildly retarded more frequently than any other ethnic group (Reschly, 1988).

Children of the poor are sometimes raised without early childhood experiences needed for success in school. Poor children may begin school with delayed language development, inadequate reading readiness, and short attention spans. Some are latchkey children. When they finish school for the day, they return to empty homes where they must care for themselves. The gut-wrenching reality of poverty is that formal education has little meaning to a youngster whose daily existence is a struggle for survival.

In *The Longest Mile* (1969), Rene Gazaway documented the inexorable slide towards mental retardation that occurred in small Appalachian communities or "hollows," where the most commonplace amenity of middle-class life is nonexistent. In Duddie's Branch, Gazaway found rampant illiteracy, malnutrition, disease, and isolation. The culture was so impoverished that for some time Gazaway thought that many adults were mute. In the course of a day, a typical family exchanged no more than a half dozen words. Children under six showed little curiosity or imagination, and parents provided no education or stimulation. Children spent most of the day together without the benefit of adult guidance or playthings. Gazaway provided the following description of a youngster's life in Duddie's Branch.

> *Hollow parents are completely indifferent to the expanding demands for more formal and informal educational experiences. Not one child from Duddie's Branch has ever seen a sandbox. None has played with finger paints, puzzles, or blocks. Their "toys" consist of broken bottles, sharp metal, discarded tin cans. Ask them about Goldilocks, and they will look at you in bewilderment—they never heard a fairy tale. I made a bean bag from an old rag and asked some of the older boys to catch it. They had difficulty. With an old string ball and a heavy stick, I tried to involve them in batting practice. I was unsuccessful. Not only do games fail to interest them, they are almost completely unable to participate in most activities. They could not be taught to whistle, or even sing a simple tune. (Edgerton, 1979, 55)*

Gazaway went on to describe the inability of these children to count, draw a geometric shape, discriminate right from left, or identify pictures of common animals. In this community, characterized by disease, hunger, lack of stimulation, neglect, and minimal verbal interaction, few children could be expected to score over 70 on an IQ test. Duddie's Branchers are trapped in an unchanging cycle of mental retardation. Adults with mild mental retardation parent children who will soon become retarded themselves, and the cycle continues.

Duddie's Branch is an example of how poverty infects a community and its inhabitants. Yet one does not need to travel to Appalachia to witness the ravages of poverty. Look around your community. Are there areas where you would not walk or where you lock your car doors as you drive through? Your fear is a common reaction of many citizens to a face-to-face encounter with poverty. Yet poverty does not change with the scenery. It endures. A 1977 report to Congress, *Preventing Mental Retardation—More Can Be Done*, noted that a poor child was fifteen times more likely to be identified as mildly retarded than a child from a middle-class family.

Most poor children are not mildly retarded, but they are disadvantaged. It would be a mistake to characterize all poor families as uncaring or unable to promote the development of their children. In *The Myth of the Deprived Child* (1972), Herbert Ginsburg observed that disadvantaged children are different from middle-class children. They are not deficient thinkers. The problem for many poor children, according to Ginsburg, is the mismatch between the adaptive demands of their neighborhood and school. The skills poor children acquire in order to succeed outside of school are, in many instances, different from the skills needed to succeed in school. Formal schooling demands conformity and adherence to a structured curriculum. Yet many poor children must learn at an early age to fend for themselves. The aggressive child who succeeds in the ghetto may be a discipline problem in school. While school rewards such passive skills as reading and writing, success in a poor community is often the result of quick action and independent problem-solving. Schools reward individual participation in academic clubs and athletic teams. Poor youngsters, who grow up in tough neighborhoods, may receive more recognition from their peers for wearing their gang "colors" than a debating club pin.

For the children of poverty, success or failure will hinge on the teacher's ability to adapt to the students' needs. This begins with an understanding of a poor youngster's life outside of school. When a student can see a connection between life in and outside of school, then there is a reason to learn. There are too many distractions on the streets for poor youngsters to sit still for eighteen yearsof unmeaningful formal schooling. The identification of a youngster as mildly retarded ensures the delivery of special education services. Yet provision of special education is no guarantee of success. Rather, it is the quality of these services that will make a difference. The task for both regular and special educators is to convince poor youngsters that there is a good reason to persevere in school.

Functional Domains

The following sections describe learning characteristics of students with mild mental retardation. The sections are divided into functional domains. The first, cognitive ability, reviews the research on the development of thinking skills. Academic achievement explains how students with mild retardation succeed or fail in school. The language/communication section describes the relationship of language ability to school achievement. The perceptual–motor section explains how attention and memory influence learning. The next section,

---

HIGHLIGHT 3–1   A Profile of Poverty

In a large northeastern city, one elementary school encapsulated the miserable union of poverty and inadequate schooling. The neighborhood around the school resembled the aftermath of a battle scene. Shop windows were boarded, cannibalized automobiles lined the streets, and the stamp of despair was etched in the faces of middle-aged men hunched in doorways. The school playground looked like a suburban landfill. Mattresses, old tires, and appliances were piled high amid broken bottles and overfilled garbage bags. Any child who played in this area risked serious injury. The outside of the school resembled a fortress with heavy metal doors and wiremesh windows. It was a cheerless yellow building covered with graffiti.

Teachers, the majority of them white, punched time cards and talked of weekends away from the chaos of the inner city. In one classroom the teacher made several tentative attempts to get his sixth grade charges to sit down and have a group lesson. After it was clear that no one was listening, he sat down with two students in the corner of the room and helped them with some math problems. The rest of the "class" wandered around or amused themselves with solitary activity. A teenage girl doodled on the blackboard. She carefully drew an arm with a clenched fist. A hypodermic needle jutted from the bulging bicep. Another girl stared into the tiny holes of an oval pencil sharpener attached to the wall. For fifteen minutes she slowly turned the handle as she peered inside, occasionally giggling to herself. When queried about the total disorder, the teacher's response was plain, "I'm just happy they come to school, at least they are safe for a while; anything after that is a bonus."

---

processing skills, describes how students with mild retardation interpret, store, and use sensory information. Finally, the section on social/adaptive skills discusses the special problems of living with the label "mildly retarded." Through a review of each of these sections you will find that students with mild retardation are more similar than different from students without disabilities. Variations between learners with mild retardation and other students are differences in degree of ability rather than differences in kinds of ability.

Cognitive Ability

What is intelligence? This is a question that continues to confound scholars in science and education. While scientists study the brain, educators study the mind. Neuroscientists calculate that the brain is composed of 10 to 100 billion neurons, with an infinite number of connections between these microscopic carriers of information. At the molecular level of brain function, thoughts are electrical impulses coursing through neural networks at the speed of light. Direct observation of brain function through such techniques as positron emission tomography (PET) scan or electroencephalogram (EEG) are incapable of distinguishing the brain of a person with mild mental retardation from that of a nondisabled person. Yet teachers in classrooms, psychologists in research laboratories, and employers in business provide ample descriptions of the different thinking abilities of individuals with mild retardation. These descriptions of different thinking skills vary depending on the point of view of the observer. For example, a teacher might describe attention problems, while a psychologist will report a subaverage mental level. An employer, meanwhile, might complain about tardiness.

Within the context of everyday life, a suitable definition of intelligence is the ability to adapt to the demands of specific settings and individuals. This social systems view of intelligence, with its emphasis on adaptation, is different from the psychometric (i.e., IQ) concept of intelligence that prevails in schools. In the former, intelligence is a function of survival and getting along with others; in the latter, intelligence is a score on a test.

Psychometry is the measurement of intellectual ability by mental tests. Mental tests provide an intelligence quotient (IQ) and mental age (MA) but scant information about how an individual thinks. Because the first mental tests devised by Binet and Simon were meant to screen dull students, revisions of the original IQ test continue to focus on school-related skills. The Wechsler Intelligence Scales for Children-Revised (WISC-R) measures verbal and performance skills including information questions, arithmetic, memory, and speed in putting together puzzles. To judge intellectual capacity based on performance on fourteen subtests on the WISC-R is a limited view of the nature of intelligence.

Sternberg (1990) described student cognitive ability in terms of thinking styles. Many learning problems could be eliminated, according to Sternberg, if teachers examined more carefully the mismatch between their teaching style and their students' thinking style. He maintained that any subject can be taught in a way that is congruent with a student's thinking style. Students who prefer what Sternberg calls the "executive" thinking style like to be told what to do and are good at recalling facts. These students make a good match with teaching methods that emphasize memorization and objective examinations. On the other hand, students who are more "legislative" in their thinking respond best to learning tasks that require imagination, planning, and creative problem-solving. Teachers may confuse thinking style with quality of intelligence. When a "legislative" thinking student is taught by an "executive" style teacher, the student is at a disadvantage. According to Sternberg, teachers need to pay closer attention to the differences in how their students think.

Piaget

The cognitive theory of Jean Piaget (1950) offers an alternative method for understanding the development of thinking. Piaget's theory describes four phases of intellectual development. Each phase is distinctively different in terms of how the individual perceives and interprets information. The *sensory-motor* stage is the initial phase of mental development. It begins at birth and typically develops through infancy. (All age indicators are only approximations. There is a good deal of variability in when individual children move onto the next stage of development.) As its title suggests, learning is linked to sensory input and evolving motor abilities. During this stage, the infant organizes and constructs a sense about how the world operates through imitation and play.

The second stage of cognitive development, the *preoperational*, begins around age two. At this point the child develops the ability to think symbolically through language, deferred imitation, games, and art. Ideas are tied to perceptions. For example, a pile of leaves that is scattered may appear to be "bigger" to a four-year-old because it covers more space than if the leaves were pushed close together. The preoperational thinker's view of the world is still characterized by the egocentrism of infancy. For example, clouds are alive because they move, and the sun sets, as a four-year-old put it, "because kids get tired."

During the primary school years (ages seven to eleven), most children are *concrete operational* thinkers. A child can mentally manipulate such symbols as numbers and words, but the child's thoughts are still tied to concrete here and now experiences. The opportunity to experiment with materials, to select topics of interest, and to investigate relationships, coupled with an increased need to share ideas verbally, characterizes thinking during this stage.

Formal operations is the final stage of cognitive development. Piaget described the onset of this stage around adolescence, although follow-up studies indicate that some college students may still be in the process of developing abstract thought (Dulit, 1972). At the formal stage, the young adult has developed the ability to reason logically, to analyze, and to search for solutions among an array of possibilities.

Unlike IQ tests, which measure *what* children think, Piaget's theory describes *how* children think. Piaget's theory of cognitive development provides the educator with insight into the student's conception of reality. The applicability of Piaget's theory in understanding the mental operations of children with mental retardation was initiated in 1943 by Piaget's colleague, Barbel Inhelder. Working with institutionalized children and adults, Inhelder (1968) concluded that individuals with mental retardation followed the same pattern of development as normal children. The difference was a slower rate of stage acquisition for individuals with a disability. Other researchers confirmed the slower cognitive development of children with mental retardation, and they discovered that mental age (MA) computed from IQ tests was a good indicator of a student's developmental level (Mannix, 1960; Marchi, 1971; Uzgiris & Hunt, 1975). For instance, a 7-year-old student with a mental age of 5 would probably be functioning at the preoperational stage of cognitive development rather than the concrete operational stage.

Piagetian research with individuals with mental retardation demonstrated that their reasoning abilities are better characterized as developmentally delayed than deficient (Henley, 1985). Stafford and Klein noted in their comprehensive review of Piagetian research:

> *An important aspect of Piaget's orientation is that it enables one to shift from the deficit notion . . . to understanding where the retarded may be in terms of developmental structures. This positive view enables us to look at what retarded children are rather than what they are not; what they know rather than don't know. (Stafford & Klein, 1977, 308)*

The major impact of Piaget's view of intelligence is that children interact and view their world in a distinctively different manner depending on their stage of cognitive development (Figure 3–1). The application of cognitive developmental theory to the instruction of learners with mild retardation requires a close look at what goes on in classrooms. Piaget described learning as interactive. Children require opportunities to learn through trial and error. They use language to compare perceptions and make adjustments to their own egocentric view of life. A teacher-directed, sit-still-and-listen classroom does not match the cognitive abilities of children at the sensory-motor, preoperational, or concrete stage of intellectual development.

Reid (1978) analyzed education methods from a Piagetian perspective and observed that many education techniques work in opposition to the natural

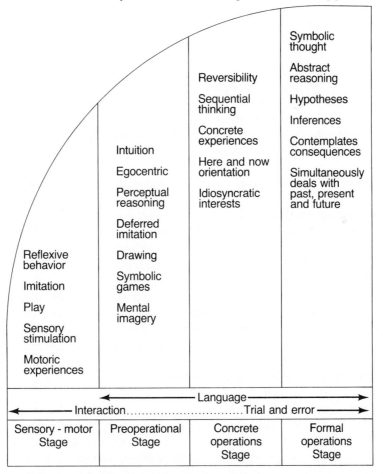

FIGURE 3–1 Cognitive Development.

Adapted from Wyne, M. and O'Connor, P. (1979). Exceptional Children, a Developmental View. Lexington, MA: D.C. Heath.

abilities of students with mild disabilities. Tightly sequenced curricula, concern for the "right" answer, drill, and memorization are formal operational strategies that overshoot the cognitive strategies of students who are at the preoperational or concrete operational stage of thinking. The neglect of educators to consider underlying developmental processes in their teaching can create a conceptual gap between the curriculum and the mediating cognitive structures of the student. The overall effect can be a loss of motivation and continued dependency on adults to provide information and solutions to problems. Educators who view the cognitive development of learners with mild retardation from a Piagetian perspective can modify classroom activities to match the learning capabilities of their students.

Academic Achievement

Traditionally, educational services for students with mild mental retardation were provided in self-contained, special classes. The curriculum was "watered down." Students were taught the regular school curriculum at a slower pace, with emphasis on drill and repetition. Students subjected to this tedious instruction frequently failed to show any significant gains in academic skills.

One way to evaluate the success of school programs for students identified as having mild retardation is to examine their status after leaving school. Edgar (1987) compared the employment condition of regular education students, students with learning disabilities, and students with mild retardation. He found the group identified in school as having mild mental retardation least capable of finding adequate employment opportunities. Of 167 students with mild retardation who left school from 1976 to 1981 (i.e., dropouts, graduates, and age-outs) in eleven school districts in the state of Washington, just 4 percent of the group with mild mental retardation were earning more than $135.00 a week. While 56 percent of the students were able to secure some type of employment over the five-year period, only 43 percent were still employed five years after leaving school.

In 1985, Polloway and Epstein asked sixty-seven educators of students identified as mildly retarded to prioritize the educational needs of their students. Vocational and career education was the first selection, postschool adjustment was second, and long-term effects of academic treatment programs was next. Clearly, these educators were concerned with the need of the school curriculum to enhance the lives of students after school.

Functional Curriculum

To succeed in life, students need to apply skills learned in the classroom to the outside world. One approach is to teach functional life skills in the classroom. Instead of emphasizing arithmetic problems on worksheets, a functional curriculum would teach budgeting and shopping skills. While reading is often treated as an isolated "subject," a functional curriculum would teach reading throughout the school day by using such everyday materials as newspapers, magazines, and job applications. Apprentice programs, where high school students spend time in the community working with "mentors" in trades and business, are examples of functional programs that integrate school with on-site job training.

A functional curriculum bridges the gap between the teaching and the application of information. It capitalizes on the cognitive abilities of students by providing learning experiences that are concrete and practical rather than abstract and hypothetical. The student can immediately see the use for new skills and gets ample opportunity to evaluate personal progress. Teachers who are successful in implementing functional curricula begin by asking the question, "What do I see this student doing five years from now?"

The more severely disabled the individual, the sooner a functional curriculum should be initiated. For the learner with mild retardation, adolescence is a good starting point. This does not mean an abandonment of academic work, but a gradual emphasis on vocational skills. The school dropout rate for youngsters with mild disabilities is over 30 percent in some school districts. As students approach the early teens, the best message educators can send is, "We have a reason for you to stay in school." A functional curriculum, with its emphasis on practical skills, gives students a rationale for continuing their education.

The Adult Performance Level Curriculum (APL) developed at the University of Texas is an example of a functional curriculum. It contains forty-two life skills objectives organized under five major categories: consumer economics, community resources, health, occupational knowledge, and law. The program ranges from elementary to high school and includes reading, writing, speaking, problem-solving, interpersonal relationships, and computation skills. Examples of tasks in reading/consumer economics for each level are as follows: elementary—look for ads in the newspaper for toys; junior high school—read an ad for a sale and find the name of the store, location, phone number, and price of the item; high school—read and compare prices of grocery store ads. The purpose of the curriculum is to develop student competencies necessary for survival in daily life (Patton et al., 1989).

Thinking

Guided teaching of thinking abilities is another approach to the education of learners with mild retardation. Goldstein (1980) advocated the direct teaching of problem-solving skills. A major hurdle for many individuals with mild retardation is adapting to the social demands of life after school. Goldstein's Social Learning Curriculum utilizes a "logical inductive strategy" to teach students a hierarchical procedure for problem-solving. Within this system, students learn to label, detail, infer, predict, verify, and generalize.

Goldstein's approach is significantly different from the traditional teacher-directed lessons so often encountered in academic programs for students with mild retardation. In a teacher-directed lesson, the teacher:

1. tells the student what is to be learned;
2. tells the student what to do (e.g., complete this worksheet);

3. calls on students to respond;
4. evaluates student answers; and
5. corrects wrong answers.

In a teacher-directed lesson, each step is controlled and monitored by the teacher. Goldstein believes that teacher-directed lessons undermine student confidence in their own thinking abilities.

The logical-inductive approach, advocated by Goldstein, encourages student input. Situations are presented to students, and the teacher guides the students' thinking by means of a series of questions. For example, the Test of Hierarchy of Inductive Knowledge (THINK) provides stimulus picture cards for classroom discussions. Students are first asked to identify details in a picture, for example, a man and boy raking a yard. Then through a guided discussion, students attempt to analyze the problem (e.g., a boy's football is stuck in a rain gutter) and come up with solutions to solve the problem. Rather than concentrating on right and wrong answers, the teacher encourages students to share perceptions and think about what they see. The teaching of critical thinking skills to all students, both those with and without disabilities, has strong support in the educational community.

Students with mild retardation are sometimes characterized as field dependent in their thinking (Bica, Halpin, & Halpin, 1986). This means they do not trust their own perceptions or judgments. They are easily influenced by peers and authority figures. By emphasizing individual problem solving, critical thinking programs such as Goldstein's logical-inductive strategy can help develop selfreliance and improve the reasoning abilities of students with mild retardation.

Early Intervention

Preschool programs, such as Head Start, provide academic interventions for children aged three to five. The ability of preschool programs to achieve positive, long-term results with students at risk of mild mental retardation was documented in *Changed Lives* (Weikert, 1984), a 22-year longitudinal study of poor, African-American children in Ypsilanti, Michigan. As adults, the preschoolers outdistanced peers who had no preschool experience in several criteria for success including: high school diplomas, employment, and functional skills. The number of teenage pregnancies among the preschoolers was half that of the control group and trouble with the law was reduced significantly among the preschooler group. In 1986, Congress passed P.L. 99-457 (The Infant/Toddler Program, Part H) to fund early-intervention programs for preschool children with disabilities and to offer incentives to school systems to develop programs for disabled infants and toddlers.

Successful preschool programs work with parents to continue gains made in preschool centers at home. The school-family partnership is critical because the single most reliable predictor of mild retardation is the IQ of a child's mother. Preschool programs help accelerate students at risk of school failure in cognitive, motor, language, and social-emotional development. A review of fifty-two studies of preschool programs found that 94 percent reported significant gains for children, siblings, and families of preschoolers with mild disabilities (Castro & Mastgropieri, 1986). Early intervention, particularly with poor children, is one of the most effective educational strategies to ensure school achievement in later years.

For the student with mild retardation to succeed in school, the focus must be shifted from what is wrong with the student to what is right and beneficial in the curriculum. Functional curricula, strategies for teaching reasoning skills, and early intervention are three educational approaches that enhance the school experience.

Language/Communication Development

Schools are primarily verbal environments. Secondary teachers expect students to follow oral directions, recall information from lectures, locate information in textbooks, and take notes. In elementary classrooms, students are expected to listen to the teacher, answer questions correctly, read silently, and write. The one-sided emphasis on verbal skills favors the middle-class child and handicaps the poor child. Disadvantaged learners may not begin school with the middle-class language background that is a prerequisite for successful classroom participation.

Robert Ornstein, the noted neuroscientist, once observed that students are not judged on how well they use their brains, but on how well they use their mouths. Rational thought involves more than verbal abilities. The neocortex of the human brain is divided into two halves, the left and right hemispheres. For most individuals, the left hemisphere is the language center. In the left frontal, parietal, and temporal lobes of the brain, mental activity is expressed through listening and speech. The right hemisphere is the creative, intuitive part of the brain. While the left hemisphere solves problems through analysis, the right hemisphere integrates information and searches for wholistic solutions. Neither half is superior to the other; both work together to produce rational thought.

The majority of school activity, including reading, speaking, and writing, requires a preponderance of left hemisphere, language skills. Therefore, a preschool child who is not provided with such language activities as bedtime stories, listening to music, and guided conversations with adults is at a distinct disadvantage on entering school. Because so many students with mild retardation are poor, minorities, or both, their opportunities to develop the language skills required for a successful school experience may be limited.

Reading
The teaching of reading by phonics is an example of a left hemispheric approach to language development used in schools. Phonics teaches the sounds of letters, how those sounds blend to make syllables, and the combination of syllables to make words. In the reverse procedure—decoding—students are expected to decipher new words by sounding out each letter to complete a whole word. This

auditory, analytical, sequential approach to reading is fine if it takes advantage of preexisting language abilities, but what about the child who does not master the phonics approach? For students who lack good auditory and analytic abilities, phonics and eventually reading can be difficult to master.

Marie Carbo found that economically disadvantaged readers tend to be tactile/kinesthetic learners. Their approach to reading is best described as "global." These students have excellent visual and integrative skills that enable them to acquire sight vocabularies. They demonstrate an intuitive awareness of word patterns. Carbo observed that "global learners learn to read most rapidly through such activities as writing stories, reading books of their own choosing, engaging in choral reading, writing and performing in plays, and listening to tape recordings of interesting and well written books" (Carbo, 1987, 432). The global reading style described by Carbo is an example of right hemisphere abilities and is an apt description of the approach to learning observed by teachers of disadvantaged, underachieving students (Dennison, 1969; Kohl, 1967).

Mandelbaum (1989) reviewed best practices in teaching reading and found that a combination of a functional reading lists with interesting reading material best met the needs of students with mild retardation. Several principles of effective teaching summarized by Mandelbaum are:

1. *Demonstrate Rather than Tell.* The teacher and student discuss, read, and answer questions together about a story on the student's reading level.
2. *Provide for Successful Practice.* Make sure students use reading materials that will sustain at least an 80 percent success rate.
3. *Use Direct Instruction.* Teacher-led group instruction should demonstrate the skill to be learned, provide practice with feedback, and allow for independent student practice.
4. *Plan for High Levels of Task Involvement.* Reading in unison, choral reading, and high interest readings improve fluency and comprehension.
5. *Ignore Errors that Do Not Matter. All errors are not equal.* Every word does not have to be read correctly. Focus only on errors that change the meaning of a sentence. Provide sufficient time for a student to analyze a word and decode.
6. *Give Independent Assignments that Relate to the Lesson.* Most workbooks and dittos focus on isolated skills unrelated to stories. Avoid the drudgery of worksheets unless relevant and necessary.
7. *Integrate Subject Matter.* Use themes or webbings to cluster concepts.
8. *Measure Behavior Change.* Plot and graph reading improvement in terms of median of number of words read correctly each minute.
9. *Provide Opportunities to Learn Achievement Formats.* Formats vary widely, and students need practice with the procedures that will be used to evaluate their skills.

Language Deficient versus Language Different

Bernstein (1961) described poor children's language as a "restricted code," which was ill-suited for subtle shades of thought or meaning. Poor children, he said, were improperly prepared for rational thought by uneducated parents who dealt with them in an authoritative, impulsive manner. The disadvantaged child fails to learn such abstract concepts as causality and long-range planning. Bernstein's view of the deficient language development of poor children was used by some educators in this country to explain the inadequate school performance of poor African-American children.

Bereiter and Englemann (1966) believed that a deprived environment retarded speech and deficient speech led to deficient thought. School failure was the cumulative result. The "language deficient" perspective of African-American children's speech focused attention on remedial efforts to teach them "white standard English." For instance, DISTAR, a tightly structured preschool program was used to teach language development to poor inner-city children. The popular TV show "Sesame Street," which is designed especially with poor children in mind, adopted the deficient language hypothesis by teaching new vocabulary, labeling objects, and other basic school readiness skills.

The assumption that poverty causes deficient language, which leads to deficient thinking skills, was challenged almost immediately by researchers in the field of psycholinguistics. Robinson (1965) found that the "restricted code" hypothesis is a better description of poor children's performance than of their competence. From his studies Robinson discovered that poor children choose to speak in dialects that are accepted by their peers even when they are capable of more elaborate, middle-class speech. To test his hypothesis, Robinson asked a group of lower- and middle-class students to write a letter to a friend and to a school administrator asking for a favor. While the informal letters reflected the children's social class speech patterns, the formal letter to the educator contained few elements that could be attributed to lower-class language deficiencies. Robinson concluded that when poor children chose to use more elaborate middle-class language, they could do so. More recently, Farley (1986) found that students with mild retardation were capable of age appropriate, fluent writing.

Lobav, Cohen and Lewis (1968) reported that poor and middle-class students are more alike than different in the way their language develops. Lobav carefully scrutinized how poor African-American children learn to speak. He found that their language, which he described as "Black Standard English," progressed through a logical sequence of syntax and structure. Lobav reported that the speech of poor African-American children followed a normal pattern of development. Their language was not deficient, only different from white middle-class language. The "language different" hypothesis advocated by Ginsburg (1972) highlighted the structural and functional conflicts between how poor children speak and the expectations placed on them by schools embedded in middle-class language. One example of structural conflict is the use of "White Standard English" in reading texts. A poor African-American child may have difficulty because the teacher expects the child to pronounce words as they appear in the text. Functional conflicts occur when, as Robinson noted, poor children persist in using speech in school that is accepted by peers because to do otherwise would be considered unmanly.

English as a Second Language

When English is a second language, it is difficult to determine if mild disability exists. Language assessment of non-English-speaking or limited-English-proficient students is improving, particularly for Spanish-speaking youngsters. Still it is difficult to identify a language deficit in a bilingual youngster. Assessment of language disorders analyzes a variety of skills including auditory discrimination, articulation, verbal expression, and comprehension of complex relationships. According to Langdon "the purpose of testing a non-English or limited English proficient student is to determine his or her proficiency in the native language and to compare it with the performance in the second language, when appropriate" (Langdon, 1983, 39). The objective is to determine if lack of proficiency in English is due to a general language disorder or a reflection of normal difficulties in learning a new language.

As numbers of non-English speaking students strain the resources of public schools, determining the source of academic problems will continue to challenge educators. For instance, in California, there are ninety distinct language groups and nearly 400,000 limited English proficient students in public schools (Cegelka, Lewis, & Rodriguez, 1987). When these students fail to progress satisfactorily, standard testing procedures used to identify mild mental retardation will almost certainly indicate a disability, unless special measures are used to take language differences into account. This is because most standardized tests of intelligence primarily assess language skills. Misdiagnosis can take two forms: false positive and false negative. In the former, students are incorrectly assessed as mildly retarded, whereas in the latter situation, mild learning disabilities are overlooked.

To accurately assess a language disorder among non-English speaking students, both languages are assessed by a clinician who is fluent in each. Assessment instruments are translated into the student's native language, and if a language disorder is found, remediation begins with the student's native language (Langdon, 1983). Table 3–3 contains a list of tests translated into Spanish.

The itenerant life-styles of many non-English speaking students make it difficult to assess mild retardation and other disabling conditions. Baca and Harris (1988) estimated approximately 80,000 migrant children in need of special education. They concluded that only 8,000, or one percent, of these children receive special education services. Because of limited English proficiency, poverty, and inadequate health conditions, migrant children are especially vulnerable to mild mental retardation. In a study of migrant education, Barresi (1984), found that:

1. Only 10 percent of children with mild disabilities were identified.
2. Identification occurs late in the school career.
3. Students were placed in the wrong special education programs.
4. Gaps in services existed because of different administrative procedures between school districts (Baca & Harris, 1988).

TABLE 3–3   Some Tests Used by School Systems That Are Translated into Spanish

Bilingual Syntax Measure
Ber-Sil
Dos Amigos Verbal Language Scales
Del Rio
Leiter International Performance Scale
Language Assessment Scales
SOMPA
WISC-R
Boehm Test of Basic Concepts
Carrow Test of Auditory Comprehension of Language
Peabody Picture Vocabulary Test
Woodcock-Johnson Psychoeducational Battery
Bender-Gestalt
PEOPLE
Austin Spanish Articulation Test
Columbia Mental Maturity Test
Raven Progressive Matrices
Woodcock Language Proficiency Battery

The number of culturally and linguistically diverse students will continue to increase in our nation's schools. By the year 2,000, an estimated 40 percent of public school students will be from such ethnically diverse backgrounds as African-American, Hispanic, and Asian (Ramirez, 1988). Urban schools, in particular, will be faced with increased numbers of underachieving students with cultural and language differences. Schools need to keep pace with the changing student population. If teaching techniques do not change to take into account such meaningful events in children's lives as their language and culture, special education will become inundated with children identified as mildly disabled. Most of these children will not have intellectual deficiencies. Rather, they will be the product of an educational system that was unable to adjust to the changing needs of its student population.

Teacher Talk
Given the array of language-different children who populate classrooms and the amount of listening students are expected to do, teachers face a formidable challenge instructing their students. Teachers, however, are sometimes unclear in their lessons. An analysis of teacher talk by Nelson (1984) found that false starts, repetitions, lack of clarity, and abstract language were common aspects of teacher talk. Students with mild retardation may have attention and memory deficits that further impair their ability to understand teachers' explanations.

Robinson (1989) recommended the use of advance organizers to help alert students to important material. She proposed the following guidelines for the use of advance organizers:

1. Alert students to the transition to a new activity.
2. Identify topics or activities students will do.
3. Provide an outline or other organizational framework.
4. Clarify teacher expectations for student participation.
5. Provide background information regarding how this lesson relates to previous activities.
6. State the concepts to be learned.
7. Give examples of concepts.
8. Highlight the relevance of topic.
9. Introduce new vocabulary.
10. Specify the desired general outcomes of the activity.

These ten steps provide the student with a direct and simple framework for listening and understanding teacher expectations for successful classroom participation.

Student memory can be enhanced through the use of verbal rehearsal and self-questioning. Rehearsal requires the student to repeat directions silently several times. This strategy can help a student follow teacher directions. Self-questioning is a strategy useful for all students. After a passage is read or a lesson is taught, the student reviews key elements by asking:

> *What is the story (lecture) about?*
> *Who is in the story (lecture)?*
> *Where did the events take place?*
> *When did they take place—in what order?*
> *Why is this information important or useful? (Robinson, 1989, 150)*

Teaching is more than simply standing in front of the room and saying whatever comes to mind. It requires clarity. Many students, including those with language differences or deficits, need help in listening and remembering. The simple technique of asking students what they learned in class today can help a teacher determine what students do or do not understand.

Writing
"Eighty percent of all high school students write inadequately, over one-half do not like the process of writing, and approximately four-fifths cannot write well enough to insure that they will always accomplish their purpose" (Decker & Polloway, 1989, 111). Writing is one of the most difficult and creative mental activities. Over the years, electronic media have replaced writing as a principal means of communication. Why then should students write in school?

Writing is a means of personal expression. It is a means of communicating. Through writing, one learns and understands material more thoroughly. Writing is a creative outlet. It increases vocabulary. Writing in the classroom complements and accelerates reading skills. Most important, writing provides students with a vehicle for expressing their thoughts, feelings, and attitudes. Writing is a pathway to future success in life.

There are two basic types of writing—creative and functional. Creative writing is comprised of compositions, stories, poetry, personal journals, letters, and plays. Functional writing includes business letters, reports, records of events, essay tests, applications, and note taking. One weakness in writing instruction is overemphasis on mechanics. When spelling, punctuation, and grammar take precedence, students lose the will to write. As Graves (1985) observed:

> *Most teaching of writing is pointed towards the eradication of error, the mastery of minute, meaningless components that make little sense to the child. Small wonder. Most language arts texts, workbooks, computer software, and reams of behavioral objectives are directed towards the "easy" control of components that will show more specific growth. Although some growth may be evident on components, rarely does it result in the child's use of writing as a tool for learning and enjoyment. (Decker & Polloway, 1989, 116)*

Handwriting instruction is a good example of what Graves refers to as mastery of minute components. Legible handwriting is a skill worth striving towards; perfect handwriting is not. How many hours are wasted in classrooms as students labor over writing handbooks trying to get their *t*'s, *f*'s, and *l*'s similar in form and shape? Yet, as adults very few of us demonstrate "perfect" handwriting.

Spelling is another area that requires a common-sense approach. When teachers hand back student essays that are red lined with spelling errors, a student's desire to write is squelched. Spelling errors and spelling disabilities are best dealt with functionally. Keeping lists of commonly misspelled words or encouraging students to use a spelling tool such as *Webster's New World Speller Divider* helps students learn to cope with spelling problems. Writing is a creative act that requires nurturing. When teachers become fixated on the mechanics of writing, it is unlikely their students will progress as effective writers.

Perceptual/Perceptual-Motor Skills

Perception is a combination of attention, memory, and thinking. As an illustration, without looking, list the names of the authors of this textbook. Even though you look at the cover of this book on a regular basis (at least your professor hopes this is the case), you probably found naming each author a difficult task. Perception begins with selective attention. You can look at many features of your environment day after day (e.g., the color of the walls in your classrooms), but if you do not concentrate and willfully commit the sensory input to memory, your brain will not encode the information, and it is forgotten.

Familiarity, interest, color, and movement are a few of the factors that influence perception. As infants mature, they learn to discriminate specific details from a background of competing stimuli. This figure-ground discrimination is an essential perceptual skill for successful school performance. Students with poor figure-ground discrimination skills may have trouble selecting individual letters from a line of words, become confused by oral directions, or become distracted by movement in a classroom.

According to Hebb (1966), early childhood experience plays a key role in the development of perceptual skills. Hebb theorized that environmental stimulation accelerates the growth of brain tissue and connections among neurons in the brain. Conversely, environmental deprivation will adversely affect brain tissue development and subsequent mental processing of information in later years. In applying Hebb's theory to children with mild mental retardation, Wyne & O'Conner noted,

> *Some have argued that Hebb's theory, which stresses sheer experience to stimulation and variation in perceptual stimulation early in life, fails to account for deviant cognitive development of disadvantaged infants who grow up in slum conditions, absolutely bombarded with stimulation. On the contrary, this may not be at all inconsistent with Hebb. Hebb's theory is built on the proposition that repeated stimulation is necessary for learning to occur, and that selective attention to those stimuli is crucial. It is now thought that some children growing up in such intense slum conditions may be so bombarded with stimuli of all kinds as to force them to tune out much of it from their awareness, and that this may be part of their cognitive deficit—the failure to selectively attend. What appears to be inattentive, off-task behavior in school aged disadvantaged children may have its origins in a disruptive, noisy, disorienting environment in infancy.* (Wyne & O'Conner, 1979, 237)

Learners with mild retardation may have deficits in short- and long-term memory. Researchers use the term "rehearsal" to describe the unconscious cognitive strategies students use to remember. Rehearsal is comprised of various verbal strategies including repetition, rhyme, subvocal speech, and verbal self-instruction. Students with mild retardation are less likely to use spontaneous rehearsal techniques. When they are taught rehearsal strategies, short- and long-term memory improves (Scruggs & Laufenberg, 1986).

Inadequate teaching is often overlooked as a contributor to presumed deficits in attention and memory. Students who are expected to maintain attention during dull and repetitive lessons are unlikely to remember what they read or heard only moments before. Ineffective teachers use general characteristics of students with mild mental retardation as a rationale for individual learning problems. A vicious cycle of low expectations and unsuccessful learning evolves when teachers use mild mental retardation as an explanation for a student's learning difficulty. A teacher who remarks, "Well, Susan simply can't retain concepts because she's mildly retarded," is overlooking the significant role of effective teaching in helping students learn. Teaching that includes active student involvement with learning tasks, guided practice sessions, and systematic error correction procedures will produce successful results that can overcome deficits in organizing perceptual information (Algozzine & Maheady, 1986).

The ability to coordinate perception with movement is a fundamental skill required for learning. The fact that he named the first phase of intellectual development the sensory-motor stage is a clear indication of the importance Piaget attached to early perceptual-motor experiences. Lack of perceptual-motor stimulation at a young age may delay intellectual development. The delay can be so subtle that negative consequences may be overlooked until the school years, when a youngster is compared to peers in such tasks as reading, writing, and physical education.

Perceptual-motor problems can manifest themselves in a variety of ways, including poor coordination and inadequate fine-motor skills. Research on motor skill performance of students with mild mental retardation consistently reports difficulties with such activities as running, throwing, and jumping (Dobbins & Rarick, 1977; Holland, 1987). Poor performance in physical education classes can negatively affect student self-confidence and motivation to persevere. Conversely, physical education and recreational skills can promote student self-confidence by enhancing awareness of body coordination and performance. Such programs as Outward Bound and rope climbing increase perception and attention skills of students while providing them with challenging and successful experiences.

Mental Processing Skills

Thinking is a complex process. Suppose a stranger asks you for directions. As you picture a route in your mind, the visual center of your occipital lobe is activated. Then you mentally translate your vision into a series of steps while your left hemisphere analyzes each part of the stranger's journey. Words take shape next, and instantaneous messages flash back and forth between the parietal lobe and frontal lobe. The mouth region of the motor cortex fires signals to your tongue, jaw, and larynx. Finally, as you speak, the auditory cortex of the temporal lobe tracks your words and sentences to ensure that you are accurately describing the correct route.

This brief illustration describes the multiple tasks the brain performs in "processing" the steps of a simple communication. When a deficit exists in these processing skills, even everyday tasks can become overwhelming. Much of the pioneering research on processing skills was done using patients who had suffered head injuries. Researchers would pinpoint the damaged area of the brain, determine what processing skill was impaired, and draw a conclusion that the damaged area was responsible for that specific processing disability. With individuals who had no obvious brain damage, judgments about deficits in processing skills were hypothetical. Ellis (1963), for example, theorized that individuals with mental retardation were deficient in some processing skills and had normal abilities in other processing skills. The challenge for researchers was to determine which processing skills were intact and which were deficient.

Testing is one technique employed by educators to identify processing deficits of students with mild retardation. However, most tests that are used to measure mental processing skills have considerable validity and reliability problems. Teacher observations are the most common source of information about mental processing problems. Deficient memory skills, short attention span, distractibility, and impaired abstract thinking are commonly attributed to students with mild retardation in school. Yet teachers' observations of student actions are biased by their expectations for "normal" classroom behavior. In a teacher-directed classroom, where students spend inordinate amounts of time sitting, listening, and writing in workbooks, even small amounts of bored or distracted behavior can be misinterpreted as a problem.

Accurate identification of the processing skills needed to succeed in school is far from complete. Until the 1970s, attempts to evaluate processing skills and deficits were hindered by overreliance on the need to infer abilities from samples of behavior. Sometimes the behaviors were answers to questions on a test; other times the behaviors were actions in the classroom. The difficulty with these indirect assessments of processing skills is that there were other factors, such as teacher bias and inadequate theory, that distorted judgments about processing skills.

With the advent of positron emission tomography (PET scans), neuroscientists can directly observe the brain in action. Through the use of computer-enhanced imagery, physicians are able to observe the brain of a patient in the act of thinking. A radioactive tracer in the bloodstream lights the computer projection of the patient's brain in vivid colors that correspond to the part of the brain that is engaged. When the patient is talking, the left frontal lobe and motor cortex are highlighted in red. When the patient is listening, the left temporal lobe projection turns red and surrounding inactive brain tissue is colored a dim blue on the computer monitor. While this procedure is too expensive to use in schools, the knowledge gained from PET scan research on mental processing and learning is certain to benefit future educators in their work with students.

Social/Adaptive Skills

Categorical labels, such as mild mentally retarded, reinforce the tendency to classify students in terms of the single dimension ascribed by the label. The social needs of students with mild retardation may be overlooked because their "problem" is viewed in terms of subaverage intellectual functioning. Yet there is nothing retarded about the emotions of these students. Students identified with mild retardation have normal feelings. They want to be liked, accepted, and valued as human beings. Their self-esteem is strongly influenced by their status and day-to-day activities in school (Dupont, 1978).

Many students spend a significant portion of their day out of the mainstream of normal school activities. A study of students with mild retardation in northern Illinois found that more than 90 percent of the students were in regular classrooms less than half the day (Polloway et al., 1988). The stigma of spending most of the day in a special education classroom, isolated from normal school activities, can have an erosive effect on a youngster's self-esteem. Like all other students, youngsters with mild mental retardation want to be liked and accepted, yet studies of regular education students' perceptions report nonacceptance or rejection of students identified as mildly retarded (Kuveke, 1983; Sabonie & Kaufmann, 1987).

Erik Erikson (1963) in *Childhood and Society* described the beginning school years, ages seven to eleven, as crucial to a youngster's sense of competence. During these first years of school, a child seeks to master tasks that are prized by the world outside the family. While the need to accomplish and produce is strong, there is an equal pull towards regression to the safe harbor of play and dependence of earlier years. The polar psychological demands to achieve in order to overcome feelings of inadequacy require successful school experiences for a positive outcome. Acceptance by peers plays a key role in the child's evolving self-concept. The successes or failures that a youngster experiences during these early school years will affect future endeavors throughout adolescence and adulthood.

The majority of students with mild disabling conditions are identified by an educational assessment after entering school. At the precise time in their young lives when they are most in need of success, these youngsters experience failure and the added indignity of being identified with such labels as learning disabled or mildly retarded. The stress of dealing with school failure, peer rejection, and segregation as a learner with mild retardation can cause students to lose faith in themselves as competent individuals. Failure in school leaves a strong impression. Educators use the term "learned helplessness" to describe student lack of confidence in their own abilities. When Reynolds and Miller (1985) compared students identified as mildly retarded with nondisabled students, they found the special-needs students showed significant signs of depression and learned helplessness. The findings suggest that students with mild retardation are vulnerable to emotional disturbance because of their failure in school and their prolonged exposure to peer disapproval (Epstein, Cullinan, & Polloway, 1986).

The "New" Mildly Retarded

Until the mid-1980s the category of mild mental retardation was almost exclusively the domain of disadvantaged children who demonstrated no sign of organic retardation. In recent years, some school systems have identified a "new," more organically involved student with mild mental retardation. The gradual transition in characteristics of mild mental retardation to more multiply disabled students is due to several factors.

1. The American Association of Mental Retardation refined its definition of mental retardation in an attempt to eliminate hard-to-teach students from the classification retarded. With the decrease in "borderline" students from the category of mild mental retardation, there has been a corresponding increase of lower functioning students included in this classification.

2. Due to the widespread implementation of special education preschool programs, students who previously might have scored in the moderate range on IQ tests are scoring in the low, mild range.

3. Since the mid-1980s, there is an increase of children disabled in utero by drug use of pregnant women.

4. As society's expectations for children with organic disabilities improve, so does school performance. For instance, it is no longer unusual for a student with Down syndrome to score in the mild range on an IQ test.

5. In states (e.g., California) that divide special education programs into mild and severe categories, parents of students with organic types of mental retardation push for classification of their youngsters in the mild category. (MacMillan, 1989)

A survey of students identified as mildly retarded provides an illustration of a changing mentally retarded population. Forness and Pollaway (1987) reported that out of eighty-four students identified as mildly retarded in California, nearly 80 percent had multiple disabilities. The most frequent cited combination was intellectual, behavioral, and speech impairments.

The more disabled condition of these students raises questions regarding characteristics and educational services. For instance, will the multiple nature of these students' disabilities be used as a justification to keep students with mild mental retardation out of regular classrooms? If placed in regular classrooms, will these students' learning be disrupted by frequent "pull-outs" for such special services as speech therapy and adaptive physical education? How will nonorganically involved students feel about special instruction placements that have them sitting alongside students with obvious disabilities?

Underlying these instructional concerns is the confusing picture about how students with mild mental retardation are identified. Individual states and school systems continue to use different diagnostic criteria. A study of five Ohio cities by Smith (1984) indicated that three of four students assigned to programs for the mildly retarded were African-Americans. The high percentage of African-American students identified as having mild retardation in Ohio follows the historical pattern of poor and minority overrepresentation of students in programs for the mildly retarded. Clearly, concerns about different characteristics of the "new" mildly retarded population need to be dealt with on a state-by-state basis.

Suggestions for Teaching Students with Mild Mental Retardation

1. Expect to see progress; mild mental retardation is not a permanent, unalterable condition.
2. Many students come to school without readiness skills; don't assume they know what you are talking about.
3. Identify a student's level of cognitive functioning (i.e., preoperational, concrete, operational), and match teaching approaches to learner characteristics.
4. Always connect abstract ideas to student life experiences.
5. Avoid dull, repetitious work. Provide novelty in lessons.
6. Provide maximum opportunities for learning in the least restrictive environment.
7. Remember that the label "mentally retarded" is demeaning and provokes stereotyping.
8. Keep in mind that IQ tests don't measure intelligence.
9. Insist on a measure of adaptive behavior before a student is evaluated as mentally retarded.
10. Provide adolescent students with functional, career-oriented learning experiences.

Summary

Mild mental retardation is both a social and an educational problem. The majority of children identified as mildly retarded are poor, with African-Americans overrepresented in many states. While many students with mild mental retardation have no identifiable organic or neurological problems, the health-threatening conditions of poverty clearly put poor children at greatest risk. The deleterious effects of such factors as low birth weight, deficient diet, and improper prenatal care can be offset by health and educational intervention for children and their families.

Characteristics of children identified with mild mental retardation can vary from one region to another. Although the American Association of Mental Retardation (formerly the AAMD) published guidelines for identifying mild mental retardation, individual states establish their own criteria. Consequently, the prevalence of students identified as mildly retarded varies from state to state. This means that some students who need special education services may go without, and other students who are not mildly disabled possibly receive services.

Students with mild retardation are characterized by slower cognitive development; academic deficiencies, especially in reading; and deficits in adaptive behavior. Because success in school depends so much on verbal skills, some students, poor children and children from non-English speaking families in particular, encounter difficulties. An individual student may demonstrate specific learning problems in mental processing, social adaption, and perception. However, students with mild retardation show a great deal of variability in learning characteristics, and generalizations about their abilities or disabilities can lead to stereotypes and negative teacher expectations.

Students with mild retardation score in a range of 75 to 50 on IQ tests, and they have deficits in social skills outside the school setting. In most states they are placed in special education programs for students with EMR (educably mentally retarded) based on the results of intelligence tests and measures of adaptive abilities outside of school. Quality of educational programming depends on the teacher's ability to motivate students who have a history of school failure. Academic programs that emphasize functional skills provide adolescents with a reason to stay in school. Younger children learn best when teachers match instruction to their cognitive abilities. Programs that attempt to remediate specific deficiencies, such as poor memory, through drill and repetition fail to consider the point of view of the learner. Students with mild retardation need practice in developing their own thinking abilities. School programs that help students with mild retardation gain confidence in themselves as learners are most successful in helping them to adapt to life after school.

The cycle of destitution that has characterized mild mental retardation throughout the past century will be broken when disadvantaged learners graduate from school with employable skills. Education is the best offensive strategy in the war on poverty. When regular and special educators work together to keep learners in the mainstream of school life, teacher and student expectations for success are enhanced. As Lloyd Dunn eloquently pointed out, the interests of poor children are not served by labeling them retarded and relegating them to isolated special education classrooms. Ultimately it is the quality of educational programming, not the label pinned on the student, that determines success or failure.

Chapter 4

Students with Behavior Disorders

Advance Organizer

When you complete this chapter, you will be able to:

1. Give examples of students with behavior disorders.
2. Describe the characteristics of students with behavior disorders.
3. Discuss how the treatment of behavior disorders has changed over the years.
4. Explain the biophysical treatment model for behaviors.
5. Describe the pros and cons of drug treatment for behavior disorders.
6. Describe the psychoanalytical treatment model.
7. Discuss how the psychoeducational treatment model has influenced teaching practices.
8. Identify characteristics of effective and ineffective behavior modification programs.
9. Discuss problems in defining behavior disorders.
10. Explain the distinction between disturbing and disturbed behavior.
11. Explain the ecological model of intervention.
12. Describe cognitive, academic, communication, and social characteristics of students with behavior disorders.
13. Make specific recommendations for teaching students with behavior disorders.

Fred Peterson has been a teacher for over twenty years: each of his classes has had at least one problem student. This year it was Amy. Amy could always find a way to avoid schoolwork. For example, one day Fred told the class to begin work on the math sheet he had provided each of them. "Excuse me, Mr. Peterson," said Amy. "Can I go to the bathroom?" Fred had a policy of letting students move freely throughout the school, so he let her go. About fifteen minutes later, she returned and asked if she could wash the blackboards. Fred mentioned it was probably a better idea to start on her worksheet. At this suggestion, Amy grew angry. She walked up to Fred, balled the worksheet in her fist, and threw it at Fred. "Do your own damned worksheet," she shouted, and she ran out the classroom door.

Alan is a senior in high school with decent grades. He is on the basketball team, and he has a lot of friends. Lately he and a few buddies have started smoking marijuana on the way to school in the morning. Alan maintains that after twelve years of boring classes, it's fun to go to "high" school. Ms. Palmer, his homeroom teacher, can tell when Alan has been smoking. His eyes are red and glassy. She has tried talking to Alan privately but to no avail. Alan either denies he smokes or he walks away. Alan's behavior in his classes is erratic. He jokes around, makes snide comments, or just spaces out. Ms. Palmer is hesitant to discuss Alan's situation with the principal because she's afraid Alan will be expelled.

Alice has been teaching kindergarten for ten years, but she has never had a class like this one. Several youngsters have neurological symptoms caused by crack use by mothers during pregnancy. Raymond, although talkative and outgoing, is unable to handle scissors or even extra fat crayons. Louis gets a sticker just for sitting still for ten minutes. He is constantly careening around the room, bumping into other children, and starting fights. Fay tries hard to do well, but she can't follow directions. She is frequently confused about what she's supposed to be doing. Alice is unable to give Fay all the individual attention she requires.

Anecdotes like these illustrate the kinds of "problems" that cause students to be identified as behavior disordered or emotionally disturbed. Disturbing behaviors, noncompliance, or an inability to adjust to classroom routines are common reasons for students to be referred for special education. Each year, Phi Delta Kappa, a national education organization, commissions a Gallup Poll of the public's attitudes towards education. In seventeen of the surveys, discipline was the number one problem identified. Recently discipline has been dislodged from the top of the list by drug abuse. In today's schools, drugs have added a new dimension to the behavior problems with which teachers must contend.

At one time or another, every student has conflicts with rules for proper behavior in school. The decision to evaluate a student for special education services on the basis of classroom behavior is a matter of frequency and intensity of the disturbing actions. The more "acting out" the behavior, the more likely a student will be referred for special education. The National Education Association identified the following behaviors as those most likely to attract unfavorable attention in the classroom:

1. Exhibits physical and verbal aggression toward classmates (fighting, instigation of arguments).

2. Exhibits verbal aggression toward teacher and the other authority figures (profanity, negative names).
3. Refuses to cooperate in classroom group activities.
4. Intentionally damages classroom materials.
5. Uses classroom materials to create disruptive sounds and noises. (River, 1977, 9)

A student who is shy or withdrawn may have a serious emotional difficulty, but if she continues to follow classroom directions and completes her schoolwork, her problems may be overlooked. Depression and suicide are far too common among today's school children to be ignored. Latchkey children (children who return home from school to empty houses), students with learning disabilities, and students experiencing chronic family problems are particularly vulnerable. Guetzloe summarized the causes of suicide among children:

Any problem that contributes to feelings of depression, worthlessness, helplessness, or hopelessness has the potential to trigger suicidal behavior in a vulnerable individual. Among the many factors that have been cited as contributing to youth suicide are isolation, alienation, loss, physical or psychological abuse, disturbance in peer relationships, substance abuse, rejection, incarceration, disorganization, availability of weapons, fear of punishment, fear of failure, knowledge of suicide, and humiliation. (Guetzloe, 1988, 22)

Among special educators there is concern that not enough is being done to help students with behavior or emotional problems. This concern is equally shared by regular classroom teachers who spend a large portion of their day trying to reach these youngsters.

Foundations of Behavior Disorders

Hyman and D'Alessandro (1984) highlighted the complex interaction of environmental and individual factors that contribute to student behavioral difficulties. They found that the causes of behavior problems often rest outside the student's ability to control.

Included among social causes are inadequate parenting, overcrowding, racism, lack of employment, overexposure to violence through television and other mass media, peer pressures, and specific social, political, and bureaucratic factors that ignore the needs of the young. Schools contribute to behavior problems through ineffective teaching, poor school organization, inadequate administrative leadership, inappropriate curricula, overuse of suspensions, and other punishments. Within the individual student, Hyman and D'Allesandro cited inborn traits, such as neurological impairments, that may disrupt interactions with others, ultimately causing behavioral or emotional disorders. Poor self-esteem and frustration with learning are also student responses that accelerate behavior problems. When attempting to understand students' problems, we must take into account the troubled systems (family, school, community) that interact with and shape children's development (Apter, 1982). Placing a student in a special education program will produce minimal results if, at the end of the school day, the youngster returns home to a sexually abusive father, a tormented mother, or a neighborhood permeated with drugs and violence.

Most of us, in our own way, walk a fine line between normal and abnormal, right and wrong, mental illness and mental health. Often the force that pushes us into one or the other of these categories does not originate in our own behavior. Others with whom we interact are instrumental in shaping, defining, managing, and manipulating our feelings and behavior. This is the crux of the human dilemma. We need to interact with others to grow and learn, yet the nature of those interactions, which are often shaped by forces outside our control, help determine the kind of person we will become.

"Behavior disordered," "emotionally disturbed," "disruptive," or "conduct problem," are all names that have been assigned to the field of study in which professionals try to explain special learning needs of students who cannot cope with the social demands of school or society. Over the years, special education has accumulated a large body of research on the causes and treatment of students with behavior and emotional difficulties. Before we discuss these different conceptual models, it would be useful to examine the historical roots of emotional disorders and their treatment.

Historical Aspects

Human history is replete with strange stories of how deviancy has been dealt with. There was a time when the treatment of insanity was worse than the condition. Early medicants believed that by boring holes in the head (a method called trephining), the devil or other evil spirits would be released and leave the body. Hippocrates first classified mental problems using mania, hebephrenia, and melancholia as terms to describe separate conditions. He also is credited with offering the first theory for the cause of mental problems, blaming an imbalance of body fluids for strange behavior (Rhodes & Tracy, 1972a,b).

Throughout the ages, theories of causation of mental illnesses or emotional disturbances ranged from witchcraft to science. One of the first environmental causes of mental illness was identified in the Middle Ages, when it was discovered that hatters were driven "mad" from the mercury they used to condition felt. When mercury use was discontinued, so was the incidence of "mad hatters." As Restak noted, "Over the centuries, schizophrenics have been burned at the stake, chained in dark dungeons, starved to death, and drowned" (Restak, 1984, 273). Discoveries that vitamin B6 deficiencies and syphilis caused mental illness helped move mental treatment out of the shadows and into the medical laboratory. About 1890, Kraeplin identified an advanced form of mental illness which he called dementia praecox. This term was used to refer to adult mental illness, and the classification system surrounding it became the forerunner of the scientific classification system that is in place today (Algozzine, Schmid, & Mercer, 1981). After Kraeplin introduced dementia, a psychologist, DeSantis, recommended that a new term be designated for the childhood version of this mental condition. He suggested dementia praecocissima, and the study of childhood emotional problems was given a life of its own.

Shortly thereafter, another psychologist, Heller, observed a severely debilitating, degenerative condition in infants characterized by a loss of motor and language abilities; this condition was labeled as Heller's syndrome. In 1943, Leo Kanner observed odd, stereotyped behaviors in young children. The children, although uncommunicative and aloof, appeared to have average or above average intelligence. This condition became known as early infantile autism. By 1952, the American Psychiatric Association produced a document listing the major types of mental disorders. Childhood disorders did not appear in the first Diagnostic and Statistical Manual (DSM-I), but the second edition (DSM-II) contained a category titled Behavior Disorders of Childhood and Adolescents. Students with behavior disorders don't exhibit the kinds of severe debilitating conditions that were first identified by early psychologists and physicians. Such disabilities as childhood schizophrenia and autism still exist; however, they are severe disabilities and are not included in our discussion of mild disabilities.

Theoretical Models

The search for understanding the causes and treatment of childhood behavior and emotional disorders has followed many roads. Each distinctive field of knowledge—biophysical, psychodynamic, psychoeducational, and behavioral—has contributed, in a synergistic fashion, to an overall understanding of behavior disorders. During the early years of special education, theorists tended to pitch their tents in a single conceptual camp. They fortified their encampments with rigorous defenses, and with equal vigor hurled verbal assaults at each other. Thus graduate students would burn the midnight oil as they debated the relative merits of Bettelheim's psychodynamic view versus Skinner's behavior modification techniques for treating troubled children.

The term "behavior disorders" is a victory of sorts for the behaviorists. Its acceptance outside the behavior modification camp indicates that psychologists and educators agree it is a faulty leap in logic to ascribe an emotional causation to all disruptive behavior. The first model we address, the biophysical, makes a clear case for understanding that behavior disorders can occur when something goes wrong with the delicate mechanism of a child's body. (Review Chapter 2 for organic factors that contribute to all three mild disabilities.)

Biophysical Treatments

Throughout history, physical and biological factors have been identified with some of the conditions that are part of the broad classification known as behavior disorders. Researchers have linked genetics and emotional disturbance; Schwartz (1979) pointed out that evidence exists to support the role of heredity in shaping behavior and personality. This conclusion is based on findings that sex-linked differences are evident in many types of behavioral disorders. For example, hyperactivity, antisocial behaviors, and conduct disorders are more commonly identified in boys than in girls.

Thomas and Chess (1977) followed several groups from childhood to adulthood and found that their behavior patterns were relatively constant. About 40 percent were made up of the "easy child" whose characteristics included adaptability, high tolerance for frustration, and positive responses to change. The "difficult" child (about 10 percent) was characterized by irregular biological functions, negative behaviors, poor adaptability, and negativism. The "slow to warm" child was characterized by limited responsiveness, flat emotional responses, and unsatisfactory interpersonal relations. These findings were presented as support for the position that behavioral characteristics are predicated on biophysical differences among people. (Note that the children described in Mary Ainsworth's research on securely and insecurely attached children in Chapter 2 also resemble the above descriptions, and Ainsworth's explanation is environmental.)

The popularity of psychoactive drugs to treat behavior disorders is testimony to the widespread acceptance of the biophysical approach. Physicians prescribe drugs, and they rely on parents and others to monitor the effects those drugs have on problem behaviors. School personnel are in a crucial position to monitor a successful drug therapy program. Teachers maintain consistent contact in situations that allow for comparisons of student behavior, so observations by teachers are exceptionally valuable. The drug monitoring process requires systematic observations and recordings of a student's behavior at various points during the school day.

Interest in using drugs is based on general knowledge about the ways chemicals influence behavior. For example, the amino acid tryptopan is converted into the neurotransmitter serotonin by chemical reactions that are regulated by enzymes (e.g., tryptophan hydroxylase); serotonin is believed to influence aggression, depression, and normal sleep patterns (Restak, 1984).

Stimulants, such as methylphenidate hydrochloride (Ritalin), dextroamphetamine sulfate (Dexadrine), and magnesium pemoline (Cylert), as well as antihistamines, such as diphenhydramine hydrochloride (Benadryl), are used to treat problem behaviors related to overactivity. Antidepressants and antianxiety drugs, such as deanol acetamid obenzoate (Deaner), imipramine hydrochloride (Tofranil), oxazepam (Serax), and chlorpromazine hydrochloride (Librium), are used to control problem behaviors related to mood disorders.

Experiments with lithium, a drug originally used to treat gout, indicate a calming effect with aggressive animals. In the laboratory, Siamese fighting fish, rats, and mice showed decreased hostile behavior when treated with lithium. Outside the laboratory, experiments with lithium have demonstrated interesting and controversial results with aggressive prisoners. In an experiment in the maximum security prisons at Vacaville and Sacramento, California, twenty-seven inmates were administered lithium. Although diverse in family backgrounds and personalities, the inmates were similar in their recurrent violent behavior and quick tempers. Restak described changes in both prisoner behavior and attitude after nine months:

> *The results showed a decline in disciplinary action for violent behavior. Among fifteen of twenty-two subjects, the number of disciplinary acts for violent behavior were reduced. Even more interesting than the decrease in violence, however, were the reports offered by several prisoners in Dr. Tupin's study. One man stated, "Now I can think about whether to hit him or not." Another said, "I have lost my anger." Each of the Lithium dosed prisoners demonstrated an increased capacity to reflect on the consequences of his actions, a quality Dr. Tupin refers to as a "more reflective mood." (Restak, 1984, 142)*

Stimulants, minor tranquilizers, and anticonvulsants commonly used for children with behavior disorders are presented in Appendix C. Each class of psychoactive medication includes generic and brand name drugs, common dosages, expected effects, and side effects. Whenever students are given drugs to treat behavior disorders, the underlying premise is that chemical body processes are being altered. Imbalances in the biochemical system are believed to be the source of the problem. Drugs are prescribed by physicians to bring abnormal body chemicals into proper levels of balance and thereby change behavior. The more disturbing the behavior, the greater the likelihood that drug treatment will be accepted as a needed procedure. In the case of students with mild behavior and emotional disorders, the use of drugs can and has created controversy.

Hyperactivity—A case study of drug treatment

Since hyperactivity was first described in 1902 by Dr. George Still as "an abnormal defect of moral control," it has been one of the most discussed behavior disorders encountered by teachers and parents. The *Diagnostic and Statistical Manual of Mental Disorders*, or *DSM III-Revised*, describes hyperactivity as a subtype of attention-deficit hyperactive disorder (ADHD). According to the *DSM III*, the onset of hyperactivity occurs before age seven, persists for at least six months, and must include eight of fourteen listed symptoms, which include some of the following: easily distracted by extraneous stimuli, difficulty in sustaining attention, fidgets with hands or feet, loses things, and fails to listen.

William Cruickshank (1986) described two types of hyperactivity: sensory hyperactivity and motor hyperactivity. Distractibility is one of the primary characteristics of sensory hyperactivity. A student with sensory hyperactivity has an exceedingly short attention span, sometimes less than a minute. The student's attention is literally tugged back and forth by the visual and auditory stimuli of classroom activity. Unable to discriminate figure-ground relationships, either visually or auditorily (i.e., separating object from background), this student encounters severe problems with the simplest task. The printed page of a book with its angled letters, spaces between letters, and pictures, is a visual mine field for a student with impaired figure-ground ability. The student is unable to stay focused on the sequential arrangement of letters and words.

Students (with motor hyperactivity) according to Cruickshank "seem to fall apart at the seams." They are constantly twisting, squirming, bending, and manipulating anything they can get their hands on. Hallways, playgrounds, or other open spaces, with the abundance of stimuli, cause the hyperactive student to overreact by running, yelling, and generally making a nuisance. Requesting such a student to sit still for ten minutes is asking the near impossible. Needless to say, a student with sensory and/or motor hyperactivity is a severe test of a teacher's patience and creativity. Cruickshank (and many other researchers) believe that hyperactivity is a neurological disorder that is outside a youngster's ability to control. With estimates of hyperactivity ranging from three to ten percent of school-aged students, it is plain to see how the problem of hyperactive students would attract teachers, pediatricians, and parents to drug treatment.

Many hyperactive students are treated with Ritalin, a potent stimulant. Ritalin is a classified as a Schedule II drug, meaning that it is regarded as a drug easily abused. Its manufacture is regulated by the Drug Enforcement Administration. Kohn (1989) reported that three-quarters of a million children are receiving the drug.

Ritalin helps some students concentrate, but recently researchers have found some negative effects:

1. Some students don't improve and others worsen.
2. While concentration may improve, the linkage with improved academic achievement has not been firmly established.
3. Placebos often (up to 40 percent of the time) work as well as Ritalin.
4. Physical side-effects such as stunted growth, elevated blood pressure, facial tics, insomnia, and weight loss have been reported.

Underlying the pros and cons of drug treatment for hyperactivity is the more basic question—is there a safer, more effective method for helping students control their hyperactivity? In some instances the problem may be the classroom. When students labeled as hyperactive are placed in school programs that promote movement and concrete activities, problems of hyperactivity may diminish. These classrooms utilize learning centers and small group activities. Students with hyperactivity are able to learn because the routines of the environment appear to match their learning style.

Other approaches to decreasing hyperactivity include elimination diets to remove allergens and decrease sugar consumption. Evidence to support diet therapy is largely anecdotal. However, widespread testimony by parents and professionals about the effect of food on behavior is difficult to ignore. Reports like the following are commonplace:

> *A nurse described the effect of nitrates, a common food preservative, "I can always tell when my daughter (7-year-old) has eaten a hot dog or baloney sandwich. She is off the walls, and it takes at least an hour for her to calm down." A college professor reported the effects of sugar on his six-year-old daughter, "Forget giving her dessert before bedtime. Just peanut butter on apple slices will keep her bouncing out of her bed and awake till 10:00 p.m." (Henley, 1986; 1990)*

Table 4–1 lists commercial foods that contain minimal amounts of sugar and preservatives.

Emotional factors can also play a role in hyperactive behavior. Life in a dysfunctional home, where a youngster is continually exposed to chaotic living situations and warped family ties, will raise a student's stress level. The normal reaction to stress is flight or fight. For a student who is experiencing chronic stress, flight in the form of hyperactive behavior may be a futile attempt to adapt to an unpredictable life style.

Researchers are unsure how stimulants help students become more focused on school tasks. The prevailing explanation is that a drug such as Ritalin facilitates the transference of neurotransmitters across neuronal pathways. Thus the stimulant is a catalyst assisting motor neuron inhibition. The apparent success of drug treatment with hyperactive students leads many to assume that hyperactivity is organically based. However, biophysical causes of hyperactive behavior have yet to be proven. Abraham Maslow, the noted developmental psychologist, once remarked that if people were given only hammers, they will treat everything they come across as a nail (Kohn, 1989). As long as Ritalin and other stimulants are treatments of choice, practitioners and researchers will assume biological causes for hyperactivity.

Psychodynamic Treatments

Some educators believe that problems related to personality development are the cause of behavior and emotional problems of children and youth (Rhodes & Tracy, 1972a,b). Generally, these professionals have received training from psychiatrists and psychologists who believe that the inner conflict principles first developed by Sigmund Freud can be used to explain and treat behavior or emotional problems. The psychodynamic view describes the evolving personality in terms of the relationship between three strong intrapsychic forces: id, ego, superego. The id is the pleasure seeking, impulsive force, that is dominant in

TABLE 4–1   Partial List of Foods—Commonly Found in Supermarkets—That Are Free of Artificial Coloring, Flavoring, and Preservatives

Cereals
Cheerios
Quaker Oats, Puffed Rice, and Puffed Wheat
Post Grape Nuts
General Mills Kix
Kellogg's Raisin Bran

Crackers
Hi-Ho
Krispy Saltines
Premium Saltines
Cheese-Its
Nabisco Graham Crackers (not Honey Graham)
Pepperidge Farm Cookies

Ice Cream
All Natural Hendries
All Natural Breyers
All Natural Dolly Madison
All Natural Stop & Shop

Canned Juices
100% juices such as: pineapple, grapefruit, cranberry, apple, tomato. Check label to be sure that no sugar, coloring, etc. added.

Salad Dressing
Walden's

Popsicles, etc.
Hoods Orange (all natural)
Welch's Grape
York Peppermint Pattie Sticks

Frozen Waffles
Golden Harvest (at Stop & Shop and Shop Rite)

Sausage
Jones or fresh ground in butcher shop

Soda
Seven-Up
Soda water
Country Club Ginger Ale

Jelly
Smuckers
Polaner

Candy Bars
Reese's Peanut Butter Cups
Mound's
Almond Joy
York Peppermint Patties
Planter's Peanut Bars
Bit-O-Honey

Froxen Juices
Minute Maid orange juice and lemonade
Stop & Shop Lemonade
Welch's Grape Juice
Many brands orange juice—look at label

Gum
Wrigley's

Cocoa
Swiss Miss Cocoa Mix
Hershey's Pure Cocoa

Peanut Butter
Teddies
Fresh Ground

Mayonaise
Cain's

Spaghetti Sauce
Prince

Sharp Cheese
"Helluva" Good Cheese

Margarine
Shedd's Willow Run
Natural food store
Margarine (colored with carotene which is natural)

Hot Dogs (without nitrates)
Wild Wind

Maple Syrup—100% Pure
Vermont Maple Orchards

childhood. The superego is the conscience—it represents moral and ethical beliefs. The ego mediates between the id and the superego. The ego shapes judgments about reality. The ego guides actions by taking into account the natural consequences of behavior. The id, ego, and superego act as a system of checks and balances on individual behavior.

Consider the following illustration of the id, ego, superego relationship. A teenager walks through a shopping mall and sees a Swiss Army knife sitting on a counter. His impulse (id) is to pick the knife up and put it in his pocket. His conscience (superego) tells him it is wrong to steal, but his id is winning the battle. "I'll go to church and it will be okay," he thinks. Meanwhile his reality testing instincts (ego) tell him to look around. He sees several mirrors arrayed along the store walls. Now the struggle is on between id and ego. The teenager walks away without the knife because he decided the knife wasn't worth the risk.

Freud described neurosis (emotional disturbance) as a conflict between the ego and the id. The person is at war with himself. The goal of psychodynamic treatment is to bring the id, ego, and superego into harmony. As Freud explained, "A man should not try to eliminate his complexes but get into accord with them; they are legitimately what direct his conduct in the world" (Seldes, 1984, 151). Over the years Freud's theory has been expanded and modified by some of the greatest thinkers in the field of psychology. A list of contributors to psychodynamic theory reads like a "Who's Who" of twentieth century thought—Carl Jung, Alfred Adler, Erik Erikson, Anna Freud, Erich Fromm, and Bruno Bettelheim are just a sample of the writers and therapists who were heavily influenced by psychodynamic theory.

Fritz Redl and David Wineman were one of the first practitioners to successfully apply psychodynamic principles to the treatment of aggressive youth. In *Children Who Hate* (1951), Redl and Wineman described how the self-control (ego development) of adolescents collapsed under the impact of specific environmental or psychological triggers. Redl and Wineman cataloged twenty-two separate self-control challenges that all children need to cope with in order to continue their emotional development. Using colorful language such as "gadgetorial seduction" and "warfare with time," Redl and Wineman presented a roadmap for identifying self-control weaknesses in specific youngsters. Their descriptions of ego functions provide classroom teachers with a clinical model for anticipating when and where a student will lose self-control (Henley, 1987).

The psychodynamic point of view underscores the need to understand *why* students are disruptive. It emphasizes the connections between how a student feels and how a student acts. The classic psychodynamic treatment is play therapy for children and individual psychotherapy for youth. For educators, who saw the value of psychodynamic principles, it was necessary to develop treatment procedures that would be useful in the classroom, where teachers must manage groups of children. Psychoeducational treatments were born out of the need to merge behavior management with psychodynamic theory.

Psychoeducational Treatments

Proponents of the psychoeducational perspective believe that problem behaviors result from underlying psychological disturbances, and that adaptive behaviors must be learned for successful accommodation in schools. Knoblock presented a succinct description: "A pychoeducational framework assumes that behavior is caused, that there are reasons why children act as they do. Early psychoeducators like Berkowitz and Rothman believed that children's feelings were the source of observed behaviors. Now it is recognized that behaviors should be analyzed in the context of specific environments as well . . . ." (Knoblock, 1983, 107). There is a balance between concern for causes of behavior and acquisition of adaptive skills in the psychoeducational treatment model.

This integrated philosophy is illustrated in the principles of Project Re-Ed (Hobbs, 1966; 1970):

1. Students should be kept busy in school; successful completion of purposeful activities are central to reeducation.
2. Students should spend as much time as possible in positive, therapeutic environments; neighborhood schools with supportive personnel are preferred in efforts to reeducate students with behavior problems.
3. Supportive teacher-student interactions are a key to establishing academic success; teachers learn this by working with students in positive relationships.

Psychoeducators believe the student-teacher relationship is the fundamental building block for change. Out of this relationship comes mutual trust and a willingness on the part of both teacher and student to accept the needs of each other. Behavior and emotional difficulties are viewed developmentally. Using cognitive and emotional developmental milestones as a guide, the psychoeducator attempts to identify developmental strengths and weaknesses. Classroom accommodations are made that capitalize on student abilities in order to move a youngster along the normal developmental continuum. Self-concept development, the teaching of social skills, and normalization of a youngster's school experience are all components in the psychoeducational treatment model.

Many programs for curriculum development, including *Developmental Therapy* (Wood, 1986), *Teaching Children Self-Control* (Fagen, Long, & Stevens, 1975), and *Skillstreaming* (McGinnis & Goldstein, 1990), have translated psychoeducational principles into functional systems for assessment, goal setting, teaching, and evaluation. Each of these models assumes that all students have the internal resources to change and that appropriate environmental supports can nourish and maintain student emotional growth. These treatments all assume that change begins within the individual and that the ultimate goal is to teach students to accept responsibility for their own behavior. A counterpoint to the psychoeducational treatment approach is the behaviorist model, which focuses almost exclusively on the manipulation of environmental conditions to shape student behavior.

Behavioral Treatments

During the 1960s, educators and psychologists recognized the importance of behavioral principles of learning. The key points of behavioral theory and practice can be summarized as follows:

1. Behaviorists view inappropriate and appropriate behavior as learned. Behavior is a response to a person's interaction with the environment.
2. Learning occurs when environmental conditions reinforce a specific behavior. Reinforcement takes several forms, including imitation, modeling, and operant conditioning (i.e., consequences that shape behavior).
3. Inappropriate behavior is learned through environmental conditioning and new, appropriate behaviors can be learned with proper reinforcement.
4. Effective implementation of behavior treatments in classrooms requires: observable descriptions of behavior to be changed, targeting of new behaviors, systematic application of reinforcers, and collection of pre- and post-data to determine treatment effectiveness.

Behaviorists do not attempt to understand behavior, nor do they ascribe specific causes to behavior. Behaviorists prefer to deal with the tangible actions of students rather than theoretical explanations for disturbing behavior. The emphasis on behavior rather than causes of behavior has been the catalyst to replace the term "emotionally disturbed" with the classification "behavior disordered." While the former term implies we know the reason for a behavior (i.e., disturbed emotional development), the latter designation makes no claim about causality but simply points out that there is a behavior problem.

The goals of behavioral treatment are to increase appropriate or adaptive behavior and to decrease inappropriate or maladaptive behavior. As Casey, Skiba, and Algozzine (1988) indicated, three primary approaches have been used to manage classroom behavior: redirecting teachers towards positive rather than negative behaviors, providing tangible rewards for positive behaviors, and providing negative consequences for inappropriate behavior.

Behavior modification has a certain intuitive appeal. After all, it's common parenting and teaching practice to reward "good" behavior and punish the "bad." Schools are awash in everyday practices that reflect behavioristic thinking. Students who learn their lessons get good grades. Teachers use stickers and progress charts to encourage students to work harder. Detentions, staying after school, and suspensions are everyday procedures for dealing with students who don't abide by school expectations for proper behavior.

When the normal corrective procedures don't seem to work for a student, it's common for a teacher to step up the reward and punishment cycle through the

TABLE 4–2   Guidelines for Behavior Modification Programs

1. Describe and count the frequency of the disturbing behavior to be changed before beginning the program.
2. If possible, enlist the student when deciding on the target behavior to replace the disturbing behavior.
3. Select a reinforcer that is meaningful to the student.
4. Avoid using sugar foods as reinforcers (e.g., animal crackers, raisins).
5. Concentrate the behavior modification on positive reinforcement rather than punishment.
6. Do a post-frequency count of the target behavior after a specified period of time to determine the program's effectiveness.
7. If the program isn't working, don't blame the student.

application of a homespun behavior modification program. Some teachers do this without training in behavior modification techniques. Consequently, errors in treatment undercut the effectiveness of the program and add to the unfortunate judgment that it's the student who is at fault. When teachers begin a behavior modification program, they should keep the seven caveats in mind that are listed in Table 4–2.

Integration of Treatment Approaches

When you look in special education classrooms today, you will probably see evidence of each of these treatment approaches used in combination. For example, one student may be taking medication to control hyperactivity; other students may be participating in a token system designed to reinforce work completion. The teacher will likely have the room organized in a manner to encourage student participation through learning centers or discussion groups. You may see many self-concept materials on display. One or two of the students may be in counseling either in school or after school at private agencies.

If you look at the teacher's lesson plans or the students' individual education programs (IEP), you should see goals and objectives that center on improving interpersonal skills and reducing behavior problems. You would also see academic textbooks and other instructional materials that are the same as those used in regular classrooms. Finally, if you observed the teacher working with the students, you would see the same type of positive teaching behaviors you would expect to see in any classroom—special or regular. The differences that have come to be identified with students labeled behavior disordered are a function of assumptions people have about the nature of behavior disorders. This perspective is evident in the diversity of definitions that are used to describe troubled students in our schools.

Definitional Concerns

The terms behavior disordered and emotionally disturbed are both found in descriptions of children with mild disabilities. Kirk (1962) suggested that a behavior deviation was comprised of actions that had a detrimental effect on a child's adjustment or interfered with the lives of other people. Pate (1963) stated that a child was disturbed when his behavior was so inappropriate that regular class attendance would: (1) be disrupting for the rest of the class, (2) put undue pressure on the teacher, and (3) further the disturbance of the child.

Bower added several aspects to the criteria when he suggested that children with emotional disabilities exhibit one or more of the following characteristics to a marked extent over a long period of time.

1. An inability to learn that cannot be explained by intellectual, sensory, or health factors.
2. An inability to build or maintain satisfactory interpersonal relationships with peers and teachers.
3. Inappropriate types of behavior or feelings under normal conditions.
4. A general, pervasive mood of unhappiness or depression.
5. A tendency to develop physical symptoms, pains, or fears associated with school problems. (Bower, 1969, 22–3)

The term does not include children who are "socially maladjusted" unless it is determined that they meet the criteria for services in emotional disturbance.

This definition is currently favored by the U.S. Department of Education and is included in the Individuals with Disabilities Education Act of 1990 under the rubric "seriously emotionally disturbed." It has the advantage of acknowledging several conceptual components of emotional disturbance and also offers operational terms (such as marked extent and a long period of time) from which to build specific guidelines. Unfortunately, it falls short of being a conceptually clear representation from which to develop meaningful identification procedures and treatment practices. For example, how do we identify "an inability to learn which cannot be explained by health factors," or what constitutes a "general pervasive mood of unhappiness"? And what about students who perform in school but still have emotional problems? Morse put it this way:

> *Note that a definition including educational performance leaves out those who have no school problems or problems that do not affect achievement, and this can be a significant number. The idea that all disturbed children must have an educational problem in behavior or achievement is a significant error. The other error lies in implying that when children have problems in school, these problems are primarily school-related. The fact is that problems are often generated outside the school environment and brought to school. (Morse, 1985, 43)*

Perhaps most contentious to some special educators is the omission of "socially maladjusted students" from the ranks of students who qualify for special education services. In addressing this problem, the Executive Committee of the Council for Children with Behavioral Disorders had this to say:

This exclusion of the socially maladjusted from special education seems to be based on several assumptions. These include: (a) There is a significant population of youngsters whose antisocial behavior is more related to a general social phenomenon than a specific handicapping condition; (b) it is possible to consistently differentiate such students from those who are truly handicapped by virtue of their behavior; and (c) it is important that special education not automatically incorporate a group specified as "in trouble" by other systems, such as the juvenile justice system. (Executive Committee of the Council for Children with Behavioral Disorders, 1987)

The position of the council is that an adjudication of delinquency does not mean a disability is present. However, some students with delinquent behavior do have mild disabilities, and they have an equal right to federal services mandated by Congress for all school-aged youngsters. Indeed, comprehensive surveys of incarcerated youngsters indicate that mild disabilities are more prevalent among youthful offenders than the general population (Nelson, Rutherford, & Wadford, 1987).

The lack of clear direction in determining who receives special education services for behavioral or emotional problems is highlighted by a study that found only twelve states used the complete federal definition in their own identification criteria (Mack, 1980). Most state definitions used to refer students with behavior or emotional difficulties tend to have several general similarities. They suggest that the disturbances or disorders that exist within the student's behavior patterns cause academic and social problems that in turn affect the youngster and peers. While these state definitions help professionals to know who should be identified as requiring special education, the actual process of identification is not facilitated by any one definition in particular. Most definitions do not have clearly stated operational criteria that can be dovetailed into a special educational assessment.

Based on an historical analysis of definitions of behavior disorders/emotional disturbance, Algozzine, Schmid and Mercer (1980) identified four operational components that can be identified as important within any criteria for determining a behavior disorder. These include:

1. A measure of alternative placements.
2. A measure of behavioral deviation.
3. A measure of behavioral interference.
4. A measure of exclusive etiology.

Algozzine, Schmid, and Connors (1980) recommend matching the above criteria with the following definition:

An emotionally disturbed child is one who, after receiving supportive educational services and counseling assistance available to all students, still exhibits persistent and consistent severe behavioral disabilities that consequently interfere with productive learning processes. This is the student whose inability to achieve adequate academic progress and satisfactory interpersonal relationships cannot be attributed to primarily physical, sensory, or intellectual deficits.

The operational criteria related to this definition can be applied across a variety of geographical areas and theoretical frames of reference. For example, the *alternative placement clause* ("after receiving supportive educational services and counseling assistance available to all students") may be related to and measured by the number of different activities attempted in order to alleviate the student's problems in school. Activities such as changing the student's class schedule, individual or group counseling, curriculum or teacher modifications, and outside agency intervention should be documented. The degree to which the behavioral difficulties are the result of situational factors may be measured by this process.

The *behavioral deviation clause* ("persistent and consistent severe to very severe behavioral disabilities") should be measured against predefined standards. Persistent may be defined as existing for three months or three years; consistent may be described as a marked similarity in behaviors within different school situations or as a result of similar incidents: for example, reacting consistently when faced with failure. Severe could be identified with occurrences more than twice a day, and very severe could mean occurrences of once or twice an hour. The actual interfering emotional and social behaviors must be delimited so that effective treatment strategies can be developed.

The *behavioral interference clause* ("interfere with productive learning processes") relates to the measurable results of the exhibited behavioral disabilities. It is possible to state objectively academic criteria (e.g., one standard deviation below school district age-mates on normative tests) as well as interpersonal problems (e.g., avoided by other children, or fighting with three children in a week). If a student's "emotional problems" are thought to be caused by a lack of school or social success, that lack of progress, in addition to the behavioral problems, can be identified clearly.

The federal definition states that the student's educational performance must be "adversely affected." To what extent remains undefined.

The *exclusive etiology clause* ("not attributed primarily to physical, sensory, or intellectual deficits") enables students whose primary disability is not emotional or behavioral to receive appropriate services. It suggests that some students have a primary disability related to interfering behaviors, and these are the students who should be identified as behavior disordered or emotionally disturbed.

A systematic application of these criteria should result in the identification of two types of troubled children. The TYPE I (Student with a Behavior Disorder) is characterized by the types of behavior problems found typically in public schools. This student may be a problem in school and not at home. The behavior may be a response to an inappropriate or unmotivating school environment, and it may be responsive to positive environmental strategies. The TYPE II (Severely Disturbed Student) may be characterized by the more comprehensive form of disturbance typically not found in the regular classroom. This student's behavior will be problematic at home and school, and it may exhibit itself with regularity in both favorable and unfavorable environments. The behavior will not be immediately responsive to environmental management strategies. The behavior may be traced to organic inadequacies, as in the case of youth with autism or schizophrenia.

Hallahan and Kauffman (1977) suggested that the conditions referred to as learning disabilities, behavior disorders/emotional disturbance, and mild mental retardation are similar disabilities. The characteristic behaviors of each condition are also similar (Neisworth & Greer, 1975). While the TYPE I behavior disordered child may be similar in many respects to students with learning disabilities and mild mental retardation, it would seem that the TYPE II child with a severe social-emotional disturbance would be unique.

A possible diagnostic comparison between TYPE I and TYPE II students with emotional and behavioral disorders based on the suggested operational criteria is presented in Table 4–3.

The application of operational criteria to a definition of emotional disturbance/behavior disorders has many advantages. The proposed components are adaptable to current treatment practices, that is, a psychoeducational as well as a behavioral statement of each component can be developed. Since a wide range

TABLE 4–3   Comparison of TYPE I Behavioral and TYPE II Emotional Disturbance

TYPE I (Mild Behavior Disorders)	TYPE II (Clinical Emotional Disturbance)
Regular class has not been beneficial; however, placement there is a preferred goal.	Regular school placements have not been successful; outside placements common.
School counseling services often prove beneficial.	External counseling services are typical.
Common behavioral problems evident in assessment records.	Clinical diagnoses and problems recorded.
Problems often reported in only one classroom or only at school.	Problems evident at home, school, and in other environments.
Evidence that interventions are effective with selected problem behaviors.	Evidence that problems are very resistant to common interventions.

of behaviors may be considered disturbing, the definitional criteria has the flexibility to incorporate variability. The inclusion of an "alternative placements" clause acknowledges the fact that appropriate behaviors are often socially derived. Behavior problems that are situational can sometimes be eliminated by an administrative placement change. However, the greatest advantage lies in the fact that the condition is clearly recognizable from a specific set of interfering behaviors. It is this set of behaviors that defines the condition of emotional/behavioral disturbance.

Prevalence of Students with Behavior Disorders

The prevalence of students with behavior disorders tends to fluctuate considerably depending on several factors. The nature of the definition and criteria used to identify students has a major impact on the rate of identification and numbers of identified students; for example, when the Bower definition was originally used, the rate of occurrence of behavior disorders was estimated to be 10 percent (Reinert, 1976).

Rubin and Barlow (1971) found that 41 percent of the students they studied had "educationally defined" behavior problems; that is, the students were identified chiefly by their inability to meet the demands of school conduct expectations. Their findings are analogous to Jane Mercer's description of the "six-hour mildly retarded student." (See Chapter 3.) The results of the Rubin and Barlow study indicated that many students may be regarded as disturbed or behavior disordered by their teachers in school. Outside of school, their behavior is adaptive to the demands of their environment.

The six-hour behavior disordered student, identified by Rubin and Barlow, is an illustration of the widening cultural gap between poor children and the demands of school. As an illustration, consider a ten-year-old who lives in a ghetto neighborhood. What are the environmental conditions that this youth must deal with on a daily basis? The widespread reports of violence, drug use, and gang membership in poverty-stricken neighborhoods suggest that survival dictates an aggressive attitude. A ten-year-old who cannot take care of himself could quickly become prey to any passerby who fancied his sneakers, jacket, or money. In order to survive, our ten-year-old must learn to stand up for himself; he must project an image of toughness and nonchalance in the face of danger.

Now let's project this same street-wise youth into a fifth grade classroom. His teacher has just demanded to know why he didn't complete his homework. The youth is trapped between the demands of the adult authority and the expectations of his classmates, who are eagerly awaiting his response. Our ten-year-old is no fool, he knows that his mettle is being inadvertently challenged by the teacher, so he replies, "Do your own homework, you red-faced cracker!" The teacher's authority has been challenged, and the teacher responds by sending the young rebel to the principal, who suspends him for the rest of the day. A cycle of hostility is now perpetuated that could lead to a special education referral because of a behavior disorder.

Prevalence rates are also affected by the instruments used to evaluate students and the individuals who are doing the evaluating. One of the earliest reported prevalence studies used teacher judgments of school-related maladjustment as the criteria; Wickman (1928) found 42 percent of the sampled students had behavior disturbing to teachers. This figure is similar to that reported by Rubin and Barlow, who also sampled teachers' attitudes toward school behavior problems. In general, higher prevalence rates are reported when teachers give their opinions of disturbing behaviors rather than matching their students to specific criteria for behavior disorders.

Higher prevalence rates are reported for "mild" than for severe forms of behavior disorders. Because teacher perceptions play such a key role in determining behavior disorders, it is understandable that more students are identified as having behavior problems after they begin school and become discipline problems. Kelly, Bullock, and Dykes (1974) reported teacher-perceived prevalence rates of 12.6 for mild behavior problems, 5.6 for moderate problems, and 2.2 for students with severe behavior disorders. This general ratio has been reported elsewhere (Glidewell & Swallow, 1968). Paul and Epinchan (1991) cite more current research that indicates a prevalence rate of 11 percent of the total school population. This amounts to an estimate of six to eight million students with behavior and emotional disorders, yet in 1989 only 377,295 students received special education services because of emotional disturbance (U.S. Department of Education, 1990).

Sex is an important factor in prevalence reports. In all studies of behavior and emotional disorders, boys consistently outnumber girls (Reinert, 1976; Rubin & Barlow, 1971; Warry & Quay, 1971). One interpretation of this data is that girls are better adjusted than boys. It is far more likely, however, that cultural experience plays a significant role. Boys tend to develop aggressive ways of expressing emotional problems, while girls learn to express anger and hostility in a more covert fashion. Promiscuity, drug abuse, and depression are not the type of disturbed behaviors that teachers see, but that doesn't mean that they don't exist. The increasing pregnancy rate for teenage girls and the large numbers of babies born to cocaine and crack addicts is indirect evidence that school special education services may be overlooking females.

Between 1977 and 1989, there was a 37 percent increase in students identified as behavior disordered nationwide (U. S. Department of Education, 1990). As we look towards the twenty-first century, several factors indicate that the prevalence of students with behavior disorders/emotional disturbance will continue to escalate.

Item: By the year 2000, one out of every four children will grow up in poverty. Poverty contributes to broken homes, proliferation of drugs, violence, and homelessness. Millions of American children will be required to adapt to desperate environmental demands. The same behaviors that are adaptive on the streets will be disruptive in school.

Item: The incidence of infants born to mothers who are addicted to alcohol, crack, cocaine, and other drugs continues to climb. These children will present a whole new category of behavior disordered students.

Item: As we move into the twenty-first century, we are becoming a bilingual nation. While schools attempt to deal with the steady increase in non-English speaking students, the cultural gap between home and community continues to widen. Students will be alienated from the affairs of schooling, and this alienation will be acted out in classrooms.

Item: Inner-city schools continue to present the greatest challenge to educational reform. Some schools have degenerated to the point that metal detectors are placed at the schoolhouse door to screen students for weapons. A principal in Newark, New Jersey, controlled his high school by walking the halls with a baseball bat and bullhorn. The social and emotional turmoil that infects these schools requires the best teachers available. However, few young people who enter the teaching profession want to risk their psychological or physical safety teaching in ghetto schools. Without a massive infusion of educational and social support, inner city schools will become hotbeds of chaos.

Item: Violence and neglect permeate the lives of many American children. *The Wall Street Journal* in 1987 chronicled three months in the life of Lafeyette Walton, a twelve-year-old Chicago youngster. His experience included almost daily gun and submachine gun battles in his housing project, beatings and maimings of relatives and friends, rapes, gang recruiting, cocaine-running by a nine-year-old female cousin, and several murders. (Zinmeister, 1990, 50)

The psychological and emotional fallout from poor children's violent lives presents an overwhelming challenge to American policymakers. However, there is no national agenda with the specific aim of creating safe havens for children. According to the *National Needs Analysis in Behavior Disorders* (Grosenick & Huntze, 1979), "The most glaring concern that exists in the area of behavior disorders is the staggering number of children with behavior problems who remain unserved"(Apter, 1982, 7).

To summarize, many students are identified each year as requiring special education due to behavioral or emotional disturbance. Yet many other children go unserved chiefly because their behavior is not disruptive in the classroom or their behavior does not fit categorical criteria for special education (e.g., socially maladjusted, disadvantaged, school dropouts). America's children and youth are in a state of emergency. As children become more vulnerable, the need for effective educational and community programs will continue to grow.

Disturbed or Disturbing?

When a student is disruptive in a classroom, does that mean the student has a disability? Are there alternative explanations? Consider the following behaviors: talking out of turn, swearing at the teacher, throwing objects, running out of the room, or refusing to do an assignment. Those behaviors are commonplace in chaotic classrooms, but they occur infrequently in classrooms where teachers demonstrate effective group management skills.

Fredric Jones (1987) studied teacher-student interactions in hundreds of elementary and secondary classrooms. Many of his observations were done in inner-city schools and alternative programs for students with behavior disorders. One might expect Jones to report many examples of behavior disorders such as hostility, impulsiveness or aggression. He didn't. Jones and his colleagues characterized the majority of student activity as "massive time wasting." Students walked around the room, "goofed off," and talked whenever they felt like it. In poorly managed classrooms, these behaviors occurred every twenty seconds. In well-managed classrooms, the same behaviors were noted once every two minutes. Jones found that teachers in poorly managed classrooms lost 50 percent of their instructional time dealing with disturbing behaviors (Charles, 1989, 90). Jones concluded that many disruptive behaviors were symptomatic of mismanaged classrooms.

The classic study by Wickman (1928) is the first major investigation that attempted to identify specific behaviors that educators percieved bothersome or disturbing in their work with children. Behaviors identifed were characterized as those that offended moral standards (e.g., stealing, cheating, untruthfulness) and challenged teachers' authority (e.g., defiance, impertinance). Ramsey (1981) analyzed 33 replications that followed this seminal study and concluded that classroom orderliness and recognition of authority are of primary importance to teachers so that they can do their job which is to teach students.

The notion that teachers can actually cause behavior problems is underscored by Jacob Kounin's research. Kounin (1971;1977) found classroom disruptions were correlated to teacher expertise. Kounin reported that the following teacher behaviors contributed to discipline problems: making verbal comments about minor disturbances such as dropping a pencil, getting sidetracked by a single student's behavior, forcing students to do boring and repetitious activities, and becoming angry or punitive when students misbehaved. Conversely, Kounin observed that teachers positively influenced appropriate classroom behavior by smooth transitions between lessons, keeping track of all student behavior in the classroom at the same time, and providing novelty in lessons. Teachers who were liked by their students had the least behavior problems.

The interactional perspective of disturbing/disturbed behaviors underscores the need to evaluate both the individual and the setting. Behavior is a function of the individual interacting within the environment. While disturbing behavior may begin with the individual student, the way in which the teacher responds is crucial in preventing further disturbances. Organization of classroom space, routines, and lessons influence student behavior. Imagine a seven-year-old youngster with hyperactivity attempting to conform to a classroom where students are expected to sit quietly at their desks and complete assignments consisting of workbooks and ditto exercises. In this classroom, the student is handicapped by her disability. She is unable to sit still and concentrate. Why force a student to do something that is outside her limits? Suppose we move the same student into a classroom where she can walk around and work at learning centers that feature manipulative materials. In the latter classroom, our seven-year-old is no longer restrained and she is engaged in concrete tasks that match her developmental abilities.

When a student's behavior is properly evaluated, the context within which the behavior occurs is examined. Special education has historically provided individual services for students rather than classroom support to the regular classroom teacher. The entire special education service delivery system is geared to find something wrong with the student. Yet for years special educators have recognized that disturbance is often in the eye of the beholder. In 1967, William Rhodes remarked that behavior is often more "disturbing" than "disturbed." He contended that disturbance is a function of where and with whom a student interacts (Rhodes, 1967; 1970).

School records and case histories brim with examples of the influence of adult expectations and perceptions on the lives of students classified as behavior disordered or emotionally disturbed. For example, Hewett and Taylor (1980) provide the following description of a "disturbed" student.

> *We worked with an adolescent boy with an IQ of approximately 80. He has the misfortune to be born into a family of extremely high achievers who expected him to go to Princeton University. He was attempting an academic program in high school and failing miserably. From his father's point of view, he was just lazy. His mother babied him. His older brother teased him. His teachers criticized and demeaned him. He stayed up long hours to study but couldn't keep up. His health began to suffer. Finally, he became deeply depressed and attempted suicide. Fortunately, following this episode, a careful examination of this boy's ecosystem (home, family interactions, community, school, teacher behavior) resulted in greater understanding on the part of all parties concerned. (Apter, 1982, 72)*

In analyzing this story, it is difficult to identify the source of the problem. Did the family's expectations and behaviors produce the student's problems? Did his behavior and expectations influence others' perceptions of him? Would he be a problem in another family? Would he be a problem with other teachers? The complex nature of human interactions clearly leaves the source of the disturbance unresolved in this case study.

The Ecological Model

When trying to understand troubled students, one can get caught up in the chicken or the egg syndrome. Does the behavior problem lead to negative responses from others, which ultimately result in an emotional disturbance? Or are the behavior problems caused by an emotional disturbance? Or is the student simply a disruptive individual without an emotional problem? These questions may seem to be rhetorical verbal games best suited for clever banter; but, in fact, how teachers and administrators view students and determine the answers to these questions can mean the difference between a student getting special education services, no help at all, or becoming a school dropout.

What is conspicuously absent from the regular-special education connection is a focus on prevention. (We will discuss prevention in more detail in Chapter 8.) More help for the classroom teacher would improve classroom management practices. Community centers would provide mental health and networking services for troubled families. More attention to the needs of children in general would produce a concentrated effort to mobilize national attention and resources to battle such childhood perils as loneliness, fear, abuse, addiction, and school failure.

The view that treatment of behavior disorders and emotional disturbance must take into account all features of a student's life (including school, family, and community) is called the ecological model. Educators who embrace the ecological perspective believe that in order to understand troubled children, we need to consider all facets of their lives.

> From this outlook emotional disturbance is not seen simply as the necessary result of intrapsychic conflict (psychodynamic model) nor as the inevitable product of inappropriate social learning (behavior modification model). Instead, according to the ecological model, disturbance resides in the interaction between a child and critical aspects of that child's surrounding environment, that is, the child's system. More specifically, ecological theorists believe that what we know as emotional disturbance or behavior disorders actually result from discrepancies between a given child's skills and abilities and the demands or expectations of that child's environment. (Apter, 1982, 2)

The ecological model emphasizes the need for comprehensive preventive systems within and outside school to make adjustments in the parts of a student's life that can cause behavior and emotional disorders. As Apter (1982) acknowledged, change strategies should be aimed at increasing competence instead of reducing deficits. Well-baby clinics, parent effectiveness training, community development programs, sex and drug education programs, and teenage counseling programs are examples of change strategies that focus on prevention while increasing the competence of young people (Heller & Monahan, 1977)

Clearly the ecological model cannot work without community and political support. The long range view of looking at troubled social systems requires a broad based constituency. It requires a commitment to social change and social policies that are often not shared by politicians or the populace in general. The road to social change is riddled with pitfalls.

A case study in the pitfalls of prevention is illustrated by the work of Spencer Holland, a psychologist at Morgan State University in Baltimore. Holland recommended educational intervention specifically aimed at African-American male students. African-American males have the highest dropout rates, get the lowest grades, and exhibit more discipline problems than any sub-group of students. Holland argued that lack of adequate male role models was a primary cause of troubles encountered by African-American males.

> *The most common reasons cited for the academic and social failings of young black males are that such boys come from poor, single-parent, female-headed households; that they have no positive male role models; and that they view the (school) as feminine and not relevant to their daily lives. (Chmelynski, 1990, 16)*

One extension of Holland's reasoning is that referral for special services for behavior problems may be related to females teaching males. Teacher ratings of behavior is the most influential component in school evaluations of behavior and emotional disorders. Teachers rate boys as "acting out" more often than girls, and boys are more likely to be evaluated as having a behavior disorder (Algozzine, 1977). When one matches the overrepresentation of boys in the category of behavior disorders with the overrepresentation of females among teachers, a likely hypothesis is that referrals for behavior and emotional problems are gender related.

Some schools, influenced by Dr. Holland's work, took a hard look at gender issues in classrooms. Several school systems responded to this problem by providing African-American male students with positive male role models. African-American businessmen, professionals, and tradesmen volunteered as role models for students in Baltimore, Detroit, Miami, Milwaukee, San Diego, and Washington, D.C. schools. The role models tutored students, took them on field trips, and provided them with the male mentoring that was conspicuously absent in the youngsters' lives.

These volunteer programs proved so popular that school officials in Dade County, Florida, and Detroit considered starting African-American male academics. The possibility of schools just for African-American male students quickly produced widespread critical reactions. Specters of sexism and segregation raised by the National Organization of Women (NOW) and the National Association for the Advancement of Colored People (NAACP) caused many advocates to reconsider education programs that single out only African-American boys. Proponents of the programs contended that the situation for young African-American males was so dire that radical measures were in order. Holland argued that while African-American girls have role models in their mothers and teachers, boys searching for role models in their inner-city neighborhoods find that the only successful males are drug dealers or criminals

(Chmelynski, 1990). As this case study of prevention illustrates, it is easier to refer a disruptive student for special education services than it is to try to change school practices or redirect social policies.

The advantage of the ecological model is that it focuses attention on the interactional aspects of behavior disorders. David Witcher is a teacher at Batchler Middle School in Bloomington, Indiana; his comments in the August 1988 issue of the Council for Children with Behavior Disorders newsletter are revealing:

> *For the past eight years, I have been a public school teacher in special education programs for so-called emotionally handicapped children and adolescents. Even after working on over a hundred cases, I still cannot tell why one student qualifies for my special services while another does not.*

As long as ineffective teaching practices continue, and urgent social issues are ignored, many students whose behavior problems could be prevented will be classified as disturbed or behavior disordered and placed in special education programs.

One strategy for short-circuiting misreferrals to special education is to discriminate those students who have behavior disorders/emotional disturbance from students whose behavior is disturbing to the classroom teacher. Henley recommends the following criteria to distinguish students with emotional/behavior disorders from those who are disturbing. A student with behavior disorders will exhibit the following characteristics:

1. The disturbing behavior occurs in a variety of settings, not just the classroom.
2. The student is unable to develop and maintain peer relationships.
3. The student is unhappy.
4. The disturbing behavior is fixed, rigid, and predictable.
5. The disturbing behavior is self-defeating; the student shows no sign of emotional growth.
6. The disturbing behavior draws attention and emotional responses from others (Henley, 1986, 2).

The above criteria does not focus on causes: consequently, it is as useful for identifying students whose problems are biophysically based and students whose problems result from unfortunate social-familial circumstances. It also serves as a guide to determine if the disruptive behavior is a function of the student or the classroom. If the same behavior is noted in other settings (i.e., home, community), then clearly the trouble resides within the student. However, if a student's behavior is only disturbing in the classroom, intervention strategies should be directed within the classroom setting rather than at the student. A more complete description of students with behavior disorders is presented in the following section, "Functional Domains."

Functional Domains

Students with behavior disorders exhibit a wide variety of characteristics. A description of functional characteristics is hampered somewhat by the differences in professional perceptions of these youngsters. We all interpret what we see, hear, and understand in terms of the assumptions we hold about the world around us. Keep this in mind when you hear professors and teachers discussing students with behavior disorders. A professional who is solidly in the behaviorist camp does not recognize feelings as important aspects of a student's behavior. If a behaviorist would describe the functional priorities of a youngster, feelings would be at the bottom of the list. At the same time, a professional who is devoted to the psychodynamic treatment approach would describe a youngster's functional abilities in terms of inter-psychic conflicts between id, ego, and superego. The observable actions that are the foundation of the behaviorist treatment model are minimal in the psychodynamic view. A key point to remember is the power of the observer (i.e., teacher, professor, psychologist) of student's behavior to determine if a behavior is disturbing or disturbed.

Seriously emotionally disturbed students are identified by their severe deficits in perception, communication, and behavior. Such behaviors as delusions and lack of affect are marked examples of the extreme behavioral disturbances in seriously emotionally disturbed students. Students with mild behavioral/emotional disabilities are quite different. Before they entered school, the majority of these youngsters seemed capable of adapting to the social demands of formal education. (We hope at this point this theme sounds familiar.) Basically students with behavior disorders exhibit behaviors that interfere with productive interpersonal relationships; they are unable to adapt to classroom routines; and they cause classroom disruptions. These students have behavioral excesses or differences that make regular school progress difficult to achieve without special education.

Consider this example: Mrs. Stone, a junior high school teacher, has just passed out a sheet of math problems to be completed by each of her students. Frank's response is clearly excessive. He looks at the paper, throws down his pencil, and angrily states, "What do you think I am, a genius or something?" After this preamble, he proceeds into a harangue supported by four-letter words and no-holds barred attacks on Mrs. Stone's professional and personal integrity. He ends up with an ultimatum suggesting that "nothing or nobody" can make him do the worksheet.

In this episode, we see grist for everybody's theoretical mill. Frank's behavior is clearly inappropriate, and a behaviorist would work to eliminate outbursts and reinforce appropriate school behaviors. The psychodynamic oriented professional examines the relationship between Frank and Mrs. Stone. Counseling might be directed at helping Frank cope with females in authority positions. From a psychoeducational point of view, Mrs. Stone is setting Frank up for failure by using typed dittos when Frank is developmentally unable to handle such abstract work. Classroom modifications that include work-related functional skills and supported employment would be directed at changing Frank's attitude towards school. The biophysical model suggests that we examine Frank's medical history. Perhaps he is allergic to ditto fluid, and the fumes set off impulsive and aggressive behavior.

In the following sections, we will describe functional characteristics on which most all professionals agree regarding mild behavior disorders. The brevity of this section is testimony to the need of professionals to consolidate theoretical models in order to present a less fractured and more comprehensive description of students with behavior disorders.

Cognitive Ability

Students classified as behavior disorderd or emotionally disturbed usually score in the low average range (75-100) on standardized tests of intelligence. Some professionals argue that emotional problems can cause individual students to perform poorly on intelligence tests. Anyone who is accustomed to taking standardized tests readily reports feelings of anxiety prior to and during testing. For children with minimal ability to cope with stress, an IQ test can be overwhelming. These students will give up, guess wildly at answers, or refuse to continue.

Students with behavior disorders proceed through the same stages of cognitive development as other children: sensory-motor, preoperational, concrete, and formal (see Chapter 3 for a more thorough discussion of Piagetian stages of development). Selman (1980) applied Piaget's developmental scheme to social perception, and he suggested that children go through four stages before they are fully capable of socialized thought. Paul and Epanchin summarized Selman's model:

> First, the child is in a fully egocentric state and is unable to differentiate the points of view of others. Second, the child can consider other people's ideas in a rudimentary way and realizes their thoughts can be different from his own. However, he has difficulty understanding exactly what the differences are. Third, although the child cannot consider others and his own perspectives simultaneously, he can sequentially consider first his own perspective and then another's perspective. Finally, the child is able to think about both perspectives at the same time in an integrated manner, as well as having a "third person" perspective in which he can figuratively step back from the interaction and examine both sides' point of view. (Paul & Epanchin, 1991, 195)

As children develop cognitively they are more capable of understanding a situation from another's point of view. They recognize how their behavior affects others. They are able to identify their own feelings, and they empathize with the feelings of others.

Students with emotional and behavior disorders are delayed in their social cognitive development. They literally forget their own contributions to conflict. Their memories seem to evaporate when they are asked to recall how their actions contributed to a classroom disruption (Redl & Wineman, 1951). They seem only to be able to recall the behavior of others while they remain steadfast in their own innocence. These students cannot apply past experiences to present situations. As often as a student will experience peer retribution for teasing or belittling others the student does not change tactics that goad others into retaliation. They don't understand how their behavior affects others in a negative way. Students with social cognitive delay are unable to learn from the experience of others, and they possess minimal strategies for solving social problems. If another youngster is disapproving, the student with emotional problems will maintain a fixed and predictable response such as a temper tantrum, sulking, scapegoating, or fighting.

These students need practice in developing social problem-solving skills and assessing social reality. They are unable to use their own experiences to advance their social skills in a useful manner; consequently, they remain egocentric and socially isolated from their peers with no sense of what they are doing wrong.

Academic Achievement

One characteristic of students with mild disabilities is low achievement. Most students with behavioral and emotional difficulties don't like school. Some professionals believe these students fail because they have not developed academic survival skills (e.g., finishing tasks, following directions, adjusting to classroom routines). Other professionals maintain that emotional problems (e.g., anxiety, low self-esteem, depression) prevent students from doing well. While researchers tend to focus on independent variables, for example, task engagement, in reality a given student could be limited by all the above characteristics.

For the classroom teacher, the main difficulty is motivation. These students have limited faith in their ability to learn. Their whole school experience has been testimony to their inadequacies. Because their behavior has been a consistent liability, they have internalized feelings of worthlessness. This makes learning a formidable task. Suppose you were on a ski slope taking your first lesson, but you were absolutely convinced you were going to fall. How far do you think you'd make it down the slope without falling? When it comes to learning, students with behavior and emotional difficulties are always falling down.

More than anything else these students need success in school. Learning requires risk-taking and a willingness to change; students with behavioral/emotional problems have spent much of their lives resisting change. Sameness, even if it's unpleasant, provides security. For a student with an emotional disability, learning to read can be a fearful experience. Reading may mean loss of control because it is change, and if one thing about a person's life changes, what is next? Fritz Redl and David Wineman (1951) called this resistance to change "newness panic." The student is overwhelmed by apprehension when confronted with new or different experiences. This makes teaching students with behavioral/emotional disorders difficult.

A secure classroom environment is the first priority. Unless psychological and physical safety is maintained, the student will be overcome by real or imagined threats. The ensuing anxiety will disrupt learning. Next, the students need to derive some personal meaning from school activities. As we discussed in the previous section, students with behavioral and emotional disorders are egocentric. Schoolwork that relates to their day-to-day lives enables students to personalize their learning. Teachers can make learning relevant by emphasizing students' interests, using humor, and developing functional lessons to teach skills. Activities such as rope climbing and challenge courses help to develop risk-taking behavior and enhance self-confidence. Finally, students need reminders of their progress. Positive feedback about emerging skills helps to consolidate gains and encourages perseverance.

Think of student development as a series of upward spiraling circles. Be prepared for regression following progress. This natural cycle of growth and backsliding is normal (Long, 1986). When teaching students who have emotional problems, it is easy to overlook how far they have come. Others who have a long range view, such as administrators or counselors, can help keep intermittent reversals in perspective.

Many special education teachers are cloistered with eight to ten emotionally disturbed students in a single classroom. These teachers are expected to bring their students up to grade level, while also teaching them how to behave properly. This is a difficult task. Students are put in special education programs because they need to learn new behaviors. In a special class, there are no models for appropriate behavior. Regrettably, the reality of the situation is that the teacher is "keeping the lid on" a group of youngsters that other teachers won't tolerate in their classrooms. The burnout rate among teachers of students with emotional and behavioral problems is extremely high.

Despite the negative programmatic aspects of self-contained classrooms, these socially isolating environments serve the administrative purpose of making the problem go away. Unless the emphasis in regular classrooms changes to preventive discipline and the teaching of prosocial behaviors becomes a legitimate part of the curriculum, the label "behavior disordered" or "emotionally disturbed" will continue to be a one-way ticket into segregated, self-contained special education programs.

Language/Communication Development

For students with behavior or emotional disorders, words are both sword and shield. Their verbal outbursts of hostility outrage others, while their facile excuses keep them, in their own minds, free of responsibility. The inability to communicate feelings in a socially appropriate manner results in resentment and misunderstandings between these students and others. Resentment, fear, apprehension, and other tumultuous feelings are acted out rather than discussed. At the same time, students with behavior disorders can use language in finely executed performances of manipulation. Students who are hostile know just what to say to get others to respond in kind. For example, students who whine and complain cause others to withdraw from them.

Like a crafty salesperson, troubled youngsters solicit feedback that reaffirm their position. The more angry or caustic the teacher or student response, the more secure a youngster is in the knowledge that others are indeed out to get him. The student with emotional disturbance needs negative feedback to keep his world steady and predictable. Why change one's behavior if it is clear that others are unable to change theirs? As long as teachers threaten, criticize, and shout, a student with a behavior disorder remains in control. The student pulls the strings, and the adults and peers in the classroom put on the show.

Ginott believed teachers can short-circuit this closed system of emotional turmoil through "congruent communication." Charles (1989) defined congruent communication as "a harmonious and authentic way of talking in which teacher messages to students match the students' feelings about situations and themselves" (Ginott, 1971, 57). Students need teachers to model communication methods that highlight verbal expression of feelings in appropriate ways. For example, Ginott advocated "sane messages." When addressing student disruption, sane messages describe the situation rather than criticizing the student. Sane messages give students the opportunity to assess a situation and to understand why a behavior is disruptive. Sane messages describe the area of concern rather than blaming, preaching, or criticizing students. As an illustration, two students are arguing about who is first in line; an "insane message" is, "You two are always causing trouble; both of you sit down and wait for everybody else to leave." In this situation, the students may feel attacked, and they have no opportunity to learn from the situation. A contrasting sane message would be, "When you act like that it takes longer for all of us to get to lunch; you have to take turns." The explanation provides insight into *why* the teacher is disturbed and describes a more acceptable behavior.

According to Ginott, through modeling, the teacher helps students to express their feelings and communicate their needs. "I-messages," for example, help students understand that teachers do indeed have feelings. Statements like "I am disappointed" or "I am angry" are better than "You are a nuisance" or "You ruin everything for everybody else." Teachers accept and acknowledge feelings when they avoid negative communication modes such as sarcasm and verbal insults. One of Ginott's more novel observations is the perils of praise. Praise creates a dependence on others for approval. Judgmental praise such as "You are a good girl" or "I really like the way you are acting" reinforces the need to look to others for self-worth. What of the student on the other side of the room who was equally "good?" Ginott underscores the need for teachers to understand that for every student who stands in the spotlight, twenty or so are going to feel left out. Charles (1989) has summarized Ginott's main points:

1. Good classroom discipline begins with the teacher's self-discipline.
2. Use sane messages when correcting misbehavior.
3. Teachers at their worst attack and label student characters.
4. Teachers should model the type of communication they expect from students.
5. Anger and other feelings should be expressed in sane ways.
6. Avoid sarcasm and be judicious with praise.
7. The best teachers build self-esteem and help students to trust and express their own feelings.

Social/Adaptive Development

A student is referred for special education services for a behavioral or emotional disorder when a teacher notes frequent and chronic behavior that is markedly different from peers. Difference in behavior is based on teacher expectations and judgments. Authoritarian teachers prize student behavior that is compliant and conforming. Teachers who depend on workbooks, dittoes and other repetitious instructional materials view students who don't "stay on task" as disturbing. Teachers who encourage students to ask questions, express their opinions, and participate in group discussions would more likely view a passive and quiet student as disturbing.

Behavior should not be separated from the context in which it is viewed or judged. Apter emphasized the interactional aspect of behavior disorders when he commented that " . . . what we know as emotional disturbance or behavior disorders actually result from discrepancies between a given child's skills and abilities and the demands or expectations of that child's environment" (Apter 1982, 2). A student who is loud and aggressive may be disturbing in school, but on city streets he could be a leader. Students who are unable or unwilling to adapt to the expectations of classroom life are most likely to be referred to special education as behavior disordered.

Achenbach and Edelbrook (1981) distinguished between internalizing and externalizing behavior problems. Internalized problems are those manifested when a student turns inward because of emotional or social conflict. Anxiety, fears, social withdrawal and immaturity are examples of internalized problems. Aggression, non-compliance, and open hostility are examples of externalized behavior problems; they are more obvious (and get more attention) because they are disruptive.

Externalized behaviors, because they are the most difficult to deal with, are more frequently used as indicators of an emotional disturbance. While all children may fight, bully, or argue, students classified as behavior disordered engage in these behaviors repeatedly. Teachers refer students because they find disciplinary measures are ineffective in controlling or minimizing externalized behaviors. Though less frequently noted, such internalized behaviors as poor self-esteem, moodiness, depression, and social withdrawal are also difficult to change. Internalized students are often overlooked in teacher's judgments about who has an emotional problem.

As children pass through developmental stages of social maturity, they acquire self-control skills that help them to restrain their impulses, assess social reality, manage group pressure, deal with stress, and solve problems in relationships. Impulse maintenance includes the ability to deal with frustration, to self-regulate behavior, and to understand that temptations are accompanied by consequences. When assessing social reality, youngsters need to be realistic about rules and routines, evaluate the effect of their behavior on others, take responsibility for their possessions, and remain reasonable about such gratifications as praise and attention. Group pressure skills include staying calm when others have lost control, managing competitive challenges, and participating in and furthering group activities. Stress management requires coping with anxiety, adjusting to new situations, separating past trauma from present events, and accepting responsibility for actions. Finally, social problem-solving skills include learning from experience, noting one's effect on others, and drawing inferences from others' experiences (Henley, 1987; Long, 1989; Redl and Wineman, 1951). (These skills will be discussed in more detail in Chapter 8.)

The less capable a student is in each self-control skill, the more likely the youngster will encounter social problems in school. Teachers who understand that the misbehavior they encounter in the classroom is based in frustration or stress are likely to demonstrate what Fritz Redl and David Wineman (1951) referred to as "symptom tolerance." Simply stated: when teachers don't personalize disruptive behavior but try to understand not only the behavior but the child as well, dealing with the behavior is easier. When teachers believe a child is intentionally being disruptive or mean or selfish, it is difficult to squelch the adult impulse to "put the kid in her place"; "show him who is boss"; or "not let the kid run all over me." No child chooses to be unhappy in school. Every child wants to be liked and admired. By working to understand the students you deal with, you will find the best way to deal with their behavior.

Suggestions for Teaching Students with Behavior Disorders

1. Recognize the differences between disturbing and disturbed behavior.
2. Look for classroom routines, lessons, and discipline practices that may contribute to behavior problems.
3. Consider diet, allergies, and other physical causes for disturbing behavior.
4. With hyperactive students, change classroom routines before going along with drug treatment.
5. Trust is the basis for social-emotional growth. Work to develop a trusting relationship with a disturbing student.
6. Use behavior modification in a systematic fashion. Don't use behavior modification as a way of rationalizing punishment.

7. Make a home and neighborhood visit of each student in your class and determine adaptive skills required for environments outside of school.

8. Present lessons in a format that connects to the personal experience of your students.

9. Assess the impact of such real life issues as teenage pregnancy, drugs, and depression on your students.

10. Model the language and behavior that you want to foster in your students.

Summary

Students with behavior or emotional problems are one of the three prevalent mild disabilities identified in schools. Students are referred for special education programs when their behavior is perceived to be disturbed or disturbing. There are no absolute standards to judge the presence of normal or abnormal behavior. Frequently, judgments represent opinions about the appropriateness of behavior in a specific classroom. Normality and abnormality are relative concepts that are derived from the interaction of the actor, the observer, and the environment. Reactions to behavior vary according to the skills, expectations, and tolerance of the teacher. A signal indication of the relativity inherent in the category of behavior disorders is the variance in state prevalence figures and differences in state criteria for identifying students.

Over the years, the study of emotional and behavioral problems has been based in four theoretical viewpoints. The biophysical perspective emphasizes the relationship between body chemistry and behavior. The psychodynamic is concerned with feelings, family history, and relationship building. The psychoeducational framework is developmental in nature. It integrates clinical insights in behavior with practical methods for managing behavior. The behaviorist position views observable behavior as the critical element. Treatment strategies are focused on modifying environmental factors that reinforce appropriate behavior.

A synthesis of these models highlights the interactional nature of behavior and emotional disorders. The ecological model promotes the notion that children are influenced by many different environments and that any attempt to help children with behavior or emotional problems must focus on all key elements in a youngster's life.

C h a p t e r **5**

Students with Learning Disabilities

Advance Organizer

When you complete this chapter, you will be able to:

1. Identify types of learning disabilities.
2. Define specific learning disabilities.
3. Know the major concepts and key phrases in defining learning disabilities.
4. Describe how brain research can provide explanations for the causes of learning disabilities.
5. Discuss the prevalence of learning disabilities in our schools.
6. List the causes of mild learning disabilities.
7. Identify developmental domains of functioning and the characteristics associated with each domain.
8. Explain the treatment models that have evolved.
9. Make suggestions about teaching students with learning disabilities.

David, an active and friendly child, progressed through preschool with some minor behavior problems. His year in kindergarten was without incident, although his parents later recalled that he was less keen about going to school than they had expected. He had some difficulty sitting still and listening to the teacher, but his parents chalked it up to "being an active boy."

During first grade, David's parents were disappointed by his poor report card grades. Finally, in third grade, David was referred by his classroom teacher for a special education evaluation. The school psychologist explained to David's parents that the scores from the intelligence test he had administered to David indicated normal intelligence. However, there was a significant discrepancy between David's ability (i.e., intelligence quotient) and his academic performance. David's behavior, particularly his inability to concentrate and follow directions, was interfering with his learning. David, the school psychologist concluded, was learning disabled.

Specific Learning Disabilities

Until the mid-1960s, learning disabilities was unknown as a specific disability. Since that time, the term "learning disability" has become commonplace. Of the eleven disability categories named in Public Law 94-142, it is the fastest growing and most controversial. Since 1975, millions of students have been identified as "learning disabled" and treated in public schools and clinical programs by educators, psychologists, and physicians (Coles, 1989). For example, in 1989, 1,973,291 school-aged youngsters with learning disabilities were identified and treated in the public schools (U.S. Department of Education, 1990). In almost every public school classroom, there is at least one student identified as learning disabled.

The study of learning disabilities can be traced to several diverse disciplines including psychology, medicine (i.e., ophthalmology, otology, neurology, pharmacology), linguistics, and education (Lerner, 1985). Researchers and practitioners in all of these specialized fields have made important contributions to the study of learning disabilities. Paradoxically, these diverse contributions have played a significant role in confusing understanding of learning disabilities. Because each profession tends to view phenomena from a distinctive perspective, it is difficult to get professional agreement about what a learning disability is and how it should be treated. To a pediatrician, a learning disability is a mild neurological disorder. To an otologist, a learning disability is an auditory discrimination problem. To a teacher, a learning disability is a reading or math deficiency. To an ophthalmologist, a learning disability is a visual tracking problem. To a pharmacologist, a learning disability is a metabolic disorder. Each of these professionals will evaluate, describe, and treat learning disabilities in terms of his or her own professional point of view. Much of the confusion can be cleared up by recognizing there are many types of learning disabilities. Throughout the past forty years, many different terms have been used to indicate a learning disability (Table 5–1).

One type of specific learning disability is dyslexia, an impairment in reading ability. A dyslexic student may see letters backwards, reverse letters, or skip over letters while reading. Students with dyslexia have difficulty with reading comprehension. A youngster who reads "saw" for "was" *may* be dyslexic. It is important, however, not to jump to conclusions too quickly about the diagnosis of dyslexia. Children will reverse letters and numbers as their nervous systems are maturing. It is commonplace, for instance, for young children to confuse the let-

TABLE 5–1   Alternative Terms Used to Describe Learning Disabilities

Attention Deficit Disorder	Perceptual Handicap
Minimal Brain Dysfunction	Behavior Disordered
Hyperactivity	Hyperkinesis
Educationally Handicapped	Impulsive
Strauss Syndrome	Strephosymbolia
Dyslexia	Word Blindness
Psycholinguistic Disorder	Multisensory Disorder
Neurologically Handicapped	Slow Learner
Reading Disability	Dyscalculia
Dysgraphia	Dysphasic
Organic Brain Dysfunction	Puzzle Children
Minimal Cerebral Palsy	Neurologically Immature
Developmentally Delayed	Mildly Handicapped
Hypoactivity	Language Disordered
Delayed Learner	Neurophrenia
Congenital Alexia	Diffuse Brain Damaged
Association Deficit Pathology	Organicity
Primary Reading Retardation	Maturation Lag

ters "b" and "d." Many educators believe dyslexia is caused by crossed signals in the area of the brain that interprets and gives meaning to words. The term minimal brain dysfunction ascribes a neurological etiology for dyslexia. It is important to note that minimal brain dysfunction is a hypothetical explanation for dyslexia and other types of specific learning disabilities and is difficult to prove.

Terms used to identify specific learning disabilities typically begin with the prefix *dys*, which means an impairment in a particular ability as in dysfunctional (Table 5–2). Minimal brain dysfunction cannot be proven by a standardized test. A neurological examination (including a detailed medical history, an examination of cranial nerves, an assessment of motor function, and an electroencephalogram (EEG)) *may* be able to confirm a neurological basis for a student's learning problems.

Other types of learning disabilities are more generalized in terms of behavior or cognitive difficulties. Students who are hyperactive or distractible are sometimes characterized as learning disabled. Students who are disorganized and have difficulty following directions may be identified as learning disabled. Poor coordination, problems with short-term memory, perceptual problems, limited concentration, speech deficits, inadequate verbal skills, and problems with becoming easily frustrated are just a sample of characteristics that have been attributed to learning disabilities.

TABLE 5–2   Specific Learning Disabilities

Each of these specific learning disabilities is generally believed to be caused by an impairment in nervous system functioning.

Dyslexia—An impairment in reading ability. An individual does not understand clearly what he or she reads.

Dysgraphia—Difficulty in writing or forming letters. Mirror writing is a severe form of this impairment.

Dysacusis—Impairment in understanding speech and deriving meaning from speech.

Dyskinesia—Clumsiness or poor coordination.

Dyscalculia—Impairment in mathematical ability.

Dyslogia—A linguistic disturbance characterized by faulty formation or expression of verbal ideas.

Dysphasia—An impairment in the ability to produce or comprehand language. It can affect either written or spoken language function.

Dysnomia—Difficulty in searching for and thinking of a word to express a thought or idea.

Dysrhythmia—Poor rhythm or the loss of ability to move with rhythm.

Attention-deficit-hyperactivity disorder—An impairment in sustained attention including fidgeting, distractibility, excessive talking, poor listening skills, difficulty in completing activities, and impulsivity. Onset before age seven. Defined in the the DSM-III-Revised Manual (American Psychiatry Association, 1987).*

*There is a good deal of controversy about whether this disorder is a learning disability. We believe it is.

Distinguishing the true learning disabled child from the underachiever is a major challenge facing educators today. Resource rooms are overloaded with children who have been identified as "learning disabled" based on unreliable evaluation procedures. As of 1989, almost 4.5 percent of the school population of students aged six to seventeen received special education services because of a presumed learning disability. Most experts agree that a range of 2 to 3 percent is a more reasonable prevalence figure for learning disabilities. Clearly, many students are misdiagnosed learning disabled.

In a relatively brief period of time, learning disabilities has emerged as a major explanation for underachievement in school. Its historical antecedents are rooted in neurological research on brain injury and brain dysfunction. Its contemporary growth has branched out into education, linguistics, psychology, and medicine. Like an apple tree, learning disabilities, with the benefit of lots of attention, has grown quickly. But the growth is wild, and the fruit is spotty. The time has arrived to do some pruning. Unless school systems become more adept at varying instruction to meet individual needs and the different learning styles of students in the regular classroom, students identified learning disabled will continue to fill special education classrooms. These students will overtax special education resources and make it difficult to provide adequate services to students who are truly learning disabled.

Defining Learning Disabilities

Congress delayed the passage of the Education for All Handicapped Children Act several months while it wrangled with experts and parents over a suitable definition for learning disabilities. The saying that a camel is a horse created by a committee aptly applies to the federal definition of a learning disability. It appeases everyone but pleases no one. It is extremely vague in some parts and too specific and exclusive in others.

> *"Specific learning disability" means a disorder in one or more of the basic psychological processes involved in understanding or in using language spoken or written, which may manifest itself in an imperfect ability to listen, think, speak, read, write, spell, or to do mathematical calculations. The term includes such conditions as perceptual handicaps, brain injury, minimal brain dysfunction, dyslexia, and developmental aphasia. The term does not include children who have learning problems which are primarily the result of visual, hearing, or motor handicaps, or mental retardation, or emotional disturbance, or of environmental, cultural, or economic disadvantage . . . (Federal Register, 1977, 65083)*

Major Concepts and Key Phrases

The federal definition for learning disabilities has been criticized because it is broad-based and includes undefined terminology. It is helpful to understand the thoughts and concerns that existed when the major concepts and key phrases were written in 1975.

HIGHLIGHT 5–1 What *Is* a Learning Disability?

In order to help you understand the difficulty in defining a learning disability, we are going to give you a brief quiz. (Don't worry— your score won't count towards your final grade.) First question—what is a table? Nice going— you figured that out without much trouble. When you can see, feel, and eat off something, it's not hard to define. Let's try another. What is the wind? That's a little harder. You can't see the wind, and you don't use it very often (except for some kite flying or sailing if you're fortunate); but you can feel the wind, and it's a common part of life. But did you give a specific definition or did you just describe what it means to you? The more abstract a concept, the further removed from direct experiences (our senses), the harder it is to come up with one definition. Let's extend this thinking to one more question. What is eternity? Now there's an abstract concept. We'll have to accept a lot of different views on this one. We have the same problem with the term learning disabilities. It is a very abstract idea, and it is interpreted many different ways.

Basic Psychological Processes

This phrase has yet to be specifically defined but refers to the processing functions that any learner must have intact in order to receive, integrate (i.e., organize, associate, store, retrieve), or express information. It infers that learning problems of students in this category are of a neurological nature and that development is uneven due to subtle disorders of mental processing. Chalfant and Scheffelin (1969) describe "mental processes" as sensing information by listening, looking, or touching; integrating sensations through such cognitive functions as attention, discrimination, memory, integration, concept formation, and problem-solving; and responding through speech or body movements.

Language-Based

The federal definition states that the disorder is language-based and occurs in learning situations that involve oral language, listening comprehension, written composition, writing, spelling, reading (i.e., vocabulary, word-attack skills, decoding, comprehension), or arithmetic (i.e., calculation, reasoning, general problem-solving). Due to each student's specific processing deficit, uneven abilities are manifested in these language-based areas highlighted in academic tasks.

Inclusion Clause

The federal definition specifically includes examples of presumed central nervous system deficits like perceptual handicaps, brain injury, minimal brain dysfunction, dyslexia, and developmental aphasia. These deficits are representative of more severe disabilities, and are not typically identified during educational assessment of students with mild learning disabilities.

Exclusion Clause

The federal definition excludes mental retardation, emotional disturbance, visual impairments, organic hearing dysfunctions, and motor disabilities as primary causes of learning disabilities, even though these conditions can coexist with learning disabilities. According to the definition, a learning disability cannot be attributed to conditions such as environmental, cultural, or economic disadvantage. This part of the exclusion clause is particularly perplexing because it is difficult to determine if a student's underachievement is due to a subtle central nervous system disorder, delayed developmental growth, inadequate teaching, or a lack of environmental opportunities.

Because the federal definition is ambiguous, another definition was written into federal regulations. This alternative set of criteria was established to complement the previous definition and to spell out a *functional* method for determining if a student has a learning disability. The second definition is referred to as the discrepancy formula. It states:

a. A multidisciplinary team may determine that a child has a specific learning disability if:

1. The child does not achieve commensurate with his or her age and ability levels in one or more of the areas listed in paragraph (a) (2) of this section, when provided with learning experiences appropriate for the child's age and ability levels, and
2. The team finds that a child has a severe discrepancy between achievement and intellectual ability in one or more of the following areas:
    i. Oral expression;
    ii. Listening comprehension;
    iii. Written expression;
    iv. Basic reading skill;
    v. Reading comprehension;
    vi. Mathematics calculation; or
    vii. Mathematics reasoning.

b. The team may not identify a child as having a specific learning disability if the severe discrepancy between ability and achievement is primarily the result of:

1. A visual, hearing, or motor handicap;
2. Mental retardation;
3. Emotional disturbance; or
4. Environmental, cultural, or economic disadvantage. (*Federal Register*, 1977, 65083)

This definition is referred to as the discrepancy formula because it focuses attention on the gap between a youngster's academic achievement and intellectual ability. It is more useful for educators because it provides functional guidelines. Simply stated, this definition hypothesizes that a severe discrepancy between intelligence and achievement indicates a learning disability. Because both intelligence and achievement can be measured by testing, the discrepancy definition has been widely accepted. All states include the discrepancy formula in their learning disabled identification procedures (Smith, 1991). This nationwide acceptance has not solved all the problems in identifying students with learning disabilities. Two key concepts in the discrepancy definition require closer inspection.

Intellectual Ability
For many years, William Cruickshank, a pioneer in the field of learning disabilities, argued against assuming that only children with average or above average intelligence have learning disabilities. The way the present discrepancy formula is written, it appears as though students with mental retardation or other disabilities cannot have learning disabilities. It is not uncommon to hear teachers define a learning disabled student as a youngster with *average* intelligence who is underachieving. This is very misleading, and the results show up in educational programming. As an illustration, a child with Down syndrome has a clear neurological impairment, but rarely does one hear learning disabilities discussed as an

explanation for academic problems. Any learning problems a student with Down syndrome has with reading or math is attributed to mental retardation. The possibility that the student might have dyslexia or some other specific learning disability is often overlooked.

Severe Discrepancy between Achievement and Intellectual Ability

As Farnham-Diggory (1978, 5) pointed out, "A learning disabled child is presumably not up to a 'grade level' that can be specified in terms of achievement test scores. Grade level work is what 50 percent of the children in a particular grade are doing." If grade level measures are accurate, half the class will always have a discrepancy between their ability and achievement. This leaves us to ponder what a *severe* discrepancy is. According to Smith (1991), 57 percent of the states provide guidelines on how to quantify severe discrepancy. Two or more years below grade level is common. Some states use three or more years below grade level. In almost half of the states, the meaning of "severe discrepancy" is left in the hands of local school systems.

Overreferrals to special education programs are a major problem that has evolved from the discrepancy notion. Many students are under grade level. If teachers take below grade level to mean that students need special education, referrals are quick to follow. A special education teacher reported her frustration this way.

> Last week a teacher came into my classroom distraught because her fifth grade class had a median grade equivalent reading score of 4.6. This type of scene has happened with three other teachers since the school year began. They are regarding any child below 5.1 grade equivalent level as too slow to teach effectively. "I have at least six of thirty-three students, within one year of fifth grade reading level, with no discernible learning disabilities. My resource room is becoming a low track learning group. Few children have a legitimate disability. With these unnecessary placements, I cannot effectively teach the children who truly need special education." (Henley, 1991)

Public Law 94-142 was originally titled the Education for All Handicapped Children Act (EHA)—*not* the Education for All Slow Learners Act. Emphasis on the purpose of Public Law 94-142, to serve students with disabilities, was further supported through renaming the law Individuals with Disabilities Education Act (IDEA). Yet throughout the country, a domino effect is taking place. Slow or unmotivated learners are overcrowding special education programs, and students with real learning disabilities are not getting the help that they have a legal right to expect. These students have intellectual and learning potential and need special help for deficits that hinder their learning abilities.

The discrepancy formula fuels overreferrals to special education. Because there is no consensus about the characteristics of a student with a learning disability, special educators continue to accept hard-to-teach students into their classroom. As long as the discrepancy formula continues to be widely accepted as an evaluation guideline, the quality of special education services will be diluted, and general educators will have no need to reexamine ineffective teaching practices.

General Problems with the Federal Definition

Some other problems with the federal definition of learning disabilities follow.

1. The learning disabilities definition implies that the disability rests within the individual, and we need to remediate or treat the student. It ignores the possibility that the tasks students are expected to perform, the presentation and instruction of these tasks, and the learning environment in which these tasks are performed might aggravate or even cause the learning problem. By placing the deficiency in the student, schools are excused from blame and from searching for educational alternatives (Bateman, 1974).

2. Unlike the AAMR (American Association on Mental Retardation) definition of mental retardation, the federal definition makes no mention of age. Sole reference is made to "children," thus it does not specifically recognize learning disabilities in adolescents or adults. It implies that children with learning disabilities have similar etiologies (i.e., causes) and symptoms (i.e., characteristics), and therefore similar treatment methods should be used with all.

3. The federal definition does not address how school curricula can maximize postschool vocational and school adjustment so that the student with a learning disability can become an employable and productive citizen (Smith, 1983).

4. Teaching methods are not addressed in the federal definition (Senf, 1978). No guidance is given about how to plan or implement treatment in the school setting (Keogh, 1977).

When the category learning disabilities was in its formative stage (1950s to 1960s), individuals were identified with learning disabilities based upon neurological "soft signs." Examples of soft neurological signs are such problems as distractibility and perceptual difficulties. Stevens and Birch (1957) found that on the mild level, slow learners are often identified and misclassified as learning disabled. And at a more severe level, students with neurological deficits are often identified as emotionally disturbed rather than learning disabled.

New Definitions Proposed

Many attempts have been made to develop a new definition for learning disabilities (Kirk & Kirk, 1983). In 1981, The National Joint Committee for Learning Disabilities was formed by representatives of six professional associations: American Speech-Language-Hearing Association (ASHA), Association for Children with Learning Disabilities (ACLD), Council for Learning Disabilities (CLD), Division for Children with Communication Disorders (DCCD), International Reading

Association (IRA), and the Orton Society. The following definition was written and agreed upon by the member groups:

> *Learning disabilities is a generic term that refers to a heterogeneous group of disorders manifested by significant difficulties in the acquisition and use of listening, speaking, reading, writing, reasoning, or mathematical abilities. These disorders are intrinsic to the individual and presumed to be due to central nervous system dysfunction (i.e., neurological). Even though a learning disability may occur concomitantly with other handicapping conditions (e.g., sensory impairment, mental retardation, social and emotional disturbance) or environmental influences (e.g., cultural differences, insufficient/inappropriate instruction, psychogenic factors), it is not the direct result of those conditions or influences. (Hammill et al., 1981, 336)*

This proposed definition was an attempt to clarify ambiguity in the existing federal definition. Spelling is subsumed under written expression, and reading and mathematical abilities are not subgrouped into categories. No effort was made to include specific neurological deficits, such as dyslexia. An attempt is made to clarify the fact that learning disabilities may coexist with other disabilities. It states that underachievement in academic or cognitive functions is due to a neurological dysfunction within the person.

This definition did not satisfy everyone. Members of The Association for Children and Adults with Learning Disabilities wrote their own definition. Members of this organization are parents of children with learning disabilities and professionals.

> *Specific learning disabilities is a chronic condition of presumed neurological origin which selectively interferes with the development, integration, and/or demonstration of verbal and/or nonverbal abilities (Bryan, Bay, & Donahue, 1988, 24).*

This definition uses the term "chronic" in an attempt to eliminate "slow learners" from being erroneously identified learning disabled. The word "presumed" is added to acknowledge the inability of educational assessment tools and most medical diagnosis to document neurological dysfunction. "Selective interference" infers that specific disabilities may occur during normal development. The inclusion of "nonverbal skills" refers to problems with performance that are not based in language, linguistics, or reading.

Both of these definitions include references to neurologically caused learning disorders. Bryan et al. conclude that professionals in the field clearly intend for the category of learning disabilities to "describe children whose learning and behavioral problems are the result of central nervous system involvement" (Bryan et al., 1988, 24). Perhaps future brain research will help to provide the technology needed to verify the existence of a neurological basis for learning disabilities.

Early Research on Learning Disabilities

Barsch was one of the first professionals to point out the need to look more closely at learning disabilities as a possible explanation for the failure of some children to make adequate progress in school.

> *The failing learner is no longer a statistic of minor significance. Academic fail-ure, learning inefficiency, anxiety barriers, dismissals, expulsions, dropouts, reading retardation, and a host of other problems are rampant on the educational scene. The percentages of failing students is increasing annually. . . . The prob-lem is immediate upon the educational terrain: the confrontation is compelling and vibrant and the pressure for action is inescapable. (Barsch, 1968, 7,10)*

Barsch's remarks, which appeared in the first issues of the *Journal of Learning Dis-abilities*, signaled a shift towards considering the possibility that some problem learners had a learning disability. Barsch's comments linked 30 years of research with brain injured individuals to remedial services for students in public schools.

Misclassified Mentally Retarded Students

In the 1950s, Samuel Kirk discovered that a number of persons had been mis-classified mentally retarded at the Wayne County Training School in Northville, Michigan. Kirk could not justify classifying these pupils as having mental retar-dation for several reasons. First, the intelligence quotient (IQ) scores of these stu-dents were too high; second, after intensive remediation in reading, they made extraordinary progress. Similar gains were rarely made by their counterparts with mental retardation.

> *All of the children I taught . . . were classified as mentally retarded. In all of these cases my purpose was to show through the results of remediation that these children should have been classified as learning disabled instead of mentally retarded, since they were normal in some respects but had specific disabilities. (Kirk, 1976, 260)*

Many of these individuals eventually left the institution and became self-supporting (Kirk, 1976). These misclassified individuals inspired Kirk to do fur-ther research to determine the nature of their disabling condition. Kirk's findings paralleled earlier research on patients with brain injuries. In the early 1930s, Kurt Goldstein had observed perseveration, figure-ground confusion, and forced responses to stimuli in adults who had suffered brain injury (Goldstein, 1942).

Heinz Werner (1944) and Alfred Strauss and Laura Lehtinen (1947) followed similar research avenues. They identified and described exogenously brain dam-aged (i.e., point of origin of disability outside the body), retarded children. The disabilities of these children could not be traced to genetic causes. Their behavior was characterized as perceptually disordered, impulsive, distractible and repetitive. This condition became known as Strauss syndrome. Later, during the 1960s, William Cruickshank (1967) was instrumental in changing the focus of research from exogenously retarded children to minimally brain damaged (MBD) children with normal intelligence. Cruickshank's identification of Strauss syndrome characteristics in children without mental retardation (i.e., average intelligence) was a pivotal turning point in the study of learning disabilities (Table 5–3).

Supporters of Learning Disabilities

The movement to gain recognition for children without mental retardation took a giant step forward in 1963 when Samuel Kirk first proposed the term "learning disability" in a speech at a special education parents' conference. Previously, professionals used many different terms to identify the same children. By using the term learning disabilities as an umbrella concept to cover children who had been

TABLE 5–3 Strauss Syndrome, Characteristics of Brain Damaged Children

These are general behaviors that Strauss and Werner believed characterized brain injured children. These characteristics influenced the later work of William Cruickshank with nonretarded children and led to treatment in classrooms that were devoid of distractions. Study carrels, which are still found in many resource rooms, are artifacts of instructional programs that were designed to focus the attention of students who exhibited Strauss syndrome characteristics.

1. Forced responsiveness to stimuli—Any noise or movement distracted the child: a pencil dropping on the floor, the sound of cars driving outside a window, a student passing by. This is different than distractibility caused by boredom.
2. Pathological fixation—The child perseverated. Once engaged in a motor task, the child repeated movements over and over. An example is a student who rubs a hole in a work sheet with an eraser. Perservation can affect thinking, talking or movement.
3. Disinhibition—Excessive motor activity. Now commonly referred to as hyperactivity. Strauss found that children with brain damage were attracted to specific features of objects. The "bounciness" of a ball or the "jabbiness" of a pencil would seduce the child into bouncing or jabbing.
4. Dissociation—The child was unable to integrate or see the "whole picture." For example, a student would have difficulty seeing how the parts of a puzzle fit together. The child was disorganized. This integration problem inspired Werner's famous Marble Board experiments where students were asked to repeat patterns of red and black marbles on eleven inch squares with ten lines and ten holes to each line. Children who were unable to copy the patterns were identified as dissociated in their conceptual reasoning.

Derived from *Learning Disabilities: A Psychological Perspective* by Sylvia Farnham-Diggory; *The Developing Child Series* (1978), Jerome Bruner, Michael Cole, Barbara Lloyd, Harvard University Press.

called minimally brain damaged, perceptually handicapped, minimally brain dysfunctional, or language delayed, advocates were able to join forces and push for federal legislation to provide remedial school services for those students.

Critics of Learning Disabilities

The category of learning disabilities evolved as a means of addressing a disabling condition that did not fit into preexisting classifications of exceptionality (e.g., mental retardation, emotionally disturbed). Some educators think that the label is a convenience because students with learning disabilities usually have average intelligence, no sign of emotional disturbance, and they primarily come from middle-class backgrounds. The critics believe that the identification of a learning disability is a way for students to get special education services without anyone being held accountable for the problem. The student is blameless because the problem is assumed to be neurological in nature. Parents are blameless because the learning problem is not caused by inadequate parenting. Finally, teachers are blameless because the student's presumed neurological impairment, rather than inadequate instruction, is the reason for school failure. According to Kronick,

> Learning disabilities is a cosmetic label which white, middle-class parents prefer because it implies that their children are not mentally retarded or disturbed, that parenting was not faulty, and that their children are not responsible for their behavior and so cannot be called "lazy" or "unmotivated" (Kronick, 1988, 33).

Coles (1989) suggested that the field of learning disabilities is popular because it explains and justifies poor school performance by focusing upon presumed characteristics and attributes found within the child. Bartoli (1989) suggested that the following causal factors be considered as alternatives to neurological dysfunction: curriculum, testing, classroom dynamics, school climate, community values, teacher-parent relationships, and poverty. A comparison of Bartoli's observation with the federal definition provides a good example of how little consensus there is regarding the nature of learning disabilities.

Brain Research

Learning disabilities were first described as caused by "minimal brain damage." The disability was classified as a neurological dysfunction (Bartoli, 1989; Sigmon, 1989). The federal definition of learning disabilities states that a mental processing deficit exists, but it does not define "processing deficit." Generally, mental processing refers to thinking skills such as generalizing, abstracting, classifying, and integrating (Kelly & Vergason, 1978). The brain (i.e., neurological system) is the site of mental processing. Some experts in the field contend that the federal definition of learning disabilities cannot be successfully put into practice (Algozzine & Ysseldyke, 1983; Ysseldyke, Algozzine, & Epps, 1983). This is because neurological impairments that cause processing deficits and would confirm the diagnosis of a learning disability are subtle and microscopic. Standard educational testing procedures lack the precision to provide valid or reliable data about whether or not a student has a neurological processing deficit.

It is possible to detect brain anomalies in persons with severe learning disabilities. In 1861, Paul Broca, a French neuronanatomist exhibited the brain of a deceased patient who had a severe communication impairment. His intelligence was average and he showed no indication of emotional disturbance. Broca called his patient "Tan-Tan" because those were the only words the man could utter. Tan-Tan understood speech and communicated through gestures. Only Tan-Tan's speaking ability was impaired. The brain Broca exhibited had observable damage in a circumscribed two-inch area of the left hemisphere. Broca ably convinced his colleagues that Tan-Tan's speech impairment (today known as aphasia) was the result of this insult to the brain. Broca was one of the first contributors to the theory that language ability is localized in the left hemisphere of the brain (Restak, 1984).

The Russian, Aleksandr Luria, is regarded by many professionals as the greatest psychologist of the twentieth century. Luria believed, as Broca did, that certain mental abilities were localized in specific areas of the brain. For instance, we recognize visual images are centered in the occipital lobe in the brain. Any damage to the occipital lobe will result in a vision impairment. Luria's work on memory, particularly with his most famous patient "S," documented the relationship between visual imagery and memory.

Luria's work with patients who suffered from dyscalculia (impaired ability to do arithmetic) demonstrated how defects in spatial logic, mathematical planning, and calculating could be traced to defects in specific areas of the brain. For example, Luria presented the case of an artillery commander who lost the ability to add, subtract, divide, and multiply after a bullet wound. Surrounding brain tissue was unblemished and other mathematical skills such as counting and logic were unaffected. In another illustration, Luria described a female patient who was unable to plan how to solve sequential problems. She became confused when given a three-part problem like: a boy is eight years old; his father is thirty years older; and the mother is ten years younger than the father—how old are they? Luria reported that this patient's thinking ability improved after surgical removal of a brain tumor (Farnham-Diggory, 1978; Reetak, 1984).

Today it is generally accepted that specific areas of the brain control discrete thought processes (Figure 5–1). Robert Sperry's (1978) work with split brain patients detailed the different ways that the right and left hemispheres of the brain process information. Sperry studied individuals whose corpus callosums were severed by surgery in order to diminish uncontrollable seizures. The corpus callosum is the bundle of nerves that connect the left and right hemispheres of the brain. It is the line of communication that allows the hemispheres to communicate with each other. Sperry found that the left hemisphere is specialized for dealing with things in sequence; the right hemisphere deals with things all at once. The left hemisphere is often characterized as the logical, verbal, analytical half of the human brain. The right hemisphere is characterized as the intuitive, holistic, visual half of the brain.

Robert Ornstein, who studied under Sperry, found that his subjects were right or left hemispheric oriented; that is, they had a preferred mode of thought. Using EEG measurements of electrical activity in individuals from different occupations, Ornstein discovered that artists relied more on their right hemisphere even when the task required left hemisphere capabilities. The opposite was true of lawyers; that is, even when the task required right hemispheric

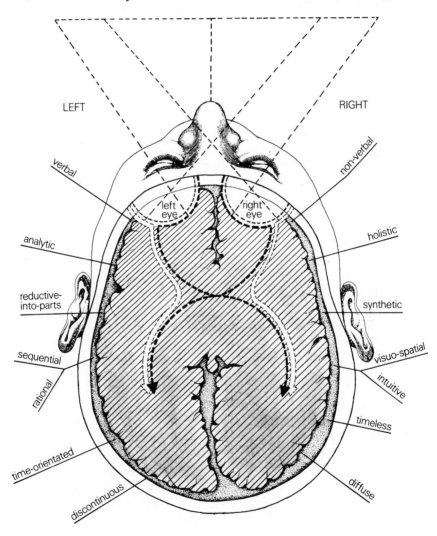

FIGURE 5–1 Areas of the Brain.

From: Charles Hamptden-Turner, *Maps of the Mind*. Mitchell Beazley, London, 1981. Reprinted with permission.

thought, the lawyers tended to process the information through their left hemisphere. Ornstein concluded that the hemispheres are specialized for information processing and individuals gradually develop a hemispheric preference.

Ornstein also found that the hemispheres of most right-handed people are specialized for specific types of thought along the lines outlined by Sperry. But, left-handed individuals, according to Ornstein, sometimes did not follow the standard left-right hemisphere localization of function. According to Ornstein,

> *Left-handers often show a reverse specialization, in which some information is processed in the opposite hemisphere from the one used by right-handers. Some left-handers appear to have brains organized like those of right-handers, while others show no specialization at all. Ambidextrous people seem to have the least specialization of all the groups we have tested. (Ornstein, 1978, 81)*

Some learning disabled students have a developmental history of mixed dominance (i.e., a condition in which neither side of the body is consistently used). Perhaps the "reverse specialization" that Ornstein discovered in left-handers may provide a clue as to why left-handed children are identified as learning disabled at a greater rate than right-handed youngsters. In applying his findings to schools Ornstein observed:

> *Even a casual look at the results of hemisphere research shows that the ways of thinking that seem to be primarily the province of the left hemisphere are used extensively in the basic subjects of the school curriculum. The realization that schools spend most of their time training students in what seem to be left hemisphere skills, and that most educators and taxpayers regard what seem to be right hemisphere skills as frills, has caused many people to wonder whether our educational system is unbalanced. (Ibid. 82)*

Ornstein's research indicated that there may be a mismatch between how students process information and how information is presented by teachers. If some students have a preferred mode of right hemispheric thinking, they will be at a distinct disadvantage in classrooms where the teacher relies heavily on sequenced learning, verbal skills, and analysis of problems (i.e., left hemispheric material). This supposition is supported by the work of Sally Smith (1988) at the Lab School, a special school for students with learning disabilities in Washington, D.C. Smith has found that her students respond to activities in which the arts (right hemispheric thinking) are used to teach academic skills. Smith's observation that . . . "the child with the hidden handicap of learning disability also has a hidden talent in an artistic area because he has learned unique ways of looking at things," sounds very much like Ornstein's description of individuals who prefer right hemispheric modes of thought.

The human brain weighs less than six pounds, and it can store more information than all the libraries of the world. In appearance it resembles a soft, wrinkled walnut. It communicates with itself through ten billion neurons and a hundred billion neuronal connections (Restak, 1984). It is capable of painting the Sistine Chapel, inventing the atom bomb, and committing murder. Neuroscientists approach the study of the brain with the same awe most of us reserve for space travel and exploration of the universe. We have much to learn about brain function, thinking, and learning disabilities. Modern technology, through the use of computerized axial tomography (CAT) scans and positron emission photography (PET) scans, can provide a detailed picture of brain function in living patients. Unfortunately, these medical techniques are far too complex and expensive to be helpful to school evaluation teams. In the future, however, we can expect that private grant and federally funded research activities will uncover more specific information about how children with learning disabilities process information and think.

A portion of the children identified as learning disabled do have some degree of neurological dysfunction that interferes with learning and academic achievement; however, the number is far less than the almost two million children who have been identified as learning disabled (Adelman, 1989; Coles, 1989). As Rourke (1989) put it, we cannot assume that brain damage or neurological dysfunction is the only plausible explanation for learning problems in students with average or above average intelligence. As long as school systems are unable to differentiate between hard-to-teach students and neurologically impaired students, these two groups will continue to be lumped together and identified as learning disabled.

Prevalence of Learning Disabilities

There are more students with learning disabilities reported each year than any other special education category (Algozzine & Ysseldyke, 1986; U. S. Department of Education, 1990). Biklen and Zollers (1986) state that youngsters identified by schools as learning disabled comprise over 40 percent of students placed in special education services. Gartner and Lipsky (1987) provided another frame of reference when they pointed out that between 1977 and 1985 there was a 16 percent increase in students with special needs, while during the same period, the number of students classified as learning disabled rose 119 percent!

Prevalence of learning disabilities, that is the number of existing cases, depends upon multiple factors. Because of this, reliable figures are difficult to obtain. Only generalities about numbers of students identified and served can be accurately stated. Numbers of students depend upon methods and criteria used for identification and classification (Lerner, 1985). As a result, the number of students classified as learning disabled varies from state to state (Algozzine & Korinek, 1985). Much of this variation is a result of the discrepancies in the eligibility guidelines used by states (Algozzine & Ysseldyke, 1987). The more stringent the criteria, the fewer students with learning disabilities are identified. Therefore, a student determined eligible for services in one school district or state may not meet requirements in another.

Unreported are adults with learning disabilities, many of whom attend post-secondary facilities (e.g., junior colleges, four-year colleges, community reading projects). Federal counts identify the number of preschool, elementary and secondary level students receiving services and their funding allocations. The actual number of persons identified as learning disabled who receive special services as they pursue an education (i.e., preschool through college) is higher than the reported prevalency figures each year.

Data reporting the numbers and percentages of children and youth receiving special education and related services have been published by the U.S. Department of Education since school year 1976–1977. These statistics are based upon student count data submitted by states and territories; Hardman, Drew, Egan, and Wolf (1990) cite the 1989 Report to Congress as reporting over 4.1 million exceptional children served in special education in the nation's schools during 1987-1988. Of this number, 1.9 million were classified as learning disabled, representing 44 percent of the exceptional population. A continued trend of increases to the category of learning disabilities is attributed to:

1. The vagueness of the federal definition for learning disabilities.
2. Social acceptance and preference for the learning disabilities classification (rather than mental retardation or behavior disorders).
3. Differing criteria used by states for qualification for services (Sigmon, 1989).

Perhaps there is much truth in the statement made by Ysseldyke, Algozzine, and Thurlow that "learning disabilities is whatever society wants it to be" (1983, 145).

Etiology of Learning Disabilities

Specific learning disabilities have been attributed primarily to neurological disorders. As we stated earlier, technology is not readily available to verify these assumptions. Thus, researchers have classified causes for the disorder in two groups: organic and environmental factors (Reid & Hresko, 1981; Smith, Price, & Marsh, 1986). Organically based causes are physiological in nature (i.e., endogenous) while environmentally based causes result from negative environmental or social factors such as inadequate diets or poor pedagogy (i.e., exogenous).

It is difficult to isolate the two groups of organically and environmentally learning disabled. The federal law does not recognize environmental, cultural, or economic factors as primary reasons for a learning disability; however, these factors do impact upon youth and can cause subsequent disorders. For example, a child born into an impoverished environment may have parents who are economically deprived and educationally deficient. Lack of knowledge about nutrition, or the ingestion of harmful substances (e.g., paint with lead or mercury) can result in delayed development or neurological damage. Insufficient prenatal or inadequate perinatal care, as well as maltreatment of postnatal diseases or trauma (e.g., infections) are contributors to learning disorders. Thus, detrimental environmental factors and biological conditions are interrelated (Smith et al., 1986).

Many of the organic origins of mental retardation can overlap as possible contributors of specific learning disabilities and behavior disorders as well (Ramsey et al., 1986). For example, postnatal disorders of encephalitis and meningitis can result in attention disorders, behavior disorders, and mental retardation. Hyperactivity, visual impairments, and deafness can be caused by measles or whooping cough. Anoxia or oxygen deprivation can cause brain damage with resulting learning or behavior disorders. Furthermore, genetic factors may precipitate learning disabilities. (See Appendix C for "Genetic, Pre-, Peri-, and Postnatal Disorders.")

Silver (1989) reported findings from a study of children with learning disabilities who were attending the TRI-Services' Center School in Chevy Chase, Maryland, the Chelsea School in Silver Springs, Maryland, and Pine Ridge School in Williston, Vermont. He calculated the frequency of learning disabled children was 4.5 times higher among adopted children. According to his study, 17.3 percent of adopted children are learning disabled versus 3.9 percent of biological children. He reported that many adopted children are born out of wedlock to indigent, young women. Such mothers are likely to receive less adequate nutritional and medical care during pregnancy and insufficient emotional support. Pregnancies of young, indigent mothers are usually stressful, and Silver concluded that the mother's tension and anxiety could adversely affect the fetus. Children born to such mothers are slow to mature, and sometimes develop learning disabilities.

Environmental effects take many forms and are likely contributors to learning disabilities. These effects include deprived learning experiences during infancy and preschool years. Teachers who do not have concern or tolerance for slower maturing and developing children or who do not adequately compensate for these learning gaps perpetuate school failure and underachievement.

Treatment Models

Contemporary treatment practices in learning disabilities stem from four major theoretical models: the medical model, the psychological process model, the behavioral model, and the cognitive/learning strategies model (Poplin, 1989). In general, treatment models evolve in response to how the problem of learning disabilities is conceptualized. Authorities within each model highlight different student characteristics. Early conceptualizations and corresponding treatment practices were based on the assumption that underlying causes of learning failure were neurological.

Then the behaviorists brought in the environmental perspective. They believed behaviors were learned and those behaviors could be altered through conditioning. More recent practices reflect an interrelated view. Regardless of whether the cause is neurological (e.g., intrinsic disorders, developmental lag), school-based (e.g., ineffective teaching), or environmental (e.g., "learned helplessness"), the student can be taught to be a more self-sufficient, independent learner. An overview of these theoretical models is shown on Table 5–4.

Medical Model

During the late 1940s and 1950s, the medical model developed with an emphasis upon diagnosis and treatment of neurological symptoms. Diagnosis included: (1) thorough reviews of case histories, (2) extensive anecdotal records, (3) tests of neurological functioning (involuntary motor reflexes), (4) lists of characteristic symptoms, (5) intelligence tests, (6) electroencephalogram (EEG) tests, and often, (7) the administration of medication. Students typically attended private facilities or institutions where they were taught in a structured, stimuli-free environment. These early programs misclassified students with learning disabilities as mentally retarded or brain-damaged (Wiederholt, 1974). The specific category learning disabilities was unknown to these early researchers.

Psychological Process Model

In the 1960s, emphasis shifted from the medical realm to the educational arena. This was due to three primary factors: (1) the recognition of the existence of students with disabling conditions within the public schools, (2) insufficient evidence that neurological examinations could reliably differentiate neurologically impaired youth from the normal population, and (3) a lack of evidence that neurological interventions alleviate school learning problems (Coles, 1989; Poplin, 1989). Treatment, however, continued to be given in controlled and structured pull-out programs or special classes. Emphasis was placed upon remediation of perceptual skills. Teachers were trained in methods for educating students with minimal brain dysfunction. They focused on changing behaviors described by such terms as distractibility, inadequate figure-ground discrimination, and impulsivity. Psychological process tests and remediation materials proliferated. In 1971, Newell C. Kephart described the student with perceptual disabilities in the preface of his book, *Slow Learner in the Classroom*.

> He does not see what we think we show him; he sees something different. He does not hear what we think we are saying to him. He does not make the connections as we do between bits of information which we think we are presenting in such a beautifully organized fashion. His central nervous system is treating these items in a different way.

Regular classroom teachers sometimes referred to these students as "lazy," "unwilling to try," and "inattentive"! Kephart attempted to dispel such negative references and to help teachers understand how these students perceived things

TABLE 5–4 Overview of Theoretical Models: 1950–Present

	Medical Model (1950s)	Psychological Process Model (1960s)	Behavioral Model (1970s)	Cognitive/Learning Strategies Model (1980s)
Emphasis	Neurological pathways.	Prerequisite skills for academic success.	Academic product or consequent behavior.	Information processing and metacognition necessary for academic success.
Etiology	Brain damage or dysfunction.	Minimal neurological dysfunction.	Lack of learned behaviors or learned nonadaptive behaviors.	Insufficient strategies or study skills with which to process information necessary for school success.
Diagnosis	Largely neurological.	Soft neurological signs, psychological process testing, some intelligence and academic tests, or modality frame of reference.	Discrepancy between IQ and academic achievement, criterion-referenced tests, and observation of specific academic and social school tasks.	Discrepancy between IQ and academic achievement, with cognitive skills tests and/or observation of specific strategies.
Assessment	Academic assessment, largely anecdotal case studies.	Psychological process; some basic academic skills.	Testing of student behavior against task analysis of skills, examination of reinforcement contingencies.	Testing of student behavior and processing against known cognitive and/or learning strategies used by successful learners, often task analyzed.
Instruction/ Treatment	Extremely structured, clutter-free environment; motoric and other neurological training; some basic skills emphasis; some medication.	Psychological or psycholinguistic training with less emphasis on actual academic skills; medication, sensory integration, and/or modality training.	Direct instruction using task analysis of skills (behaviors) and application of reinforcement principles.	Direct instruction in strategies used by school learners; also use of principles of reinforcement, particularly self-management and self-task.
Goals	Function in community.	Function in school; less community emphasis.	Almost exclusively school-related goals, some social but primarily academic mainstream.	Almost exclusively school-related goals, some social but primarily academic mainstream.
Some Major Figures	Werner, Strauss, Lehtinen, Cruickshank	Kirk, Frostig, Minskoff, Kephart, Barsch, Wepman.	Lovitt, Camine, Jenkins, Haring, Bateman.	Torgesen, Hallahan, Deshler, Schumaker, Alley, Meichenbaum, Feurestein, Wong.

Source: M. S. Poplin, "The Reductionist Fallacy in Learning Disabilities: Replicating the Past by Reducing the Present," *Journal of Learning Disabilities*, 1989 Vol.21, No. 7, p. 391.

in a different way. The shift in perspective from apathetic student to different type of learner advocated by Kephart was a major contribution to educating the public about learning disabilities.

Helmer Myklebust was recognized for his work in determining a relationship between neurological disorders and language development. He coined the term "psychoneurological learning disorders." This term refers to students with reading and other language impairments. He maintained that if the central nervous system is dysfunctioning, there may be a learning disorder of one or more of the following types (Myklebust, 1964; classroom problems by the authors).

1. Perceptual disturbance: Inability to identify, discriminate, and interpret stimuli. (Classroom problem: Poor recognition of everyday sensory experiences [e.g., reading letters, following directions].)
2. Disturbance of imagery: Inability to recollect common experiences although they have been perceived. (Classroom problem: Deficiencies in recalling words and other information provided.)
3. Disorders of symbolic processes: Inability to express experiences symbolically. (Classroom problem: Children with aphasia, dyslexia, dysgraphia, dyscalculia, and language disorders have difficulty using letters and numerals.)
4. Conceptualizing disturbances: Inability to generalize and categorize experiences. (Classroom problem: Problems classifying ideas.)

Behavioral Model

In the 1970s educators became disillusioned after seeing slight progress being made by students who were assessed and taught by psychological process model methods. Test results were unsuccessful in differentiating the learning disabled from the non-learning-disabled population, and psycholinguistic and perceptual process training models were unable to provide evidence of improved ability to perform academic tasks. The behavioral model emerged from a need for social skills training coupled with a general lack of academic achievement in regular classrooms.

Proponents of the behavioral model proposed direct instruction of academic and social skills. Prerequisite processing abilities were minimized in delivery of special education services. The remediation of inadequate sensory processes was replaced by a functional approach to teaching. The discrepancy clause written into Public Law 94–142 made processing tests less important in assessment. The discrepancy clause states that there must be a significant difference between potential and achievement. This is determined by administering tests of intelligence and tests of academic achievement and then comparing results between these two types of tests. Programmed texts, short-term objectives, task analysis, and criterion-referenced tests were developed as educational materials during this decade (Poplin, 1989). The purpose of these materials was to provide the classroom teacher with a functional, sequenced approach to academics.

Behavioral Approaches

Norris G. Haring, while director of the Children's Rehabilitation Unit at the University of Kansas Medical Center, argued for the use of behavior modification because it deals with observable behaviors and deemphasizes mental types of remediation. According to Haring, achievement oriented behaviors increased when events (i.e., reinforcers) were arranged to follow targeted behaviors (Haring & Phillips, 1962). Careful arrangement of reinforcers, Haring maintained, was a more practical way to teach students with learning disabilities.

Ogden Lindsley taught the use of "precision teaching" in instructional settings while at the University of Kansas. According to Lindsley (1964), precision teaching is a type of instruction that directly measures student performance on a daily basis. Students are administered probes (i. e., skill samples) each day that correspond to their instructional objectives. These frequent measurements provide a systematic method for planning instruction. In addition, Lindsley encouraged the use of contingency management, which is similar to behavior modification. Contingency management is an "if-then" type of arrangement, which incorporates carefully selected reinforcers to follow specified target behaviors.

Behavior modification, precision teaching, and contingency management were transferred from the laboratory setting into the classroom in an effort to identify observable and measurable student behaviors. The goal was to teach by contingency (i.e., an "if-then" type of reinforcement) rather than concentrating upon undetectable neurological causes. By looking at task requirements, adding contingencies, and observing the learners' responses, behaviorists believed that students could be more effectively taught. Observable behaviors related to learning (such as staying on-task, being in seat, or raising one's hand to talk) were targetted for reinforcement.

Academic Achievement

During the 1970s, studies of brain functioning, which were characteristic of the medical model, were replaced by measurements of academic achievement. Persons attempting to instruct students with learning disabilities were teachers, not clinicians. Academic achievement was the primary concern of educators. Further support for the academic point of view was provided by the development and early utilization of standardized tests which, though imperfect, could measure academic skills (e.g., KeyMath Diagnostic Arithmetic Test [1971], Gates-MacGinitie Reading Tests [1972]). The academic model rejected the concept of mastering mental processing skills as prerequisites to academic achievement. Many of the instruments developed to measure mental processing abilities were proven inadequate (Myers & Hammill, 1982). The academic achievement camp remained the primary force in teaching students with learning disabilities in the 1980s. The notion that instruction for students with learning disabilities should focus upon acquisition of academic skills and the application of these skills into everyday functioning skills became widely accepted among special educators. Still, the academic remediation approach had its limitations. It was characterized by critics as teacher-directed and student-passive. Critics maintained that behavioral treatments bred student dependency. Poplin (1989), for instance, felt that students should develop autonomous ways of learning in order to adequately prepare for self-sufficiency after school.

Cognitive/Learning Strategy Models

Teaching students how to learn, how to manage their own behaviors in the learning environment, and how to generalize information from one setting to another is a present-day emphasis in learning disabilities. Initiated in the early 1970s, this approach is called *metacognition*. The metacognition movement was cobbled from previous research in psychological processing dysfunctions, information processing, cognitive psychology, metacognitive theory, tenets of general education, and self-reinforcement principles in behaviorism. Metacognition ties together the past with the present. Cognitive strategists recommend that students be taught "strategy behaviors" necessary to perform academic tasks.

Cognitive strategists emphasize a self-monitoring approach to learning. Self-questioning, self-checking, self-correcting, self-evaluating, and self-reinforcing are components of cognitive strategies. Students are taught learning skills such as outlining, organizing time, memorizing, studying, and generalizing conceptual information from one setting to another. Teaching students "how" to learn is paramount (Reid & Hresko, 1981). Presently, two cognitive/learning strategy models predominate: cognitive behavior modification and the cognitive strategy model.

Cognitive Behavior Modification
Donald Meichenbaum at the University of Waterloo in Ontario, Canada, is a primary contributor to the cognitive behavior modification approach (CBM). Meichenbaum (1977) emphasized teaching students a variety of self-instructional strategies (e.g., self-questioning, self-checking), a variety of self-guidance strategies (e.g., "What do I have to do? I have to find the main idea in this paragraph."), and a variety of executive strategies (e.g., reflection about one's own array of strategies and selecting the strategy most appropriate to the task at hand). The goal is to train students to use verbal statements and images that prompt, direct, and maintain their behaviors (Lovitt, 1989).

In Meichenbaum's "What's my problem? What's my plan?" problem-solving program, students are taught to verbalize statements of self-correction, self-evaluation, and self-reinforcement (Meichenbaum & Goodman, 1971). Hallahan and Kauffman (1982) outlined Meichenbaum's self-instructional procedure:

1. *Cognitive modeling.* The adult model performs a task while verbally instructing himself.
2. *Overt, self-guidance.* The student performs the same task imitating instructions spoken by the model.
3. *Faded overt self-guidance.* The student softly repeats the instructions spoken by the model.
4. *Covert self-instruction.* The student performs the task while silently instructing himself.

Tarver (1986) theorizes that gradual fading of speech from overt (outward) to covert (inward) will change the student's spoken language into the inner language that typically regulates thought. According to cognitive behavior modification advocates, modeling and imitations of inner language improve thinking skills.

Cognitive Strategy Model

Another type of metacognitive approach teaches such study skills techniques as scanning, outlining, taking notes, and time management. The model is derived from cognitive psychology and information processing literature. The cognitive strategy model incorporates theories based in student learning styles, cognitive styles, thinking skills, and cognitive behavior modification research. Torgesen (1977) hypothesized that passive learning is a characteristic of many students with learning disabilities. Thus, cognitive strategy researchers addressed how students approach learning.

A descriptive scheme was devised by Kinsbourne and Caplan (1979) for distinguishing between learning disorders of cognitive "style" and those of cognitive "power." The first, those of cognitive style, refer to children characterized as having attention deficits. These students exhibit difficulties with impulsivity, distractibility, and other symptomatic behaviors of inattention. By contrast, students who display disorders of cognitive power experience difficulty grasping particular types of concepts or remembering certain kinds of information. Examples of cognitive "power" problems include dyslexia (reading disability), dyscalculia (mathematical disability), and perceptual-motor impairment (Bohline, 1985).

Knowing how one knows, metacognition, is also stressed in the cognitive strategy model (Wong, 1979). Brown (1978) summarized metacognitive processes as including the identification and analysis of the task at hand, the reflection on what one does and does not know about the situation that may be necessary for solving the problem, the designing of a plan for dealing with the problem, and the monitoring of one's progress toward solving the problem. Other assumptions in the cognitive strategy model are: (1) the learning strategies students need are relatively stable across learners and tasks, (2) the act of verbalizing a strategy assists learning, and (3) knowing how one learns is advantageous to further learning (Poplin, 1989). The following guidelines detail Meichenbaum's (1985) techniques for teaching metacognitive strategies:

1. Teachers need to adopt metacognitive outlooks. They should have the attitude that self–instructional thinking skills exist and can be taught.
2. It is important that teachers be aware of their own metacognitive skills and make students aware of these. Teachers let students down when they fail to assist students in developing metacognitive skills that they themselves find effective.
3. Teachers need to conduct a task analysis of the skills to be taught. This requires reducing the desired metacognitive skills into a series of simpler subskills.

4. Teachers must be aware that generalization of the learned metacognitive skills will not simply occur; learning opportunities that cut across various settings (e.g., home, community, work) must be employed.

A major criticism of treatment models for students with learning disabilities programs has been the lack of generalization and maintenance skills (Lovitt, 1989; Poplin, 1989). What is taught in one training site or classroom has not proven to carry over or generalize sufficiently to other settings or circumstances. When skills do not carry over, maintenence, or sustained use of them diminishes. Some suggestions for assuring generalization include tasks that place responsibility for learning on the student. These include (1) student self-instruction, (2) student self-rehearsal, (3) practice in multiple settings, (4) dividing skills into manageable portions, (5) student self-monitoring, (6) teacher feedback about performance, (7) skills taught to mastery level, and (8) teacher reinforcement of skill acquisition.

Contemporary thinking about best practices for teaching students with learning disabilities combines academics with metacognitive learning strategies. In other words, it is important that teachers focus upon academic skills; however, this can be effectively accomplished through teaching students how to learn, how to manage their own behaviors in school, and how to generalize information from one setting to another. In the following section, some suggestions are given for teaching students with learning disabilities.

Functional Domains

Student characteristics can be categorized within functional domains. These domains include cognitive abilities, processing skills, academic achievement, communication development, perceptual-motor skills, and social-adaptive skills. All domains interact; no functioning areas operate alone.

Each student needs to be viewed holistically. If one part of an auto malfunctions, the rest of the vehicle will not function properly either. Compensations can be made, but the malfunctioning part affects the overall service the car gives; for example, have you ever tried to go somewhere only to find that your car would not start because the battery was dead? You quickly learned that the best performing engine will not function at all because the starter would not turn over. You may have used a jumper cable to start your car—which means you were able to temporarily bypass the main problem. But sooner or later, the battery had to be replaced. The learning disabled are a heterogeneous group of individuals that have deficits in one or more of the functional domains. The problem can be bypassed or overlooked for a period of time—but sooner or later, the specific disorder has to be addressed.

Students with mild learning disabilities do not usually have a simple, easily identifiable problem. We cannot assume that the problem simply resides within the student. We have to look at all of the interactive components within the child's learning environment; for example, what task is the child required to perform? If it is above his or her functioning level or if instruction is inappropriate, the student may fail. Curricular and task components should be analyzed as assiduously as learner behavior. Learner characteristics by functional domains are presented on Table 5-5, along with general instructional interventions for teaching students with learning disabilities.

Cognitive Abilities

The existence of a learning disability is often detected in a particular function such as reading (Swanson, 1988) or a mental process like attention or memory (Jacobs, 1984). If the student displays deficiencies across several academic areas and has adaptive and/or social problems, the individual is showing characteristics more like that of a child with mild mental retardation.

There is overlap between cognitive functioning, intellect, and processing of information. Cognitive refers to a wide spectrum of thinking skills (e.g., memory, analysis, deduction). Jacobs (1984) defines cognition as the active process of mental awareness and thinking. Some of these skills are sampled by an IQ test.

Children without disabilities approach learning by asking themselves questions, organizing information, and using environmental cues. This process of thought is called metacognition (Ryan, Short, & Weed, 1986). Students with a learning disability typically do not acquire the skills of learning how to think through problems naturally. These students can be taught how to organize their thoughts through metacognitive training.

Students who don't utilize metacognitive strategies while learning may appear to be apathetic or passive. Torgesen (1977) reported that teachers described students with learning disabilities as dependent, lazy, impulsive, and disorganized. A negative cycle occurs when a student's academic progress is

TABLE 5–5 Teaching Students with Learning Disabilities

	Cognitive	Academic	Adaptive	Social	Perceptual/ Peceptual Motor	Language
Learner Characteristics	Normal or above average intelligence.	Uneven pattern of academic performance.	Some degree of field dependency.	Susceptible to distraction. Social imperception.	Difficulties with learning modalities and eye-hand coordination. Inadequate gross or fine motor skills.	Difficulty in reading or language skills.
Instructional Intervention	Adapt instruction to individual cognitive abilities.	Identify entry level skills for each academic area.	Emphasize independent strategies for learning.	Teach self-management skills. Make social skills training situational.	Adjust instruction to individual learning styles and physical capabilities.	Provide opportunities for language stimulation activities.

limited by his or her inadequate learning strategies. The person becomes soured towards learning, and teachers come to expect the student to be a passive learner. This cycle of failure can be changed if students are taught learning strategies.

Metacognitive training emphasizes teaching students *how* to learn rather than teaching them specific content (Tarver, 1986). Deshler et al., (1983) suggested teaching students such study skills as scanning, outlining, note taking, time management, and questioning. Tarver (1986) stated that metacognitive training includes instruction in various (1) self-monitoring strategies (e.g., self-questioning, self-interrogatives, self-checking); (2) self-instructional strategies; and (3) executive strategies (e.g., selecting the strategy most appropriate to the task or problem at hand).

Lloyd (1980) emphasized the positive benefits of using self-instructional training, sometimes called academic attack strategy training. This involves training in self-verbalization of academic strategies. The student is taught to ask himself or herself: "Am I paying attention?" "What is the problem asking me to do?" "What is my plan for solving this problem?"

Deshler, Schmaker, and Lenz (1984) look at cognitive skills as highly interactive with academic achievement, and contend that students with learning disabilities are deficient in both. Their view is supported by factors such as the high number of students with learning disabilities who (1) reach an academic plateau of fourth or fifth grade level in the tenth grade, (2) have not passed minimal competency tests, and (3) are school dropouts. Most of these students are unable to generalize what they have learned across subjects or settings. The fact that these students are reported to be less satisfied with their personal social lives and continue to live with parents after secondary school years supports the contention that they need to acquire the cognitive tools necessary for life after school.

Processing Skills

Students with learning disabilities may experience problems when attempting to process knowledge and information. Learning problems can occur during any step of the processing sequence: receiving information through the senses (e.g., visual, auditory, haptic); using integrative skills to organize, store, react to, or retrieve acquired information; and responding through movement or speech. According to the definition in Public Law 94–142 (EHA, 1975) and its amendment, Public Law 101–476 (IDEA, 1990), specific learning disability means "a disorder in one or more of the basic psychological processes involved in understanding or in using language, spoken or written" (*Federal Register*, 1977). As we have pointed out, the specific disorder is assumed to be neurological in origin, but cannot be identified (or even proven to be the cause) due to lack of access to technological procedures that can pinpoint the specific spot in the brain where a neurological dysfunction is located. Perceptual-motor deficiencies and disorders in listening, thinking, speaking, reading, writing, spelling, or mathematical calculations are typically the means by which educators or clinicians infer mental processing problems. The assumption is that some type of "blockage" is occurring along the perceptual neuro-pathways that transmit and integrate information within the brain during the act of thinking (Ramsey, 1988).

Processing skills relate directly to cognitive skills. As noted, a problem may occur in one or more of the perceptual neuro-pathways activated during learning. In school, these perceptual neuro-pathways are primarily visual or auditory. Educators use terms such as visual or auditory discrimination, visual or auditory memory, visual or auditory closure, visual or auditory sequencing, and visual or auditory blending to describe the interplay between perception and mental processing. Difficulties can occur at any point along the perceptual processing continuum: reception (input), integration (association), or expression (output).

The receptive process utilizes subskills that are essential to learning. These include attending to task, and being able to discriminate what is heard or seen (Ramsey, 1988). Attending relates to one's knowing what to pay attention to and what to ignore (Tarver, 1986). Distractibility is sometimes confused with attending as the student may be thought to be not attending when he or she is actually attending to the distraction. Learners must enhance appropriate attending skills in order to be proficient in the classroom (Tarver, 1986).

Discrimination refers to the ability to differentiate one thing from another (e.g., an object, an item, a sound). When asked to identify the letters "m" and "n," the child must visually perceive that there are two humps in "m" and only one in "n. " Children learn to discriminate by color, shape, pattern, size, position, and brightness. Eventually students must be able to visually discriminate letters and words to learn to read. This requires more intricate visual processing skills than some students with learning disabilities may have.

Subskills directly related to the auditory receptive process include auditory attending, auditory awareness, and auditory discrimination. Sometimes it is necessary for the teacher to eliminate auditory distractions within the classroom. In order to read, a child must be able to perceive individual phoneme sounds and correspond these sounds with correct letter symbols. These skills are necessary for decoding written (and spoken) languages (Ramsey, 1988).

Academic Achievement

The continued decline over the school years of the academic attainment of students with learning disabilities has been the focal point of much research (Deshler, 1978; Koppitz, 1972-1973). The impact that delayed developmental cognitive functioning has on academic progress was addressed in a study by Speece, McKinney, and Appelbaum (1986). They concluded that students with learning disabilities, even though they showed average intelligence on tests, did not catch up with their peers after 3 to 4 years of remedial services.

The disparity between academic performance and intellectual ability characterizes students with learning disabilities. The federal definition specifies academic areas in which learning disorders are manifested during school experiences. Reading, mathematics, spelling, and writing are listed. For students with learning disabilities, resource rooms serve as primary settings in which specific academic problems are addressed by special educators.

Instructional procedures must match the learning style of students in order for them to achieve success in learning to read (Ratekin, 1979). Since reading skills are necessary in every subject area (e.g., science, history, geography), Wong (1985) suggests that learning strategies be combined with teaching school subjects. Palinesar (1982) suggested, for example, that reading comprehension can be improved by teaching students self-monitoring strategies such as reciprocal questioning and summarization skills (i.e , metacognition). However, to use self-questioning skills, a student must have an adequate knowledge-base in the particular subject matter. The acquisition of knowledge may be hampered due to inattention, decoding problems, vocabulary deficiencies, poor reading comprehension skills, and inadequate instruction in content areas (Wong, 1985). It is essential that passive or inactive adolescents learn effective thinking and studying strategies, such as the cognitive strategy approach proposed by Alley and Deshler (1979).

Edge and Burton (1986) cite studies in which many students with learning disabilities are able to perform such computational skills as adding, subtracting, multiplying, and dividing, but they lack the ability to use these computational skills in problem-solving situations. These authors further point out that students need to know how to apply computational skills to financial situations that occur in everyday life.

Spelling problems are sometimes the initial reason for student referrals. In some instances, the teaching of spelling has been integrated into a broader language arts curriculum (Reid & Hresko, 1981). This tends to make the spelling task easier for students with learning disabilities. Spelling and other language-related disorders have been studied by a number of researchers. A major type of difficulty that has been pinpointed in students with learning disabilities is the incorrect utilization of standard rules in a phonics approach to spelling. Boder and Jarrico (1982) refer to these errors as phonetically inaccurate (PI). PI spelling errors contain inaccurate phoneme-grapheme (i.e., sound-symbol) correspondences. Letters of the alphabet (i.e., symbols) that correspond with phonemic sounds are not used in the spelling of words. Cicci (1983) considered these errors to reflect an underlying language disorder. Horn, O'Donnell, and Leicht (1988) determined that an excessive number of PI disorders is characteristic of persons with learning disabilities; however, other factors, such as inattention and carelessness, might also contribute to this problem. Eighteen percent of the young adult learning disabled sample in this study were characterized by PI spelling and deficient speech sound perception.

Language/Communication Development and Usage

Experts have identified specific stages of language and communication development. These stages begin with early responses to and imitations of sound, continue with one to several word sentences, go through grammatical refinement, and extend into abstract realms. Children with mild disabilities typically lag behind in language and communication skills, whereas children who excel in intellectual ability are observed to progress more rapidly through the stages.

Youngsters with learning disabilities may have specific disorders related to the general processing of language-based information (Ramsey, 1988). Like any type of processing skill, language disabilities can occur anywhere along the cognitive continuum (i.e., reception, integration, expression). Language disorders usually interfere with academic achievement, not only in subject areas like reading, spelling, language arts, and mathematics, but also in listening, thinking, and expression. Notice how language is identified as the broad-based disorder in learning disabilities in the federal definition

> *Specific learning disability means a disorder in one or more of the basic psychological processes involved in understanding or in using language spoken or written, which may manifest itself in an imperfect ability to listen, think, speak, read, write, spell, or to do mathematical calculations* (Education for the Handicapped Law Report, *1981;* Federal Register, *1977;).*

Language is a complex phenomenon. It refers to the ways in which a person receives, comprehends, and transfers thoughts to another person and to oneself (Ramsey, 1988). Five components are traditionally identified in the study of language: phonology, morphology, syntax, semantics, and pragmatics. Youth with learning disabilities may have difficulties with basic speech sounds (phonemes), units of meaning (morphemes), sentence structure (syntax), relationships between words, grammatical forms, and underlying meaning (semantics), and everyday context usage (pragmatics).

In the receptive channel, phonology refers to how well a person can discriminate speech sounds. Quite often, proficiency, or lack of it, is observed as a child attempts to form letter-sound associations. In the expressive channel, phonology refers to the production or articulation of speech sounds. Misarticulation is a major problem area in verbal expression for many children (Bryen, 1982; Lund & Duchan, 1988). Morphology refers to the linguistic structure of words and how word units (i. e., prefixes, suffixes, tense and comparative endings) change the meaning of the word. Syntax includes grammatical usage of word classes, word order, and transformational rules for the variance of word order. In other words, syntax refers to the arrangement of words within sentences. Semantics relates to the understanding and use of word meanings and vocabulary, respectively, when viewed in terms of receptive (listening and reading) and expressive (speaking and writing) abilities. Receptive and expressive skills in semantic functioning include vocabulary, categorization, ability to define, identification of synonyms and antonyms, and detection of ambiguity or absurdity. One's listening vocabulary and level of spoken vocabulary may be determined by assessment of semantic receptive and expressive skills (Bryen, 1982; Lund &

Duchan, 1988). Pragmatics is the practical application of language. It is concerned with the way language is used to communicate rather than with its structure (Owens, 1992).

Perceptual-Motor Skills

The ability to process (or use) information received through the sense organs of the body is necessary for learning. Deficits within this functioning domain may stem from the perceptual realm and underlie cognitive and motoric functions. For example, a child may incorrectly copy simple geometric designs. If she cannot "see" her errors, a problem might exist in her perceptual (input) mechanism; whereas, a child who can acknowledge her errors, but cannot correct them may have a deficiency in her motoric (output) mechanism. Likewise, a child who is unable to "write" on a paper at his desk what he "sees" on the chalkboard or in a textbook may be experiencing cross-modal difficulties. The difficulty rests in the ability to transfer from one modality to another (e.g. , visual to motor, auditory to expressive). Keep in mind that the perceptual-motor hypothesis described above is only one of the several possible explanations for a child's behavior.

According to Jacobs (1984), perception, memory, and attention are integrative processes and are used collectively to obtain information from the environment and make it meaningful. Perception is the differentiation of distinctive features with filtering of irrelevant information. Attention is affected by a person's capacity to organize and make sense of information (Reid & Hresko, 1981). Memory is dependent upon attention and how well information has been received and associated with experience. Perception, attention, and memory are necessary prerequisites for learning. Jacob suggests that each individual uses unconscious metacognition strategies to organize and remember new information.

Some students with learning disabilities have coordination problems. They may appear awkward or clumsy when attempting ordinary childhood activities like riding a bicycle, skipping, and jumping rope. Children with learning disabilities frequently develop these skills, but later than their age-mates. Problems with fine motor skills may become apparent when these children are cutting with scissors and manipulating small objects. Motor problems are most evident in school during physical education and during handwriting and art activities (Lewis & Doorlag, 1987).

Dysgraphia is a term that describes impaired handwriting skills some children demonstrate when attempting to form letters of the alphabet. The child can see accurately what to write but cannot manage correct writing movements (Bush & Waugh, 1982). An example is mirror writing. Each letter is symmetrical but backwards. This condition is not to be confused with children who have poor handwriting skills of a temporary nature due to late maturation or those who write poorly due to carelessness or lack of practice.

During the formative years of learning disabilities research (1950s–1960s), perceptual-motor differences in underachieving children with average intelligence were considered indicators of a minimal brain dysfunction. When hard-to-teach children were unable to match peers in such tasks as copying geometric shapes, researchers believed that a learning disability represented by perceptual-motor processing difficulties was present. Treatment programs were developed based on the premise that the presumed perceptual-motor dysfunction would be remediated by having students practice such worksheet tasks as connecting dots, tracing lines, and finding hidden objects in pictures. Perceptual-motor training declined in the early 1970s when basic assumptions of this approach were unsupported by research. Perceptual-motor training failed to improve academic skills, and tests used to identify perceptual-motor dysfunction were found to be unreliable.

Adaptive-Social Skills

Contrary to definitions for mental retardation and behavior disorders, there is no mention of adaptive behavior in the definition for learning disabilities. This omission is noted by experts in the field of learning disabilities (Mercer, 1983; Strawser & Weller, 1985; Weller, Strawser, & Buchanan, 1985) The researchers contend that failure to consider social skills difficulties as a trait of learning disabilities contributes to mistaken placements of students with learning disabilities in programs for students with mild mental retardation or behavior disorders.

Social skills underlie one's ability to adapt to the environment. Students with learning disabilities demonstrate adaptive behavior problems through such difficulties in school performance as lack of self-control, poor self-esteem, and inadequate interpersonal relationships. Adaptive behavior skills shape friendships, communication, and vocational choices (Weller et al., 1985). Social competence has been operationally defined as the ability to act appropriately in social situations. This is an area in which youngsters with learning disabilities may exhibit difficulties (Bryan, 1978; Carlson, 1987; McConaughy, 1986). Social competence comprises an umbrella of social skills that one needs in order to be accepted in social situations (Hops, 1983; McFall, 1982). A socially adept person selects appropriate skills in particular circumstances, and uses social skills in ways that lead to positive outcomes (Deshler & Schumaker, 1983; Larson & Gerber, 1987). Making appropriate actions and responses in social situations requires the use of adequate social perception, social knowledge, and social performance. Some individuals with learning disabilities lack the ability to perceive social situations correctly, show deficiencies in social "know-how" skills, and fail to act appropriately. These students require instruction in the use of social skills (Wojnilower & Gross, 1988).

Several factors have been suggested as contributors to social problems of children with learning disabilities. Carlson (1987) reported studies that showed those with learning disabilities have processing deficits in social comprehension and misinterpret social situations. Specific cognitive functions may be affected in some persons with learning disabilities that cause an impaired ability to understand or empathize with another person's feelings, make inferences about social cues, or predict and evaluate consequences for social behavior (Schumaker &

Hazel, 1984). Margalit and Shulman (1986) concluded that individuals with learning disabilities exhibit anxious behavior due to dependency needs. They sometimes misinterpret information from their environment and misperceive social cues (Fine, 1987). Both are problem areas related to perceptual and cognitive deficiencies. Such students adopt an egocentric perspective and exhibit an inability to shift the focus away from themselves (Derr, 1986). An overwhelming number of studies indicate problems including social competence, personal failure in social interaction (Bryan, Donahue, & Pearl, 1981) and peer relationships (Bruininks, 1978; Bryan, 1974).

Researchers report that delinquent behaviors and antisocial acts characterize a significant number of adolescents with learning disabilities (Bryan, Werner, & Pearl, 1982; Larson & Gerber, 1987; McConaughy, 1986). Even as children, these youngsters evidently lack the skills and inner control to handle age-appropriate tasks and to manage their own behavior (McWhirter, McWhirter, & McWhirter, 1985). Because of this, they may receive negative feedback from family and neighbors. Messages like this lessen feelings of self-worth (McConaughy, 1986). Thus, by adolescence, it is not surprising when students with learning disabilities exhibit behaviors that are out of step with prevailing values.

Zigmond, Levin, and Laurie (1985) reported tardiness, absenteeism, and off-task behavior by high school students with learning disabilities. Ysseldyke and his colleagues (1982) observed no differences in the classroom behaviors of elementary nonlearning-disabled children and those with learning disabilities. Contrary to this finding, other researchers found that children with learning disabilities, when compared to nonlearning-disabled elementary students, spend more time off-task (McKinney et al., 1982) and engage in more non task-related behaviors (Sherry, 1982).

Suggestions for Teaching Students with Learning Disabilities

1. Teach the student to organize materials and assignments. Use lists to establish work priorities. Teach study skills.

2. Help the student to think through steps in completing a task. Use questions such as the following as a guide: "How much time do I have to complete a task? What materials will I need? Who can I ask for help?"

3. Overlook such minor errors in written work as spelling and handwriting. Emphasize quality of ideas and perseverance .

4. Provide right hemispheric activities such as art, drama, and images to represent ideas. Don't overemphasize such left hemispheric functions as verbal reasoning, logic, and sequential arrangement of ideas.

5. Provide emotional support to help ease the frustration of a learning disability.

6. Provide options during tests such as untimed or oral exams. List answers to multiple choice questions vertically rather than horizontally.

7. Give clear and concrete directions. Have the student repeat instructions back to you.

8. Link new ideas to the student's experience.

9. Use multisensory materials. Repeat concepts, but use novel presentations rather than drill.

10. Collaborate with parents.

Summary

The search for appropriate terminology that would identify learning disabilities continues to challenge educators. The first terms used to describe this population emphasized medical and neurological processing deficits. The most popular and widely accepted name was "minimal brain dysfunction," or "MBD."

In 1962, Kirk suggested the name "learning disabilities." This new classification was intended to distinguish persons with learning disorders and average intelligence from other exceptionality categories, especially mental retardation. Many students were identified as mentally retarded during the 1940s and 1950s, because the category learning disabilities didn't exist. The classification "learning disabled" was adopted following Kirk's use of this term to link together students with average intelligence and presumed mild neurological disorders.

The current federal definition of learning disabilities was formulated in 1968 by the National Advisory Committee on Handicapped Children. This definition served as the basis for the Learning Disabilities Act of 1969, and was subsequently included in Public Law 94–142, the Education for All Handicapped Children Act of 1975. Thus, this definition is widely used in providing appropriate public education to students who are eligible for services because of a learning disability. The functional part of the federal definition is referred to as the discrepancy formula.

The prevalence of learning disabilities has been reported by states to be between 2 and 5 percent of the school-aged population. The number of existing cases eludes accuracy because methods and criteria used for identification differ from state to state. In lieu of data reported by respective states showing otherwise, federal estimates have remained at 2 percent.

The etiology of learning disabilities has been classified into two groups: organic and environmental. The majority of students identified as having learning disabilities have no demonstrable organic problem, thus their causes are assumed to be environmentally based. These cases result from inadequate or negative environmental factors, including poor instruction and a schooling system which makes few allowances for developmental differences within like age-groups of children. The case for organic based learning disabilities is much stronger for students with specific, localized conditions such as dyslexia, dysgraphia, and dysnomia. These conditions are more universally known, described, and documented.

Characteristics of students with learning disabilities are classified by developmental domains of functioning. These functioning domains include cognitive skills, academic achievement, language and communication development, perceptual and perceptual-motor skills, and social-adaptive skills. Students with learning disabilities demonstrate learning difficulties in at least one of these functioning domains.

From the 1940s to the 1990s, treatment models evolved in response to theories about the causes of learning disabilities. For example, the medical approach of the 1940s and 1950s advocated the use of heavily structured and controlled learning environments to offset presumed neurological deficits. Programs were developed during the 1960s which attempted to ameliorate perceptual deficits. This approach is called the psychological process approach.

Interaction between the learner and the environment was the major emphasis during the 1970s. This is the behavioral approach. Arranging the environment, reinforcing appropriate behavior, and using systematic instructional approaches in the teaching of academic skills are components of this model. Contemporary thinking, brought over from the 1980s into the 1990s, states that it is important to teach academics, but it is also necessary to teach students how to learn, how to manage their own behaviors in school, and how to generalize information from one setting to another. Cognitive/learning strategies models emphasize the need to produce self-sufficient, independent learners for a lifetime.

$$Chapter \quad 6$$

Mainstreaming

Advance Organizer

When you complete this chapter, you will be able to:

1. Explain the relationship of mainstreaming to the least restrictive environment.
2. Describe the range of special services for students with special needs.
3. Describe strategies for successful mainstreaming.
4. Compare the benefits of peer tutoring and cooperative learning.
5. Explain the role of the consulting teacher.
6. Compare and contrast instructional practices that facilitate mainstreaming.

   The Whole Language Approach to Reading
   Adaptive Learning Environment Model
   Career Education
   Direct Instruction
   Open Education
   Skillstreaming
   Computer Assisted Instruction

7. Explain pros and cons of the Regular Education Initiative.
8. Discuss areas of mutual reform interest for both regular and special educators.
9. Explain how special and regular educators can benefit from collaboration.

Frank Williams could name the exact day he decided to quit teaching students with mild disabilities. It wasn't that he didn't like teaching his special class at Jackson Elementary

School. For the first time in their lives, Frank's students enjoyed school. They were learning new skills and gaining confidence in themselves. By all measures Frank was a success. His special class for students with learning and emotional disabilities had received accolades from numerous professionals including education professors from the nearby university. Frank seemed to be doing all the right things, but it all ended abruptly for him on Tuesday, January 27.

It was an ordinary morning, but Frank knew there was going to be trouble when Ben climbed off his school bus and stormed into the classroom. "They called me retarded," Ben said as he slammed his books on his desk. Mark filed in next. "The kids on the corner say we ride the 'retard bus'." Mark's face was red and he appeared ready to explode. The boys' anger set off a chain reaction among Frank's other students as they described the humiliation of riding a special education bus to school.

That afternoon while Frank was driving home, he came to a simple but powerful conclusion. Any success he had as a teacher would never offset the stigma his students felt because of their placement in a special class. The neighborhood kids were wrong; his students were not retarded. But what difference did the label make? The fact remained that his students wanted to be accepted as normal kids. This was more important to them than reading, math, or a high school diploma. Frank's world was turned topsy-turvey when the magnitude of his situation sunk in. By developing a model special education program, Frank was contributing to the segregation of his students. Sure he was planning to mainstream some of them soon, but Frank knew that as soon as a few moved out, the school system would quickly replace them with others. As the weeks passed, Frank realized he could no longer teach special education students in a self-contained, special education program. At the end of the year, Frank resigned and entered graduate school.

Frank, like many other good special education teachers, was caught in a Catch-22 situation. If he continued to develop an exemplary special class program, he would get more referrals and placements. As his reputation grew, it would be easier for his school system administrators to convince parents that a special class was the best choice for their children; yet Frank's goal was to mainstream his students into regular classrooms. He was enough of a realist to understand that special education classes were dead-end solutions. The longer a student stayed in a special class, the less likely he or she would ever return to a regular education program. As Frank saw it, the cards were stacked against kids who didn't fit into the system. It was ironic, he thought, that the better he became as a special educator, the more he would contribute to limiting his students' opportunities.

Frank's story illustrates a basic principle of human nature. Each of us wants to be viewed as normal. When students are categorized and shipped into special classrooms, they are viewed as deviants by their peers and eventually by themselves. During the civil rights struggle of the 1960s and 1970s, many people fought, and some died, in order that others could be integrated into the mainstream of society. Today individuals with disabilities are fighting those same battles and the stakes are just as high. In 1954, the Supreme Court ruled in *Brown* v. *The Topeka Board of Education* that separate but equal was unconstitutional. Yet separation of disabled and nondisabled is a commonplace occurrence in public schools. In 1989 over a million students with special needs were segregated by categories of disabilities in separate classrooms and special schools.

The integration of students with special needs into the regular classroom is called mainstreaming. It is one of the most discussed and least understood concepts in special education. When Public Law 92–142 known as the Education for All Handicapped Children Act was passed in 1975, the media dubbed it the "mainstreaming law." Many educators believed mainstreaming meant students with mild to severe disabilities would be placed in regular classrooms.

The worst fears of educators who viewed the federal law as an intrusion into the regular classroom never materialized. Rather, an opposite trend began to build—the movement of students out of regular education into special education programs. In 1977, 3,708,601 students received special education services; ten years later 4,421,601 students were identified as disabled and receiving special education services (Jordan, 1989). While the total special education population grew by 700,000, the number of students with mild disabilities skyrocketed. For example, in 1977 there were 797,226 students with learning disabilities identified in the public schools. By 1989, the number of students with a learning disability rose to 1,973,291 (U.S. Department of Education, 1990).

Rather than more special education students put in regular classrooms, we are witnessing a reverse trend—more regular education students are placed in special education programs. We estimate that approximately 15,000 students are referred each week for special education services. During the 1980s in Massachusetts some urban school systems reported 20 percent or more of the entire student population in special education programs. Where did all these special education students come from? Were they sitting undetected in regular classrooms, or have special education mandates provided a fast track out of regular education for problem learners?

The Least Restrictive Environment

The term mainstreaming does not appear in federal legislation; rather, the mandate for keeping special education students in regular education comes from the "least restrictive environment" provision of the law. When students are educated in the least restrictive environment, they are taught in classrooms that most closely approximate a normal learning situation. For many students with mild disabilities, the least restrictive environment is full-time placement in a regular classroom. For students who require more intensive remedial help, the least restrictive environment would be part-time resource room instruction with the majority of their school day spent in the regular classroom. When students with special needs are segregated in full-time special classes or alternative special education programs, they are in the *most* restrictive environment. Their opportunities to associate with nonspecial needs children are severely limited.

When a student with a mild disabling condition is placed in a special education program, there is a presumption that it is a temporary situation. Placement in a special education program is no badge of distinction for child or parent. Indeed, if parents suspected that once identified as having a special need their youngster would be permanently tracked in special education, it is unlikely that they would be so cooperative and eager to have their child receive special education services.

When Gartner and Lipsky requested data from the federal government on numbers of special education students who return full-time to regular education, they received the following reply.

> *Thank you for your letter in which you ask about data concerning children who had been certified as handicapped and have returned to regular education. While these are certainly very interesting data you request, these data are not required in State Plans nor has the Office for Special Education Programs collected them in any other survey. (Gartner & Lipsky, 1987, 367)*

The absence of data on the success rate of students returned to regular education raises questions about program efficacy and the ability of special education services to remediate learning difficulties.

In a study of three American cities—Milwaukee, Wisconsin; Charlotte, North Carolina; and Rochester, New York—researchers found that over a two-year period 17 percent of youngsters with special needs terminated special education services and returned full-time to the regular classroom. The remaining 83 percent of students remained in special education (Walker et al., 1988). The majority of the students in the study were identified as speech impaired, mentally retarded, learning disabled, and emotionally disturbed. Students identified as speech impaired (33 percent) were most likely to return to regular education. Children identified as learning disabled had the next highest return rate (14.9 percent). Students with emotional or behavioral problems were more likely to be reclassified than returned full-time to regular education classrooms. Two years after initial placement, less than one in ten students with emotional disturbance returned to regular education.

When students with disabilities are kept out of the mainstream of normal school life, it underscores the differences between them and students without disabilities. Indeed many separate special education programs are classified by such categories of disabilities as emotionally disturbed, mentally retarded, or behavior disordered. When a student is grouped with eight to ten other "emotionally disturbed" students, taught in a program by a teacher who is trained in "emotional disturbance," and isolated in a special classroom that is located in a secluded area of the school, it is unlikely that the student will either feel or act "normal."

The intent of the least restrictive environment provision of the law is to assure that a student's special education program is as normal as possible. Each school system is required to provide a continuum of special education placements. Figure 6–1 lists special education programs for learners with special needs ranging from least to most restrictive environments. Once the bold line is crossed, a student is out of the mainstream, and the prospects for return to a normal school experience are bleak. This might be a good time to return to Chapter 1 and review the descriptions of each type of special education placement.

Successful Mainstreaming

Teachers want their students to develop the skills and self-confidence necessary for successful adjustment to life after school. Research journals and special education textbooks contain many references to mainstreaming. These articles and essays describe the advantages of integrated schooling; for example, students with mild disabilities develop better academic and socialization skills when they are educated in well-organized mainstreamed classrooms (Guralnick & Groom, 1988; Wang & Baker, 1986). Yet there are reports about failed mainstreaming and teacher concerns for students who are "over their heads" or "lost" in regular classrooms. As Susan Ohanian states, it takes more than good intentions and

Least Restrictive

INTEGRATED

1. Full-time regular classroom placement with support services.

2. Resource room (pull-out) program for part of the day.

SEGREGATED

3. Full-time placement in self-contained special classroom in regular school.

4. Special day or alternative school program outside of regular school.

5. Homebound/Hospital.

6. Residential facility.

7. Correctional facility.

Most Restrictive

FIGU RE 6–1 Range of Special Education Placements

administrative fiat to make mainstreaming work. In the following excerpt from "P.L 94-142: Mainstream or Quicksand," she highlights the folly of unplanned mainstreaming endeavors.

> *When following the mandates of P.L. 94-142 we need to figure out just what it means to mainstream children "to the maximum extent appropriate to their needs." Many school districts lump all children with learning problems together in a sort of academic twilight zone. The educable mentally retarded [i.e., students with mild mental retardation], the low normal, the learning disabled (whatever that means this week), and the emotionally disturbed are all sent off to regular English, science, social studies, and mathematics classes—until the situation becomes too traumatic either for the child or for the teacher. I always figured my district had to see blood before it would demainstream a child. (Ohanian, 1990, 219)*

Mainstreaming works if benefits are accrued by students with special needs, regular education students, and their teachers. A regular education teacher who is asked to take a youngster with a mild disability into her classroom might legitimately ask, "What's in it for me and my students?" After all, is it fair to ask regular educators to teach special education students at the expense of the other students? The answer is unequivocal—no. A mainstreaming program that does not have something for everybody is headed for failure. Teachers, administrators, and parents will not tolerate the education of a minority of students if it takes away from the learning of the majority.

Wang and Baker's (1986) meta-analysis of eleven empirical studies on mainstreaming indicated that mainstreamed students consistently achieved better than non-mainstreamed students with comparable disabilities. The paradox of students with special needs doing better in regular rather than special education programs can be explained by several factors.

1. The research on the ineffectiveness of tracking students by ability groups demonstrates that students perform better academically in heterogeneous groups than in homogeneous groups (Lewis, 1990; Massachusetts Department of Education, 1991).

2. Modeling enhances learning. Students naturally imitate their peers. Good peer models provide teachers with success examples that can help encourage students with learning problems to strive harder.

3. Teacher expectations for success go up in relationship to perception of a student's capability. Mainstreamed students may benefit from increased teacher expectations because the student is perceived to be ready to succeed in the regular classroom.

4. Teachers who were used as mainstreaming research subjects may try harder to succeed with their students. The "Hawthorne Effect" (i.e., trying harder

to excel because of the perceived special status of being a research subject) is well-documented in research annals.

5. How students feel about their abilities has a lot to do with success. Students in special education programs may feel stigmatized. This can affect motivation and perseverance, two crucial elements in school success.

6. Teachers who agree to accept mainstreamed students may be more skilled than their colleagues.

One of the major rationales for mainstreaming is that it provides a better academic environment for students with mild disabilities than either pull-out (resource room) programs or separate special education classes. Students in special education programs can be caught in a paradox when the primary criteria for mainstreaming is attainment of skills that are best learned in the regular classroom.

Careful planning precedes the implementation of successful mainstreaming programs. Ronald Brandt's observation that the freeway of American education is littered with the wrecks of famous bandwagons aptly applies to mainstreaming. Mainstreaming will not work if teachers are coerced to comply or if special and regular educators are not given ample time to plan together. The research on mainstreaming provides enough illustrations of failed mainstreaming programs to make the point that mainstreaming is not a panacea. Students cannot be mainstreamed with the expectation that simply seating students with mild disabilities next to other youngsters in a regular classroom is a formula for success. There are five basic strategies that help ensure a mainstreaming program will work for both teachers and students. By following these guidelines, teachers will increase the probability of a successful mainstreaming program.

Establish Entrance Criteria

Full-time placement in the regular classroom begins with identification of criteria for mainstreaming. Criteria might include such classroom behaviors as "follows directions" and "works independently." When regular and special educators work together to develop criteria for a particular classroom or school, a mainstreaming program has the best chance for success (Morsink, Thomas, & Correa, 1991).

While some educators recommend academic criteria for mainstreaming, this approach should be used cautiously. For the majority of youngsters with mild disabilities, it was lack of academic skills that prompted their removal from regular classes in the first place. Strict academic criteria for mainstreaming, such as reading at grade level, may in fact act as a screening system to keep students out of the regular classroom. The notion of grade level as an academic goal is misleading because the statistical concept is based on 50 percent of a student population reading below the standard set for grade level!

Understand Student Needs

Full-time entry into a regular classroom can be an anxiety provoking experience for a student. Special education programs provide a safe haven from the demands of normal school routines, and a mainstreamed student may experience "newness panic." Some students withdraw, while others act out in uncharacteristic ways. It is not unusual for a recently mainstreamed student to regress to disruptive behaviors that the special education teacher thought were eliminated. The first few weeks is not the time to evaluate the viability of the mainstreaming decision. The mainstreamed student needs reassurance that a few bumps in the road will be tolerated.

When a student is identified as having a mild disability, it is sometimes difficult to remember that the student has the same developmental needs of other children. Students with mild disabilities are more alike than different from nondisabled students. A student with dyslexia has difficulty reading, but this academic activity is a small slice of a youngster's daily experience. Students with dyslexia play Little League, get into trouble, and sing in church choirs, just like other children. All adolescents share a common need for group approval and independence from authority. These developmental needs are just as immediate in a youngster with an emotional or behavior disorder as with other adolescents. Interpreting a youngster's behavior from a developmental perspective rather than an assigned school label provides a clearer picture of a youngster's actions.

Prepare for a Change

Regular and special education classrooms differ in many respects (Deno, Maruyma, Espin, & Cohen, 1990). A self-contained special class, for instance, ranges from eight to twelve students. In the special class, a youngster has an individualized academic program and constant adult attention. Regular classrooms, on the other hand, contain large groups of twenty to thirty-five students. In the regular classroom, students must follow directions, wait for teacher assistance, and concentrate on learning tasks with minimum adult supervision. Before a student is mainstreamed, it makes sense to begin a transition program to help prepare the student for the upcoming change.

Because educational materials, routines, and behavioral expectations are different in the regular classroom, the student can begin adapting while still in the special education program. The special educator can teach practices that are routine in the regular classroom. For example, the regular classroom teacher might require note taking or homework. The use of textbooks, and regular classroom assignments, can begin in the special education program. The student needs success with new routines and activities in the secure confines of the special program in order to build confidence for regular classroom performance.

Adequate preparation requires communication and planning between special and regular educators (Schulte, Osborne, & McKinney, 1990; Zigmond & Baker, 1990). Before and after the student is mainstreamed, meetings between teachers provide a basis for problem-solving, goal-setting, and evaluation of student progress. As an illustration, the special and regular teachers may decide to begin mainstreaming gradually. The student begins by spending forty-five minutes a day in the regular classroom for the first month. The teachers decide to pick a high interest time, such as science, where the special education student would work on a small group project with her new classmates. This plan would decrease student anxieties about academics, while providing an opportunity to make friends. During the initial month, the special and regular educators evaluate progress and make adjustments in classroom routines.

Mainstreaming places an additional burden on the regular classroom teacher. Before a student is mainstreamed, the classroom teacher, special education teacher, and building level administrator need a plan to provide support for the regular classroom teacher. Support could include additional planning time, consultation, team teaching, new instructional materials, or a teacher aide.

Every class develops its own character, and the entrance of a new student is bound to disrupt the group dynamics. This is a normal function of all groups and is not a signal that something is wrong. The manner in which the student is accepted by the rest of the class is a crucial determinant of success. Films, role playing, class discussions, visits by adults with disabilities, disability simulations, and books about children with disabilities are a few ideas that have helped regular education students adapt to the entrance of a new student. These preparations help foster acceptance of a student with a mild disability.

Evaluate Student Progress

Enormous amounts of time and money are spent by school systems to assess the educational status of children referred for special education. Norm-referenced tests measure how they compare in academics to their peers. Criterion-referenced tests pinpoint specific strengths and weaknesses in academics. Psychological tests attempt to determine if a student has mild mental retardation, a learning disability, or an emotional disturbance. Observations detail learning styles and student ability to adapt to classroom routines. These are the most common evaluation procedures used to identify and place youngsters in special programs.

Once a student has moved full-time into the regular classroom, the need to evaluate progress does not diminish. However, evaluation methods shift to curriculum-based assessment. Samples of student work, observations of student interaction, and charting of student progress provide detailed evaluative information. The student's individual education program is reviewed to match student learning objectives with classroom work. Evaluation also includes assessment of teaching behavior. Does the teacher provide enough time for the student to answer questions? Are classroom materials adapted to meet student needs? Is the student seated in an area of the room that makes it easier to concentrate and follow teacher directions? Is the teacher providing enough hands-on activities to help students master specific skills? These are a sample of questions that could guide observations of teaching methods with mainstreamed youngsters.

Communicate with Parents

Parents play a vital role in student achievement. Parents of students with mild disabilities attend individual education program conferences, participate in decisions regarding type of special services, and approve placement changes. Lack of communication between teachers and parents can foster misunderstandings and adversarial positions. Parents are concerned about their youngster's progress in school. They want to be kept informed and need to know that the teacher respects their views.

Sometimes parents have ambivalent feelings about schools and teachers. They may have had difficulties in school themselves, which cause them to feel apprehensive when dealing with school personnel. Some parents feel guilty that they have failed their youngster, and the identification of their child's special need reinforces feelings of inadequacy. Single parents, in particular, face a problem of dealing with numerous child raising issues.

Often the only time parents hear from the teacher is when something is wrong. A weekly note indicating classroom successes, a home visit, or a monthly phone call to review student progress can bridge the communication gap between home and school. Parents can provide information on a student's interests, likes, dislikes, and time spent outside of school. When parents feel that the teacher values their input, crossover learning between school and the family is more likely to occur. A productive teacher-parent partnership can be a powerful alliance for change and growth in a youngster's life. We discuss teacher-parent partnerships in more detail in chapter 9.

Mainstream Models

Every profession has models for putting theories to work. Economists have supply and demand models for explaining changes in financial trends. Psychologists use developmental models to explain human behavior. Like a blueprint, a model provides a set of instructions for the application of an idea. Education has many models. There are instructional models, assessment models, and discipline models. In education, a model is judged in terms of its usefulness. An elaborate model of instruction may be well-researched in terms of how children learn, but if it requires too much teacher time or is too expensive to implement, teachers will look someplace else for ideas. Teachers like practical ideas that increase student competence. A good idea for one teacher may seem esoteric or nonfunctional to another. Teachers adopt models that match their professional philosophy and personal values.

Mainstreaming has been a national topic since the passage of Public Law 94-142 (EHA) in 1975. This concept was reaffirmed by the passage of Public Law 101–476 (IDEA) in 1990. Over the ensuing years, many educators have attempted to develop a blueprint for successful integration of students with and without disabilities. A set of guidelines for mainstreaming qualifies as a model when it has proven effective in a variety of educational programs. This is no easy task because circumstances vary so much from region to region, system to system, and from school to school. The following three topics: collaborative learning, consulting teacher, and instructional practices describe mainstreaming models that have proven useful in many classrooms.

Collaborative learning programs have the advantage of increasing learning time of both disabled and nondisabled students. It capitalizes on the most valuable classroom resource—the students. The consulting teacher model has strong appeal because it offers the promise of cost effectiveness, while improving educational services. Instructional practices describe specific teaching approaches that bridge the gap between regular and special education classrooms.

The three approaches to mainstreaming: collaborative learning, consulting teacher, and instructional practices have produced results throughout the country in secondary, elementary, and preschool classrooms. Each model can stand on its own or be combined with other models and strategies. Ultimately, the choice of a mainstreaming model depends on how well it matches the needs of students, teachers, and parents.

Collaborative Learning

How much time out of a typical school day are students actually learning? This is a question that garnered the attention of educators during the 1980s. There is a significant correlation between time spent engaged in learning and academic achievement. Engaged learning means that students are doing something that demonstrates they are thinking about the task at hand. Writing or oral reading are examples of engaged learning. Sitting quietly and looking at the teacher is not an example of engaged learning. The students could be daydreaming. Educators who study how time is used in the classroom report students spend from 40 percent to 26 percent of their day actually engaged in learning (Rich & Ross, 1989; Ysseldyke & Algozzine, 1990).

Why don't students spend more of their school day engaged in learning? One reason is student passivity. In teacher-directed classrooms, students are unable to proceed with their learning without teacher permission. Students spend large chunks of time waiting for the teacher. When twenty to thirty students depend on one person for instruction, feedback, and permission, then significant periods of time are wasted.

Collaborative learning is a method for increasing student engaged time by having students teach other students. There are two types of collaborative learning: peer tutoring and cooperative learning. There are three types of peer tutoring: cross-age tutoring, same age tutoring, and youngsters with and without disabilities tutoring each other. Cooperative learning is a teaching strategy that groups students together to work towards common instructional objectives. Peer tutoring and cooperative learning promote the idea that students are capable of contributing to the intellectual life of the classroom.

Peer Tutoring

One of the best ways to learn something is to teach it to someone else. Cloward (1976) reported that high school students in a New York City antipoverty program gained nearly five months on grade level for each month they tutored another student. Peer tutoring can be equally effective for students with and without mild disabilities. For example, Maheady, Sacca, & Harper (1988) established a classwide peer tutoring program for fifty tenth-grade social studies students. The students ranged in age from fifteen to seventeen years. Weekly study guides developed by regular and special education teachers were used as the basis for half-hour tutoring periods, three times a week. Progress was measured by weekly quizzes. The researchers reported that the implementation of CWPT (classwide peer tutoring) resulted in an increase in test scores for both special and regular education students.

Peer tutoring places the responsibility for learning on the student. This is a potent change for students with mild disabilities who are often passive learners. With a tutor, students accustomed to sitting alone at their desks waiting for the teacher are directly involved in their learning. Peer tutoring provides individualized instruction. The non-threatening aspect of peer tutoring encourages students to admit a lack of understanding without concern about adult evaluation. Working with another student provides a youngster with opportunities to discuss, question, practice, and evaluate learning with immediate feedback. Jenkins and Jenkins (1981) described seven steps to implement a peer tutoring program.

1. *Determine which children are to be tutored.* Start small. Begin with four or five students who like to work with other children. Slow development of a tutoring program gives the teacher opportunities to restructure tutoring sessions as needed. Tutoring is not for everyone. Students who are serious behavior problems may not respond well to working with fellow students.

2. *Prepare the school for tutoring.* The principal and teachers who are involved in the program must be convinced that a tutoring program will not disrupt regular school activities. A written proposal outlining scheduling and monitoring procedures will insure that all participants are clear about each person's role. Accountability is a major issue in schools. The tutoring program developer should reassure the other teachers that time used for tutoring will not detract from the tutor's classroom performance.

3. *Determine a time for tutoring.* Daily sessions of one half-hour produce the best peer tutoring results. Peer tutoring within the classroom does not present the scheduling difficulties that occur when two separate classes are involved. Working out a program between classrooms requires careful negotiation of time and space—two valuable commodities in schools. Establish a set time each day for tutoring sessions. When a program is initiated, adjustments in plans are almost always required. This is a normal consequence of implementing a novel idea. Build in a first week evaluation, with the expectation that adjustments in schedules will be needed.

4. *Inform parents about the program.* Parents are always curious about school programs that vary from traditional teacher instruction. In public schools, even minor changes can have a ripple effect. Some teachers, particularly those who are not involved in the program, may be suspicious of its value. It is best that parents receive written notice about peer tutoring rather than hearing about it from their children or other parents. Such a letter would contain a brief description of the program skills that students will learn, program supervision methods, and evaluation procedures. Invite parents to school to observe the tutoring program in action.

5. *Design lessons and a measurement system.* Decide what content tutors are to teach; then specifically detail tutoring methods. For example, a reading lesson might involve five minutes of listening to oral reading followed by the tutee writing a list of words she found difficult. Then the tutee could write a sentence containing each word. Tutors need clear guidelines for their work. Avoid unstructured tutoring sessions where the students are not sure of their responsibilities. Detailing student progress on daily charts is a recommended procedure for keeping track of program effectiveness.

6. *Conduct tutor training.* Although tutorial skills will vary with age and content, there are some general training needs applicable to all tutors. Each tutor should be clear about punctuality, confidentiality, and positive regard for the tutee. Schoolwork needs to be evaluated in a systematic manner. The tutor will need to understand how progress is measured. Daily charts, percentage of correct answers, or random samples of behavior are examples of data that tutors commonly are asked to maintain.

The tutor will require training. A natural tendency to prompt or do the work for a tutee can be addressed by the teacher modeling proper instructional behavior. The tutor is a helper. This requires the ability to interact in a positive manner. Some key interpersonal skills are active listening and praising good effort. Change behaviors that intimidate or cause the tutee to feel incompetent. Model error correction behaviors that encourage sustained effort.

7. *Maintain tutor's involvement and interest.* Frequent reminders of the tutor's positive contributions can be gleaned from tutee progress charts. Special recognition at assemblies or through the awarding of certificates will serve the dual purpose of rewarding tutors and encouraging other students to be involved with the program. Teaching is no less a difficult endeavor for a youngster than it is for an adult. Periodic group meetings with tutors can provide the program developer with opportunities for refining the program and boosting morale.

Peer tutoring is cost effective, and it provides a student with individual attention. If conducted in a thoughtful and systematic manner, peer tutoring can increase school achievement and motivation of both students.

Cooperative Learning

According to William Glasser (Gough, 1987), when students lack control over their learning, motivation to persevere is undermined. Glasser contends that student cooperation and motivation demonstrated in extracurricular activities can be transferred into the classroom. Cooperative learning is a method of structuring small groups of nondisabled and disabled students so that all the individuals achieve a learning goal through mutual planning and decision making.

Cooperative learning can be used with all age groups to teach any part of the curriculum. Putnam and her colleagues (1989) compared fifty studies of cooperative, competitive, and individualistic learning situations. Cooperative learning produced more instances of positive relationships between students with and without disabilities. Benefits from cooperative learning include: increased student motivation, higher test scores, and enhanced social skills (Johnson & Johnson, 1986; Putnam, Rynders, Johnson, & Johnson, 1989; Slavin, Madden, & Leavey, 1984; Smith, 1987).

There are 4 steps to establishing cooperative learning groups in the classroom:

1. *The teacher selects members of each learning group.* Cooperative learning groups are heterogeneous in composition with a balance between males and females, high and low achievers, and active and passive students. A typical group would include three to six students with no more than one student with a mild disability. The balance of the groups is crucial to insure that each group has strengths to offset individual academic or social weaknesses.

2. *The teacher directly teaches cooperative group skills.* Most students are conditioned to earn grades based on individual work, often in competition with other students. Such familiar refrains in classrooms as, "Pay attention to your own work," or "no talking while we are working" are antithetical to cooperative learning. The teacher who uses cooperative learning wants students to talk and work with each other. Cooperative learning requires such interpersonal skills as the ability to trust and work with others; good listening skills; acceptance and support of others; and the ability to resolve conflicts constructively (Johnson & Johnson, 1990).

Some students may have difficulty making the transition from passive, teacher directed learning, to cooperative learning activities. Roy Smith (1987) found he needed to teach his junior high school students how to work cooperatively. He described six steps for teaching cooperative skills:

a. Identify the specific skills group members will need to demonstrate; for instance, listening or providing information.
b. Help students become aware of the need for cooperative skills.
c. Help students gain a clear understanding of each skill.
d. Provide students with situations to practice cooperative skills.
e. Give students descriptive feedback on their performance of each skill.
f. Persevere in practicing the skill. Role playing, group discussions, brainstorming sessions, and observer feedback of group activities are a sample of classroom methods that help students acquire and reinforce cooperative group skills.

3. *The teacher assigns cooperative group activities.* There is a difference between small group work and cooperative learning. In typical small group activities, students are given an assignment with little attention paid to how they will work together. A common complaint about small group activities is that a few students do all the work. In cooperative group activities students work together towards a common goal, and the group tasks are equally divided among group members. One approach to subdividing group participation is the "jigsaw" strategy. The group is given an assignment, and each member has part of the materials needed to complete the task; for instance, the assignment could be a group report on drugs. Each student would have a different source of information, such as a medical reference book, newspaper clippings, magazine articles, and an encyclopedia.

Another approach for beginning cooperative groups is to assign each member a specific role to facilitate the group work. One student would be responsible for reviewing suggestions, another would question individual members to elicit their ideas, while a third group member could be responsible for keeping the group on track. When students are experienced in cooperative learning, it is possible to turn virtually any part of the school curriculum into a collaborative learning experience.

4. *The teacher evaluates group efforts.* In cooperative groups, students learn that they sink or swim together. There are two levels of group assessment:

    a. Did the group accomplish its goal?
    b. How well did the group work together?

Products such as a classroom presentation or tests where individual scores are averaged to give a group score are examples of ways teachers have evaluated group goals. Self reporting by groups or observer feedback on group dynamics can provide information on group interaction. Group evaluation should be criterion-referenced. Before the group work begins, the teacher should clearly outline the criteria used for group evaluation. For example, a cooperative group activity on drug abuse could conclude by members summarizing each other's contributions.

Tanteyama-Sniezek (1990) cautions against investing too much enthusiasm in cooperative learning as a tool to increase academic achievement of students with mild disabilities. She points out that more studies need to be undertaken that include students with mild disabilities in cooperative learning groups. Stevens and Slavin (1991) took issue with Tanteyama-Sniezek's findings. They pointed out that when group rewards and individual accountability are both included in cooperative learning activities, the outcomes for students with and without disabilities are positive.

Both peer tutoring and cooperative learning groups capitalize on students as classroom resources. The active involvement of students in their own learning enhances mainstreaming efforts by fostering social relationships between students, increasing student motivation, and supporting the acquisition of skills.

A poster in a teacher's classroom, who used cooperative learning activities, summarizes the impact of collaborative learning strategies. It simply states, "None of us is smarter than all of us," (Smith, 1987, 664).

Consulting Teacher

One of the most often cited criticisms of the teaching profession is the lack of career options for those who are not inclined towards administration. Teachers can spend thirty years in a classroom with few opportunities to share their wisdom or expertise. The consulting teacher is a role that can enhance teacher effectiveness by replacing direct special instruction of students with collaboration between special and regular education teachers. Consultation enables teachers with diverse expertise to generate creative solutions to mutually defined problems (Idol, Paolucci-Whitcomb, & Nevin, 1986).

The consulting teacher model is an alternative to the pull-out approach to special education services (Phillips & McCullough, 1990). Instead of working directly with special needs students (for example, in a resource room), the consulting teacher plans with the regular classroom teacher to facilitate mainstreaming. Some of the responsibilities of the consulting teacher include observing in the regular classroom, sharing materials with the regular classroom teacher, demonstrating instructional techniques, coordinating programs, and presenting inservice workshops for regular educators.

The consulting teacher model provides intervention at the site of the learning problem. Both the student with the learning problem or the instructor with the teaching problem can be helped within the regular classroom. Consultation can remedy such disadvantages of pull-out programs as fragmentation of instruction and stigmatization of students. It provides a viable means for regular and special education to jointly own the problem of a difficult learner. Through a process of shared problem-solving, collaborative consultation crosses over boundaries that have traditionally separated regular and special educators.

In Winooski, Vermont, a single department of pupil personnel services integrated all remedial programs, including special education. Special education professionals provided services by team teaching with regular classroom teachers. In Montlake, a Seattle elementary school, pull-out programs were eliminated. The regular and special education teachers team taught multi-age reading and math groups. No distinction, in either of these two programs, was made between special and regular students (Villa & Thousand, 1988).

When Jenkins and Heinen (1989) asked remedial and special education students if they preferred help from their regular classroom teacher or a resource room teacher the students chose their regular teacher. An interesting footnote to the student preference study was their choice of resource room services over special education instruction in the regular class. It seems that leaving the classroom for remediation is less embarrassing than having a specialist work directly with the student in the regular classroom. This is an important piece of information for educators who favor direct special services (e.g., one-to-one aides) to students in the regular classroom. It is clear from this study that students do not wish to draw attention to their learning problems, and, given the choice, they would choose the less stigmatizing alternative of leaving the classroom.

The consulting teacher concept seems to offer clear advantages to both teachers and students. It consolidates services, provides expertise in hard to reach rural areas, and can save school districts money while improving educational services to students. Yet the consulting model presents its own set of problems that must be addressed in order to gain the desired results.

Consulting requires careful scheduling and administrative support. Consulting is ineffective if the classroom teacher and consulting teacher do not have adequate time to plan. The building principal controls each classroom teacher's schedule. Administrative support in terms of release time and a nonjudgmental view towards teachers who are working with a consultant are two prerequisites for successful implementation of this model.

Consulting requires diplomatic communication skills on the part of the consultant and a readiness to cooperate on the part of the consultee. Any "helper" has a power advantage over the person who is being helped. The need for consultation, if not handled properly, can imply weaknesses in the ability of the recipient. Imagine the following scenario. A 24-year-old special education teacher has just completed graduate training as a teacher consultant, and her first assignment is a teacher who is a 20-year veteran of the public schools. The teacher was selected by her principal because she has a higher than average referral rate for special education services, and the principal wants to mainstream two students with mild disabilities into her regular classroom. It is clear, without drawing out this illustration any further, that a successful outcome is problematic. How will the regular classroom teacher feel about this "youngster" observing in her classroom and offering suggestions for changes in instruction? How will the consultant deal with the regular classroom teacher's attitude towards outside help? Can consulting work when the regular classroom teacher has not directly requested outside assistance?

Consulting works when there is genuine collaboration among all parties (e.g., regular classroom teacher, consultant, special services teachers). There are superb and poor teachers in both special and regular education. For the consulting teacher model to be useful, there needs to be a commitment to sharing of expertise and resources on both sides of the fence (Pugach & Johnson, 1989). Trust must precede collaborative problem-solving. Consultant teachers should be selected from the ranks of the most experienced and respected teachers in a school system. Pinning the title "consultant" on a teacher who lacks the expertise or interpersonal skills to work with classroom teachers will disrupt rather than facilitate mainstreaming efforts.

The consultant teacher model seems well-suited to facilitate the mainstreaming of students with mild disabilities. It is designed to provide services to both students and teacher in the regular classroom. Through consulting, special educators can advance the integration of both their students and themselves. It is a holistic approach to what has become a very fragmented instructional pattern in public schools—the removal of hard-to-teach students from their normal class-room setting. Ultimately, the success of the consulting teacher model depends on a mutual sharing of ideas, methods, and responsibilities between regular and special educators.

Instructional Practices

Teachers never cease to puzzle about how to teach students with varying abilities. Students are so different in personality, motivation, work habits, and interests that even the best teachers are challenged to keep all their students involved in learning. The selection of the following instructional practices is based on the flexibility each provides for teaching students who are different. These are merely a sample of worthwhile instructional practices for maintaining students with mild disabilities in the regular classroom.

The Whole Language Approach to Reading

The National Assessment of Educational Progress (NAEP) noted an improvement in reading ability of students between 1971 and 1984, yet there are still many students, particularly economically disadvantaged youngsters, who struggle over the printed word. The NAEP data for 1984 indicated that 40 percent of 13-year-olds could not read or understand their textbook with ease. About two-thirds of the nine-year-old students interviewed in the National Assessment of Educational Progress reported that their teachers did most of the reading for them. Teachers pointed out the hard words, read parts of stories aloud, and told them how to find the main idea before they read the story (Lapointe, 1986).

The whole language approach remediates reading deficiencies by integrating reading with writing. The achievement data presented by the NAEP supports the premise that reading and writing skills are tied together. Better readers are better writers. In whole language classrooms, reading and writing are not taught as separate subjects. Students improve their skills in both areas by engaging in holistic activities like journal writing and choral reading. Students are enveloped in reading materials. Emphasis is placed on children's literature along with basal reading texts. Whole language teachers have found that authors such as Maurice Sendak, Chris Van Alsburg, Jane Yolen, and Mercer Mayer create stories that enchant young readers and instill the desire to read. Creative writing is encouraged in whole language. Priority is given to student imagination and expression rather than such editorial skills as spelling and punctuation.

Whole language offers an alternative to the lock-step phonetic approach common in many classrooms. Phonics are not eliminated, but the teacher recognizes that endless drills like "the fat cat sat on the tan hat" does not enliven a child's desire to read. More attention is paid to the quality of children's literature, discussion of stories, and student initiated reading-writing activities. Intuition, visual imagery, and spontaneous learning all play a part in whole language instruction. Students are encouraged to describe their experiences, write them down, and read them to others. Whole language increases student motivation by linking reading to real life experiences.

Adaptive Learning Environments Model (ALEM)

The Adaptive Learning Environments Model is a mainstreaming program designed to adapt regular classrooms to meet the needs of both special needs and nondisabled students. According to Wang and Birch, "The ALEM is designed to create school environments that maximize each student's opportunities to master basic academic and social skills" (Wang & Birch, 1984, 392). Since 1968, the ALEM has served as a guide for the National Follow Through Program, a federally funded early childhood program for economically disadvantaged students.

There are two major components of the Adaptive Learning Environments Model. The first is a highly structured diagnostic-prescriptive program for teaching academics. The second component promotes social and personal development of students through open-ended, exploratory activities.

The ALEM is designed to facilitate mainstreaming of students with mild disabilities through the following procedures: (1) early identification of learning problems, (2) description of learning needs rather than labels or categories of mild disabilities, (3) individual educational plans based on student strengths and learning needs, and (4) instruction of self-management skills to help students accept responsibility for their learning (Berres & Knoblock, 1987). In the ALEM program, the identified special needs student remains in the regular classroom.

Research on the effectiveness of the ALEM presents equivocal results. Fuchs and Fuchs (1988) found insufficient data to view the ALEM as a full-scale mainstreaming program. Slavin, Karweit, and Madden (1989) stated achievement gains in reading and math were not significant, but they also describe increased engaged learning time and enhanced student self-perception. Wang and Walberg (1988) stated that the ALEM is based on extensive positive research in such practices as cooperative learning, mastery teaching, and student self-monitoring. Moreover, the authors cite numerous independent evaluators who have attested to the effectiveness of the ALEM to facilitate mainstreaming efforts. Some reported advantages to the ALEM include parental participation, data-based decision-making mechanisms, and an ongoing staff development component.

Career Education

One of the most perplexing problems facing educators today is how to keep students from dropping out of school. One out of four students who begins high school does not graduate with his or her senior class. Students who experience school failure through elementary and junior high school are prime dropout candidates by their sixteenth birthday. Slavin (1989) noted that by the time a student has reached third grade, reliable predictions can be made about who will drop out and who will remain in school. Moreover, one-half of all high school graduates, over twenty million students, will not attend college. For these students, "the forgotten half," many school reforms (such as higher academic standards), inhibit rather than facilitate their adjustment from school to employment (The William T. Grant Foundation Commission on Work, Family, and Citizenship, 1988).

Career education attempts to provide a meaningful school experience for students by bridging the gap between the curriculum and work. Students are taught employable skills while in school. The most effective career education programs are those that either simulate real life experiences or place a student in direct, supervised work experience. One approach is to assign students to work with "mentors" in community businesses. A student might attend academic courses in the morning, spend three afternoons in vocational skills classes learning such trades as carpentry and plumbing, and spend two afternoons working with an experienced craftsman at a local building site.

Career education differs from vocational education by providing career counseling and teaching work habits that will enhance a student's marketability. Promptness, appearance, ability to follow directions, and perseverance are a few of the attributes employers value in their employees. Data from a detailed assessment of a student's abilities in school subjects, leisure activities, occupational preferences, and personal characteristics can help instructor and student choose an appropriate educational plan to prepare a youngster for life after school.

Open Education

The goal of the open education method is to teach students to take responsibility for their own learning. Open education was spawned as part of the counter-establishment movement in the late 1960s and early 1970s. It has roots in the Progressive movement of the 1930s and the British informal school system. Each of these educational practices viewed teaching and learning as a process that linked student experience to activity-based instruction. Student initiation and discussion of classroom events are valued; rote learning, drill, and such passive learning materials as worksheets and dittos are used sparingly.

While open classrooms are not as numerous as in the past, open education methods are still prevalent. Peer tutoring, cooperative learning, activity centers, and discovery learning are a few examples of open education methods used in classrooms throughout the country. With its emphasis on student participation and the classroom as a "community," open education methods provide a good foundation for mainstreaming efforts. The problems of overactive and restless students are diminished, for example, when they have opportunities to move about the room while working at learning centers. Students who have difficulty remaining quiet will not become disruptive in open classrooms where students are encouraged to exchange ideas. Barnes and Knoblock (1973) observed that the open classroom, with its emphasis on democratic group procedures, is particularly well-suited to respond to the needs of students who have conflicts with authority, problems in establishing relationships, and feelings of loss of control over their feelings and behavior.

One of the primary criticisms of open education is the difficulty in measuring student learning. Standardized achievement tests are geared more to teacher-directed methods than student-centered techniques. When students are allowed to follow their interests in reading, math, or writing, their learning will not coincide with tests matched to curriculum guides. As a result, the beneficial effects of open education methods on student achievement are difficult to prove (Slavin, 1989). However, increased student motivation and greater attention to student feelings are a few of the unmeasurable benefits attested to by teachers, students, and parents who have been exposed to open classroom practices.

Skillstreaming

The ability of students to conform to classroom expectations for appropriate behavior is one of the most important criteria for a successful mainstreaming program. Unfortunately, when students with mild disabilities return to the regular classroom on a full-time basis, such disruptive problems as withdrawal, aggression, or immaturity can impede successful integration. Because of negative classroom behaviors, students may be ignored or rejected by their classmates. Gresham and Reschly (1986) compared the social behaviors and peer acceptance of one hundred nondisabled students with one hundred mainstreamed youngsters with learning disabilities. They reported the mainstreamed students persisted in negative social behaviors at home and school. Specifically, the youngsters with learning disabilities had difficulty attending to tasks, completing tasks, staying on task, following directions, and completing independent work.

Skillstreaming (McGinnis & Goldstein, 1984) is a program designed to teach prosocial behaviors to mainstreamed students. The guiding assumption is that students with mild disabilities lack "behavioral flexibility," (that is, they are unable to adjust their behavior to different situations). McGinnis and Goldstein describe their system of Structured Learning as a combination of behavioral and psychoeducational techniques designed to teach prosocial behaviors through modeling, role playing, performance feedback, and transfer of training. The Skillstreaming program includes assessment profiles, teaching methods, and a sequenced prosocial curriculum ranging from classroom "survival" skills to skills for dealing with stress.

Research on the effectiveness of the Skillstreaming approach is not included in the program. Like many therapeutic intervention programs, its validity rests heavily on teacher belief in the knowledge and experience of the authors. Both psychoeducational and behavioral approaches to change student behavior have been used extensively in schools over the past fifty years. The detailed analysis of prosocial skills and lesson plans for teaching the skills provide a useful framework for organizing a self-control curriculum for difficult students.

Computer Assisted Instruction

The history of education is replete with examples of technological innovations that never fulfilled their original promise. Television, for instance, was supposed to revolutionize education by hooking students up to a worldwide network of experts in every discipline. When personal computers first were introduced in schools in the early 1980s, gloomy tales of machines replacing humans in the classroom became a staple for teacher lounge debates. The computer literacy movement helped dispel the darker images of how computers would subvert education. Rather than replacing teachers, many school computers are under-utilized (Wagschal, 1984).

Computers can fill an important niche in mainstreamed classrooms by providing students with a tool for expression and learning. For a student with handwriting, reading, or spelling problems, word processing is an excellent alternative to labored composition efforts. Seeing one's ideas printed cleanly and concisely can provide a student with the incentive to persevere with creative writing. Interactive software can promote both reading and problem-solving skills. Hypertext provides students with access to supplementary information by layering pages on the computer screen. Placed on the perimeter of a classroom as a learning center, a computer can prove a valuable resource for a teacher who follows a few simple guidelines for computer application in the classroom:

1. Think of a computer as a stereo. The machine is useless if you don't select software (i.e. music) that you like and need.
2. It's unnecessary to know how to program in order to use a computer. The basic computer skill is typing.
3. Different computers run different software. Be certain the machine you select for your classroom can accommodate the software you want.
4. There are many adaptive devices available that make a computer accessible to students with physical, visual, and auditory disabilities.
5. Talk with other teachers who use computers in the classroom. New software and computer applications are continually being developed.

Good teaching is the selection of an instructional practice that best suits the needs of students. Effective teachers use a variety of instructional practices in their classrooms. When students are having difficulty learning, it makes more sense to vary the teaching approach than to assume there is something wrong with the learner. Each instructional practice offers an alternative method for helping hard-to-teach students in the regular classroom. No one approach is best for all students and teachers. Used in combination, these practices can match the diverse needs of a mainstreamed classroom.

The Regular Education Initiative

The Regular Education Initiative is a movement designed to bring special education services into the regular classroom. This is a significant change from the traditional practice of having students receive special services in resource rooms or self-contained special education classrooms. Some advocates take the Regular Education Initiative a step further and propose a merger of regular and special education.

In 1986, Madeline Will, the Assistant Secretary for Special Education and Rehabilitative Services, reported on the status of educational programming for hard-to-teach students. She noted that despite intensive efforts to remediate learning difficulties through remedial education, Chapter 1, bilingual education, migrant education, and special education students were still dropping out of school at a 25 percent rate per year. She also noted that 30 percent of high school graduates were functionally illiterate. Will concluded that a merger of special education and regular education services would enhance the ability of the public schools to educate students at risk of school failure.

According to Will, four obstacles to effective educational progress are unintentional by-products of special education services.

1. *Fragmented instruction.* Students who do not meet eligibility criteria for specific remedial programs "fall through the cracks" and receive no special help. Financial incentives determine program choices. School systems "put the child where the money is with too little regard for educational need." Many who receive special services are put in "pull-out programs"; others in self-contained classrooms. Meanwhile there is a lack of coordination between regular and special educators. Consequently remedial and special education students fall further behind in their studies. Each minute they spend in a special program, students miss a minute of regular classroom instruction. Meanwhile, students who could use extra help are overlooked because their learning problems are not severe enough to qualify for remedial or special education. The present system of special education emphasizes remediation rather than prevention of learning problems.

2. *Dual systems.* Special and regular education have separate administrative structures, distinct budgets, and separate training for teachers. The duality of these systems creates a gap between the regular and special educator. Building principals do not feel ownership of special programs because of separate financial, administrative, and decision-making procedures. Special education teachers feel estranged from regular teachers because they tutor students in resource rooms or teach small groups of students in self-contained classrooms. Physical isolation of special education classrooms minimizes contact, communication, and mutual problem-solving. With these constraints it is difficult to foster a sense of shared responsibility for the instructional needs of special learners. Learning becomes jeopardized when special and regular instruction do not complement each other.

3. *Stigmatization of students.* Schools are social environments. Isolation of students from their peers can decrease self-esteem and increase negative attitudes about school. All children want to be accepted and feel they belong. Low expectations for success, failure to persist on tasks, learned helplessness, and continued school failure are some of the negative consequences of separating students into categories of "special needs."

4. *Placement decision as battleground.* The Individuals with Disabilities Education Act is based on the premise that parents have much to contribute in making school-based decisions. Confusing requirements for special programs can place teachers and parents in opposing positions. Parents get stereotyped as "pushy" if they fight to get a youngster into special education and "uncaring" if they don't attend school meetings. The cumulative effects of these misunderstandings are "a series of adversarial, hit-and-run encounters" between parents and educators.

Will summarized her position on the need for coordination between special and regular education by pointing out that the "major flaw" in school practice is the belief that improvement in student performance is dependent upon the creation of new educational environments. Instead of viewing a learning problem as a deficiency in the student, Will recommended a reevaluation of the classroom setting where the learning problem is first observed and a reallocation of resources to maintain students in the regular classroom.

Beginning in the mid-1980s the Regular Education Initiative was a goal of many special educators. The strategy of merging regular education with special education and other remedial programs appeared to be an idea whose time had arrived. Criticisms of special education programs for students with mild disabilities had mounted over the preceding years. Hobb's (1975) position that classifying students by disabling conditions was "a major barrier to efficient and effective delivery of services" seemed more valid than ever. Wang, Reynolds, and Walberg (1986) reported that only 20 percent of special education students were classified according to rigorous physical and physiological measures. Will (1986) pointed out that the proliferation of "pull-out" programs had created a fragmented approach to educational intervention that failed to meet the educational needs of learners with mild disabilities. Stainback and Stainback (1984) recommended a unitary system of education to replace the splintered approach of providing help through regular, special, remedial, migrant, bilingual, and Chapter 1 education programs.

The Regular Education Initiative targeted a restructuring of education services for all hard-to-teach students. While mainstreaming focused on integrating specific students into regular education classrooms, the Regular Education Initiative advocated the elimination of pull-out programs for remedial populations. Personnel, money, and material resources would be reallocated for the use of all educators. Regular education teachers, with support, would take on greater responsibility for the education of special populations. However, the Regular Education Initiative faced many obstacles.

Not all educators were convinced that a merger of regular and special education was a good idea. Opponents of the Regular Education Initiative cautioned against a complete overhaul of the existing system. They were concerned about putting students back in the regular classroom, which was the source of their original learning problems. Vergason and Anderegg (1989) wrote that a dismantling of special education without any substantial improvements in regular education was the same as throwing out the baby with the bath water. Shumaker and Deschler (1988) warned against a wholesale application of the Regular Education Initiative without recognizing key differences in learners, curriculum, and organizational variables. Kaufmann, Semmel, and Gerber (1988) agreed with the broadly stated goals of the Regular Education Initiative, but questioned whether it was possible to distribute the instructional resources needed to achieve desired educational outcomes.

Semmel et al., surveyed teacher perceptions of the Regular Education Initiative. They found that generally teachers were satisfied with the current special education service delivery system. Specifically, respondent teachers preferred pull-out programs. The teachers were concerned that existing special education resources might be threatened by Regular Education Initiative changes. Finally, regular education teachers seemed unsure of their ability to adapt their instruction to meet the needs of students with mild disabilities. The researchers reiterated an often cited criticism of top-down education reform proposals.

> *Of particular concern is the reasonably high probability that the problems in current special education practices, as perceived by distal academicians and policymakers, may be radically different from the perceptions of the educators called on to implement policy. . . . Such initiations must be directly guided by the perceptions and attitudes of the service providers responsible for ensuring successful implementation of innovations (Semmel et al., 1991, 21).*

Perhaps the most realistic caveat was presented by Mitchell (1988), who observed that regular and special educators had different perspectives about what needed fixing in public schools. Mitchell pointed out that regular and special educators were not talking to each other about education reform. She compared the focus on educational reform without a shared vision to the construction of a modern version of the Tower of Babel. According to Mitchell, regular and special educators shared a number of concerns including: attending to the problem of high risk learners; the realization that fragmentation of remedial services interferes with teaching; and an understanding that the organization of schools into self-contained units of instruction fostered isolation and inhibited collegiality. These mutual concerns of special and regular educators seemed like a good starting point for connecting the two systems of education.

Recently regular and special educators have been more focused on respective in-house concerns than on mutual problems. By 1988, two years after Madeline Will's proposal for a merger of regular and special services, most regular educators had still not heard about the Regular Education Initiative. At the same time that special educators were heatedly discussing the Regular Education Initiative, the attention of regular educators was diverted by a series of reports that criticized the general education of all public school students.

In 1983, the U.S. Department of Education released *A Nation at Risk: The Imperative for Education Reform*. This document presented strong criticism of regular education. Its most heralded excerpt stated, "If an unfriendly foreign power had attempted to impose on America the mediocre educational performance that exists today, we might well have viewed it as an act of war" (Orlich, 1989, 513). *A Nation at Risk* recommended stricter coursework requirements for high school graduation, higher admission standards for college, and longer school days. *In A Place Called School,* John Goodlad (1984) characterized public schools as "mindless." Other reform documents (*A Nation Prepared: Teachers for the 21st Century,* 1986 and *Tomorrow's Teachers: A Report of the Holmes Group,* 1986) called for merit pay for teachers based on student test scores, a revamping of teacher preparation with more emphasis on liberal arts, and the development of a national test to measure teacher competency.

Regular classroom teachers seemed to be placed squarely on the horns of a dilemma. While special educators were advocating integration of low achievers in the regular classroom, critics of public schooling were lambasting teachers for failing to educate nondisabled students properly. The choice seemed to come down to equity or excellence in education. Should regular education treat all students equally by educating them in the regular classroom, or should regular education adopt more stringent educational practices that pushed for higher achievement for the brightest students?

The "effective schools" research of the 1970s and 1980s indicated that schools may be able to achieve both goals without sacrificing the values of equity or excellence. Ronald Edmonds (1979) described four features of schools that were capable of educating both underachievers and good students. Effective schools were characterized by:

1. Strong instructional leadership that established a climate for learning,
2. High expectations for *all* students,
3. A pleasant and orderly learning atmosphere,
4. Emphasis on the acquisition of basic skills through direct instruction. (Orlich,1989)

To summarize, according to proponents of the Regular Education Initiative, categorical special and remedial programs do not serve the best interests of students nor the teachers who work with them. Special and regular educators agreed that: many students were underachieving and "falling between the cracks" of specialized services; the "pull-out" method of providing special services interfered with teaching and learning by fragmenting instruction; and the organization of schools into self-contained "regular" and "special" units fostered teacher isolation and inhibited cooperation (Mitchell, 1988). Opponents of the Regular Education Initiative pointed out that change for the sake of change was irresponsible. Special education had come too far since 1975 to "give the store away." Surveyed teacher perceptions about current special education services presented a strong caution against dismantling special education practices.

Working Together

Schools must change in order to meet the demands of the future. As we move into the twenty-first century, demographic trends indicate increased poverty among students. A growing proportion of students will be non-white and non-English speaking, and there will be an increase of students from single parent families. If the schools of the future are to meet the growing demands of hard-to-teach students, changes must occur in present school practices that serve to separate students (and teachers) into groups of "haves" and "have nots."

Regular and special educators can work together to teach all children. There are contact points where key issues faced by regular and special educators rub together. All educators, whether they are special or regular, must deal with problems of: teacher expectations, standardized tests, classroom organization, discipline, and dual systems of administration. The ability of educators to meet these challenges and solve them together will set the course for an improved educational system for the students of the twenty-first century.

Teacher Expectations

Research on effective instruction indicates the powerful effect of teacher expectations, both positive and negative, on student performance. When students are labeled as deficient and put in "special" programs, the message is clear—there is something intrinsically wrong with this student. Labels like mentally retarded and learning disabled become explanations for why a student is difficult to teach. Students are then grouped with other "deficient" learners, and teacher expectations for the group decline. Conversely, when teachers believe that learning problems are temporary hurdles that can be overcome by adaptions in teaching methods, there is an expectation that success will come with hard work. When teachers have high expectations, the performance of all students is enhanced.

But what about teacher expectations of themselves? Two Rand Corporation studies found that positive teacher opinions of their own ability had a beneficial effect on students' learning (Armor et al., 1976; Berman et al., 1977). McDaniel and DiBella-McCarthy described the teaching style of these confident teachers.

> *High efficacy teachers maintained high academic standards, had clear expectations for students, concentrated on academic instruction, maintained on-task behavior, and demonstrated "withitness." They combined a secure classroom environment with a strong academic orientation. . . . High-efficacy teachers allocated twice as much time to whole group instruction as did low-efficacy teachers.(McDaniel & DiBella-McCarthy, 1989, 35)*

Teachers who believe in their own ability have good group management skills. They encourage student participation and have less discipline problems. Perhaps most important, high-efficacy teachers are problem-solvers. They view a student's learning difficulties as a temporary problem, and they try different teaching approaches until they get results. Teacher preparation programs that concentrate on developing high-efficacy skills will provide young teachers with the tools needed to help all learners in the regular classroom.

Classroom Organization

Between kindergarten and twelfth grade a student will spend more than 11,000 hours in school. How much of this time is actually spent learning? According to researchers who have studied life in schools, only a fraction of a school day is allocated to instruction, and students spend even less time engaged in learning activities. Out of a typical 390-minute school day, teachers spend less than half that time teaching. In their survey of second, third, and fourth grade classrooms, Ysseldyke and Algozzine (1984) found that students have few opportunities to do independent work, and they spend a lot of time in such passive activities as listening and waiting.

Students spend as little as 12 percent of their school day questioning, reading, writing, or engaged in some other activity that reflects active learning. Goodlad (1984) reported that a good deal of what goes on in schools is like painting by numbers. The teacher gives directions, and students follow them in robot-like fashion. He described the emotional tone of these classrooms as flat. The climate of these rooms lacked joy and warmth. Goodlad noted that while teachers verbalize the need for students to become independent thinkers, many teachers have a need to control student decision making.

More attention needs to be directed on how classrooms are organized. When the teacher controls every action, from distribution of materials to collecting lunch money, precious instructional time is wasted. As students progress through school, they learn to conform to the teacher's authority. The National Institute of Education (1987) summarized the research on conditions for successful teaching-learning by reporting that students must be actively involved in their learning to succeed. Such active teaching strategies as cooperative learning projects, learning centers, and peer tutoring allow teachers to move about the room and guide student learning. By shifting the classroom instructional norm from "frontal teaching" to student-centered activities, teachers can increase instructional time and allow learning to proceed at the student's pace.

Standardized Tests

For many years, United States education has heavily favored standardized tests. Perhaps this is rooted in our competitive spirit or the mistaken belief that standardized tests provide a true "objective" measure of achievement. Standardized tests are used to compare achievement between school districts, and they are used to compare the gains made by individual students. Each year fifty million school children take standardized tests. In some classrooms around the country, instruction is test-driven. In these classrooms, teachers teach to the test, and a student's learning is summarized in a single number at the end of the year.

The billion-dollar-a-year testing industry is unregulated. There are no standards for who takes the test. In some school systems, all children are evaluated, while in other systems, students who receive special instruction are excluded. Some critics of current testing procedures have pointed out that a school superintendent can increase district test scores by placing students in special education programs. Chester Finn, past assistant United States Secretary of Education in charge of research, characterized standardized testing in America as the "Lake Wobegon" effect. He observed that in the mythical Minnesota town, popularized by the humorist Garrison Keillor, all the children are "above average." Finn's comment was prompted by national achievement scores that each year showed a rise in average test scores for all school children. In their zeal to demonstrate how much their school systems have improved, this statistical paradox has been conveniently ignored by many educators (Fiske, 1988).

Despite the rise in standardized test scores, schools continue to graduate functionally illiterate citizens (Wiggins, 1989). Neill and Medina summarized the case against standardized tests.

> *At best, standardized testing is hopelessly inadequate for promoting school reform. At worst, such testing will preclude reform. In either case, the continued domination of testing will mean that millions of students—primarily those most in need of improved education—will be dumped into dead-end tracks and pushed out of school. (Neill & Medina, 1989, 695)*

Alternatives to standardized tests are available to teachers. Curriculum-based assessment, classroom observations, and student portfolios provide more detail about student learning than standardized tests. Evaluation of student performance can improve when assessment paints a picture of a student as learner rather than student as test-taker.

Discipline

What type of classroom behavior would you find disruptive? Some teachers are disturbed by a student who constantly needs structure and direction. Other teachers resent students who don't sit still and have difficulty waiting. Which is the best student behavior—quiet, outspoken, compliant, or nonconformist? There are as many views on proper student behavior as there are teachers.

Because teachers organize their classroom routines to match their own likes and dislikes, there is no standard for determining "normal" classroom behavior. Jacob Kounin (1977) reported that some teachers actually create discipline problems in their classrooms, for example, when teachers switch topics without a smooth transition or abruptly end a lesson, classroom disruptions increase. Teachers can either prevent or contribute to discipline problems in the classroom.

Suppose Jerome is upset because he doesn't understand his homework assignment. He throws his book on the floor and announces to the class, "I'm not doing this stupid assignment; you don't hand our papers back until a week later anyway." So far there is no discipline problem, only one very angry student (anger is simply not accepted as a normal childhood feeling in many classrooms). It's the teacher's reaction that will determine the outcome of this scenario. Maybe

Jerome has a point. However, for the teacher who has no tolerance for students acting out their feelings, Jerome's anger may be interpreted as an affront to teacher authority. A sharp retort from the teacher will almost certainly escalate the problem. On the other hand, there are any number of teacher behaviors, including planned ignoring, restructuring, or humor that could defuse the situation (Henley, 1987).

Ginott (1973) maintained that the crucial factor in classroom management is teacher ability to convey an attitude of helpfulness and acceptance through teacher-student communications. When teachers feel angry, they should use "I messages" such as "I am angry" rather than statements that put students down, such as "You are always causing problems in this classroom." Teachers who are capable of responding to student feelings without getting defensive themselves are effective managers of discipline problems. According to Ginott, when a student is disruptive, the effective teacher addresses the situation rather than the character of the student. Ginott described this communication process as a sane message. Insane messages, such as "Why can't you learn to behave," undermine student self-esteem. On the other hand, a sane message, such as "It's difficult to read during quiet time if you are talking," underscores a reality need of classroom life without personally attacking the offending student.

The Phi Delta Commission on Discipline (1982) did a national survey of schools with successful discipline policies. The commission found these schools were student-oriented. Schools with good discipline concentrated on the cause of discipline problems rather than adopting isolated practices to punish wrongdoers. Routine discipline problems were handled in the classroom. When serious infractions occurred, such due process procedures as student hearings were established to give students an opportunity to present their side of an issue. Schools with good discipline emphasized positive behaviors and implemented preventive measures instead of punitive actions to improve discipline. Awards, honor days, and positive communications with parents are a few strategies used to reward well-mannered behavior.

The schools surveyed by Phi Delta Kappa were not soft on discipline; in fact, several schools had strict behavior codes. The factor that distinguished exemplary schools was their emphasis on teaching prosocial behaviors. For example, the Beta School for underachieving students in New York City reinforced positive behaviors by issuing "Commendation Cards" to selected students. The Rocky Mountain School in Marietta, Georgia, used social studies as a forum to help students learn human relations skills in the classroom.

Working and getting along with others is a basic prerequisite for a successful career after school. When teachers and administrators value the feelings of students and model effective interpersonal skills, students learn to be more responsive to the needs of others. When teachers and administrators dictate and punish, students learn the wrong lesson—might makes right. As adults we look at repressive governments and cheer on populations who fight for self-determination. Why then should we be surprised to discover that repressive school policies contribute to student discipline problems?

Each year, throughout the country, over three million students are administered corporal punishment. A long list of research studies illustrates that physical reaction to disruptive behavior rarely yields effective results—yet corporal punishment continues in many public schools, particularly in the Southeast (Hyman & D'Allesandro, 1988). If corporal punishment is prohibited by state law, then it cannot be used as a discipline procedure for special education students. However, when state law allows corporal punishment, there is no exception for special education students unless specified in a student's individual education program. Emotionally disturbed, neglected, and sexually abused students can be further traumatized by onerous discipline procedures. Teachers and parents need to work together to insure that school discipline procedures do not duplicate conditions that have led to an emotional problem. Although the National Education Association passed a resolution against corporal punishment, it is legal in many states, and the Supreme Court has repeatedly upheld the right of teachers to "paddle."

School-aged youngsters are deluged with TV shows and movies that romanticize violence. Drug abuse is a national tragedy, and 50 percent of all students will experience the hardship of divorce. Teachers and parents cannot ignore the sad truth that the "mean streets" of America also include the hallways of many schools. When metal detectors are needed to keep out weapons in some urban schools, it is clear that students are frightened and need help. By providing students with humane and fair discipline practices, teachers can instill in young people the moral values and social skills they will need to successfully cope with life after school.

Administrative Leadership

The purpose of administration is to develop policies and procedures that make schools better places to teach and learn. Principals, superintendents, and special education directors can work together so schools will meet the needs of disabled and nondisabled students. A dual system of regular and special education administration makes mutual problem-solving and planning difficult, if not impossible.

Virtually all aspects of special education programming are in the hands of special education administrators. This means that although special education programs are located in their buildings, school principals are administratively disconnected from their operation. Regular and special education have separate budgets, separate administrators, and separate teacher certification procedures. As might be expected this dual system of education creates and sustains separate priorities. When the entire special education system is set up on a separate administrative track, there are few built-in incentives to teach youngsters with mild disabilities in the regular classroom.

Chapter 1, bilingual education, migrant programs, and special education services are administered separately. The net result is a jumble of overlapping programs designed to provide remedial education. Guidelines for each type of remedial program including eligibility criteria and evaluation of student progress are imprecise and often confusing. Some of the more common educator complaints are:

1. Placement of students in the wrong program.
2. Turf issues about educational resources put program directors in competition with each other.
3. Students who don't match eligibility criteria fall between the cracks and receive no help.
4. The pull-out system of delivering remedial services causes students to fall further behind their classmates because they miss too much regular classroom instruction.

The underlying assumption of pull-out programs for remedial services is that differences between each subgroup of students requires specialized instructional techniques. Yet the meager research base for successfully matching specific instructional approaches to distinctive learner characteristics fails to justify the billions of dollars spent to maintain specialized pull-out programs.

Wang, Reynolds, and Walberg (1986) recommended "waivers of performance" as an administrative approach to integrating special and regular services in the regular classroom. The waivers would guarantee school districts categorical funds while students are taught in the regular classrooms. This plan would restructure how services are funded in order to provide incentives for regular education programming. With "waivers of performance," school districts would not lose funds by keeping hard-to-teach students in the regular classrooms. Services would follow the child into the regular classroom, rather than the child being pulled out of the classroom to receive specialized services. While the present dual system of specialized administration reinforces disjointedness and isolation, "waivers of performance" would encourage coordinated planning among regular and special educators. Such an initiative would provide a base for the creative merging of regular and special education expertise in an effort to better serve at-risk students as well as students with mild disabilities.

Summary

Mainstreaming means educating students with disabilities in the regular classroom. The legal mandate for mainstreaming is based on the least restrictive environment provision, reaffirmed in the Individuals with Disabilities Education Act. However, as Frank Williams discovered in the beginning of this chapter, mainstreaming is more than a legal concept. Each student wants to be viewed as normal by peers and teachers. When students are pulled out of their classroom for special instruction or placed in segregated "special" programs, it creates an artificial division between them and their peers.

Mainstreaming can be an effective educational intervention. A well-planned mainstreaming program helps develop both academic and social skills as well or better than pull-out or self-contained special education programs. Planning a mainstreaming program includes establishing of entrance criteria, understanding student needs, preparing students for a change, evaluating student progress, and communicating with parents.

Sound general educational practices work equally well with students with mild disabilities. Collaborative learning, peer tutoring, whole language, direct instruction, open education, career education, and computer assisted instruction are examples of instructional methods that help all students learn. Consultant teachers and specific mainstreaming models such as ALEM and Skillstreaming offer teachers and students alternative educational practices to achieve successful mainstreaming programs.

The educational tradition of viewing learning difficulties as defects in the student has created and sustained a dual system of public education in this country. One brand of education, "regular," is for students without learning problems, and another brand of education, "special," is for students with learning problems. Each year the numbers of students placed in some sort of "special" program increases. Billions of dollars are poured annually into pull-out special and remedial programs that are unable to fix the problems of hard-to-teach students.

Both special and regular educators have a stake in realigning their efforts to teach students with mild disabilities. The Regular Education Initiative breathed new life into mainstreaming efforts by focusing attention on benefits of merging special and regular education efforts for hard-to-teach students. It is clear by now that uninspired teaching does as much to create learning problems as the characteristics of individual students. By focusing attention on ways of enhancing classroom learning environments, educators can best serve the needs of all students.

Chapter 7

Learning and Teaching

Advance Organizer

When you complete this chapter, you will be able to:

1. Discuss how student perception influences school performance.
2. Explain how a developmental perspective can provide insight into student behavior.
3. Describe the hidden school curriculum.
4. Explain how classroom time management affects learning.
5. Outline the components of curriculum-based assessment.
6. Contrast the following instructional models:

   Direct Instruction
   Precision Teaching
   Student Centered Learning
   Learning Strategies

7. Explain how discrete instructional strategies can be integrated into a comprehensive approach to instructions.
8. Provide practical suggestions for modifying classroom practices to meet the needs of students with mild disabilities.

With all the literature dedicated to learning and teaching, it would seem that by now schools would be getting the job done. Yet reports of uninspired teaching and troubled learners permeate descriptions of United States classrooms (Goodlad, 1984; National Commission on Excellence in Education, 1983). Hispanic (32 percent) and African-American (15.5 percent) youngsters are dropping out of school at an alarming rate (Gage, 1990). Urban schools are in disarray

(Maeroff, 1988). Special education referrals and placements climb each year (U.S. Department of Education, 1990). What can be done to stem this apparent tide of mediocrity? We can begin by looking at schools through the eyes of students. What does school mean to the graduates, the dropouts, and the students with special needs? The experience of the consumers can provide insight into how to improve schools.

In any organization that is having difficulty meeting its goals, it is good managerial practice to find out more about how the employees spend their time. Through a discussion of time management in school, we will discuss factors that contribute to and take away from the business of education. In our description of instructional strategies and learning styles, we will demonstrate how teachers can develop a better match between teaching approaches and the learning needs of students. An explanation of learner characteristics and instructional materials will provide a framework for making decisions about how to modify teaching for students with and without mild disabilities.

Teachers are professionals; and, like doctors and lawyers, they need a variety of skills to do their work in a purposeful manner. The more capable teachers are in managing time, utilizing an array of instructional approaches, and modifying materials—the better suited they will be to meet the individual needs of all students.

The School Experience

Each morning, forty-eight million youngsters troop off to school. They arrive on foot, in cars, and in an armada of yellow school buses. Bells ring; children file into classrooms; the teacher closes the classroom door, calls for attention, and another school day begins. What happens next? Outside of sleeping, and watching television, no other activity demands as much of a youngster's time as school. Even though teachers and students spend almost a thousand hours together each year, our knowledge about what transpires inside classroom walls is fragmentary.

Public school classrooms are oxymorons. They are actually private places. The teacher works alone. The students are there, but they are quiet consumers. Students rarely complain about bad teachers. To whom would they address their complaints? And what would be the purpose? The next day the same teacher would be standing in front of them. This is because teachers, once they have achieved tenure, have almost total job security. Barring an economic downturn that can lead to layoffs, teachers have the assurance of continuing their profession with minimum outside interference, until retirement.

Teachers are the only professionals that do their best or worst work in virtual isolation from their peers. The act of one teacher observing another teacher in the classroom is so unique that when it happens it is labeled an innovation. Occasionally the seclusion of classroom life is pierced by researchers, and the insights gleaned are informative.

What Are Schools For?

Ask any teacher what schools are for, and you are likely to get a variety of answers ranging from the basic—"Schools are to teach skills for life," to the enthusiastic—"Schools are to help kids learn about themselves and the world around them." But what about the consumers? What do the students who, from age five to seventeen, spend 12,000 hours in classrooms think about school?

Student Perceptions of School

Noyes and McAndrew (1971) interviewed students throughout the country and asked them, "What are schools for?" A typical response was:

> We go to school because it is the law. They make you stay until you are sixteen, and by then you may as well go on since you probably only have another year or two anyway. The point of it, I guess, is to get a diploma so you can go to college. (Noyes & McAndrew, 1971, 321)

The overall impression made by the students in this study was that the purpose of school was preparation for college. Students did not view school as a place that would meet their personal needs. They gave different versions of the same theme—figure out a way to get through school with the least resistance. Beat the system before it beats you.

Mallery (1971) interviewed students from eight high schools. The purpose of his study was to examine the effects of the school experience on student values. When students made spontaneous references to curriculum, they talked about the need to get good grades. Virtually all students wanted to find some purpose in their schoolwork. They singled out for praise courses that allowed active participation. They emphasized teacher personality. They respected teachers who provided opportunities to build self-confidence, independent thinking, and personal expression. According to these students, competition for grades and the pressure to be admitted to college increased as they advanced from ninth to twelfth grade.

In elementary school, White found student and teacher perceptions differed on the purpose of school. While teachers value the content of the curriculum, students pay more attention to teacher judgments of their work. In the words of one student:

> . . . you have to have a half inch margin on your papers . . . you put the headings on the right not on the left, and line it up . . . the cover should be felt if you want an A . . . you can't hand in papers that aren't neat, she'll really mark you down . . . you have to write out "remainder" or it's wrong . . . (White, 1971, 341)

Students measured their progress by grades rather than what they learned. When he was a special education teacher one of the authors had a straight-forward reminder regarding the importance of grades to students:

> *The director of our program had accepted the teachers recommendation that we substitute descriptive evaluations for grades. The students participated in assessing their learning. Students met with the teachers to determine if their work in each subject showed improvement. Peter and I had a conference at my desk about his progress. "Do you think your reading has improved?", I asked him. "What do you mean?" he replied. "You know, are you getting better at reading?" I asked. "How should I know," Peter said, "you're the teacher. It's your job to give me a grade so I'll know if I've learned anything."*

Peter's comment illustrates the distance between teacher and student perspectives about school. Students are not connected to their learning in the ways adults imagine. They learn the rules of school and how to get by, but curriculum as adults understand it does not have the same meaning to students. While teachers want students to learn, students want to get the teacher's approval, receive good grades, and enjoy the company of their friends. Sometimes they are excited about learning, and sometimes they are bored (Goodlad, 1984; Jackson, 1968). At all times, students realize that essentially their fate is in the hands of the teacher. Some students cope with the inequality of power and perform at a level that will satisfy both teacher and parents. Others fall by the wayside. These failures eventually are classified as students at-risk, school dropouts, or students with mild disabilities.

What Happens in School?

What are the characteristics of classroom life that create such a discrepancy between how teachers and students view learning? It should come as no surprise that students view grades as the Holy Grail of their school experience. From the time they receive their first report card until they take the Scholastic Aptitude Test (SAT) in high school, students are continually reminded of the importance of grades. As Jackson pointed out, tests are as indigenous to life in schools as chalk, blackboards, and textbooks (Jackson, 1968).

Some teachers' efforts are best characterized as test- rather than curriculum-driven. These teachers teach to improve test scores rather than to stimulate a love of learning. As long as school-based quizzes and national achievement tests continue as the key measure of success in school, students will concentrate on grades as their most important goal.

Child and Adolescent Development

"What did you do in school today?" When a father asked his six-year-old daughter Margaret this question, she answered, "Well, we had lunch in the cafeteria, we lined up for the bus, and we had folder work on Thursday and we had fun together, me, Brian, all my friends." She added, "That's not all but I forget the rest."

Margaret's response illustrates another major difference between how teachers and students view school. When she thinks about school, Margaret considers its most gratifying aspects—lunch, friends, and a side reference to her studies—"folder work." Children are not miniature adults. There are significant developmental differences between teachers and their students. One developmental distinction is in perceptions of goals.

While adults take the long view, students look at the future from short-range. Teachers are concerned with distant goals; students are concerned with here and now. For a five-year-old twenty minutes is an endless wait. Summer for a twelve-year-old seems to extend into the distance, an uninterrupted progression of sunny days and steamy nights. To the freshman and sophomore, high school appears as if it will never end. Time limits have slight meaning to teenagers who perceive themselves as immortal.

Within this context of time without end, parents and adults pound away at such themes in high school as "You need to learn math in order to get a good job," or they tell primary grade children "If you finish your work in twenty minutes, you will get free time at the end of the week." Each of these messages leaves a faint impression on students who are unable to fathom the mystery of work today for tomorrow's reward. Child and adolescent development lend weight to Einstein's view that time is relative. Discipline, grades, and learning are fundamental classroom issues that teachers approach as long range preparation for work or college, while youngsters jolt forward one day at a time with eyes cast on more substantial concerns, such as watching the clock hands on the wall slowly creep towards dismissal.

Developmental differences between students and teachers are accepted and valued in many early childhood programs, but teachers and administrators sometimes lose track of child and adolescent development as students mature. This neglect of child and adolescent development by school personnel creates a gulf between teachers and students that can have dire consequences. To paraphrase Robert Sternberg (1990), we ignore students' developmental differences at our peril—and theirs (Sternberg, 1990, 367).

Part of growing up is learning to take on the perspective of those who are older. Primary school-aged children learn to be less egocentric as they acquire the ability to perceive a situation from another's point of view. Students in elementary school are here-and-now oriented. It isn't until adolescence that students can begin to think about future goals. Each of these developmental changes occurs through a process that Piaget characterized as assimilation-accommodation. This means that changes in student perceptions occur gradually, with a good deal of regression intermingled with advancement.

Developmental needs dictate priorities to students, and these priorities can put a student in conflict with adults. For the teenager, relationships, intimacy, and getting a driver's license are major concerns. Adolescence is a time of "grandiose ascension." Teenagers fly high above the mundane matters of the everyday world as they experience new mental and physical abilities they never imagined they would possess (Bly, 1990). Many teenagers perceive parents as "old fashioned" and too strict. When bad things happen, teenagers are reluctant to face them head-on. Denial is a useful defense mechanism for skipping over the hardships of a family's divorce, a mother's addiction, or a father's neglect. This is why depression and drug abuse are such developmental hazards for adolescents. Adolescents are more likely to act out their emotional struggles than to reflect or talk to others.

In high school, acceptance by one's peer group can be more pressing than getting homework done. The teenager confronts the social dilemma of breaking free from the bonds of adult authority at precisely the same time that parents and teachers are demanding "responsible behavior." This pulling in opposite directions usually leaves both adults and adolescents perplexed. Even though developmental changes are at times baffling, these changes help explain why the meaning of school is interpreted differently by teachers and students.

The Hidden Curriculum

Much of what transpires in school is dictated by what Phillip Jackson (1968) described as "the hidden curriculum." While the visible academic curriculum channels schedules and routines, the hidden curriculum comprised of praise, power, and crowds more subtly exerts its influence. In classrooms, students must learn to accommodate themselves to the hidden curriculum. Students' ability to adapt to the three unpublicized features of classroom life—praise, power, and crowds—will, just as surely as achievement test scores, determine school success or failure.

Praise
Learning to live in a classroom requires learning to perform successfully under constant adult supervision. Students must elicit praise from teachers. They must learn to sit still, wait their turn, follow directions, and do well on tests. Successful students learn to please their teachers. While teachers may be disappointed by errors in academics, students soon learn that violation of classroom rules for behavior causes teachers the greatest aggravation. Students receive praise based on their ability to follow the organizational guidelines laid down by their teachers. Students who garner reproof rather than praise in their attempts to adapt to the norms of classroom life may eventually find themselves referred for special education.

Power
The evaluative norms in classrooms contribute to an unequal balance of power. While children are accustomed to bending to the authority of parents, school presents a different situation. The intimacy and duration of contact that is character-

istic of parent-child relationships is absent in school. As Jackson (1968) put it, "For the first time in the child's life, power that has personal consequences for the child himself is wielded by a complete stranger." At the precise time in their lives that developmentally they are ready to take on the world and demonstrate their capacity for mastery, five-year-old children are sent to school, and placed under the authority of a "teacher" (Erikson, 1963). In developmentally based classrooms, students are given time and opportunity to explore their personal abilities. In teacher-centered, curriculum-based classrooms, students are immediately pressed into compliance. In the latter settings, students are expected to follow directions, get the "right" answers, and master the curriculum.

The contrast between student compliance and teacher power is subdued in democratic, student-centered classrooms, but the essential institutional power of schools is invariant. Students must go to school. They must listen to the teacher. Their lives are regulated by bells, schedules, and routines. They cannot decide when they will eat lunch. They cannot decide when it's time to stop their studies. They cannot go to the bathroom without permission.

This is not a criticism of schools; rather, it is a description of institutional life. Schools manage large numbers of children with limited space and resources. Student behaviors such as tractability, obedience, and conformity are prized by administrators. Nonconforming behaviors, rebelliousness, or lack of attention are dealt with swiftly and surely. It is no wonder that "good students" seek to create a favorable impression on teachers.

One approach is to curry favor. The extreme example is the apple polisher who realizes that teacher evaluations can be enhanced by anticipating and fulfilling teacher expectations. This ability to appraise social reality is a valuable skill in the workplace as well. However it is conspicuously absent in students with mild disabilities, who are not as adept at deciphering social cues as students without mild disabilities.

John Holt, in his book *How Children Fail* (1970), catalogued the many strategies students devise to avoid teacher disapproval. Holt observed that students display remarkable ingenuity and cunning in bluffing teachers. According to Holt, teachers unconsciously give children clues about correct answers through eye movement and by body language. By watching these nonverbal signs, students can make a good guess at the right answer. While teaching in a special education program, one of the authors discovered how students go about the business of faking.

> *One day I was doing a math drill with a small group of five students with learning disabilities. I showed them a flash card and one after another they came up with the right multiplication answer. I felt great. I thought I was finally making progress. At recess I took Timmy aside and told him how pleased I was with his multiplication work. He looked at me sheepishly and said, "We didn't really know the answers; you were sitting with your back to the window, and we could read the answers on the other side of the cards each time you held one up."*

The students' insouciance was unnerving. It was as if every student in the group, without any prior discussion, was in on a secret plan. Clearly students do a great deal of thinking in school as they try to tip the scales of power in their direction.

Crowds

The third aspect of the hidden curriculum is crowds. Classrooms are crowded places where, for the most part, students work alone. Additionally, students must adapt to delays, interruptions, and waiting. According to Jackson (1968), the typical elementary school teacher engages in 1,000 interactions a day. When researchers have cataloged how teachers and students utilize their time together, the results have been astonishing. For example, Ysseldyke and Alogozzine (1990) reported that out of 390 minutes in an elementary school day, 170 minutes was time lost to lunch, recess, physical education, and similar activities. Of the remaining 220 minutes, forty minutes was spent in free time, lunch counts, roll call, and other "housekeeping" activities. Eighteen minutes was spent in "fetch and put away" activities. Out of the entire school day, a student averaged two minutes of individual time with the teacher. Students and teachers spend large chunks of time together, but the crowded conditions of schools and the ensuing artifacts of organizational life play havoc with instruction and learning. Educational researchers are beginning to appreciate that time management is a critical element of effective classroom instruction (Berliner, 1979, 1988; Good & Brophy, 1986; Rosenshine, 1979).

Time Variables

In 1983, the National Committee on Excellence in Education recognized "time as a critical learning variable" and they included time in their recommendations for improving schools. Specific time variables addressed by the National Committee on Excellence in Education were: time management, allocated time, engaged time, and academic learning time.

Time Management

Data about time management are based primarily on research in general education classrooms. Researchers are interested in finding out how learning is influenced by teachers' use of time. Rich and Ross (1989) found that teachers are allocated approximately 55 percent of the classroom day for instruction, but only half of that time, or 25 percent of the entire day, is utilized by students engaged in learning tasks. How is it that out of an entire school day only one-fourth of the time is spent learning?

Jacob Kounin's (1977) research on classroom organization in elementary and secondary schools bears testimony to how time is wasted in classrooms. Kounin found that many teaching behaviors disrupt lessons. He used such terms as "thrusts," "dangles," "truncations," and "flip-flops" to describe common time wasters. "Thrusts" refers to intrusions in lessons. Principal announcements over the loud speaker are an example of "thrusts" that interrupt lessons and make it difficult for teachers to get back on track. One inner-city school teacher was so distracted by PA announcements that his first action of the new school year was to disconnect the speaker from his classroom wall! This minor act of rebellion nearly cost him his job.

"Dangles" occur when a teacher leaves a lesson in midair, for example, when a visitor comes to the classroom door. Students may be left with a perfunctory remark like, "I'll be out in the hall for a minute. Turn to page 36 in your workbooks and complete the problems." It is the rare group of students who would not take a teacher's momentary absence as an invitation to relax and catch up on some classroom gossip. The ensuing reprimand upon the teacher's return usually wastes more time and creates an unpleasant mood. After such an incident teacher and students are hard pressed to rejoin the lesson with their original enthusiasm.

Teachers "flip-flop" when they reverse directions in a lesson. Flip-flops may be fostered by strategically minded students who would rather hear how Mrs. Jones spent her summer vacation on Cape Cod than hear a lecture on the "mollusk family." Teacher anecdotes turn into tangents and digressions, which entertain both teacher and students, while instructional time is sliced into smaller pieces. When teachers flip-flop, students with mild disabilities become confused and dispirited. The teacher who begins a lesson on multiplication of fractions and then realizes that some review in fractions is needed may move back and forth too abruptly for students to keep track of the central ideas. Students with weak listening or attending skills will give up and lose the teacher's train of thought.

"Truncations" occur when a teacher abruptly ends a lesson and moves on to something else without alerting students to the change. The conclusion of a lesson and transition to the next topic is one of the most critical parts of instructional time. Many behavior problems occur because of disorganized transitions. Dealing with classroom disruptions is a major time-waster. By moving smoothly from one lesson to the next, the teacher diminishes management problems and focus students' attention on the next lesson.

Kounin found that teachers who were able to maintain a group focus were most successful in using instructional time. These teachers were able to monitor the entire class without being distracted by minor incidents that could cause the entire class to become diverted, like stopping a class discussion because there is a piece of paper on the floor or because someone isn't paying attention. Such teachers demonstrate "withitness" and "overlapping." They are able to work with an individual student without losing track of the rest of the group. Students describe a teacher who demonstrates "withitness" as having "eyes in the back of her head."

Allocated Time

Allocated time refers to the amount of time scheduled for a specific subject. State and school districts generally mandate a minimum number of minutes per day or hours per week for curriculum topics such as reading and mathematics. The actual time teachers spend on subject matter within these allocated blocks of time varies. Different beliefs about what is important for students to learn, along with teachers' likes and dislikes for teaching specific subjects, shapes how time is allocated in classrooms. A teacher's enthusiasm for a subject is an indicator of how much time will be allocated for covering that curriculum area.

Even when time is allocated for a subject, weak organizational skills can bleed precious instructional minutes from a lesson. Berliner illustrates this point.

> *Let us suppose, by law, that forty minutes a day is the minimum amount of time to be devoted to mathematics in the second grade within a particular school district. Let us also suppose that this mathematics time begins at 11:15, after a recess, and that the time period devoted to mathematics ends at noon. The teacher, principal, and superintendent may well feel the state minimum requirements are being met and exceeded. But careful observation will reveal otherwise. A ten-minute delay in the start of work, called transition time...may occur before the mathematics curriculum is really in effect. Toward the end of the allocated time students are putting workbooks, contracts, and Cuisenaire rods away, getting lunches out, and lining up for dismissal at noontime. Another ten minutes may be lost. Functional time for mathematics is now twenty-five minutes, which is 60 percent under the legal requirements. (Berliner, 1988, 129-130)*

Good time management begins with measurements of time allocation. A colleague observing in the classroom can help determine average number of minutes allocated to each subject or topic. From a qualitative perspective, colleague observation can target such instructional interferences as thrusts, dangles, and truncations. This feedback can help a teacher make necessary adjustments in order to increase allocated time.

Engaged Time

Engaged time refers to the amount of time that a student is working. Engaged time is a significant indicator of achievement (Berliner, 1988). Engaged time can reflect whole group involvement, or the time a student is working alone. Time measures begin from the time students initiate an activity up until they finish. Engaged time depends upon such variables as a teacher's classroom management ability, how effectively the teacher matches instruction to student learning styles, and how well students understand what is expected of them. Students can be wasting time and give the appearance of being engaged in their work. As an illustration, put a blank piece of paper over this and the previous page. Now answer the following questions. What is allocated time? Who is the researcher who identified such teacher skills as withitness and overlapping? How do transitions affect allocated time?

Do you get the point? You allocated time to sit and read this text, but how engaged were you? Going through the motions of reading words and turning pages doesn't automatically lead to learning. How many times have you had the experience of reading twenty pages of text only to realize after you close the book that you don't remember anything! Engagement requires active involvement with learning materials. When students are doing something—moving, talking, writing, counting, measuring, questioning, drawing—their level of engagement is heightened. When students are required to be passive—listening, reading, completing workbook pages—their level of engagement is questionable. Students may look like they are engaged in the learning task, but, as we all know, looks can be deceiving.

Students with mild disabilities, in particular, have difficulties with engaged time. They often lose track of teacher directions or misunderstand an assignment. They might be anxious about something that happened at home. Such students are feeling distress. The biophysical distress reaction is fight or flight. Since there is no way to fight frustration, and fleeing from the classroom is a last resort, students with mild disabilities will withdraw into the false antidote of daydreams. On the outside they may seem a model of classroom decorum as they quietly turn pages or scribble notations on their worksheets. Yet their minds could be light-years away from the task. Their moments of engaged thinking are focused on bluffing the teacher into thinking they are working.

Fisher, Filby, Marliarc and Cahe (1978) found that engagement rates varied from 50 to 90 percent of allocated time depending on the classroom. They report:

> *One hour of allocated mathematics instruction, then, can result in either 30 minutes or 54 minutes of actual delivered instruction to students. In a single week, differences of such a magnitude can yield a difference of about two hours in the amount of mathematics that is actually engaged in by students. It is no wonder that in reading, mathematics, or science, at any grade level, large variations in engaged time by students is a strong predictor of achievement. (Berliner, 1988, 13)*

Thus the amount of time engaged in learning may be quantitatively different from time allocated to learning. Educators agree that increasing engaged time can improve achievement of students with and without mild disabilities.

Academic Learning Time

Beliner defines academic learning time (ALT) as "time engaged with materials or activities related to the outcome measure being used (e.g., an achievement test), during which a student experiences a high success rate" (Berliner, 1988, 15). When teachers evaluate students specifically on subjects in which students were engaged, academic learning time will improve. If this sounds confusing, let's look at it from a different point of view.

Suppose a sixth grade teacher allocates sixty minutes a day to whole language instruction of reading. She has selected this teaching method because she gets high student involvement. At the end of the year, the school system administers a standardized reading achievement test. There is a vocabulary section where students are required to give the meaning of solitary words. Also included are timed reading comprehension sections, which include paragraphs of increasing complexity. As the teacher reviews the test, she feels an icy tingle down her spine. The test clearly favors students with strong phonetic skills! Her students are going to do poorly on this test because it is measuring a different set of skills than they were taught. If academic learning time is to improve, curriculum, instruction, learning, and evaluative measures must mesh. The amount of time a student spends demonstrating a specific skill is important to school success. Teachers who are able to monitor student progress through observation, pre-post testing, informal testing, and student portfolios are most effective in enhancing academic learning time. This procedure is called curriculum-based assessment.

Once evaluative measures (i.e., tests) are matched with the curriculum, teachers concentrate on student classroom performance. Materials that are too difficult impede academic learning time. This is a particularly nettlesome problem for teachers of students with mild disabilities. What do you give a fifteen-year-old, street-wise, inner-city youth, who is on a first grade reading level, to read? How do you reteach fundamental math concepts to eighteen-year-olds who need manipulative materials? One solution is high-interest library books (perhaps with brown paper on the covers) for reading and functional lessons (measuring, check writing, grocery budgets) for mathematics. Students who have failed with the traditional basal texts are not going to improve through drill and repetition with similar materials.

To improve academic learning time, students require opportunities to practice skills in novel situations. They need to see how skills can be generalized, and they need to demonstrate skills in different settings. It doesn't help to teach students to read if they are never going to pick up a book to read for enjoyment or if they don't know how to read the classified section of the newspaper. Berliner illustrates the interrelationship between allocated time, engaged time, and academic learning time.

> *If 50 minutes of reading instruction per day is allocated to a student who pays attention about one-third of the time, (engaged learning) and only one-fourth of the student's reading time is a high level of success, the student will experience only about four minutes of ALT—engaged reading time at a high success level. Similarly, if 100 minutes per day is allocated for reading for a student who pays attention 85 percent of the time and is at a high level of success for almost two-thirds of the time that student will experience about 52 minutes of ALT (academic learning time). (Berliner, 1988, 17)*

There are many reasons why students experience lesser amounts of academic learning time. Distractibility, inadequate study skills, emotional problems, disorderly classrooms, and disorganized instruction are samples of the reasons ALT is minimal for students. Students with mild disabilities are placed in double jeopardy when they are pulled out of their classroom for special education services. Unless the resource room teacher is duplicating materials and instructional strategies utilized in the regular classroom at the time of the student's absence, academic learning time will be lost day after day, week after week, month after month. This is a strong argument for mainstreaming.

Curriculum-Based Assessment: A Promising Practice for Teaching Students with Mild Disabilities

Standardized assessment practices are often criticized for a lack of relevance to instruction. Assessment procedures linked to what is taught in school have reemerged as promising alternatives to standardized assessment (Blankenship, 1985; Deno, 1985, 1986, 1989; Tucker, 1985; Wesson, 1991; Ysseldyke & Algozzine, 1982, 1991).

Advocates of curriculum-based assessment point out the need to target evaluation procedures on content that is taught in the classroom (Algozzine, Ruhl, & Ramsey, 1991). Standardized achievement tests are comprised of a limited sample of questions that the test-makers believe reflect the classroom's curriculum. If the standardized test-makers are wrong in their hypotheses, the student is evaluated on content she or he was never taught. Curriculum-based assessment is defined as, "The practice of obtaining direct and frequent measures of a student's performance on a series of sequentially arranged objectives derived from the curriculum used in the classroom" (Blankenship, 1985, 234).

An illustration of curriculum-based assessment follows: Carol, a kindergarten teacher, decided to teach her students a unit on frogs. Before beginning her lessons she asked her students a series of questions about the amphibians. She tabulated their responses. After the unit, she again quizzed her young charges. She found that they could answer 75% more questions about frogs after the unit than before. By evaluating student progress based on their ability to learn the classroom curriculum, Carol was practicing curriculum-based assessment.

Evaluating Student Competency

Curriculum-based assessment involves repeated measurement of a student's performance on a sequenced curriculum (Research Brief for Teachers, 1988). Counting and graphing are the best means of tracking student progress. For example, a teacher could ask a student to read a passage from a story that seems to match his present reading level. Each incorrectly read word is marked. A final tally reveals that the student knew two-thirds of the words in the story. This 66 percent figure provides base-line data to measure future progress. Every few days, after instruction, the student's progress in reading is again measured.

Graphing the results of each measurement provides a visual means of efficiently marking progress.

Curriculum-based data is collected "prior to instruction, immediately following instruction, and throughout the year to assess long-term retention" (Blankenship, 1985, 238). Assessment of student progress in relationship to the classroom curriculum has several uses:

1. Various instructional procedures are evaluated and, if necessary, changed.
2. The data can provide information to support special education referrals.
3. Current performance, goals, and objectives for individual education plans (IEPs) are written in a straightforward language; this enhances communication between parents and administrators.

Practice of Curriculum-Based Assessment

Gickling and Havertape (1981, 55) state that curriculum-based assessment is "a procedure for determining the instructional needs of a student based on the student's ongoing performance within existing course content." The practice offers great promise as a procedure for meeting the inadequacies identified in standardized achievement tests (Deno, 1985, 1986, 1989; Deno & Mirkin, 1977). According to Tucker:

> There is nothing new about curriculum-based assessment. In many respects, it is like coming home to traditional classroom instruction. Under the rubric of curriculum-based assessment, some novel ideas are being proposed and reported, and several practical tools have emerged, but the basic idea is as old as education itself. It is unfortunate that good practice in education is often cast with the framework of "new" theories and "new" terms used to describe what has become a tried-and-true approach to teaching since the dawn of education. (Tucker, 1985, 199)

One modified form of curriculum-based assessment includes: (1) direct observation and analysis of the learning environment, (2) analysis of the strategies used by students in approaching tasks, and (3) examination of pupil products (Ysseldyke & Algozzine, 1990).

Analysis of the Learning Environment

In curriculum-based assessment, the teacher evaluates the learning environment in several ways. One of these involves analyzing the kinds of instructional materials being used. It also includes looking at ways in which instruction is organized and at the sequencing of concepts within the curriculum. Teachers look for possible mismatches between teacher instructional style and student learning style.

In curriculum-based assessment, considerable effort is devoted to systematic analysis of several situational variables; for example, the ways in which groups are used to facilitate instruction are evaluated, as is the involvement of students in instructing peers. The ways in which volunteer personnel are used to work with individual students is evaluated, and considerable emphasis is placed on evaluating the structure of the school day. In this latter instance, diagnostic observers systematically analyze the amount of time allocated to instruction and the amount of time the pupil is engaged with academic materials.

Evaluating Task Approach Strategies

Rather than immediately assuming that students who perform poorly do so because something is wrong with them, the teacher doing a curriculum-based assessment begins by looking at ways in which students approach tasks. Meta-cognitive strategies, such as the think aloud protocol, help both teachers and students identify shortcomings in how the student mentally goes about completing a task. The teacher evaluates student problem-solving strategies, student attention to task, and the extent to which students understand instructions.

Evaluating the Products of Instruction

Teachers regularly examine student products in curriculum-based assessments. They do this in order to pinpoint instances in which students are having difficulties. Students produce products in the form of written essays, completed worksheets, and tests or quizzes. Error analysis of these products involves systematic examination of types and frequency of mistakes.

For example, a student who makes multiple errors on a math sheet may not understand a specific component such as carrying. It would be poor teaching and unfair to the student to mark all incorrect answers wrong. An analysis of error patterns may reveal that the student correctly solved each problem but used the wrong arithmetic procedures. Looking at the student's work from an error analysis point of view provides a qualitative evaluation and suggests alternative remedial help. Rather than practicing the same math problems over again, the student simply needs to learn the correct arithmetic procedure—in this case, carrying.

Curriculum-Based Instructional Planning

All students with mild disabilities must have an individual education program (IEP) to document student current performance and instructional goals. Fuchs and Shinn (1989) identified two categories of problems associated with using non-curriculum-based assessment methods to write IEPs. First, IEP goals are typically vague and global (e.g., . . . will improve one year in reading) or overly specific, covering small details. Second, without curriculum-based assessment, IEP goals are written so that substantive and procedural compliance with federal requirements related to multidisciplinary evaluation procedures are inadequate. Fuchs and Shinn (1989) suggest that instructional planning can be improved by writing curriculum-based IEP objectives.

Formulating Objectives

Curriculum-based objectives specify (1) the conditions under which performance is obtained, (2) the learning behavior being performed, and (3) the criterion for success (Mager, 1962). Rather than stating that Alex will decode words at the second grade level, which is really a global objective or goal, each objective describes specifically one discrete skill that will move Alex closer to the goal. Consider the following example: Given a written list of one syllable words, Alex will sound each out with 80 percent accuracy. The condition (i.e., Given a list of one syllable words) describes the context for observing Alex. The behavior (i.e., will sound each out) describes the action Alex is expected to perform, and the criteria (i.e., with 30 percent accuracy) identifies how Alex's skill will be evaluated. A list of four to five such objectives would be arranged in a hierarchical fashion, culminating with the stated goal of improving Alex's decoding skills. Teacher accountability, student progress, and program effectiveness can be scrutinized on a more professional level when instructional objectives are stated in a clear, observable, and lucid fashion.

Deno (1986) described a three step process for formulating curriculum-based IEP objectives. First, current performance data are collected. Next, a level of the curriculum is specified (e.g., employment skills for a secondary student), conditions and behavior are identified, and a date for review of progress is established. Finally, a criterion for success is specified based on curriculum standards or individual performance records. Having done this, the process of actually writing objectives is straightforward.

Curriculum-Based Program Monitoring

Some educators express concern that much of traditional special education practice represents a "refer, classify, place, and forget" to students with special learning needs (Algozzine & Ysseldyke, 1983, 1986; Algozzine, Ysseldyke, & Christenson, 1980; Ysseldyke & Algozzine, 1982, 1984, 1990). Curriculum-based assessment practices offer considerable promise for improving periodic and annual reviews used to decide whether to continue or terminate special education services (Allen, 1989; Marston & Magnusson, 1988; Shinn, 1985). Assessment activities for periodic and annual reviews are similar; annual reviews tend to be more thorough and typically are documented with a formal written report (Allen, 1989). The focus of these activities is assessing the general benefits of special education services and deciding whether to continue or modify current levels of service to meet special learning needs.

In determining benefits of special education, teachers make curriculum-based comparisons of student performances before and after entering special programs. Comparisons of special education and regular education progress are used in deciding when to terminate special programs. If a student's performance falls within the average range of performance for grade-level peers (e.g., within one standard deviation above or below their mean), return to regular class placement would seem appropriate (Allen, 1989), but as Marston (1968) points out a grade-level standard is too strict a criterion for mainstreaming. Performance of other low-achieving students may be a more appropriate standard (Allen, 1989; Salvia & Ysselkdyke, 1986).

Curriculum-based assessment is not a panacea for all problems with assessment. However, it does offer a number of advantages over traditional psychometric practices. First, gathering performance indicators in classroom-based curriculum materials and comparing them to similar scores obtained by peers clearly goes a long way in making assessment relevant for instruction. Too often, skills measured by items on standardized tests bear little relation to daily classroom activities (Good & Salvia, 1987; Jenkins & Pany, 1978; Salvia & Ysseldyke, 1986).

Instructional Strategies

There is a commonly held perception that students with mild disabilities require instructional strategies that are distinctive from effective regular education teaching methods. This assumption is based on the "medical model" perspective that characterized the formative years of special education. Just as medicine is geared towards treating diagnosed disorders, the medical model applied to special education was oriented towards matching an educational treatment to specific types of mild disabilities. Students were placed in special education programs based on the assumption that there was something intrinsically wrong with them and that special education instruction would help remediate learning problems symptomatic of specific disabling conditions.

While some mild disabilities, such as dyslexia, are individually based, many mild disabilities are the result of a variety of overlapping issues that are interactional in nature. Poverty, lack of school readiness skills (e.g., mild mental retardation), disorganized classrooms, dysfunctional families (e.g., behavior disorders), and mismatch between instruction and student learning style (e.g., learning disabilities) all contribute to a cycle of school failure that can result in a special education placement.

Jenkins, Pious, and Peterson (1988) wanted to determine if students with mild disabilities were different from other students. The researchers analyzed differences between students identified as learning disabled and students identified as underachievers. They compared instructional levels, learning rates, and learning styles of each group. They found more similarities than differences between the two groups of students. Students with and without disabilities had identical achievement levels. Individual students in each group demonstrated considerable overlap in learning rate and instructional level.

The history of special education is replete with attempts to match instruction to specific disabilities. As Jenkins and his colleagues reported, attempts to remediate specific impairments in such areas as perception and cognition generally have met with failure. There is no "cure" for dyslexia. The most effective programs teach youngsters how to cope with their mild disability by teaching them functional and organizational skills. These educational programs target practical skills that will help students overcome the problems presented by the disability; for instance, a student with dyslexia needs help in understanding how the disability impairs reading ability. In some instances, auditory processing skills are deficient, and negative effects can be overcome by switching from a phonics to a whole language approach to reading. In most cases, students with mild disabilities will progress when they are taught by talented teachers (general or special) who know how to match teaching and learning styles.

Classifying students into specific categories of mild disabilities supports the notion that these students are qualitatively different from each other. An examination of instructional practices in self-contained classrooms for students with mild disabilities presents a different picture. Algozzine, Morsink, and Algozzine (1988) investigated the "conventional wisdom" that special education programs have mutually exclusive treatment programs for students differentiated by separate categories of mild disabilities. They did systematic observations of instruction in forty self-contained classes for students with learning disabilities, mild mental retardation, and emotional disturbance. The students were assigned to the special education classes for at least twenty-five hours a week. The teachers in each of these classrooms provided similar instruction in terms of how they structured student time, provided student feedback, and gave directions. The teachers didn't use different instructional strategies matched to specific disabilities. Their approach was eclectic; for example, teachers certified to teach emotionally disturbed students used techniques originally formulated for students with learning disabilities, and teachers certified to teach students with learning disabilities used instructional strategies developed for students with emotional problems.

The findings that teachers in categorical self-contained classrooms use similar instructional strategies regardless of disabling condition suggests that separation of students based on instructional needs is a long held educational tradition that should be reexamined. Stainback and Stainback emphasized that *good* instructional strategies work for all students.

> There are not two discrete sets of instructional methods—one set for use with "special" students and another set for use with "regular" students. As used here, instructional methods refer to basic instructional processes, such as the development of behavioral objectives, curricular-based assessment procedures, task analysis, the arrangement of antecedents and consequences, and open education/discovery learning methods. While some methods need to be tailored to individual characteristics and needs, few, if any, can be clearly dichotomized into those applicable only for special students or only for regular students. (Stainback & Stainback, 1984, 103)

Best teaching practices for regular education students are also best teaching practices for students with mild disabilities. Teachers in both regular and special education have at their disposal instructional strategies to facilitate the learning of students with mild disabilities.

When we talk about students with mild disabilities, underachievers, and other hard-to-teach students, qualitative distinctions among groups are difficult to detect. The challenge for general and special educators is to implement instructional strategies that can change school failure to success for all students. The following models for instruction have proven effective with students in both general and special education settings.

Instructional Models

Trying to find the best way to teach unsuccessful learners is a major goal for twentieth century educators. Educational journals brim with debates about which system of instruction is most effective for students who have difficulty with reading, math, writing, and behavior. Table 7–1 summarizes several special education instructional strategies matched to types of mild disabilities.

As the pendulum of educational reform swings from left to right, priorities change and so do instructional approaches. The late 1960s and early 1970s were a time of widespread social change. The "establishment" was challenged through civil disobedience, war protests, and rock music. Student-centered learning, with the counter-culture theme of "freedom to learn," flourished during this period. The name given to educational reform during this period, "open education," underscored the goal of flexibility in classroom instruction. Later, during the more conservative 1980s, direct instruction and the effective schools research emphasized basic skills and testing for student mastery.

The search for the best way to teach is tied to many factors. Among these are local leadership, politics, economics, and public support. Education is more like law than medicine. Absolute cures for educational ills are almost nonexistent. Rather, like law, education must change and adapt to the needs of society; for example, educational policy is shaped at the local level by superintendents, who are hired by school committees. School committees are elected by voters in the community. Consequently, introduction of educational change, along with the necessary budgetary adjustments, must eventually have public support.

Each of the following instructional models has been used successfully with students with mild disabilities and nondisabled students. None is foolproof. All have supporters and detractors. As Robert Slavin (1989) noted, other applied fields have clear indicators of progress such as return on investment, yield per acre, or mortality per 1,000 patients, but there is considerable lack of agreement about what constitutes progress in education. Should we lower the dropout rate, raise achievement test scores, or teach students with mild disabilities full-time in the regular classroom? Each goal presents its own set of criteria for success and suggests different instructional models. Direct instruction, for example, will raise achievement test scores, while student-centered learning offers more possibilities

TABLE 7-1 Summary of Instructional Strategies by Functional Domains

	Mild Mental Retardation	Learning Disability	Behavior Disorder
Cognitive	1. Identify stage of cognitive development. 2. Match teaching style to student level of development and learning style.	1. Teach meta-cognitive, "how to learn" skills. 2. Teach study skills. 3. Don't confuse I.Q. with low intelligence.	1. Provide decentering activities to teach students to share perceptions of others.
Academic	1. Provide early childhood education. 2. Teach thinking/problem-solving skills. 3. Teach functional/career skills.	1. Teach students self-monitoring strategies. 2. Analyze products & performance for learning disability clues.	1. Focus on enhancing motivation to learn. 2. Provide emotional support. 3. Build on student experiences.
Language	1. Emphasize intuitive skills and high interest in reading. 2. Use systematic analysis of skills and progress. 3. Respect cultural differences.	1. Utilize alternatives to phonics such as whole language and right hemispheric activities. 2. Identify specific language processing deficits and teach coping skills.	1. Emphasize congruent communication: "sane" and "I" messages. 2. Accept student feelings; promote expression of feelings.
Social	1. Emphasize activities to build confidence and self-esteem. 2. Teach social skills	1. Teach social perception skills. 2. Teach social behavioral skills.	1. Establish a systematic behavior management program. 2. Teach self-control skills

to potential dropouts. The selection of an instructional model should come after a careful review of educational goals, school-wide resources, and student need.

Direct Instruction

Direct Instruction, also referred to as mastery learning, refers to a variety of carefully sequenced, teacher-directed methods. The term was originally used to describe *Distar*, a teaching guide for reading and mathematics. More recently the term direct instruction has been used by researchers to describe a set of procedures derived from the effective schools research of Rosenshine and Stevens (1984). Their research indicated that when teachers followed a hierarchy of instructional steps in their lessons, low achieving students demonstrated increased academic achievement in basic skills.

Direct instruction encourages the use of teacher demonstration, guided practice, and feedback. According to Larivee, "Design components of direct instruction include mastery learning, carefully designed sequential instruction, flexible skill-level grouping, adequate opportunity for practice, and periodic review of previously learned concepts" (Larivee, 1989, 307). A teacher would utilize direct instruction by:

1. Teacher demonstration—Provide clear, controlled presentations of new material. Model each step of the material to be learned.
2. Guided practice—Following the demonstration, ask questions and check student understanding of material.
3. Feedback—Circulate among students as they work on independent activities related to the new material. Provide corrective feedback on their work. Use frequent cumulative review.

The work of Madeline Hunter and her Instructional Theory into Practice (ITIP) instructional model is an example of a direct instruction program that was implemented in hundreds of schools throughout the country. Hunter stated that teachers were first and foremost decision makers, and teaching decisions should be informed by educational research. Hunter's ITIP system divided teaching into practical lists and sublists that teachers could follow as they made decisions regarding how and what to teach; for example, she organized the teaching act into seven components:

1. Knowledge of human growth and development
2. Content
3. Classroom management
4. Materials
5. Planning
6. Human relations
7. Instructional skills

These components identify the kinds of decisions a teacher makes minute-by-minute in the classroom. Hunter wanted teachers to understand how cause and effect influenced learning within each component. She encouraged teachers to use data from learning situations to augment teaching decisions and increase student mastery of content. Hunter summarized her approach in an interview with Mark Goldberg, ". . . all of the 5,000 decisions a teacher makes every day fall neatly into three categories: what you are going to teach, which we call a content category; what the students are going to do to learn it and to let you know that they've learned it, which we call learning behavior category; and what you as the teacher will do to facilitate and escalate that learning, which is called a teaching behavior category" (Goldberg, 1990, 41).

In their summary of direct instruction for students with mild disabilities, Bickel and Bickel (1986) noted, "Effective teachers take an active role in creating a positive, expectant, and orderly classroom environment in which learning takes place." Teachers' control time management, signal when academic work will begin, maintain a group focus, expect students to be accountable, and provide a variety of instructional tasks. Direct instruction is based on teacher control of instruction and close supervision of student work. It has produced good results in teaching basic skills, particularly with low achievers. Critics maintain that direct instruction stifles student initiative and that it doesn't teach higher level thinking skills. Critics also express concern that direct instruction undercuts motivation by reinforcing student dependence on the teacher (Knap, Turnbull, & Shields, 1990).

Precision Teaching

Jamie is a fifth-grade student at Somewhere Elementary School, U.S.A. Four days a week, Monday through Thursday, Jamie reads aloud, answers math problems, and spells words dictated by her teacher. Each of these tasks is timed, and Jamie plots her own scores on separate graphs for reading, math, and spelling. A line is extended from the points where other scores have been plotted. This procedure enables her teacher to visually track Jamie's learning rate. Jamie and her classmates are participating in precision teaching. Their teacher is measuring their learning performance daily. By seeing the changes in students learning each day, Jamie's teacher, and others who utilize precision teaching, can adjust their instructional plans as needed (White, 1986).

Ogden Lindsley is the founder of precision teaching. Lindsley observed that learning can be enhanced by frequent, self-recorded responses on standardized charts. He encouraged teachers to concentrate on rate of responses instead of percentages of correct responses. Lindsley recommended that teachers teach their students to self-record their own rate of learning on standardized charts (Lindsley, 1990).

Lindsley designed precision teaching around a framework of operant conditioning and methods of behavior analysis developed by B.F. Skinner. This framework consists of seven basic components:

1. By assessing daily performance, teachers can directly measure performance and monitor learning.
2. Calculating rate of response (i.e., the number of correct responses per minute) establishes a consistent measure of behavior.
3. A standard chart format provides a visual display of performance patterns.
4. Definitions of behavior are descriptive and functional.
5. Analysis of instruction is ongoing.
6. The emphasis is on building appropriate and useful behavior, rather than focusing on doing away with undesired or inappropriate behavior.

When students like Jamie are assessed daily, their changes in performance from one timed assessment to the next guide instruction. The more frequently the timed assessments are made, the more often decisions can be made about the effectiveness of instruction for an individual student. Timings are done each day, thus students have sufficient opportunities to demonstrate skills.

Educators traditionally look for accuracy in student responses. Daily timed assessments provide the data to measure both the accuracy and the rate of learning. Wolking (1991) provided the following description of Jamie.

At the beginning of this unit of study, Jamie answered 20 subtraction fact problems in a minute. She got 13 correct and made 7 errors. Twelve school days later

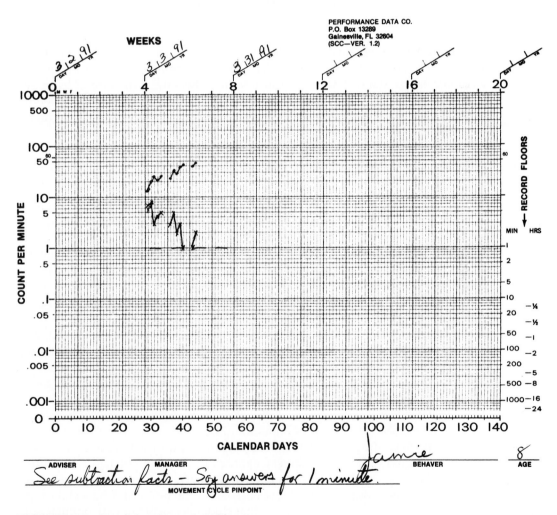

FIGURE 7–1 Precision Learning Chart.

Contributed by William Wolking.

she answered 47 subtraction facts in a minute. On this timing, she got 45 correct and made 2 errors. The learning line for her correct responses showed that she was improving at a rate of 65% per week. The learning line for her error responses showed she was reducing her errors at a rate of about 70% per week. Overall, Jamie's correct responding has improved by 246% (from 13 to 45 per minute correct), and her error responses have decreased by 250% (from 7 to 2 errors per minute) in just twelve school days.

Precision teaching requires plotting scores on a chart so that changes in student learning can be tracked. This chart is a ratio or logarithmic scale, and referred to as the "standard celeration chart." The logarithmic scale displays performance values that are recorded as number of responses per minute. When scores are plotted, an individual's pattern of learning can be seen by drawing a line through the dots. This line of connected points is called a learning line. Generally, the steeper the learning line, the faster learning is occurring. Conversely, the more horizontal or flatter the learning line, the slower the rate of learning. The chart is called a standard or celeration chart because the same rate of learning is always displayed by the same slope.

Student-Centered Learning

In his widely acclaimed book *A Place Called School,* John Goodlad (1984) laments the lack of vigor in United States classrooms. He describes teachers as "frontal" in their style. By this he meant they seemed rooted to the front of the room, where they oversee all classroom activity like a captain on the bridge of a ship. In describing the culture of school, Goodlad characterizes the teacher as the central figure, a virtually autonomous person who controls almost every aspect of classroom life. Students labor alone, solitary figures in groups, with little to say about how they spend their days. Students, Goodlad said, engage in a narrow range of passive behaviors such as listening to the teacher, writing answers to questions, and taking tests or quizzes. Goodlad was not the first educator to describe public schools as havens of autocracy that demand conformity. Demands for changing schools to be more student-centered seem to follow every reform movement that insists teachers get back to the basics. For every point about empowering teachers, such as Hunter's direct instruction model, there is the inevitable counterpoint to empower students.

Glasser (1985) argued that schools should become more responsive to student needs. According to Glasser, student apathy and unwillingness to participate in classroom activities is a direct response to student impotence. As an illustration, Glasser pointed out that no one has to coerce students to work hard at extracurricular activities. Yearbooks, science fairs, athletics, and debate clubs represent a few manifestations of activities that students engage in with enthusiasm. Glasser maintained that the opportunity to exercise control of extracurricular activities increases motivation and involvement. He articulated four student needs that schools should strive to fulfill in the classroom:

1. Students need to belong. They need to feel a part of a larger community and to feel that they are valued by the group.
2. Students need power. They need to make decisions and have responsibilities.
3. Students need freedom. They need to feel self-reliant and in control of their own destiny.
4. Students need fun. They need to have joy, humor, and they want to work for personal satisfaction.

Notice none of these needs relates to specific parts of the academic curriculum, rather Glasser is focusing on deeper, developmental needs. It's at the developmental level where student-directed and teacher-directed advocates split. Teachers who formalize student-directed learning in their classrooms assume a developmental view of education. Preschool education is presently the only sector of public education that holds to a strong developmental outlook. Once students begin first grade and continue through middle and high school, developmental views on how young people learn and what their psychological needs are get mired in a curriculum logjam (Elkind, 1986). Teachers wilt under the pressure to get a student "ready" for the next grade. Basal readers, spelling tests, and an endless array of workbooks provide the grist that students must grind their way through in traditional, curriculum-centered classrooms. In high school, the winds of curriculum pick up pace as teachers bend to pressure to prepare students for graduation and college entrance requirements.

In a student-centered classroom, it is unlikely that students would select the same topics mandated by the school system for each grade. Here lies the dilemma for the developmental teacher. What is the priority—specific curriculum requirements that are best taught through teacher-directed lessons, or student-centered activities that may overlook content measured in standard tests of achievement? A negotiated solution is workable. Teachers can merge both approaches. Direct instruction on the periodic table is more likely to grab a student's attention after a few experiments in a chemistry laboratory. Classroom discussions about the pros and cons of abortion can provide the same insight into the judicial system of our country covered by a mundane chapter in a social studies text. Cooperative learning projects can cover the same content as a lecture on algebraic equations.

Student-centered classrooms look different than teacher-directed classrooms. Furniture is arranged to enhance student conversation in small groups; cooperative learning and peer tutoring are commonplace. Myriad objects for concrete learning experiences are arranged on tables. While students work, the teacher moves about the room encouraging, providing feedback, and giving directions. Some students are engaged in small groups; others work independently. Work schedules are arranged to allow students to study different topics at the same time. Rote learning, drill, and passive materials such as worksheets and dittos are shunned.

A common misconception of student-centered classrooms is that they are unstructured. A visitor to a student-centered fourth grade might observe the following scene. Adults and students are scattered throughout the room. In one corner, a parent volunteer is listening to three students take turns reading. Along the perimeter of the room, students in pairs are working at several tables that are labeled "math center," "science center," "art center," and "writing center." In another corner of the room, a student is playing a math game at a computer. Two students are cleaning the gerbil cage. Four students are sitting on pillows and reading library books in the "quiet corner." A student teacher is standing in front of the blackboard reviewing fractions with a group of five students. Finally, the visitor spots the teacher in another corner. Around her is a group of seven students. She is doing a phonics lesson. The room is a beehive of activity. People are talking and walking about. Everybody is busy.

To the untrained eye, the scene may appear disorganized, but there is a complex structure that holds everything together. A student-centered classroom requires a well thought out plan for moving students from one center to another; materials and themes at the centers need continual refurbishing; volunteers need direction; student progress must be monitored; and the daily schedule must insure that all students have a blend of direct and indirect learning experiences. A teacher in a student-directed classroom must be capable of supervising several simultaneous activities.

As long as teachers view direct instruction and student-centered learning as philosophical opposites, the debate about which is the best way to teach will continue indefinitely. A ten-minute slide show on the history of United States education would resemble a dance with strobe lights. Following every slide of students frozen in their seats listening to the instructor, there would be a slide picturing students spread around the room involved in different activities. Since the early 1900s the educational pendulum has traced a well-worn track back and forth between direct and student-centered instruction. Teachers who are capable of integrating both approaches into their lessons on a daily basis can attend to the demands of curriculum without forsaking the developmental needs of their young charges.

Learning Strategies

A twelve-year-old given the task of remembering a list of objects (e.g., milk, bread, soda, candy) will say the words over and over again in order to commit them to memory. This automatic use of repetition is the essence of learning strategies (Pressley & Harris, 1990). Learning strategies (also referred to as cognitive strategy, cognitive behavior modification, and meta-cognitive skills) are unconscious mental schemes for memorizing, solving problems, planning, or organizing. Many individuals independently learn these strategies in the normal course of development; others never acquire these strategies on their own. The lack of learning strategy development may be the basis for many of the learning problems students with mild disabilities encounter.

Alley and Deshler, practitioners in the field of special education, identified learning strategies as ". . . techniques, principles, or rules that will facilitate the acquisition, manipulation, integration, storage, and retrieval of information across situations and settings" (Alley & Deshler, 1979, 13). These authors support the need to teach students how to use learning strategies to improve comprehension and retention of classroom content. Equally important is teaching students how to generalize learning strategies outside of school.

> *The adage "Give me a fish, and I can eat for a day. Teach me to fish, and I can eat for a lifetime" summarizes the goal of this approach. The intent is to teach students skills that will allow them not only to meet immediate requirements successfully but also to generalize these skills to other situations over time. (Alley, 1979, 13)*

Learning strategies help students learn to cope with mild disabilities by providing them with a set of directions for improving their ability to learn. Pressley and Harris present the following guidelines for using learning strategies to improve reading comprehension:

1. Summarize the story. Dialogues and classroom discussions enhance memory of plot and characters.
2. Construct an internal visual representation of the story. This procedure can be enhanced through art activities.
3. Relate student experience to a story.
4. Make up questions about the story while reading. (Pressley & Harris, 1990, 32)

The teaching of learning strategies begins with the teacher modeling the strategy in the context of a meaningful classroom assignment. Students might be assigned an essay, for example, and the teacher would begin by demonstrating how to write an intuitive outline (see Figure 7–2 on page 242). The purpose of the intuitive outline is to get ideas out before listing them in a sequential outline. An intuitive outline is completed by a student sitting at a desk for ten minutes and brainstorming by herself. She begins by placing the theme or main idea in an oval, and then writes each idea associated with the main thought on lines that branch out from the center. As a new idea comes to mind, it is added to an existing branch or a new branch is started. Just as a tree branches out spontaneously in different directions, the intuitive outline grows to accommodate the natural progression of ideas. This learning strategy (sometimes called mapping) can help solve common problems such as "writer's block" or test anxiety.

Another example of a learning strategy is mnemonics, a system of memory training that helps students remember important concepts by associating ideas to visual stimuli. A student might remember key principles of the U.S. Constitution, for instance, by going for a memory walk down his street and mentally "picking up" due process from the delicatessen, freedom of the press from the newspaper machine, and the right to bear arms from the department store mannequin.

Mann and Sabatino (1985) recommend the following steps for incorporating a learning strategies approach in the classroom:

1. Describe the strategies needed to solve a classroom problem. (One way to do this is through task analysis—break the solution down into specific steps.)
2. Measure a student's use or nonuse of strategies.
3. Help students implement selected strategies and adjust and revise as needed.
4. Monitor how well the strategy is working.
5. Motivate students to use the strategy. (Scott, 1988, 33)

Selecting the best type of learning strategy is a key element in utilizing the learning strategy approach. Scott (1988) recommends teaching problem-solving skills demonstrated by successful students. She identified concentration, independence, reflection, self-direction, active learning, and persistence as core learning strategies students with mild disabilities could learn to improve their classroom performance. Scott presented a variety of activities to teach each learning strategy to a student. For instance, concentration can be taught by playing chess or other games. Reflection could be taught by having students count to ten before they give an answer.

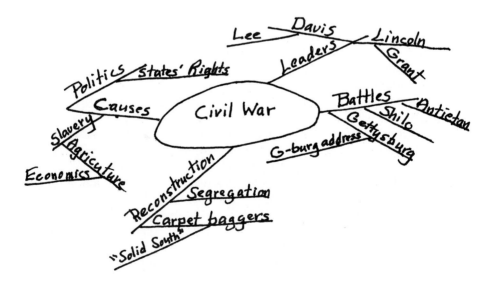

FIGURE 7–2   Intuitive Outline

Learning strategies teach students how to learn. Learning strategies help students to organize their thinking and teaches them skills they will use throughout their lives. However, one should be cautious about jumping too quickly on the learning strategies bandwagon. Much of the seminal work in this area has been conducted under experimental conditions that are unlike classroom conditions. Further research on learning strategies will provide insight into: how to teach learning strategies that students can use in different settings; how to integrate learning strategies into the curriculum; and how to design texts to support strategy instruction (Harris & Pressley, 1991).

Integrated Teaching

Madeline Hunter emphasized that teaching is decision-making. Each instructional method is like a tool in a mechanic's kit. Just as a mechanic will select an adjustable wrench for a particular problem and then move on to other tools, a teacher can select direct instruction to teach specific concepts and then follow up with student-centered activities or learning strategies. The more tools in the instructional kit, the better equipped a teacher is to choose the best instructional strategy for a given situation.

Glickman (1987) draws a distinction between "effective" schools and "good" schools. Effective schools sponsor teacher-directed learning. They narrow the academic focus. Students are taught in large groups from prescribed instructional objectives. Reviewing, demonstration, checking for student understanding, and frequent tests are standard procedures. Glickman asks the question—should there be more to school than Scholastic Achievement Test (SAT) scores; and if a school is effective, does that necessarily mean it's a good school? To illustrate his point Glickman related the following story.

> *A special education teacher recently told me that she had asked her supervisor for permission to take her students on a five-minute walk to a grocery store to observe transactions at the check-out counter. The supervisor immediately asked, "Which specific objectives will this walk accomplish?" The teacher replied, "I don't know. I simply want my students to see transactions involving real money. Besides getting out of the classroom for awhile would be fun." Responded the supervisor, "I'm sorry. If it's not one of our curriculum objectives, we don't do it!" (p. 623)*

Glickman's point is well made. His concern about the overemphasis of one instructional strategy to the exclusion of others is shared by many educators and researchers. Moreover, Ronald Brandt (1990) observes that teachers have difficulty making changes in their teaching style "like so many compliant windmills on a Kansas prairie." A more comprehensive view of instructional strategies is needed to help teachers integrate seemingly disparate teaching methods.

Harris and Pressley (1991) point out that student-centered and teacher-directed strategies are false dichotomies. Students do indeed need opportunities to construct their own knowledge (i.e., student-directed), but that does not obviate teacher-directed lessons. As Harris and Pressley point out, students will direct their own thinking even when exposed to direct instruction.

> . . . *children engaged in the rehearsal of mathematics operations may construct new procedural forms, such as arithmetic shortcuts, while practicing. As students develop skill and proficiency, they do not do exactly what they have been taught. This construction of personalized learning has been well recognized among (learning) strategy researchers. (Harris & Pressley, 1991)*

Another element in the discussion of the merits of direct and indirect instruction is the uneasy hypothesis that teachers gravitate towards instructional strategies that reflect their personal learning styles. Claudia Cornett observed that teachers tend to choose instructional strategies based on their personal educational philosophies (Cornett, 1983). The research in this area is thin, but there is ample anecdotal evidence that authoritarian teachers prefer teacher-directed strategies, while student-centered strategies are preferred by teachers who have a developmental view on teaching and learning. More research in this area might produce some uncomfortable insights. While researchers labor to determine the effectiveness of specific strategies and college professors promote strategies based on their utility, it may be that teachers select instructional strategies based on conscious or unconscious personal preferences.

Harris and Pressley (1991) described how learning strategies are compatible with student-directed learning. They point out that good learning strategy teachers help students to construct their own problem-solving approaches. They keep students actively involved in tasks that are meaningful and personal. Guskey (1990) provided the following framework for synthesizing diverse instructional strategies:

1. All instructional strategies should share common goals.
2. Recognize that no single strategy can do everything.
3. Strategies should complement each other.
4. Time should be taken to experiment and adapt strategies to particular schools and classrooms.
5. The combined beneficial effects of combined strategies will surpass the effects of any single strategy.

Strong and a small group of colleagues created a framework to integrate five different instructional strategies: ITIP (Hunter's model of direct instruction), learning strategies, student learning styles, cooperative learning, and reading and writing in content areas (Strong et al., 1990). Each member of the group identified a basic operating principle that represented the core premise of an instructional strategy. They called these core principles their "declaration of interdependence." From teacher-directed ITIP, they derived the principle that teachers' decisions should be based on verified educational research. From the learning strategy approach, they highlighted the need for teachers to incorporate reasoning skills in lesson designs. From the research on student learning style, they emphasized flexibility in using a range of instructional strategies. Collaborative learning underscored the social dimension of learning; that is, the sum total of learning in a small group will surpass the learning each student could accomplish working alone. Finally, from the reading and writing across the curriculum literature, they highlighted the need to appreciate the artfulness of teaching.

In order to make use of Strong's integrative model, teachers need to understand how each system works, have knowledge of the learning characteristics of students, and have administrative support for experimentation. Any time a teacher tries something different in a classroom, there is an element of risk. Change is anxiety provoking, and schools are organizations (some would say bureaucracies) that have many built-in mechanisms that resist change. Schedules must be adhered to; school norms must be followed; and principals have most of the power. In a school where teacher-directed learning is the norm, the teacher who attempts to set up student-centered activities is risking failure and ridicule. Without administrative support, teachers must struggle in isolation against the odds. Only in schools where innovation and experimentation are valued will teachers succeed in providing the best of all worlds for their students.

The notion that there is one best way to teach is naive and delimiting. The voluminous research evidence that documents students have different optimal ways of learning should give any teacher reason to pause before wholeheartedly adopting one method of classroom instruction to the exclusion of others.

Student Learning Styles

Just as there is no right way to teach, there is no right way to learn. Students who are primarily verbal learners generally do well in school. They follow verbal directions; they listen; they participate in class discussions; and they have good reading comprehension skills. Some educators have pointed out that school work is primarily left hemispheric oriented. The right and left hemispheres of the neocortex process experience and information in different ways: the left hemisphere is the verbal, logical, abstract side of the neocortex; the right hemisphere is visual, intuitive, holistic, and insightful in the way it handles information. Students whose learning style is left hemispheric oriented have an advantage, while students who are right hemispheric oriented are at a disadvantage in school. If the school curriculum emphasized creative activities like art, drama, and spatial reasoning, students who were right hemispheric oriented might excel.

Sally Smith (1980) found that students identified as learning disabled do better when the school curriculum is taught through the arts. In the Lab School, Washington, D.C., teachers use art to develop organizational skills, strengthen memory, and promote academic readiness. Art activities provide Lab School teachers with opportunities to observe a student interacting with many different mediums of expression. This provides teachers with insights about educational needs and information about how a child learns most effectively. Experimental programs in New York City, Oakland, California, and Columbus, Ohio, resulted in higher standardized test scores in reading and math when teachers incorporated both right and left hemispheric activities in their lessons (Grady & Luecke, 1978).

Marie Carbo reported that the phonics method of learning to read is unsuitable for some children. Phonics is a left hemispheric oriented instructional strategy. It requires sequential processing and reproducing of sounds. Students must learn to sound out individual letters and then analyze how each sound combines to make a complete word. For a youngster who is right hemispheric oriented, this predominant left hemispheric strategy is burdensome and could lead to reading failure. Carbo states that ". . . many global/visual students derive little, if any benefit from phonics instruction because their strong intuitive abilities enable them to perceive the patterns of entire words or phrases with relative ease" (Carbo, 1987, 56). Notice that Carbo does not describe global/visual (right hemispheric) students as deficient. Their learning style is different. When teachers use only phonics instruction to teach reading, global/visual learners encounter difficulties. It is the mismatch between instructional strategy and learning style that gives the appearance of student inadequacy. Carbo describes global/visual learners as students who do well when: reading books of their own choosing, participating in choral readings, writing their own stories to read, and listening to tape recordings of interesting books. Drill and repetition of such reading skills as decoding bore these children. They perform better with whole language reading instruction.

In the formative years of special education (1950–1975), a variety of tactile/kinesthetic approaches to reading were designed for students identified as having learning disabilities. Grace Fernald's multisensory approach to reading continues to be widely used in resource rooms. The Fernald approach requires the student look at a word as it is pronounced by the teacher; say the word while tracing it; copy the word while saying it; and write the word from memory. The teacher reinforces word knowledge by using the rehearsed word frequently during reading instruction. The Fernald approach was based on the premise that the student had a learning disability, probably neurological in origin, that impaired ability to read through conventional instruction (usually phonics). It is important to note that in most instances it was impossible to verify the neurological impairment, rather the impairment was inferred. The logic, in many instances, was circuitous. Learning disabilities, it was believed, were neurological impairments. So when a student was identified as learning disabled by the school, educators illogically concluded a neurological impairment was present.

While it is clear that some students do have a subtle neurological impairment and a learning disability, it is also evident that many students are misidentified as learning disabled, or mildly retarded, or behavior disordered. The problem is not within the student but the overreliance on a single instructional strategy (e.g., phonics or direct instruction) that creates a mismatch between student learning style and teacher methods. This sort of standoff is no contest; the student will be placed in special education and the teacher will continue blithely on her way heedless to her lack of instructional flexibility. The most effective teachers are able to match instructional strategy to learning style. This coupling of instruction and student, however, can present a confusing array of approaches because of the myriad ways that learning styles are described in the research literature.

Research in learning (also called cognitive) styles has been going on for forty years. Convergent and divergent thinkers; field dependent and field independent learners; analytic and thematic styles; legislative, judicial, and executive styles are just samples of the diverse terminology used to explain preferred learning styles of students. In order to assist teachers sort through various options, Charles (1976) synthesized the research on learning styles. He described three types of learners: adventurers, ponderers, and drifters. He suggested that each style requires a different approach to teaching. An adventurer is similar to the divergent thinker. This student moves quickly through materials and ideas. The adventurer is right hemispheric oriented. Learning is intuitive, creative, and spontaneous. The adventurer is tolerant of ambiguity and indifferent to finding the "right" or "wrong" answer. Teacher latitude in structure works best for the adventurer who feels hemmed in by too much teacher control. This individual responds best to student-centered learning that provides opportunities for discovery and experience activities. The adventurer needs flexibility and encouraging feedback.

The ponderer is reflective and analytical (left hemispheric preference). A convergent thinker, this student looks for details and "correct" answers. The ponderer likes facts and generally does well with standardized achievement tests. A student with these qualities learns best when expectations are clear and direct. The ponderer works well with teacher-directed activities and responds to praise. The ponderer conforms well to classroom rules and expectations for behavior. This student is a convergent thinker. Using art as a metaphor, the adventurer could be compared to the many spontaneous hues of the impressionist, while the ponderer reflects the clear, crisp lines of an Andrew Wyeth painting.

The drifter, as the name implies, is an uncertain learner. The drifter does not display the self-confidence or initiative of the adventurer and ponderer. This student requires more attention from the teacher. Assignments often go unfinished. Without teacher encouragement and intervention, the drifter loses interest in schoolwork. The drifter leans on adult authority to overcome feelings of learned helplessness. We used paintings as a metaphor for the adventurer and ponderer. Andy Warhol, with his ironic view of modern pop culture, symbolizes the drifter. This individual is an oxymoron—a pupil who is out of place in school. Even though surrounded by the security of a predictable learning environment, the drifter is befuddled. Each learning task is approached with apprehension and a sense of foreboding. Bereft of the tools for classroom success, the drifter approaches schoolwork in an aimless and lackluster manner.

Each of these learning styles suggests a need to modify instructional strategies. The adventurer learns best in an environment that offers latitude and the opportunity to have some control over activities. Cooperative learning and activity centers are examples of student-centered instructional strategies that would respond to the learning needs of the adventurer. The ponderer would do well with the clearcut structure of teacher-directed instruction. Hunter's model (ITIP) or other strategies that provide sequential steps to skill development give the ponderer a predictable path to success. The drifter doesn't know how to learn in a classroom situation. The drifter needs encouragement and support. This student requires immediate feedback about classroom performance. Precision teaching and learning strategy techniques would match the needs of the drifter.

Identifying students learning style is a good beginning for instruction, but teaching is not a mechanical one-to-one correspondence activity. We cannot fit students to instruction like so many eggs nestled in a carton. To some extent all students need some control over their environment, as well as teacher-directed group instruction, and assistance in how to learn.

Rather than emphasizing the "right" way to teach, learning style literature underscores the fact that students are different. Student learning style is a unique blend of individual development and life experience. Teachers who understand learning styles respect the capabilities of their charges. The literature on learning styles provides a sharp contrast to the traditional school norm of student conformity to a single standard of instruction or behavior. As John Holt remarked, "Children are not only extremely good at learning, they are much better at it than we adults are. As a teacher it took me a very long time to find this out" (Holt, 1970, 232). By utilizing an array of instructional strategies, the classroom teacher builds a bridge between the student and the curriculum. Research on instructional strategies and learning styles helps us to grasp the complexity of learning and to appreciate the need for teachers to remain flexible when deciding how to teach.

Specific Recommendations for Helping Students with Mild Disabilities Adapt to Classroom Routines

Many students with mild disabilities have low self-esteem. Others have unreliable study skills and weak organizational skills. These problems have been reported repeatedly in the literature as common characteristics of students with mild disabilities (Meyen, Vergason, & Whelan, 1988; McCoy & Prehm, 1987; Polloway et al., 1989).

Students with these problems can be helped to function more productively in the classroom. Teachers can assist students who manifest difficulties with self-esteem, study skills, and organizational skills.

Self-Esteem

Teachers may have negative perceptions of students with mild disabilities; likewise, expectations of these students are less than what is expected of other students (Coleman, 1985; Siperstein & Goding, 1985). Other students often pick up on their teachers' perceptions and develop similar negative expectations toward classmates with mild disabilities. Equally important, students with mild disabilities develop poor self-concepts.

Teachers can serve as positive role models—that is, model positive reactions toward students with mild disabilities in order to create an environment of acceptance and support. Teachers do this by conveying that they want to work with the students and by supporting students' efforts.

> *Example: Sara and Jane have low self-esteem due to their learning problems. Both girls are in their early teens, come from middle-class backgrounds, and are popular with their peers. Sarah experiences difficulty comprehending what she has read. Even though she rereads a passage several times, she still has problems answering questions about what she has read. Jane, on the other hand, has difficulty with written expression. She reads assigned subject content with ease, can tell you what she has read, but cannot write legible responses to short answer or essay type questions. Sarah has withdrawn and become quiet in class; whereas, Jane acts belligerent and sassy.*

Both of these students would benefit from successes in the areas in which they are experiencing difficulties. There is a relationship between achievement and self-esteem. How Sarah and Jane perceive themselves is related to their feelings of failure (Whelan, de Saman, & Fortmeyer, 1988). What strategies can help these students achieve some measure of success with their respective academic problems? By following these practical suggestions, a classroom teacher can help students such as Sarah and Jane.

First, assign tasks in which the students can succeed, and make certain that the assignments are understood so they can be carried out successfully. Point out something favorable about each student's daily work, and praise successful attempts toward desired goals, even if progress is small. Whenever offering constructive criticism, recognize the effort that was made and explain the desired outcome rather than just calling attention to shortcomings. These suggestions may sound simple and commonplace, but praising effort reinforces student perseverance.

Much of a youngster's self-esteem is tied to social acceptance. Students can make contributions to class discussions by explaining a concept or discussing a topic with which they are familiar. Simulations and role play activities help students to rehearse social responses; cooperative learning provides opportunities to learn with other students. Peer tutoring develops feelings of satisfaction in helping other persons. Grouping students with low self-esteem with classmates who have similar interests enhances social conversation so they can more easily work together on class projects. Providing time for students to share positive accomplishments with classmates and to write daily happenings in a private journal also builds self-confidence.

Encourage students to use word processors so that writing can more easily be edited. Word processing encourages trial, error, and practice. Mark and give credit for students' correct and acceptable work, not just their mistakes and errors (e.g., circle or put checks by correct responses, indicate number correct with a plus symbol).

Study Skills

Knowing how to study is essential to successful performance in school. Students with mild disabilities demonstrate poor study skills (Polloway et al., 1989; Reid & Hresko, 1980). Many teachers are either unaware that study skills must be taught to these students or do not know how to teach these kinds of skills (Scruggs & Mastropieri, 1986).

> *Example: Jack, a sixth grader, exemplifies this problem. During early elementary school years, Jack had no problem reading assigned stories, doing basic math operations, and spelling weekly spelling words. Therefore, Jack's parents were perplexed when he began bringing home low grades in science and social studies. There was no doubt that Jack was reading the assigned chapters in his science and social studies textbooks—but he made failing test scores in these subjects. His parents and teacher discovered that Jack's lack of effective study skills left him ill-prepared for tests in these classes.*

One way to find out if students need to improve their study skills is to ask them questions about their study habits. Stephens, Blackhurst, and Magliocca (1988) recommend using a checklist for this purpose. See Table 7–2 for the Study Habits Checklist.

Often, students like Jack read the pages but don't comprehend what the written passages mean. Several researchers found the SQ3R method of study effective in helping students to better comprehend what they are reading (Cheek & Cheek, 1983; Mercer & Mercer, 1985; Wallace & Kauffman, 1986). The SQ3R study skill teaches students to:

- survey or scan the material: read the title, first paragraph, subheadings, and last paragraph.
- develop questions: change the title and subheadings into questions.
- read the material: find answers to the questions.
- recite both the questions and answers.
- review the material: recite questions and answers daily.

TABLE 7–2 Study Habits Checklist

_____ Do you have a regular place where you study?

_____ Do you keep a chart that shows the time you spend studying?

_____ Do you have a regular time to study?

_____ Do you keep a homework assignment book?

_____ Do you keep a calendar of tests, reports, and projects?

_____ Do you keep a notebook or folder for each subject?

_____ Do you take class notes?

_____ Do you make notes or highlight material while reading?

_____ Do you review class notes and reading notes regularly?

_____ Do you outline or summarize what you read?

_____ Do you make note of and look up new words?

_____ Do you keep for review all returned papers and tests?

_____ Do you visit and use the library regularly?

Adapted from: Stephens, T.M., Blackhurst, A.E., and Magliocca, L.A. *Teaching Mainstreamed Students* (2nd Edition, 1988, Pergamon Press, 160–161).

The SQ3R method of study can be modified and used to help students better understand math problems (Georgia Department of Education, 1989). The student procedure is as follows:

- survey or scan the whole problem to determine what needs to be done.
- change the math problem into a series of questions.
- determine the facts that need to be answered.
- determine processes needed to answer the facts.
- perform computation to solve the problems.
- question the answer by checking the computation.

Reading comprehension is enhanced when students can relate their personal experiences to what they are reading. Since each reader's background will vary, involve students in first-hand experiences (e.g., field trips) when possible. Another method is to stimulate students' thinking about a topic before oral or silent reading begins (Wilson, 1983). Polloway and colleagues (1989, 229) suggest having the teacher introduce a reading selection by saying, "As you read, think about what you would do if you were caught in a flood as Van is in this story." This helps a student personalize a story.

Active reading is encouraged when a teacher initiates a discussion related to the selection the students are about to read. For example, encourage students to comment on a passage by giving their opinions or by having students read a passage and justify or change their original opinions (Polloway et al., 1989). When students make predictions about the story and generate their own questions, their comprehension is improved.

Students with mild disabilities frequently feel overwhelmed with the amount of material they are expected to learn. The teacher can reduce the amount of written work that is presented or assigned (Carbo, Dunn, & Dunn, 1986; Schulz, Carpenter, & Turnbull, 1991). Students can demonstrate mastery of learning material through projects (Lewis & Doorlag, 1987). For example, students can track the position of planets in relation to the sun by constructing a mobile on which styrofoam balls representing the planets are scaled in size and distance from a sun. Projects enhance interest in learning.

Organizational Skills

Being organized is important for success in the regular classroom. Students with mild disabilities have organization problems. Particular areas in which organization assistance might be needed include: (a) keeping track of materials and assignments, (b) following directions, (c) completing class assignments, and (d) completing homework assignments.

Keeping Track of Materials and Assignments

Example: Billy, a fifth grader, exhibits problems keeping track of his materials and homework assignments. One day his English teacher gave him a slip of paper that excused him from that evening's homework in her class. He had earned this waiver by receiving good grades on a specified number of prior homework assignments. When handed this paper, Billy jammed it into one of his pants pockets. The next day, his teacher asked the students to turn in either their homework assignment or their homework waiver. Billy suddenly realized that he had neither the excuse nor the homework.

What can be done in the classroom to help students like Billy learn responsibility? Billy could keep all of his schoolwork in a large loose-leaf notebook and not in single folders that could be lost. Students with mild disabilities may not have the materials and supplies necessary to begin their classwork. This is especially a problem when students move from one classroom to another for different subjects. These students need to be shown how to organize and plan ahead for classroom needs. One way to help students develop judgment and planning skills is to teach them strategy games like monopoly, checkers, or chess. Mnemonic devices and lists help students organize priorities (McCoy & Prehm, 1987).

Following Directions

Example: Jack has problems following classroom directions. Invariably, Jack answers the wrong set of questions, uses the wrong type of paper, or in some way, exhibits difficulties following directions.

Before giving directions to students like Jack, have them clear their desks of distracting objects. A cleared desk helps students to focus attention, as does maintaining eye contact while stating directions. A variation is breaking directions into parts one, two, and three. Support directions with visual cues. For example, write key words or steps on the chalkboard or on a large chart. Ask students to restate the directions as they understand them. If directions are written, underline or circle directional words. Gloecker and Simpson (1988) caution against giving directions to a group several times. Students may "tune out" the initial instructions because they have learned that the directions will be repeated. In addition, the instructions may be reworded the second time, and thus become confusing. Encourage students to ask for clarifications if part of the directions are missed or misunderstood.

Students sometimes experience problems in proper sequencing. To assist with this difficulty, keep the number of directions in a sequence to a minimum. Check to see if the student understands the order in which the directions were given. This can be done by listening to him or her repeat the directions in sequence (Gloeckler & Simpson, 1988).

Completing Class Assignments

Example: "Class, you have ten more minutes to finish your assignment," said Mrs. Green. Even that won't help Janice, she thought, as she walked by the girl's desk. Look at her paper--she hasn't even written six math problems on it! I wish I knew what I could do to get her to finish her class assignments!

All teachers encounter students like Janice who have difficulty completing class assignments on time. Before looking for strategies that might be helpful with particular students, teachers might analyze how they are going about assigning work. First, is adequate time being given to finish assigned tasks? Not everyone works at the same pace, and some students require more time than others. Therefore, as in Janice's case, Mrs. Green could assist her in pacing her work. After advising students of exactly how much time is being allowed, Mrs. Green could help Janice set a kitchen timer on her desk that shows her just how much time she has spent on a particular assignment, and how much time is left. Or Janice could be given an assignment sheet with two blank clocks, one for the teacher or student to fill in hands to signify time to begin and one for drawing hands to end that task. With either of these time reminders, a reward system for completed work would help reinforce student efforts.

There are several other strategies that help students with mild disabilities complete work. Students need to know exactly when assignments must be turned in. Mini-deadlines set throughout the day alert students periodically to work that is due. Scheduling a brief free-time period before work is due allows some catch-up time if needed.

Completing Homework Assignments

Example: Completing homework assignments is a problem for Sandra, a fourth grader. It's not that Sandra won't do the work—she does what she can. Her problem is that the homework assignments given by her teacher cover new con-

cepts she has yet to master. So why don't her parents help her? Well, her father is a sales representative and travels during most week days. Her mother works part-time as a nurse at one of the nearby hospitals. The family with whom Sandra stays during the evenings her mom works is so busy with their own activities that no help is possible there.

The tasks assigned by Sandra's teacher are in the category of new tasks—not practice tasks. Because her teacher is overlooking this basic principle, she is handicapping Sandra. Sandra's teacher has overlooked another basic tenet that relates to Sandra's ability level. Students should only be assigned homework that they are capable of completing successfully. Tasks that are too difficult instill feelings of frustration and hopelessness in students.

Cooper (1989a, 7) defines homework as "tasks assigned to students by school teachers that are meant to be carried out during nonschool hours." He states that homework helps students to understand academic work and to remember what they have learned (Cooper, 1989b). More indirectly, homework helps in the improvement of: students' study skills, attitudes toward school, and an aware-ness that learning occurs in other places than school. Other nonacademic benefits, named by Cooper, include the fostering of independence and responsibility. Homework involves parents in the school process, makes them more aware of what their child is studying, and signals support of their child's education.

Unfortunately, there can be a negative side to homework, says Cooper (1989b). For example, too much work on the same topic leads to boredom. Homework should not deprive a youngster of recreational activities. If parents try to assist their child with homework, their use of different methods from that of the child's teacher can cause confusion. Not understanding what or how to do a homework assignment can result in copying or cheating.

Homework too often accentuates inequities in home environments. For instance, some children do not have quiet, well-lighted places to do their home-work; some do not have the necessary materials; and some, like Sandra, do not have someone to answer their questions or monitor them.

So what can be done to reap the benefits of homework yet make sure indi-vidual student abilities and home situations are considered? First, remember that only practice tasks should be given as homework. Second, when deciding upon the amount of homework, the objective is for the student to practice things learned at school; thus, too much homework, especially if practiced with errors, can be harmful.

England and Flatley (1985) encourage teachers to talk with their students when homework problems arise. They suggest that teachers ask their students if they need help or if they are confused about a homework assignment. There may be legitimate reasons that preclude completing a particular homework assignment.

Some homework do's and don'ts listed by England and Flatley (1985, 36–37) are:

1. Do not give homework as punishment.

2. Do not make up spur-of-the-moment homework assignments.
3. Do not assume that because there are no questions asked about a homework assignment that students understand the assignment.
4. Do not expect students (even your best students) always to have their homework assignments completed.
5. Do understand that not all types of homework assignments are equally valuable for all types of students.
6. Do explain the specific purpose of every homework assignment.
7. Do listen to what students say about their experiences in completing your homework assignments.

Coordinate homework with parents. One way to do this is to have students keep a special notebook or folder in which homework assignments are recorded. Such a log would include type of assignment, specific instructions, when it was taken home, and when it was completed. Parents might sign the page on which the day's homework assignments are recorded. Keeping a homework log would ensure that parents know each day what their child is assigned for homework. An alternative is to ask parents to sign the actual homework papers, either before they are turned in or after they have been graded and returned to the youngster. Encourage parents to reward successful completion of homework assignments.

Selection of Instructional Materials

Teachers are faced with difficult decisions about which instructional materials to select for students, especially those with mild disabilities. When given the choice, Ramsey (1988) discovered that teachers most often select materials with which they (1) are most familiar, (2) have been trained to use, (3) can find available, and (4) can identify with their teaching style.

Smith (1983) maintains that the most appropriate materials for a teacher to use with students who have learning problems are those which:

- have a logical, hierarchical sequence of instructional objectives,
- are adaptable to a variety of learning styles (e.g., adventurer, ponderer, drifter),
- are adaptable to individualized, small-group, and large-group work,
- cover the same objectives in multiple ways,
- review previously learned objectives,
- present content in a consistent, understandable way,
- offer ideas for task analysis and alternative teaching strategies,
- pretest to determine where teaching should begin,
- have a built-in evaluation mechanism for determining mastery of instructional objectives,
- allow students to proceed at their own rate and even skip objectives they have already mastered,

- include several evaluation formats (e.g., projects, multiple-choice tests or essay exams, oral reports, homework assignments, self-checking keys, etc.),
- have reinforcement activities.

To this list, Ramsey (1988) adds a few additional criteria for the selection of instructional materials. Stories should contain characters who are the same age, gender, and race as the readers. Young readers will be more interested in reading stories when they see pictures and other illustrations that are representative of themselves, their friends, and their families. Likewise, content and vocabulary need to be at their reading levels. Last, instructional materials should meet the learning needs of students, as noted on their individual education programs (IEPs).

Modifications and Adaptations of Selected Materials

Students with mild disabilities sometimes require modifications in materials. One type of modification that is often needed is a reduced number of problems for classroom seat work. For instance, why have Johnny, who works at a pace much slower than his classmates, work out 20 long division problems when he can show he knows how to do the mathematical operations by answering five of these problems correctly? And when Mary experiences difficulties with division, use error analysis. That is, pinpoint what she is doing procedurally that is causing the same error to occur in several problems. By applying error analysis, the student has only one calculation error to correct.

Another type of modification is altering the response requirement. For example, the usual way that teachers give spelling tests is by oral pronunciation of words and having students write them. Instead, give students word choices that are similar and have them underline or circle the correct spelling of words from a multiple-choice format. Or use the cloze procedure where the teacher deletes selected letters which must then be filled in by students. Similarly, alter the instructional formats. Have students work at learning centers and use picture directions rather than written sentences. Or use a buddy system whereby one student reads the instructions, and the other performs the tasks.

In order to present content at secondary students' reading and comprehension levels, a teacher might write information presented in textbooks, develop chapter outlines, code paragraphs to chapter questions, and so forth. Using magic markers, highlight the main idea, topic, and specific vocabulary words or letters. Discarded books and workbooks can be put together and reassembled in ways that meet specific instructional needs of students.

Testing and Grading Systems

Tests are administered by teachers to find out what students have learned. This in turn helps teachers to know how effective their instruction has been. It is characteristic of students with mild disabilities to function academically at levels lower than their grade placement. Because of this, both testing and grading systems may require modifications.

Testing Alternatives

Methods for testing students with mild disabilities vary in type, structure, and level of response. Students can be asked to respond to tests and quizzes with written answers, verbal responses, or by demonstration. Learner characteristics often dictate the amount that can be tested at one sitting, the time needed for completion, and whether the testing results can best be achieved by giving group or individually administered tests. Responses should be monitored and expanded from simple recognition and recall (with or without cues) to higher level thinking skills, like inference, analysis, synthesis, evaluation, and appreciation.

Bauer and Shea (1989) focus upon three areas of test development: construction, design, and administration of tests. They contend that making the directions for a test clear and understandable is as important as careful development of test items. They suggest giving only one direction in each sentence and sequencing directions in order.

The design of tests is generally that of multiple-choice, true-false, matching, fill-in, or essay. Bauer and Shea (1989) suggest eliminating unnecessary verbiage. For example, in multiple-choice questions, they suggest that "all of the above" and "none of the above" be avoided in the recommended four alternatives following the stem of the question. Similarly, in true-false questions, avoid negatives and words like "never," "sometimes," and "always." Write questions at the student's level of comprehension, and define unfamiliar words. Be certain that test items reflect subject knowledge rather than reading, writing, or vocabulary skills.

When administering a test, Bauer and Shea (1989) recommend that sufficient time be given students so that they can complete it without rushing. Students with mild disabilities may have short attention spans; therefore, schedule intermittent breaks. Read test directions orally and give an example of the expected correct response. Remind students to review their tests, complete any unanswered questions, and make corrections where needed. For students who have difficulty with traditional tests, alternatives suggested by Bauer and Shea include projects, checklists, discussions, student-teacher interviews and student-developed portfolios designed to demonstrate student knowledge and understanding of content. Finally, giving brief, frequent tests increases students' opportunities for success.

Grading Systems

Much debate has centered around how the performance of students with mild disabilities should be graded. Carpenter (1985) suggests using the following questions to guide grading decisions: "On what criteria are grades based? What type of medium (e.g., letter grades, pass-fail) should be used? Who should participate in the grading process? How frequently should grades be given?"

Teachers generally include class participation, seat work, tests (e.g., daily, weekly, unit), homework, and special projects in student evaluations. More than one grade could be given to reflect other student attributes such as effort, attitude, or study skills. Supplement number or letter grades with oral and written information.

A major dilemma for teachers is how to grade work that is completed on the student's functioning level in the regular classroom, but not at his or her grade level placement. It is generally agreed that student work which is performed satisfactorily should be reinforced if it is at the student's functioning level and not his or her grade level. One practice is to link grades to the goals and objectives in a student's IEP (Brantlinger & Guskin, 1988). Schultz, Carpenter, and Turnbull (1991) suggest using a criterion-referenced skill list so that specific objectives can be checked as "mastered" or "needs improvement."

Another means of assigning grades is to reward students with the grades earned but coded with actual functioning levels. For example, a fourth grade student with mild learning disabilities earns an "A" in reading at the second grade level (the student's actual functioning level in that subject)—thus an "A2" appears on the student's report card as his grade in that subject.

Special educators are encouraged to meet with regular teachers on a regular basis to discuss student progress and achievement. Meetings provide the opportunity to convey to the classroom teacher a clear description of a student's strengths, weaknesses, capabilities, and needs. By doing so, additional data is provided the regular classroom teacher by which to determine grades. Perhaps, most important is the inclusion of the regular classroom teacher in IEP meetings and decisions. Whenever possible, engage in cooperative grading arrangements so that both regular classroom and resource room performances are evaluated. Charting student progress can help illustrate student gains which might otherwise be overlooked. It may help to involve students in their own grading when possible.

Teacher Communication Skills

Effective teaching depends upon good communication between teacher and students (Johnson, 1972; Jones & Jones, 1986). Participants in communication are actively involved as senders and receivers. The sender is the person who communicates the message, verbally or nonverbally; the receiver is the person who ultimately responds to the message. The communication process may break down if the message cannot be heard, understood, or is misinterpreted. When any of these happen, communication exchanges usually cease.

By using good communication skills, a teacher has more assurance that the intended message is getting across to the students. By being a model of a good listener, a teacher can help students learn to listen and respond appropriately to others. Attention is the prerequisite to listening.

Attending Skills

Students sometimes need to be taught how to attend to a speaker. Some related attending skills include: (1) looking at the teacher when information or instruction is being presented, (2) listening to directions for assignments, (3) listening for answers to questions, (4) looking at the chalkboard, (5) listening to others speak when appropriate, and (6) watching audiovisual presentations.

For some students, special techniques are employed to gain and hold attention (Morsink, 1984; Jones & Jones, 1981; Ramsey, Dixon, & Smith, 1986; Stephens, 1977). For instance, the teacher might first call the student by name when asking a question to assure attending by that individual, conversely the teacher can ask the question before calling the name of a student to create greater interest or anticipation from members of the group. Selecting students at random to answer questions helps to keep everybody alert and listening. Enthusiasm and keeping lessons short and interactive assists in maintaining the attention of those students with attending problems. Some students may be better able to focus their attention when environmental distractions are eliminated or at least reduced, and nonverbal signals can be used to draw students' attention to the task. Attending skills can be taught through games that encourage active listening. Arranging the classroom so that all students can see the teacher helps direct attention to the appropriate location. Finally, by paying close attention when students speak, teachers become good models for attending skills.

Clarity of Expression

Unclear communication between the teacher and students with mild disabilities sometimes contributes to problems in academic and social situations. In the learning environment, unclear communication can add to the student's confusion about certain processes or skills he or she is attempting to master.

There are many ways in which teachers can improve the clarity of their communication (Gloeckler & Simpson, 1988; Lewis & Doorlag, 1987). One is to give clear, precise directions. Teachers can simplify verbal directions by using shorter sentences, familiar words, and relevant explanations. Asking a student to repeat directions or to demonstrate understanding of them by carrying out the instructions is an effective way of monitoring clarity of expression. In addition, clarification can be achieved by the use of concrete objects, multidimensional teaching aids, and by modeling (i.e., demonstrating) what should be done in a practice situation.

Finally, a teacher can clarify communications by using a variety of vocal inflections. The use of intonation (i.e., stresses on certain words or sounds), and juncture (i.e., spacing of words) can add clarity to a message. For example, pausing before stating key words or stressing those that convey particular meanings helps students.

Teacher Feedback

Feedback that is given just after a behavior occurs is called immediate feedback; whereas, feedback that is given some time after a particular behavior occurs is called delayed feedback. There are appropriate times for using both immediate and delayed feedback (Alberto & Troutman, 1982; Gallagher, 1988; Jones & Jones, 1986; Morsink, 1984; Ramsey et al., 1986).

In situations involving behavior and feelings, the more immediate the feedback, the more helpful it is. Disturbing situations should be discussed as they occur. Collective hurt feelings and annoyances that are communicated at one time may lead to more hurt feelings and frustrations.

> *Buddy's father is a salesman and travels during the week. One Sunday evening, he told Buddy all the things that had bothered him during the weekend. His dad did not feel that Buddy had been glad to see him on Friday evening, and he thought that Buddy spent too much time with his friends instead of with him on Saturday and Sunday. Buddy felt that he was being "dumped on" and that his good traits were overlooked, so he withdrew and pouted. Communication ended and nothing was really resolved between Buddy and his dad.*

Immediate feedback is helpful in most behavioral situations like this. Had Buddy's father talked with him throughout the weekend as things occurred, perhaps his feelings of being left out of his son's life could have been resolved. Had Buddy known how his father felt earlier, he could have reassured him by doing something special with him.

In the classroom, there are appropriate uses of both immediate and delayed feedback. In general, learning is enhanced when students are provided with quick, specific feedback about their performance. When learning new skills or practicing tasks yet to be mastered, students should be provided with prompt information about the correctness of their responses. If the responses are incorrect, encourage a student to analyze and discover his or her own errors. This turns a mistake into a cooperative venture. Immediate reinforcement can relay affirmation followed with a suggested modification: "Good job! You got two correct. Now just do this one the same way."

Johnson (1972, 1978) gives several suggestions that teachers can use when providing feedback. First, only give a student the amount of feedback that he or she can understand at that time. Overloading a student with feedback reduces chances that the feedback will be used. Second, describe what happened rather than making judgmental evaluations about the situation. For instance, "You need to be sure and pronounce clearly the words at the end of your sentences," rather than, "You don't make a good public speaker." Last, give objective feedback—avoid moralizing. Do not make personal judgments about statements made by the students or their behavior. Instead, give the students descriptive feedback; for example, "Johnny, the rule says you need your pencil and paper ready to begin work," rather than, "You always forget your notebook!"

Teacher Questioning Skills

Teachers of all age groups ask myriad questions while they are teaching each day. What types of questions are teachers asking of their students? Are teachers encouraging students to think on higher cognitive levels, or are they asking for rote memory type answers? Berliner (1979) did a study in which he investigated the cognitive levels of the questions that teachers normally ask. He classified Bloom's and Barrett's Taxonomies into lower and higher level cognitive thinking skills. Questions that teachers asked were recorded and matched with thinking levels. His study found that the cognitive thinking level of the questions that teachers ask is typically low rather than high. For example, a lower level question asks for a literal answer, like "Can a person go into space?" A higher level question requires a student to apply knowledge, analyze and synthesize information, or make evaluations and interpretations. For instance, "Why do astronauts weigh less in space than on earth?" requires students to apply their knowledge of gravity. Both lower and higher level cognitive questions are relevant and are needed in classroom learning; however, teachers may need to focus on asking more higher level questions.

Asking lower level questions encourages student participation and builds factual knowledge. From these bases of knowledge, higher order questions stimulate and facilitate the development of more sophisticated thinking—like analyzing or evaluating an idea. In the long run, students achieve considerably more when their thinking is heightened and expanded (Berliner, 1989).

Regardless of the level of a question, Belch (1975) suggests strategies for improving teachers' questioning skills.

1. Ask questions that require more than a yes or no response.
2. Allow sufficient time for students to deliberate the question.
3. Reword or restate questions when students fail to respond or respond incorrectly.
4. Challenge student responses in a professional way. Avoid giving "put-downs" or other belittling responses.
5. Direct questions to all students and not just to volunteers or the brighter ones.
6. Try to sequence your questions. Encourage students to use logical thinking and build one question on another, or build one question on the answer given to a previous question.

Summary

Much has been written about student learning and how teachers should teach, yet we know little about what actually happens inside classrooms. This is because teachers primarily function in isolation.

Teachers and students sometimes differ in how they view school. While teachers are concerned with long-range successes, students are more concerned about the here and now. As children become adolescents, they are often more concerned about peer acceptance than about adult approval.

Too often, we ignore developmental differences between students and adults. Teachers like students to adapt to the often unstated norms of public school life, therefore, students with mild disabilities need to learn the hidden curriculum. Time management is a critical learning variable. The professional literature in general education has addressed several issues related to time management of students. Special educators have found these same principles apply to students with special needs. Numerous studies have noted the importance of time management, allocated time, engaged time, and academic learning time.

Effective teachers are able to use a variety of instructional strategies. In recent years, special educators have found that students with mild disabilities share many of the same learning problems. There is a growing sentiment that matching specific instructional strategies to specific disabilities is a wrong course to take. Educators are realizing that such teaching strategies as precision teaching, direct instruction, student-centered learning, and learning strategies hold promise for students with and without mild disabilities. Rather than matching instructional approaches to types of disabilities, teachers are encouraged to match instructional approaches to the learning styles of individual students.

Day to day classroom life presents teachers with students who have low self-esteem, poor study skills, and weak organizational skills. Practical strategies for dealing with these difficulties include affirmation, successful experiences, and direct teaching of organizational skills. Teachers must adapt instructional materials for students with mild disabilities. Many of these materials must be modified in line with individual learning characteristics. Appropriate modifications are needed in testing and grading practices. Modified tests more accurately assess the achievement of learners with mild disabilities. Student grades should accurately reflect individual progress, even if in small increments.

Effective teaching also depends upon good communication between teacher and students. It is important that student attention be directed toward the instruction being given, that teachers be clear in their instructions and explanations, that teacher feedback be appropriate to the purpose, and that questioning skills reflect good instructional techniques.

Chapter *8*

Classroom Management

Advance Organizer

When you complete this chapter, you will be able to:

1. Cite how teacher attitude influences classroom management.
2. Explain preventive discipline.
3. Describe the purpose and components of a life space interview.
4. List criteria for classroom interventions.
5. Outline the steps in a behavior modification program.
6. Describe nonverbal and verbal classroom interventions to manage behavior disruptions.
7. Discuss the purpose of teaching prosocial skills in the classroom.
8. Describe specific self-control skills suitable for a prosocial curriculum.
9. Identify and explain specific group management skills.
10. Discuss drawbacks of using punishment as a discipline strategy.
11. List the steps for solving behavior problems in the classroom.

Classroom management is the essential teaching skill. The most elegant lesson will fall apart if the teacher is unable to maintain a sense of order and purpose in the classroom. The first signal that a new teacher is experiencing difficulty is usually problems with discipline. Przychodgin (1981) notes, "No teacher can teach a class that is out of control, and once it is reported that the teacher cannot control the classroom his reputation in the public eye begins to decline" (Sabatino, 1987, 9).

Many special needs programs are populated with youngsters who were referred for discipline problems. Disruptive behavior in the regular classroom is the fast track to special education services. While classroom teachers may have

263

tolerance for weak academic skills, deficiencies in self-control quickly strain teacher patience. Since 1977 there has been a 32% increase in students identified as having some type of behavior or emotional disorder. These students constitute the highest proportion of special needs students in the 12–21 age bracket (Henley, 1986).

Educators have a penchant for labeling behavior problems, and those labels have a way of intimidating even the most sanguine teacher. Such terms as emotionally disturbed, attention deficit disorder, hyperactive, and conduct disordered have a common theme—the youngster needs help with discipline. How is a teacher to manage a classroom with youngsters such as these? The answer actually is quite simple—look behind the label for the child. Labels are deceptive. They obscure the truth by implying that a student is qualitatively different from others. All students, with and without educational labels have similar needs. Every student needs attention; every student needs success; every student needs recognition.

This chapter will describe behavior management practices that have proved useful with all students. Many of the strategies were designed specifically for youngsters with behavior and emotional disorders. Other strategies were developed within general education. This blend of general and special education discipline practices will provide you with a functional guide for teaching students with emotional and behavioral difficulties.

It takes more than one tool to tune a car, and it takes more than one approach to effectively manage a classroom. Our design is eclectic and practical. Theory is embedded in practice. Our goal is to help you, the classroom teacher, create an environment that is supportive of pluralism. Our schools are populated by many different students—different cultures, different languages, and different motivation to learn. The teacher who says, "I treat all students the same," and then proceeds to try to get them to conform to a rigid set of behavioral expectations will be continually frustrated. Like Sisyphus, the mythical Greek king whose eternal punishment was to roll a rock to the top of the hill only to have it roll back down again, the educator who presses for obedience will put much effort into a futile task. Young people are resilient and resourceful. They may bend to a heavy hand, but they will end up resenting any system of discipline that overlooks their culture, their personal needs, or their integrity.

Discipline—An Overview

All students, at some time, present behavioral challenges to teachers. Incidents can range from a few cases of noncompliance to serious emotional problems. All teachers, whether general or special education, need a diverse array of classroom management skills to facilitate learning. Baker reported a strong relationship between good grades and acceptable school behavior. He found that "a student whose grades were mostly D's was nine times as likely as a student whose grades were A's to have had trouble with the law, 24 times less likely to have done homework assignments, and about three times more likely to have cut classes" (Baker, 1985, 483).

Students are not the only casualties of classroom discipline problems. In their survey of teacher burnout, Feitler and Tokar (1982) reported 58% of teachers polled said that student misbehavior was the primary cause of their job-related stress (Baker, 1985, 484). The following remarks by Amanda, a graduate student working towards her M.Ed. in education, illustrates the psychological impact of discipline problems on a beginning teacher.

> *At the breakfast table last week, I was talking incessantly about how well I was doing in my courses at the college and about how all of the information I was getting about teaching was finally coming together. I was sure that I was soon going to be an English teacher extraordinaire, just like Robin Williams' character in* Dead Poet's Society. *My husband was staring at me with his cold, calculating eyes and I knew what was coming; we had this conversation before. "What will you do when some kid acts up in your first class?" he asked, a knowing smile on his lips. "Well that's easy," I said, "I will handle it in as mature and responsible a way as you would expect from someone of my obvious mental stature." And I smiled, but my husband did not. "You'll cry," he said, and then he smiled. (Levereault, 1990)*

Every teacher would like a class full of motivated, well-adjusted young scholars. But as Amanda's breakfast conversation with her husband indicates, the more realistic expectation is that public school teaching requires intestinal fortitude as well as good teaching skills.

Consider the challenge of teaching. The typical classroom teacher engages in 1,000 interactions a day (Jackson, 1968). Less than half of these interpersonal exchanges relate to teaching. The majority of time is spent trying to keep the classroom running smoothly. Maintaining a group focus, minimizing disruptions, and encouraging student participation require the organizational skills of the "one minute manager" and the human relations skills of a Dale Carnegie. Each student is a unique human being with likes, dislikes, strengths, and weaknesses. Regardless of ability or personality of individual students, the classroom teacher is expected to bring each "up to grade level." The public school classroom is one of the best examples of our democratic tradition. Public education is based on the common school principle that all students should have an equal opportunity to succeed in life. Yet all students do not start out equal. The inequity of student life experiences and student ability imposes the greatest challenge on public school teachers.

Students are impressionable human beings with complex life histories. Some inner-city schools have set up metal detectors to stop students from carrying weapons. But there is no method for screening such emotional baggage as hostility or despair. These burdens cannot be checked at the schoolhouse door. Poverty undermines hope. Drug abuse scorches intellectual ability. Dysfunctional families thwart personal development (Menacker, Weldon, & Hurwitz,

1989). Even students who are raised in the best conditions by loving parents experience emotional ups and downs.

There is no easy life. All young people must grapple with the distress that accompanies growth. The metaphor "growing pains" refers to more than pinched toes from tight fitting sneakers. Personal growth requires persistence, mentoring, and opportunity. It is hard work for both student and teacher. Growth is first an emotional and second an intellectual experience. Before students can learn, they need an emotional base of security, trust, and self-confidence. It is the classroom teacher's responsibility to nurture these feelings in some students and instill them in others.

Buffy's Dilemma

When Buffy, a beginning third grade teacher, arrived for the first day of work she was confronted with a variety of organizational tasks. Housekeeping duties such as attendance and lunch count were outlined by the principal. The first solitary hours alone in the classroom were spent inspecting textbooks, reviewing curriculum guides, and arranging furniture. The maintenance person dropped by to give some not so subtle tips about how he likes to find the room at the end of the day. Colleagues offered helpful advice about how to get along with the administration. It was an exciting time, and Buffy eagerly anticipated the arrival of her young charges.

Yet one nagging thought remained—"Can I maintain discipline?" The novice was fully aware that everybody would be watching to see if she could handle her students. Buffy's apprehension about discipline is a normal reaction to the often unstated, but nevertheless powerful, norm of public school teaching—teachers who can control their classrooms succeed, and teachers who cannot control their classrooms fail. Such suggestions as "Keep a tight rein," and "Don't smile until Christmas," when given by experienced teachers, usually add to, rather than subtract from, the novice's anxieties. Advice steeped in repressive or authoritarian tactics presents an unsettling picture of students. A new teacher such as Buffy might begin to wonder if her first students are an undisciplined bunch that must be tamed before they can be taught.

Buffy is at a crossroads. Discipline styles are established during the first days of school (Strother, 1985). The manner in which discipline is approached the first day will set the pattern for the rest of the year (Charles, 1983, 9). Buffy wants to start off on the right foot, but which foot is that? Like many other young teachers she wonders if she should "come down hard" on her students so they learn "who is boss?" Or should she try to be a friend and try to help teach her students self-control?

When she went home that evening, she took some of her college textbooks off the bookshelf. She looked up classroom discipline and found a bewildering array of "discipline models." Some discussed consequences for behavior and positive reinforcement. Others described caring and trust as important prerequisites to classroom control. Ideas from one model sometimes contradicted ideas from another. In total the ideas seemed too abstract, while her apprehensions about her first day were very real. Then Buffy read a passage from Charles's book *Elementary Classroom Management:*

> *. . . on the first day the teacher should go over with the students exactly what the basic rules for student behavior will be. Four to six rules are considered sufficient, and most teachers have these rules fairly well in mind although they wisely allow students to give input, discuss, and have at least some say in deciding how the rules will be enforced. When students participate in making such decisions, they become more likely to abide by them, see them as fair, and recognize the necessity for rules in helping learning occur better for all. (Charles, 1983, 10)*

This seemed sound advice. Take charge the first day, be assertive, but give the students input into decisions about discipline. Buffy liked this cooperative approach to discipline. It matched her intuitive belief that teaching and learning can be fun when teacher and students work together. Buffy went to bed that night resolved to work *with* her students to establish an orderly classroom ambience in order to prevent discipline problems.

Preventive Discipline

Many discussions about school discipline begin with what the teacher should do after a student is disruptive. Preventive discipline focuses on teacher actions that will decrease classroom disruptions. Preventive discipline is defined as a classroom management system designed to promote student self-control by focusing teacher intervention at the cause of discipline problems and by teaching prosocial skills. Preventive discipline requires self-knowledge and knowledge of student strengths and weaknesses.

Know Yourself

Kohn (1991) points out that what a teacher believes about the nature of his or her students can have a profound effect on how classroom management is handled. The teacher who believes students need to be taught obedience will emphasize teacher control of student behavior. Many teachers use rewards and punishment as external motivators to encourage conformity. In such classrooms the teacher makes the rules, determines sanctions, and doles out justice. Student behavior is controlled by teacher power.

The authoritarian approach to discipline is commonplace in schools and widely accepted. Some parents select schools based on the premise that their children will get "old fashioned discipline." While authoritarian tactics have admirers and detractors, the use of such teaching practices are rarely controversial. The case of Joe Clark is a notable exception.

Joe Clark was the principal of Eastside High School in Patterson, New Jersey. Each day he patrolled the halls of Eastside with a bullhorn. His motto, "There's only one way—my way," hung on his office door as a stern reminder that Joe Clark was a tough disciplinarian. Before Joe Clark came to Eastside, the school was in chaos. Fights and drug deals were routine in the halls of his inner-city school. Learning was almost nonexistent. Each year Eastside students tallied pathetically low on standardized tests of achievement.

After his arrival, Clark, a retired Army sergeant, quickly took charge. In one incident, he suspended 60 students without notifying the school board. He locked school doors, a fire code violation, to bar intruders. As a result of Clark's tough tactics, 1,900 students either dropped out or were expelled from Eastside. To some, including former Secretary of Education William Bennett, Joe Clark was a hero—an example of a no-nonsense disciplinarian in action. The remaining students at Eastside walked the school hallways without fear, and their standardized test scores improved. Other educators argued that Joe Clark did not solve problems; he merely transferred them from the halls of his school to the streets of his community. After a deluge of positive and negative media attention, Joe Clark resigned. He was commended by President Reagan and a movie was made of his exploits as principal of Eastside. Is Joe Clark a modern day pedagogical hero or villain? He got results, but did the end justify his means?

Albert Shanker, president of the American Federation of Teachers, believed Joe Clark created more problems than he solved. According to Shanker, punishments, suspensions, and expulsions become necessary when schoolwork ceases to be relevant for students. When students are made to sit still and listen quietly for 4 to 6 hours every day, when they are hopelessly behind the rest of the class with no chance to catch up, classroom disruptions are inevitable. Shanker believes many classroom disruptions can be traced to student apathy, student frustration, and lack of student control over daily events. Shanker's wry comment that teachers are the most powerful people in the world "because who else can tell 200 people exactly when they can go to the bathroom?" succinctly captures the essence of discipline codes in some classrooms.

Canter and Glasser: Contrasting Archetypes of Teacher Attitudes

The following two authorities on discipline, William Glasser and Lee Canter, illustrate different attitudes about the nature of discipline. While Glasser's views are student-centered, Canter's approach is teacher-directed. Each stands at polar points of a teacher attitude continuum. Canter, to the right of the continuum, is convinced that teachers know what is best for students and teachers have an obligation to reward and punish student behavior. Glasser, to the left, advocates student control and discipline procedures based on cooperation between teacher and students.

Glasser (1985) espouses a student-centered view of discipline. He believes that students are competent human beings who are capable of making good or bad behavioral choices. His underlying premise is that school should be meaningful to students. Students need input into school decisions that affect their daily activity. Every student, according to Glasser, has an innate need for power. When students feel powerless, they become apathetic or contentious. Glasser coined the term "control theory" to describe his principles for classroom management.

> *Control theory is based on the fact that we're internally motivated and driven by needs that are built into our biological structure, just as our arms and legs are built into our biological structure. From birth we must struggle—we have no choice—to try to survive and try to find some love, some power, some fun, and some freedom. To the extent we can satisfy these needs on a regular basis, we gain effective control of our lives. (Gough, 1987, 658)*

Teachers who share Glasser's attitude about discipline encourage student talk and reflection. Students will accept responsibility for their actions, contends Glasser, when they have opportunities to discuss problem behaviors in class. The teacher's role is to clarify student values. Questions like, "Is what you are doing right now helping others to learn?" puts the onus on the student to consider the effect of behavior. Glasser does not rule out reasonable consequences for persistent, disruptive behavior. However, he cautions teachers to be certain the punishment equals the infraction. Above all, teachers should avoid caustic language, physical punishment, sarcasm, and other reactions that demean and put down the student. When teachers utilize democratic practices, such as Glasser's, the aim is to help students learn, through their participation in the process, how to control their own behavior.

In contrast to Glasser's beliefs that students need power is Canter (1976) who believes discipline problems are caused by a lack of teacher power. In the Canter (1989) assertive discipline model, minor classroom disruptions are dealt with promptly. The teacher follows these guidelines:

First misbehavior—warning (often name goes on blackboard).
Second misbehavior—check by name (10 minute timeout).
Third misbehavior—second check (15 minute timeout).
Fourth misbehavior—third check (parents called).
Fifth misbehavior—fourth check (student goes to principal).

Canter encourages teachers to be assertive and understand that they have certain basic rights including the right to establish a classroom that is congruent with their teaching style. Students are expected to behave appropriately and accept teacher limitations and sanctions. Charles (1989) summarizes Canter's guidelines: students receive positive consequences for proper conduct; teachers establish clear limits and follow through on sanctions; teachers respond to student disruptions in non-hostile but an assertive fashion that communicates the teacher's disapproval. In Canter's system, the teacher is in total control of the classroom.

1. The teacher sets the rules.
2. The teacher determines rewards and punishments.
3. The teacher enforces the rules.

Canter and Glasser represent two ends of a continuum with teacher-directed at one end (Canter) and student-centered at the other end (Glasser). Neither is absolutely authoritarian or democratic. Glasser believes teachers should provide consequences for student misbehavior, and Canter emphasizes the humane treatment of students. However, a comparison of the two philosophies highlights how teacher attitude about teaching and students influences behavior management practices.

Values in the Classroom

Classroom management practices are "saturated in values" (Morse, 1987). Each time a teacher reacts to a classroom disruption, a hidden message is embedded in the teacher's action. Sometimes the message is autocratic, "You need to behave because I say so." With other teachers, the message is humanistic, "I care about your feelings, and I expect you to be responsible for your actions." When teachers act in anger, the hidden message is, "I can't control myself either." This is the most unsettling message of all because students first and foremost need the security of knowing the teacher is in control. When teachers punish students, the embedded message is, "You can't control your behavior, so I must do it for you." Punishment accompanied with anger creates stress among students, and increases the likelihood of further discipline problems (Kohn, 1991; Kounin, 1977).

Steel Glove or Velvet Hand?

Rezmierski (1987) distinguishes between punishment and discipline. Punishment is a penalty imposed by wrongdoing, while discipline is a response calculated to meet the needs of the child or youth. Her distinction raises a key question. Whose needs should classroom management practices meet—the teacher or the student? Rezmierski points out that it is neither the steel glove (i.e., punishment) nor the velvet hand (i.e., discipline) that makes the difference, but the maturity of the disciplinarian.

When adults feel secure, they are more capable of responding to the different developmental needs of youngsters. Conversely, insecure adults may feel threatened by disturbing student behavior that is developmentally normal. Rezmierski explains:

> . . . *adults who are still struggling to develop a sense of power or autonomy are likely to have difficulty dealing with adolescent children for whom this is a natural developmental struggle as well. Such adults may even have difficulty dealing with their two-year-olds who display what some have called the first round of adolescence . . . (Rezmierski, 1987, 6)*

Discipline practices that take developmental phases of youngsters into account emphasize the needs of the students. Some teachers are predisposed towards authority (i.e., power) practices; others are predisposed towards democratic (i.e., cooperation) practices (Lasley, 1989). Before establishing a behavior management system, teachers should understand their own psychological needs. This requires reflection and honesty. Effective discipline is emotionally disengaged from student behavior. Teachers who respond to individual discipline problems with anger, defensiveness, or hostility create stress among all the students in the classroom. This "ripple effect" will either lead to more discipline problems (Kouning, 1977) or produce a group of obedient, frightened learners.

All teachers have pet peeves. Some dislike tattling; others can't tolerate name calling. Fighting is the worst offense in many teachers' minds. *The key behavior, in effective discipline, is not the student transgression, but the teacher intervention.* Teachers who know themselves are more effective disciplinarians because they don't take misbehavior personally. Such teachers realize that students need to be taught what is expected of them. Canter (1989) says:

> *Teachers too often assume that students know how they are expected to behave. Teachers first need to establish specific directions for each activity during the day—lectures, small group work, transitions between activities, and so forth. For each situation, teachers must determine the* exact *behaviors they expect from them. . . . they (teachers) must teach the students how to follow directions. . . . they must model the behaviors, ask the students to restate the directions, question the students to make sure they understand the directions, and immediately engage the students in the activity to make sure that they understand the directions. (59)*

The aim of discipline is to teach students how to behave in a socially responsible manner. Sometimes compliance or noncompliance to classroom routines obscures the real issue. When 10-year-old Sammy consistently argues with his classmates, he is disturbing the classroom, but there is a deeper, more fundamental concern—Sammy lacks the ability to maintain relationships with his peers. Classroom discipline procedures aimed solely at stopping Sammy from arguing in school miss the point. Sammy needs to learn how to socialize with others both in and out of school. In the following sections, we will describe behavior management strategies that help teachers manage behavior problems while promoting the development of prosocial skills.

Know Your Students

The Phi Delta Commission on Discipline (1982) had this to say about good discipline practices:

> *Educators in well-disciplined schools know that behavior is caused. When misbehavior occurred, the principal and faculty tended to go beyond merely pun-*

ishing students for the misbehavior. They searched for probable causes and they addressed them. They improved discipline in their schools by taking steps to remove those causes and by establishing activities within their school and community that would result in good behavior. (12)

Discipline is a double-edged sword, and it cuts both ways. Students have an obligation to cooperate and to allow others to learn. Teachers and administrators have a duty to understand their students and to deal with disruptions in a fair and equitable manner. Teachers who believe students need to learn to be responsible for their own behavior work to help students to develop inner controls. These classrooms are characterized by a respect for student differences. Discipline is approached as a process rather than an end in itself (Henley, 1987). In this context, students are encouraged to develop social skills that will help them to adapt not only to the classroom, but also to the world at large. Cooperation, decision making, and accountability for behavior are skills emphasized by teachers who believe discipline should be a learning experience.

Developmental Differences

Knowledge of child and adolescent development is extremely useful in understanding why students behave as they do. Such giants in the field of psychology as Jean Piaget (1950), Erik Erikson (1960), and Lawrence Kohlberg (1973) have described significant differences in how children think and feel.

These researchers have described stages of cognitve, social-emotional, and moral development. As a youngster grows and matures, each stage is characteristically different from preceding stages. The domains of development are interactive. Progress in cognitive development affects moral reasoning. Social-emotional development influences and in turn is influenced by cognitive and moral acquisitions. The construction of "models" of development within specific developmental domains tends to obscure the synergistic power of human growth.

"Experts" in one area of development can be woefully naive about other areas. Consider a school psychologist who recommends placing a 7-year-old student in a special class for students with mild retardation based on a finding of "delayed cognitive" development. Cognitive development is not the only issue in this youngster's life. At the age of 7, the student is at the stage that Erik Erickson characterizes as industry versus inferiority. The child's ability to master the world outside of home is a central challenge during this period, and relationships with peers provide the impetus for meeting this challenge. From a developmental perspective, the psychologist's recommendation has created a dilemma for the student. A self-contained special class placement is stigmatizing. At the precise time in the youngster's social-emotional development when success with peers is central to further growth, the student is relegated to a special classroom for students with mental retardation.

One Teacher's Experience

Herbert Kohl took his first public school teaching assignment in an inner-city sixth grade. His 36 students were academic failures who saw no connection between their lives on the streets of Harlem and the pristine view of America depicted in their textbooks. Over time, Kohl came to recognize that effective discipline began with understanding how his students felt about school and life.

> *Each day there were incidents, and ultimately I accepted them as inevitable and impersonal. Alvin's malaise or John's refusal to work were natural responses to an unpleasant environment; not merely my class but a cumulative school environment which meant nothing more to most of the the children than white-adult ignorance and authority. There was no simple solution to such discipline problems, and sometimes it seemed necessary to learn to be patient and indulgent with a child who won't behave or refuses to work. A teacher must believe that such problems exist in his classroom because he hasn't found the right words or the right thing, and not that they lie in the heart of the child. (Kohl, 1967, 29)*

In Kohl's view, discipline begins with understanding and respect. There is always a reason for misbehavior. Boredom leads to distractibility and inattentiveness. Vandalism is anger erupting in mindless destruction. Impulsivity can signal a learning disability. Teachers who try to understand their students look for the causes of classroom disruptions. They recognize that students are complex human beings with developmental needs which can overshadow reading, writing, and calculating. By looking beyond misbehavior and trying to understand why a student is a discipline problem, a teacher can gain insight into the causes of disruptive behavior (Phi Delta Commission on Discipline, 1982).

While all students have "good" and "bad" days, some students have persistent problems in adapting to school expectations and routines. The intensity and duration of student disruptions will determine the severity of the problem. An emotional disturbance can cause a student to act out feelings of anger, hostility, or isolation. For instance, students who engage in attention-getting behaviors don't know how to relate in socially acceptable ways. Many students who receive special education services for behavior problems are identified as emotionally disturbed.

Most of the causes for emotional problems are outside the classroom teacher's reach. Time is a factor no one can overcome. A student's aggressive behavior may be caused by sexual abuse that happened several years earlier. Childhood difficulties, such as separation of parents or death of a loved one, may be overcome in a positive manner by one student or thrust another student into the depths of depression. What then is a teacher to do when confronted with the awesome obstacles presented by a student's disturbed life history?

While a teacher cannot (nor should not) pretend to be a therapist, the teacher can utilize therapeutic strategies that have proved useful with students who have an emotional disturbance. One such strategy is the life space interview (Redl, 1971).

Life Space Interview

The life space interview (LSI) is a technique for turning listening into a plan for student behavior change. If a teacher wants to understand why a student behaves a certain way, the best source of information is the student. The LSI uses crisis situations to move a youngster towards more constructive behavior. It is a four-step procedure for understanding the student perspective and helping the student to learn how to behave responsibly.

Step 1. Ventilation of Feelings.   The LSI is a conversation between student and teacher. Unlike most such conversations, the student does most of the talking and the teacher listens. The LSI is initiated by the teacher after a specific incident. It requires some privacy. A quiet corner of a classroom would do under most circumstances. If the student is very upset, he or she should be removed from the classroom for the interview.

The teacher begins by allowing the student to ventilate feelings. No moral implications are attached to what is said. The teacher is nonjudgmental and supportive of the student's feelings. Such statements as, "I can see you are angry," or "When Alex said that you must have felt hurt," emphasize empathy and communicate that feelings, even negative ones, are important. During Step 1 of the LSI, the teacher is accepting. This builds trust and helps the teacher to understand the student perspective.

The student may swear, whine, or blame others. It may seem strange not to correct these "inappropriate" comments. Some youngsters lack the verbal skills to express strong feelings in a socially acceptable manner. Strong language is a symptom of frustration. The intention at this stage is to build trust. The following steps aim at behavior change.

Step 2. Clarify the Incident.   Physical signs that the student is beginning to unwind (e.g., relaxed muscle tone; steady, calm breaths) will become evident. At this point, the incident that prompted the LSI is ready to be clarified in two phases.

First, the student is asked to describe his interpretation. The student will most likely focus blame on you, other students, other adults, anyone but himself. This is to be expected. The purpose of the LSI is to help a student learn to accept responsibility for individual behavior. If the student was in the habit of "owning up" to disturbing action, you wouldn't need the life space interview.

The student's view is significant data. Action is guided by perception. Attempting to correct the student version would eliminate an important source of information. Right or wrong, distorted or clear, the student perspective is a crucial clue in understanding behavior.

Next, the incident is reviewed again, except this time the teacher assists the student to paint a reality-based picture of the crisis situation. The student is prompted to describe the physical scene and chronological time frame. Comments such as, "Where were you standing when Cole threw the eraser?", or,

"What happened next?" help the student to recall events. A gentle reminder interjected at this point about how the adult saw events unfold can be helpful, but caution is advised because too much "reality rub" will place teacher and student at odds. The student is reflecting, an unaccustomed practice, and he or she will jump at an opportunity to argue over details, and thus derail the LSI.

Step 3. Look for Patterns. Questions such as, "Has this happened before?" or gentle reminders such as, "Last week it seemed you had the same problem with Sally," help students to gain insight into their own behavior. Many times students with emotional problems will deny their experience. They literally forget past episodes, or they may be unable to learn from experience. The student may be "stuck" in behavior patterns, continually repeating the mistakes of the past.

Up to this point, the LSI has focused on affective fallout from the incident. Looking for patterns switches emphasis to the cognitive domain. The student may be well-equipped to deny a history of problems related to the incident. Projection (i.e., finding one's own faults in someone else) and rationalization (i.e., explaining away behavior) are well entrenched defenses against change. Initially it is enough at this stage to get agreement that there does seem to be a problem. Future interviews can continue to explore disturbed behavior patterns.

Step 4. Implement a Plan. The purpose of the life space interview is to help a student assume personal responsibility. When a persistent pattern is identified by both teacher and student, the next logical step is to consider alternative ways to deal with the problem. Questions such as "What could you have done rather than knock all of your books off the desk?" or, "Are there any signals we could arrange for the next time you are feeling frustrated?" move the interview into the problem-solving stage. While the teacher provides supportive or clarifying questions, it is up to the student to do the problem-solving. The student needs to "own" the behavior and the solution.

Of course, reality rules of the school and common sense also come into play. A student may be overly zealous in terms of self-imposed punishment. Neither punishment or "consequences" are part of the solution. The plan is preventive. "Each time I feel frustrated with my work, I'll close my book and count to ten slowly." "Every time I lose my temper I'll put a check in my self-monitoring log." "If I get angry I'll blow off steam by walking around the room."

The intent of the planning stage is to get students thinking and working on their emotional or behavior problems. Student plans are not usually characterized by their elegance. It may be tempting to step in and offer a more reasonable alternative. The student may need to be reminded about such reality concerns as the implausibility of leaving the room when upset. The initial plan might require multiple adjustments, but that is the nature of personal growth. Changing habitual behavior patterns is a difficult endeavor. Whether or not the mechanics of the plan achieves the objective is secondary. The student is learning to take responsibility for behavior. In the long run, there is no more important goal. The final act of the LSI is for the teacher and student to write the plan and sign it. The "contract" increases commitment and provides a basis for future life space interviews (Fagen, 1986).

Emotional First Aid

Sometimes the situation calls for a less intensive investigation into the student's behavior and reasoning. An abbreviated version of the LSI can be used to provide emotional first aid. Just as a doctor tends to temporary physical bumps, bruises, and fractures, the teacher who uses emotional first aid tends to such temporary feelings as anger, rejection, or hostility. According to Long, emotional first aid provides support for students "when their defenses become ineffective and they find themselves overwhelmed by reality demands and/or internal conflicts" (Long, 1990, 11). The following illustration describes emotional first aid.

> Andy has just stalked out of Ms. Halpin's special class. She catches up with him in the hall. He is leaning against the wall ten feet from the classroom door. As she walks nearer it is clear he is near tears. When she tries to speak to him he covers his ears and says, "Leave me alone." Ms. Halpin knows that Andy's characteristic defense from stress is flight. Andy is eight years old. He is overweight and more immature than the other preadolescents in her special class for students with behavior disorders. Andy is often scapegoated by the other students, and he plays right into their manipulations each time he cries and runs away.
>   "I know it hurts when the others tease you," Ms. Halpin says. "I hate them," is his immediate retort. "I will give you the stopwatch," Ms. Halpin tells him. "After five minutes come back into class, and you can clean the gerbil cage." She hands Andy her stopwatch and goes back into the classroom. After four minutes he returns and walks over to the gerbil cage to begin one of his favorite activities.

Long (1990) describes five uses of emotional first aid: to drain off frustration, to support the management of strong feelings, to maintain communication during stress, to regulate social and behavioral traffic, and to provide umpire service. In this brief episode, Ms. Halpin managed all five. She allowed Andy time and space to ventilate his anger. She helped him deal with his anger by her supportive comments. Instead of punishing him for leaving the room, she maintained communication by remaining nonjudgmental and concerned about his feelings. She emphasized social regulations by giving him five minutes to return to the classroom, and she emphasized his accountability by handing him the stopwatch. Finally, she recognized that she could not solve Andy's problem for him. Like a good umpire, she remained neutral while requiring Andy to return to the classroom.

Both the life space interview and emotional first aid are directed at helping students make good choices. Each technique takes into account the student's point of view and feelings. Each provides support and ultimately points the student in the direction of personal accountability. Each also adheres to the principle that behavior management should be non-judgmental and non-punitive. They emphasize prevention of discipline problems by helping students to manage their feelings while working towards solutions to behavior problems. The life space interview is a long-range technique for helping students learn new behaviors. Emotional aid provides "hurdle help" for students who are distressed.

Managing Student Behavior

The life space interview and emotional first aid are directed at helping students manage their feelings. Each approach assumes student misbehavior is a symptom of deeper emotional problems. Over a period of time, the LSI can help students learn new behaviors to handle chronic emotional and behavioral problems. However, there are many times during the school day when the teacher needs to act quickly in order to eliminate and contain disruptive behaviors.

What follows are seven basic criteria for determining *when* to intervene; keep in mind that intervention is preventive, not punitive (Long & Newman, 1969). Interventions work best when the teacher anticipates that continued student behavior will ultimately become too disturbing to tolerate or will cause students harm, either physically or psychologically.

1. *Protection from Injury:* Adults usually see consequences for behavior before students. If a student is in danger of being hurt either physically or psychologically, the teacher should intervene. Psychological injury includes scapegoating, name calling, and isolation.

2. *Protection against Too Much Excitement:* A substitute teacher once gave into student requests to let them play records for the first ten minutes of class with the promise that they would work hard for the rest of the day. By the time the teacher finally turned off the record player, the class was totally out of control. The rest of the day the teacher tried in vain to get the students calmed and working. Overstimulation is contagious. Group excitement can unsettle a perfectly sensible class of students.

3. *Protection of Property:* Misuse of property is commonplace in today's society. Graffiti and litter are ubiquitous reminders of young people's lack of concern about property. Teachers model prosocial behavior by highlighting the need to respect both individual and communal property.

4. *Protection of On-going Program:* One disruptive student can ruin a successful lesson. In order to maintain the group's investment in a specific activity, it may be necessary to intervene. Nonverbal interventions work best in this situation.

5. *Highlighting a School Rule or Policy:* A successful teacher in a rough inner-city school had only two rules: no leaving food in class (he couldn't tolerate the smell of decaying peanut butter sandwiches) and no name calling. Rules should be limited to the necessary, and they must be enforced equitably. This means insuring that sanctions are a fair match for the violation and giving students the opportunity to express their position. Rule breaking is an excellent opportunity to teach such democratic principles as due process.

6. *Protecting the Teacher's Inner Comfort:* Awareness of one's personal needs is a basic requirement for good teaching. Professionalism means separating personal idiosyncrasies from classroom judgment. An adult may like a tidy house, but to expect the same ambiance in a classroom is unreasonable. Some teachers have a fixation on quietness and act out this need by assigning worksheets, dittoes, and other "quiet" work. An understanding of personal needs helps to avoid overreaction to disturbing behavior.

7. *Do Nothing:* Learning to permit behavior might sound like a strange way to manage a classroom. This non-sequitur requires an understanding of the power of natural consequences in child and adolescent development. Children and young adults learn to modify their behavior based on their interactions with peers. Consider the parent who steps in to negotiate each dispute between playing children as compared to the parent who steadfastly tells the children that they must work out their own disagreements. The first parent is reinforcing the adult as arbiter, while the second parent is teaching personal responsibility. The first adult is reinforcing "tattling"; the second adult is eliminating that annoying behavior.

Students need leeway to learn how to behave and work with each other. Minor arguments, testiness, and bad moods are all part and parcel of the human experience. In a well-managed classroom, the teacher respects each student's right to have a "bad day." A student's momentary loss of temper or stubbornness will soon pass if tolerated, but can be blown out of proportion if a teacher overreacts.

Much of the behavior encountered by teachers reflects the social-emotional development of students. There are developmental differences between students which need to be accounted for when managing behavior. Young students are naturally egocentric. Arguing is one of the ways they learn to take on the perspective of others. Adolescents are searching for their identity. Their burgeoning sense of independence may run counter to an adult need for obedience. As youngsters seesaw their way through emotional growth, conflicts with authority figures are inevitable. Students need some latitude as they grope their way along the difficult passage to adulthood. Appreciating developmental struggles of students helps to depersonalize the inevitable conflicts that occur when children and adults occupy the same space for five hours a day, 180 days a year.

Behavior Interventions

Once there was a school administrator who believed he had hit on the perfect plan for classroom discipline. With the assistance of his daughter, who was a graduate student in special education, he embarked on a systematic collection of interventions matched to problem behaviors. His goal was to develop an index card system, compact enough to fit into the top drawer of a teacher's desk. The cards would alphabetically list student discipline problems and briefly explain the correct intervention; for instance, if a student refused to obey, the teacher would flip through the cards, pull out the 3″ X 5″ labeled "disobedience" and read what to do. His approach was well-meaning, but hopelessly naive. Student behavior cannot be matched to interventions like dominoes. Every student is different, and every situation unique. Therefore, teachers need an array of interventions to meet the changing needs of the classroom. Each of the following strategies is research-based (Cooper, Heward & Heron, 1987; Dreikurs, Grunweld & Pepper, 1982; Ginott, 1971; Jones, 1987; Redl & Wineman, 1957). Each is useful for eliminating problem behaviors, but none is teacher-proof. Professional judgment determines the best intervention to use at any given time. Classroom interventions anticipate student disruptions and nullify potential discipline problems. Each category of interventions—behavior modification, nonverbal interventions, and verbal interventions—prevents disruptive behavior while maintaining a sense of mutual respect between teacher and student. None will work all the time. Good classroom management requires the ability to select an appropriate strategy from an array of alternatives.

Behavior Modification

Behavior modification is the application of learning theory to change behavior. Operant conditioning is a form of behavior modification used to change student behavior in the classroom. Operant conditioning is based on the premise that actions are shaped or changed by their consequences. The operant is the behavior (e.g., listening, hitting, laughing), while the consequences (e.g., praising, punishing, or ignoring) either reinforces the operant or eliminates it.

Examples of operant conditioning are all around us. One person can modify behavior of another; for instance, a parent who encourages a child to eat vegetables by offering ice cream for dessert. Individuals can modify their own behavior. Cooper, Heron, and Heward provide the following example of behavior which is modified by the consequences it produces.

> When an infant moves her arms through space, setting in motion the mobile dangling in her crib, she is literally operating on her environment. The mobile's movement and sound are stimuli produced by the child's behavior, consequences of her batting at the toy with her hands. If continued observation of the baby reveals an increased rate of arm swinging when the mobile hangs in her crib, her behavior would be described as an operant. (Cooper, Heron, & Heward, 1987, 21)

Behavior can be modified spontaneously, for example, when a student invents a shortcut to solve math problems. Or behavior can be shaped systematically, for instance, when a teacher awards tokens for finishing classroom tasks. Behavior can also be modified ineffectively, as when a teacher's verbal reprimands reinforce acting out behavior. The principles of operant conditioning are always the same—the key is knowledgeable application. Many teachers, both special and regular education, use operant conditioning practices in their classrooms on a regular basis.

Schroeder and Riddle (1991) list the basic components of operant conditioning. The following is an adaptation of their definitions.

1. *Positive reinforcement:* presenting a consequence that increases the probability of a behavior in the future. Example—a student who shares toys in a play area of a classroom because of favorable reaction from other children.
2. *Punishment:* presenting or withdrawing a consequence that decreases the probability of a behavior in the future. Examples—a reprimand (i.e., presenting a stimulus) or keeping a youngster in class during recess (i.e., withdrawing a stimulus) in order to stop disruptive classroom behavior.
3. *Negative reinforcement:* increasing the probability of a behavior by avoiding an unpleasant consequence. Example—students who complete homework for five consecutive days are excused from taking a weekly math quiz. Negative reinforcement is often confused with punishment. Example—a student is sent into the hall for disrupting the class. The teacher is negatively reinforcing the misbehavior when the child continues to act up in the future in order to avoid an unpleasant classroom activity (Cooper, Heron, & Heward, 1987, 25).
4. *Extinction:* decreasing the probability of a response by withholding a previously reinforcing stimulus. Example—classmates don't laugh when a student makes a sarcastic comment in class.
5. *Differential* reinforcement of other behavior (DRO): decreasing the probability of a response by reinforcing the omission of it; sometimes referred to as omission training. Example—a student who is disruptive is given a token for every five minutes the behavior is not emitted.
6. *Satiation:* decreasing the probability of a response by reinforcing it excessively. The reinforcer no longer maintains the behavior. Example—a teacher uses a novel reading series to encourage student effort. In a short while, student effort diminishes as the novelty wears off.

Often the above treatments are used in combination to shape behavior in the classroom; for example, a teacher might use both positive and negative reinforcement to encourage a youngster to comply with classroom rules. Positive reinforcement could take the form of verbal praise immediately following the desired behavior, and negative reinforcement would consist of a decrease in corrective comments from the teacher. A comprehensive elaboration of each component of operant conditioning is outside the scope of this book. For more details, we suggest *Applied Behavior Analysis* by Cooper, Heron, and Heward (1987), Merrill Publishing Company; *Behavior Management: A Practical Approach for Educators* by Walker and Shea (1991), Merrill Publishing Company; and *Educating Emotionally*

Disturbed Children and Youth by Paul and Epanchin (1991), Merrill Publishing Company.

Operant conditioning is regularly used to teach prosocial behavior to students with mild disabilities (Zaragonza, Vaughn, & McIntosh, 1991; Ager & Cole, 1991). Operant conditioning programs are data-based. Target behaviors (i.e., behaviors to be eliminated or shaped) must be observable and measurable. Prior to initiating a program, the target behavior is described in precise, behaviorally concrete terms. Vague behavior descriptors such as "immature," "aggressive," or "cooperate" are replaced with specific such target behaviors as "whines," "hits other students," and "shares toys." Baseline data on the frequency of the target behavior are collected for at least a week prior to beginning the program. These data serve as a comparison for determining progress at a later date. Once a target behavior has been selected and counted, the most appropriate consequence is determined (e.g., positive reinforcement, negative reinforcement, differential reinforcement of other behavior, etc.). Next a schedule to administer consequences is developed (e.g., positive reinforcement in the form of verbal praise will follow each time a student raises her hand).

The following systems: token economies, contingency contracts, timeout, and cognitive-behavior intervention are well-established in the operant conditioning literature and in special education programs.

Token Economies. A token is a general conditioned reinforcer. Tokens are paired with backup reinforcers such as special privileges or toys from a "class store." A token is given to a student to reinforce a target behavior. At a later time in the day or week, the student can exchange accumulated tokens for the backup reinforcer. The value of tokens is derived from the student desirability for backup reinforcers. For example, without goods to purchase (backup reinforcers), money (tokens) would be useless. Cooper, Heron, and Heward (1987) provide the following guidelines for implementing a token economy:

1. Select a token that is durable and cheap (e.g., rubber stamp, chips, pennies).
2. Be clear about rules and behavior(s) for earning tokens.
3. Whenever possible, use regularly occurring events or privileges for backup reinforcers.
4. Guard against bootlegging of tokens. Hoarding of tokens is often a signal that students don't understand the token's value.
5. Establish a rate of exchange; begin with a low ratio of token to backup reinforcer and increase the ratio as the program becomes successful.
6. Decide in advance how to remove the system.

The efficiency and immediacy of token economies make them an attractive alternative for motivating students.

Contingency Contracts. A contingency contract is a written agreement between a teacher and student. The contract serves as a positive reinforcer to shape a target behavior. A contingency contract specifies the responsibilities (i.e., the behaviors) of each party and the consequences associated with compliance. Schroeder and Riddle (1991) list five key elements of a contingency contract: detailed privileges and obligations, observable behaviors, sanctions for failure, bonus clauses for consistent compliance, and clear description of methods for administering reinforcers. Contingency contracts are a way of concretely emphasizing student responsibility for behavior. Salend (1987) suggests that responsible behavior can be increased by involving students in making such contractual decisions as determining the target behavior, selecting reinforcers, and evaluating systems.

Timeout. Cooper, Heron and Heward (1987) describe two types of timeout: nonexclusionary and exclusionary timeout. Nonexclusionary timeout consists of planned ignoring, withdrawal of a specific reinforcer, contingent observation, and the timeout ribbon (441). Planned ignoring is the removal of such social reinforcers as attention, praise, or verbal comments. Withdrawal of specific reinforcer means that an identified positive stimulus is removed when an undesirable behavior occurs. In one study, researchers turned off classroom music each time students left their seats, thus significantly reducing out-of-seat behavior (Ritschl, Mongrella, & Presbie, 1972). Contingent observation is the change of seating of a student for a specified period of time following a classroom infraction. During the contingent observation time period, the student is able to observe the activity of the rest of the group, but may not participate. The timeout ribbon is a paired reinforcer. When a youngster wears the ribbon, it is a signal that there are opportunities to receive positive reinforcers. When the ribbon is removed, no reinforcers can be gained.

Exclusionary timeout is the removal of a student to a room outside the classroom for a specified period of time. Release from timeout is contingent on cessation of disturbing behavior. While an effective intervention if used sparingly, exclusionary timeout can be misused and even abused. Procedures for using exclusionary timeout must be spelled out clearly to both students and parents. Exclusionary timeouts are documented with a timeout log. Such data collection protects against abuse and provides information to determine the effectiveness of exclusionary timeout as a means of extinguishing disruptive behavior.

The aim of timeout is to institute a brief, 5–10 minute isolation of a student from classroom activities because of disruptive behavior. Longer periods of timeout are not recommended for several reasons. Instructional time is lost. The student may prefer the timeout, thus it becomes a positive reinforcer. Removing a student from the classroom may be more disturbing than the behavior that prompted the timeout. Finally, timeout can be unnecessarily punitive (Cuenin & Harris, 1986).

Cognitive-Behavior Intervention. The purpose of operant conditioning is to teach youngsters social skills. According to Ager and Cole, cognitive-behavioral interventions differ from traditional environmental operant techniques in that attempts are made to influence the cognitive processes of participants in order to bring about behavior change (Aver & Cole, 1991, 276).

Deluke and Knoblock (1987) point out that thinking is a buffer between feelings and behavior. Strategies such as coaching, modeling, self-instruction, self-talk, and social problem-solving activities teach youngsters to think before they act. Despite the widespread acceptance of cognitive-behavior interventions, Gresham (1985) reported scant evidence that cognitive-behavioral techniques fostered more significant changes in behavior than more traditional environmental operant conditioning procedures. In their meta-analysis of 22 studies of cognitive-behavior training, Ager and Cole (1991) found that a lack of description of treatment procedures by researchers made replication and verification of behavior change claims difficult to achieve. Despite the methodological shortcomings, cognitive-behavior treatment continues to have strong support among researchers and practitioners.

Nonverbal Interventions

Nonverbal interventions have several advantages over verbal interventions. Silence does not draw attention to the student or inadvertently reinforce the behavior. Classroom activities proceed without interruption when the teacher manages classroom behavior unobtrusively (McDaniel, 1986). Lastly, nonverbal interventions help teachers avoid "power struggles" with students.

Body Carriage. Frederic Jones (1987) observed teachers in hundreds of secondary and elementary classrooms. He found teachers conveyed leadership through body language. Posture, eye contact, facial expressions, and gestures conveyed confidence or uncertainty. Students observe teacher body language and make judgments about what they see. Charles summarizes Jones's findings:

> *Good posture and confident carriage suggest strong leadership; a drooping posture and lethargic movements suggest resignation or fearfulness. Effective teachers even when tired or troubled tend to hold themselves erect and move with a measure of vigor. (Charles, 1989, 92)*

Teachers who convey authority naturally through body language encounter half the behavior problems of teachers in "loud, unruly" classrooms (Charles, 1989, 90).

Planned Ignoring. Sometimes disruptive student behaviors are intended to attract the attention of the teacher and other students. When teachers ignore attention-seeking behaviors, the audience is eliminated. Planned ignoring works best for minor classroom disturbances. The teacher who interrupts group lessons or activities with a continual stream of admonitions such as "sit still," or "pick up that piece of paper" disrupts learning while drawing attention to the misbehavior. Paradoxically, this "negative" attention can reinforce behavior problems.

Signal Interference.   Every adult has memories of childhood teachers who could quell minor disturbances with a flick of a light switch or a finger raised to the lips. There are numerous nonverbal signals for quieting a class—eye contact, snapping fingers, a frown, shaking the head, or a quieting gesture with the hand. Visual signals do not disturb students and emphasize the teacher's awareness of all activity in the room.

Proximity Control.   Teachers who stand or sit as if rooted to the front of the room are compelled to issue verbal directions in order to deal with disruptions. Teachers who move around the room merely need to stand near a student or gently place a hand on a student's shoulder to stop a disturbing behavior. Teaching while moving has several advantages: rather than being a separate, remote entity, the teacher becomes physically a part of the group; the teacher is able to monitor students more easily; the teacher projects more of a presence because students can't predict where the teacher will be standing at any given moment; finally, standing nearby also reassures students that the teacher is in control.

Removal of Seductive Objects.   Manipulation is a strong channel for learning, and in most instances should be encouraged. However, some students become distracted by objects. Fritz Redl and David Wineman (1951) indicated that the ability to control the impulse to handle, grab, or steal seductive objects was a basic component in the development of self-control. When teachers leave valuables or students leave toys around youngsters who are prone to "gadgetorial seduction," the objects might disappear. Removing seductive objects decreases the pressure on a youngster's burgeoning self-control system.

Verbal Interventions
Because nonverbal interventions are the least intrusive, they are preferred. Verbal interventions are useful after it is clear that nonverbal interventions have been unsuccessful in desisting a disruptive behavior.

Humor.   It may sound strange to use humor to calm a disruptive student, but it is a very useful technique. Almost every school has a teacher who is capable of defusing discipline problems with a quip or easy comment. Humor is a basic human need. People watch T.V., go to the movies, and pay to watch live performances just to laugh. The teacher who smiles and jokes in the face of adversity sets a strong model for students. A word of caution, however: avoid sarcasm, cynicism, or teasing. Rather than lightening a moment, sarcasm increases tension and creates resentment.

Sane Messages.   When teachers respond to disruptive behavior with anger, they add to student anxiety, which increases the likelihood of further behavior problems (Kounin, 1977). "I" messages let students know how the teacher feels. Such statements as, "I am frustrated because you keep interrupting this lesson," or "I am disappointed because you didn't maintain control when I left the room," describe the situation rather than attacking a student's character (Charles, 1989,

59). Sane messages are descriptive and model appropriate behavior (Ginott, 1971). Sane messages help students understand how their behavior affects others. They are a direct appeal to change behavior. "Mary, when you talk during silent reading, it disturbs everyone in your group," is an example of a sane message. "Mary, keep quiet," is an example of what Ginott calls an insane message. In the first instance, the reason for a change in behavior is explained to the student. In the second instance, the "insane message," the student feels personally attacked. Such a directive as "keep quiet" or "shut up" may get the intended results, but if the model for expressing needs is abrupt and callous, students will take the same approach in their own conversations.

Restructuring.   Restructuring means changing a lesson or activity that is floundering. When confronted with student disinterest, the best option may be to move onto another activity. Restructuring is part of the decision-making powers of a teacher. One inner-city sixth grade teacher gave a spelling test every time the class seemed restless and difficult to manage. "It was amazing," he reported; "one minute they are ready to climb the walls, and the next minute they were quietly and dutifully folding their papers and numbering lines from 1 to 20!"

Hypodermic Affection.   Each student from time to time needs a shot of caring. Hypodermic affection lets students know that they are valued human beings. Students get frustrated, discouraged, and anxious in school. Students with mild disabilities, in particular, need encouragement to persevere with tasks at which they have failed in the past. Sometimes a smile, a pat on the back, or a kind word can help a student over a psychological hurdle. Showing interest in a student's life outside of school, and plainly communicating concern are ways of building trust. A trusting relationship between student and teacher is the key to solving all discipline problems.

Praise.   Verbal praise is frequently used to reinforce positive classroom behavior. The aphorism "Catch them being good" describes the most useful approach to praise. For example, some students need attention. Praising their behavior when they are not seeking attention while ignoring disruptive behavior is a useful way to use praise in the classroom. Too much praise can undercut impact; too little praise communicates indifference. Effective praise is directed at student behavior rather than the student personally. "You really are trying hard" encourages student effort. It is a descriptive statement that gives the student guidance in terms of the type of behavior the teacher expects to see. "You are a good student" is a direct compliment about an individual's self-worth. While it may make the intended student feel good, it causes other problems.

Ginott pointed out the "perils of praise" (Charles, 1981). Praise directed at a student personally is condescending and manipulative. A statement such as, "You are a good person to have in my class," implies the teacher is making such judgments about all the students. What about the students who don't get the same compliment? Remember there is always a "ripple effect" in the classroom.

Everyone wants to be liked by the teacher. Judgmental praise may make one student feel good, and another may feel rejected. Praise works best when it evaluates behavior, instead of the student.

Alerting.   Imagine a group of students during recess playing kickball. They are hot, sweaty, and thoroughly enjoying themselves. All the running around has them excited, and they are eager to continue the game. The teacher looks at her watch and realizes she should have had them back into the classroom five minutes ago. What does she do? One approach is to abruptly end the game and rush the entire group back to class. Abrupt changes will almost assuredly result in behavior problems.

In his extensive research on classroom discipline, Kounin (1977) found the manner in which teachers handled transitions to be a key element in effective discipline. Charles succinctly summarized Kounin's findings: "Teachers' ability to manage smooth transitions and maintain momentum was more important to work involvement and classroom control than any other behavior management technique" (Charles, 1981, 33).

Alerting helps students to make smooth transitions by giving them time to make emotional adjustments to change. This is particularly true for impulsive students or students who are easily frustrated. Alerting takes many forms. One method is to count down the number of minutes before a change will take place. Usually two warnings in five-minute increments is sufficient. Alerting is useful when moving from a high student preference activity (e.g., recess) to a low student preference activity (e.g., grammar lesson).

Accepting Student Feelings.   A student walks into class in the morning radiant with the news that the family will be visiting Disneyland. The teacher is pleased to have such a happy youngster in class for the day. It is a pleasure to accept positive feelings and reaffirm their expression. The next day the same youngster walks into class furious. Her dad has been laid off his job, and the trip to Disneyland is canceled. The student is angry and frustrated. She hates her dad; she hates the teacher; and she hates her schoolwork. These feelings are not so easy to accept and reaffirm. Teachers, who have a one-sided view of student feelings, allow for the expression of positive feelings but are reluctant to accept feelings of distress.

Students need to learn how to express such feelings as anger, frustration, and impatience. Students act out these feelings when they lack appropriate verbal skills. The teacher who attempts to put a lid on student behavior that is embedded in anger or frustration is sowing the seeds of further discontent. Distressful feelings cannot be made to disappear. Suppressed feelings will resurface. By providing opportunities for students to express all types of feelings, teachers reaffirm students. Role playing, class discussions, life space interviews, and journal writing are samples of classroom methods that help students channel difficult feelings into constructive outlets.

Teaching Social Skills

Many general and special educators agree that social skills training has a legitimate place in the classroom. Participation in our changing society requires adaptability and human relations skills. Through most of the twentieth century, students graduated from high school found employment in manufacturing. Factory workers needed to follow directions, tend to repetitious work, and accept company rules. The workplace required obedience and conformity. A worker's value was judged on the ability to complete an honest day's labor. However, the blue collar world of work is slowly disappearing from the American scene. The "iron belt"—the string of automobile factories, steel producers, and mines that were once the backbone of our industrial society—is now the "rust belt."

The United States is evolving into a service economy. Most of the new jobs in the twenty-first century will require the ability to handle people instead of machines. Employers will want employees who can cooperate with others, solve social problems, and resolve conflicts. Historically, the teaching of these skills was assumed by the family and church. But the changing demographics of United States society indicate that traditional means of training children in social abilities need support from the schools.

London (1987) characterizes today's children as potential victims of a "psychosocial epidemic." He states that millions of American children are at-risk because of rents in the social fabric of childhood. London provides the following statistics: in 1982, 715,000 children were born to unwed mothers; over a million nonsexual cases of child abuse are reported each year; three million 14- to 17-year-olds may have a drinking problem; half a million children attempt suicide each year, and six thousand die. According to London, students need help in managing their lives. They need to understand how to make good choices. They need to learn to view problems from the other person's point of view. They need assistance in coping with feelings that drive them to drugs and sex.

Character Education

Schools are the only places where children are assured constant adult supervision. If today's youngster is to successfully navigate the social storms that await outside school, they will need adult help. Social skills education in the curriculum can provide a lifeline. Character education (Kohn, 1991; Lickona, 1988; London, 1987) is a term that best seems to suit the evolving notion about what a social curriculum would encompass. Proponents of character education stress the teaching of cooperation and mutual respect. Moral development, with its attendant emphasis on caring for others, is emphasized in character education, as is reflection and commitment to moral principles. London lists two primary components of character education: (1) education in civic virtue and in the qualities that teach children the forms and rules of citizenship in a just society, and (2) education in personal adjustment, chiefly in the qualities that enable children to become productive and dependable citizens (London, 1987).

The Child Development Project (Kohn, 1991), begun in 1982 in the San Ramon Valley (California) Unified School District, is an example of a character education curriculum. In the CDP program, children participate in decisions about how classes can become "caring communities." Classroom management practices are directed towards teaching prosocial skills. Classroom meetings, cooperative learning, and warm student teacher relationships are highlighted. A literature-based reading program encourages students to reflect on personal values while learning to read. The CDP program, which was recently adopted by the Hayward, California school district, has set as its overall goal—teaching children to develop self-control. According to Marilyn Watson, an educator in CDP, teachers have learned that you don't need punishment and rewards to have a well-managed classroom. The core of classroom discipline, according to Ms. Watson, "lies in teachers developing positive relationships with their students and helping them to understand the reasons behind the rules" (*New York Times*, 1990, B7).

Character education can be included in any lesson. Lickona describes how a second grade teacher merged character education with a science lesson. For a science project, the class was incubating 20 chicken eggs. The teacher suggested that the students might want to open one egg to observe embryonic development. Later that day, Nathaniel, seven years old, expressed reservations, "Mrs. Williams, I've been thinking about this for a long time. It's just too *cruel* to open an egg and kill the chick inside!" Mrs. Williams listened and decided to bring the topic up for a class discussion. Some students agreed with Nathaniel; others wondered how you could kill a chick if it hadn't been born yet. Mrs. Williams gave her students the night to think it over. The next day, the majority decided not to open the egg (Likona, 1988, 422). This brief episode illustrates a common strategy in character education—values clarification.

Values Clarification

Moral reflection requires understanding one's values. Lickona describes moral reflection in the following way:

> The word reflection refers to a wide range of intellectual activities, including reading, thinking, debating moral questions, listening to explanations by the teacher (e.g., why is it wrong to make fun of a handicapped child), and conducting firsthand investigations to increase children's awareness of the complex social system to which they belong. (Likona, 1987, 422)

When using values clarification in the classroom, the teacher encourages reflection. The purpose is to guide students in exploring personal values. The teacher does not attempt to impose his or her own value system; rather, opportunities are arranged for students to examine their own values, consider alternatives, and make future choices. Teachers who use values clarification assume that with guidance and freedom, students will identify personal values that reflect the common good. Values clarification can be a proscribed lesson (e.g., class discussion on whether or not to open an egg), or it can be embedded in the flux of daily classroom life. Students are constantly reflecting their values in unconscious ways. Examples of these are:

Attitudes: "I feel that . . ." "I don't like. . ."

Aspirations: "One day I'm going to. . ."

Purposes: "I plan to make a . . ."

Interests: "I like to . .. " "I enjoy . . ."

Activities: "After school I'm going to . . ."

Essential to values clarification is questioning. By formulating questions, the teacher can assist the student to understand personal values. Values clarification probes would include questions such as the following:

1. *Choosing Freely.*

   Where do you suppose you first got that idea?
   How long have you felt that way?
   What will you do if you don't succeed?

2. *Choosing from Alternatives.*

   What else did you consider before you picked this?
   How long did you look around before you decided?

3. *Reflective Choosing.*

   What would be the consequences of your choice?
   How much thought have you put into this choice?
   What is good about this choice?

4. *Prizing and Cherishing.*

   Are you glad you feel that way?
   What good is it?
   What do you want?

5. *Affirming.*

   Would you tell the class the way you feel?
   Do people know you feel that way?

6. *Acting on Choices.*

   What is a plan of action?
   Where will this lead you?

7. *Repeating.*

   What are your plans for doing more?
   Has it been worth the time and effort?

Values clarification is aimed at helping students learn how to think through their choices. Caution is advised about making direct statements under the guise of questioning. For example, "You don't really think that is proper behavior, do you?" is a veiled attempt to have a student conform to the teacher's values.

Goals of Character Education

While not dismissing the importance of students learning to reflect on their own values, character educators are proactive in terms of teaching students specific values. For example, Lickona (1987) cites the following goals for character education:

1. To promote movement away from individualism toward cooperative relationships and mutual respect.
2. To foster the growth of moral agency—the capacity to think, feel, and act morally.
3. To develop in the classroom and in the school a moral community based on fairness, caring, and participation—such a community being a moral end in itself, as well as a support system for the character development of each individual student.

Several variations on the above themes appear in other character education models. Edwards (1991) emphasizes a modified version of the 1921 Dalton Plan where students determine their own schedules from subject lab alternatives. The purpose of the Dalton Plan is to teach students to assume responsibility for their own learning in a noncompetitive atmosphere. Kohn (1991) stresses a caring curriculum. He encourages teachers to develop empathetic relationships with their students; to promote cooperation over competition; and to allow students to participate in the governing of the classroom. Each of these conditions, Kohn maintains, increases academic skills by investing students in their day to day learning.

Character Education—New Lyrics for an Old Song

The notion of teaching values, moral development, or social skills in the classroom is not a novel idea. Moral development is a cornerstone of Western philosophy. The eighteenth century philosopher, Immanuel Kant, believed that moral behavior was directed by reason. He provided the following "categorical imperative" to guide reason and actions, "Act only on that maxim through which you can at the same time will that it should become a universal law" (Seldes, 1985, 223). According to the categorical imperative, the rightness of behavior depended on the reasoning behind the act, not the consequences (Benniga, 1988). This focus on the internalization of judgment is what sets advocates of character education apart from teachers who believe students are best trained through external manipulation.

No educator in the twentieth century was a more ardent advocate of character education than John Dewey. In 1909 Dewey published *Moral Principles in Education* in which he advocated the teaching of initiative, courage, judgment, and persistence. He maintained that external control of students instills dependence on the judgment of authority figures. Dewey believed that the purpose of education was to help students develop social consciousness. According to Dewey, concern for the social good required nurturing. Students needed opportunities to help their classmates, participate in classroom decisions, and discuss moral questions.

Classrooms don't have to be inclined towards character education to teach values. All classrooms "are saturated in values." Either covertly or overtly, American students for generations have been instilled with values educators believed crucial to success. Consider the following excerpt from *McGuffey's Fourth Eclectic Reader* (1920):

Lazy Ned

"'Tis royal fun," cried lazy Ned.
"To coast upon my fine, new sled,
*   And beat the other boys;*
But then, I can not bear to climb
The tiresome hill, for every time
*   It more and more annoys."*

So while his schoolmates glided by,
And gladly tugged uphill, to try
*   Another merry race.*
Too indolent to share their plays,
Ned was compelled to stand and gaze.
*   While shivering in his place.*

Thus, he would never take the pains
To seek the prize that labor gains,
*   Until the time had passed;*

For, all his life, he dreaded still
The silly bugbear of uphill,
*   And died a dunce at last (cited in Benniga, 416).*

Unobtrusive artifacts of values permeate life in classrooms. For example, tests promote competition while stringent behavior codes demand conformity. Benniga provides insight on the pervasiveness of covert moral education. "Whether or not they offer specific programs, schools provide moral education. In many schools and districts the curriculum in morality is informal and unwritten. It pervades the school and classroom rules, the treatment by teachers of such individuals and groups as minority and handicapped students, and the attitudes of the community toward academics, specific curricular programs, and athletics." (Benniga, 1988). As an illustration, consider the recent change in how scholars depict Christopher Columbus. For years Columbus has been portrayed in American textbooks as a prototype of American values. Against all odds, the story goes, he altered our conception of the world and discovered America. He brought Christianity to the native "Indians" and opened the gates to a "new world." So esteemed was Columbus that the Knights of Columbus promoted him for canonization (i.e., sainthood).

Compare the traditional tale of Columbus with the view held by some Native Americans. According to Russel Means of the American Indian Movement, Columbus practiced genocide with the fervor of a despot. Under Columbus's administration, Indians living in what is now the Dominican Republic were shipped to Europe as slaves; thousands of others were raped, tortured, and murdered. Recent disclosures of Columbus's misadventures prompted the United Nations to cancel a celebration of his quincentenary. The National Council of Churches stated that the 500th anniversary of Columbus's discovery should be a time of penitence instead of jubilation. Cultural values are shaped by textbook writers and teachers. In the case of Columbus, the atrocities committed against Native Americans were paved over by historians eager to promote Columbus as an icon of American values (Wilford, 1991).

Moral education is as basic to schools as mathematics and reading. What type of moral education do we want to pass on to our students? Advocates of character education believe school should emphasize prosocial skills. These educators prefer cooperation to competition, altruism to individualism, and empathy to egocentrism.

Teaching of prosocial skills are especially relevant for students with mild disabilities. Students with mild mental retardation are characterized by deficits in adaptive behavior; students with learning disabilities have difficulty deciphering social cues; and students with emotional or behavioral disorders act out their emotions in disruptive ways. Teaching students with mild disabilities how to regulate their behavior in socially acceptable ways is a goal for educators and parents.

Teaching Self-Control

Cox and Gunn (1980) list three reasons why students have difficulty adjusting to social situations:

1. The student does not know what are appropriate behaviors.
2. The student may have knowledge of appropriate behavior but may lack practice.
3. Student emotional reactions to situations may inhibit performance of the desired behavior. (cited in McGinnis & Goldstein, 1984, 4)

Lack of social competence is one of the primary reasons that students with mild disabilities have difficulty in regular classrooms (Nelson, 1988). More than one special educator has been chagrined at how a student with mild disabilities seemed to "fall apart" when transferred from a special education program to a full-time regular classroom placement. Advocates of direct teaching of prosocial skills develop curricula to enable transition from the security of special education programs to the demands of normal school routines. Such programs as *Structured Learning* (Goldstein & Glick, 1986), *Developmental Therapy* (Wood, Gunn, Combs, & Weller, 1986), and the Adaptive Learning Environments Model (ALEM) (Wang & Birch, 1984) provide goals, instructional objectives, learning activities, and consulting guidelines. The aim of each program is to teach social skills that can be generalized beyond the secure confines of special education programs.

Each of these programs is based on the premise that social skills training of students with special needs requires cooperation between regular and special educators. Students cannot be "fixed" in self-contained special education programs and then shipped as finished products into regular classrooms. (See chapter 6 for guidelines about mainstreaming.) In order to develop appropriate social skills, students with mild disabilities need time to learn with and from nondisabled students. Social skills training requires agreement by regular and special educators on specific areas of competence to be developed.

Developmental skills, those that cut across many settings, are preferred to context specific skills. Youngsters must be able to cope with social demands in many different environments. Training a youngster with low frustration tolerance to complete three worksheets is a school context skill. Teaching the same youngster to verbalize rather than act out feelings of frustration is a developmental skill that is useful in many settings (Fagen & Hill, 1987). While following directions, completing assignments, taking notes and other "school survival skills" (Silverman, Zigmond, & Sansone, 1981) are important, unless these skills are embedded in a more comprehensive framework students will leave school without the tools to manage the broader social demands of work, family, and the community (Figure 8–1).

The Anatomy of Self-Control

Fagen and Long (1976) define self-control as the ability to direct and regulate personal behavior flexibly and realistically in a given situation. The work of Redl and Wineman (1951) presents a structural model for describing a self-control curriculum. In their quest to unveil the "anatomy of self-control," Redl and Wineman detail a list of specific self-control skills that children normally develop as they learn to restrain their impulses and relate to the world at large. Redl and Wineman's detailed descriptions provide the classroom teacher with a paradigm of self-control (Henley, 1987). As children mature, they must learn to control their impulses, assess social reality, manage group pressure, deal with stress, and solve social problems.

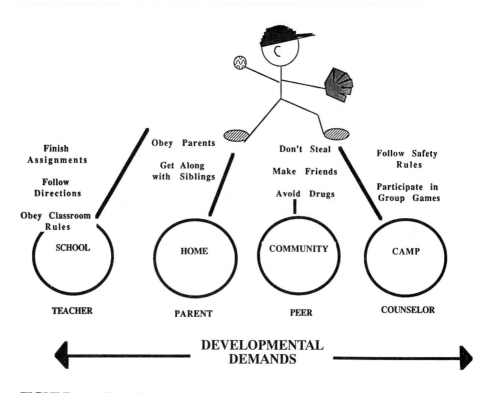

FIGURE 8–1 Developmental Demands

What follows is a brief description of the social skills entailed in each of the above areas. The items describe self-control developmental milestones. The descriptions can help the classroom teacher in the following ways:

1. To identify individual student self-control strengths and weaknesses.
2. To anticipate situations when a student might lose control.
3. To establish goals and objectives for a prosocial curriculum .

For a more thorough discussion of the components in self-control we recommend *Children Who Hate* (Redl & Wineman, 1951) and *Teaching Children Self Control: Preventing Emotional and Learning Problems in the Elementary Schools* (Fagan, Long, & Stevens, 1975).

Impulse Control
Impulses are powerful psychological motivators. A student may have an impulse to hit another student or an impulse to throw a textbook in frustration. Impulses are derived from an infant's need for immediate gratification. As children grow and mature, they learn to delay gratification. A student with self-control is capable of restraining impulses. Situations or conditions can strain the impulse con-

TABLE 8–1 Self-Control Skills

Impulse Control
Resisting Temptation
Using Materials Properly
Spontaneous Establishing of Self-Control
Tolerating Frustration

Assessment of Social Reality
Anticipating Consequences
Evaluating the Effect of Behavior on Others
Appreciating Feelings
Accepting Praise and Affection
Taking Care of Personal Possessions

Manage Group Pressure
Resisting Group Contagion
Maintaining Control Under Impact of Peer Pressure
Adapting to Competitive Challenge
Participating in Group Activities

Stress Management
Coping with Anxiety
Controlling the Floodgates of the Past
Adapting to New Situations
Relaxing

Solve Social Problems
Recalling Disruptive Actions
Learning from Experience
Drawing Inferences form Others' Experiences
Resolving Conflicts

Adapted from Redl and Wineman, 1951, *Children Who Hate* and Fagen, Long, and Stevens, 1975, *Teaching Children Self-Control: Preventing Emotional and Learning Problems in the Elementary School*, Preventive Discipline Project, Westfield State College, 1988-1992.

trol abilities of students and cause classroom disruptions. The following self-control skills are a subset of impulse control:

1. Resisting Temptation. As they grow and mature socially, students learn to control the impulses brought on by tempting situations or objects. A student who sees an examination lying on the teacher's desk and resists the urge to pick it up to survey the questions is practicing self-control. Schools are filled with alluring objects. Equipment, toys, and learning materials can present strong temptations to students who lack temptation resistance. Students with emotional problems sometimes steal with no idea about what to do with the object once it is in their possession. One youngster in a program for students with emotional problems was literally seduced by gadgets of any sort. He was so predictable that the teaching staff always knew to go to Peter's "treasure hole" under the schoolyard fence to check for missing items.

Space has its own attraction. Open spaces invite running. Enclosed spaces invite yelling. Field trips, in particular, offer myriad possibilities for disruptive behavior for a youngster who has difficulty curbing impulses.

2. Using Materials Properly. Most students understand the purpose of classroom materials. Books are for reading. Erasers are for cleaning blackboards. Clay is for modeling. Chisels are for scraping wood. Other students use classroom materials as props to act out feelings. An impulsive toss of an eraser across the room at an offensive peer or jabbing an adjacent student with a pencil illustrate how students misuse materials. These students are unable to restrain the impulse to "send a message" with the closest object available. Care should be taken to keep a close watch on materials that could be used to injure another student in a sudden outburst of anger or frustration.

3. Spontaneous Establishment of Self-Control. Many a substitute teacher has been greeted by a spontaneous, "Oh boy, a sub"; or in other words, "Let the fun and games commence." The substitute teacher scenario is an example of how in certain situations even well-mannered students can fail to spontaneously establish self-control. Controlling one's own behavior when there is no authority figure around to monitor is a sign of maturity and emotional development. Conversely, the absence of spontaneous self-control skills indicates a youngster is motivated by impulses rather than a sense of social responsibility. Organized classroom activities and routines support the student in maintaining self-control. When schedules indicate a change in routine, particularly from structured to open-ended activities, the impulsive youngster does not have the inner resources to substitute internal for external controls. Transition times, in particular, challenge the impulse control system of the students.

4. Tolerating Frustration. Frustration can be overwhelming for a youngster who lacks impulse control. Such a mundane obligation as waiting for help with a classroom assignment can culminate in a display of anger. When a four-year-old child cries because she loses in a game, that is acceptable. When an unhappy nine-year-old throws a board game aside, sending everyone's pieces flying because someone else bought "Boardwalk," there is a problem. It is quite remarkable to behold how children learn to accept minor frustrations and persevere as they mature. Learning to swim, ride a bike, and play a musical instrument are all building blocks towards perseverance, an essential quality for success in life.

For many children, frustration-tolerance happens naturally and gracefully. Others need to be taught how to handle frustration. Usually low self-esteem exemplified by an "I can't do it" attitude is characteristic of students with low frustration-tolerance.

Assessment of Social Reality

All students learn to take measure of social situations. For instance, behavior that is accepted by one teacher, may be forbidden by another. Developing children are remarkably adaptable, and their insight into behaviors that are acceptable and unacceptable is a determinant of how they are accepted by others. Well-adjusted children are capable of maintaining relationships. They interpret social cues and make adjustments in their behavior based on what a situation demands. Deficiencies in assessment of social reality will result in persistent conflicts with peers or adults.

1. Anticipating Consequences. In the classroom, as elsewhere, rules and routines organize activity and keep harmony. Students may not like rules, but they understand why rules are necessary. They know there are consequences for breaking rules. In society, norms substitute for rules, and laws are legislated codes of behavior. Social consequences follow violation of norms, and legal action is the consequence for breaking the law. Students who have an unrealistic notion of rules, norms, and laws interpret them as personal affronts to their integrity or well-being. They resent consequences. Such students, when confronted with consequences for their behavior, may become hostile.

2. Evaluating the Effect of Behavior on Others. Youngsters learn that their actions stir up corresponding reactions in others. Without this insight, a student will fail to recognize how personal behavior shapes the way that others act. A youngster who is "mean" to another may show remorse or at least understand why a friend has decided to leave. Some students with behavioral or emotional difficulties are unable to untrack their self-centered thinking. To such a student interpersonal problems are always the fault of others.

3. Appreciating Feelings. Students with emotional problems have difficulty accepting the feelings of others. This is not surprising because their own feelings are such a mystery to them. Their ability to identify and describe feelings in themselves and others is deficient. Low self-esteem coupled with a naive grasp of the significance of feelings leaves a student with emotional disturbance at a loss to contemplate his or her own life experience.

4. Accepting Praise and Affection. Trust is a basic requirement for social exchange between teacher and student. A student who has difficulty trusting adults will have difficulty forming attachments to others. Expression of care and interest may be reciprocated by hostility or resentment. Many students with emotional problems have well-entrenched defenses against what they consider a hostile world. Such youngsters need to learn to accept and give affection.

5. Taking Care of Personal Possessions. A bike that is left unlocked may get stolen. Carelessness in keeping track of assignments can mean coming to school unprepared. Personal responsibility in managing day to day activities is important for school success. Students who can manage their daily lives do well in school. Other students need to learn how to organize themselves. They are undermined by their own unintentional carelessness.

Manage Group Pressure

Virtually everything in a classroom happens in a group situation. Group dynamics have a powerful impact on young people both in and out of school. The need to belong, the need to socialize with like-minded people are strong forces that can impel a youngster to make good or bad choices. Why does one youngster join Boy Scouts, while another joins a gang? Why does one youngster look for mystical experience with drugs, and another choose religion? In many cases the answer is the power of peer pressure to shape young people's choices. The ability to handle group pressure is a hallmark of self-control. Students who are overly influenced by peer groups give up control of their lives. These students need to learn how to manage group pressure.

1. Resisting Group Contagion. Excitability is contagious. When a class is "out of control," one or more students set off others with their disruptive behavior. Overstimulated students become leaders in pandemonium, and the teacher is hard pressed to restore order. Some students have the internal strength to maintain internal control while others around them are out of control. Meanwhile, other students are swept away by the excitement. Such students need to learn how to appraise situations reasonably and to strengthen their sense of themselves as agents of their own control.

2. Maintaining Control under Impact of Peer Pressure. For young people, particularly adolescents, peer pressure is an extremely powerful shaper of attitude and behavior. When confronted with peer pressure, students may be hard pressed to make the types of decisions that adults would advocate. Self-control within groups means being able to steer an individual course of action, even though it may be the opposite of group expectations. By helping students learn to make prosocial decisions despite group pressure to the contrary, teachers not only enhance classroom management, but also provide students with the tools to deal with myriad group pressures outside of school.

3. Adapting to Competitive Challenge. Competition is a basic fact of life in our society. Keeping a balanced perspective about winning and losing is necessary to productivity both in and out of school. Winning and losing gracefully require self-control and positive self-regard. Competition in school, both obvious (e.g., tests) and unobtrusive (e.g., art displays), are factors that all students must learn to accept. Resilience, perseverance, and task commitment are sine qua nons of success. Students who avoid competition or think of themselves as "losers" need help in learning how to handle competitive challenge.

4. Participating in Group Activities.   Cooperative group work is prevalent in all levels of society. Learning to help others, resolve conflicts, and share resources are signs of personal growth. Each of these skills requires the ability to "decenter," that is, to consider the other person's perspective. While these skills develop naturally in some students, others become fixated on their own point of view. This impedes their ability to cooperate and maintain group harmony. Such students need opportunities to learn to set aside their own personal agendas and focus on the concerns of the group.

Stress Management Skills

Stress is the electricity of life. Through a combination of perception and biochemical reactions, stress energizes us to action. Schultz and Heuchers (1983) succinctly state, "All life events carry the potential for introducing stress into a person's life" (cited in Knoblock, 216). Hans Seyle (1978) defines stress as the nonspecific response of the body to any demand, pleasant or unpleasant. For a student, a pleasant prospect, such as anticipating a field trip to the zoo, causes stress just as surely as the unpleasant prospect of going to school without assigned homework.

   Learning to manage stress is an important adaptive and survival skill. Perception plays a key role in inducing a stress reaction of fight or flight. Students with emotional disabilities often misinterpret social cues. Overreaction to mild stressors is commonplace with these students. An ordinary task, such as reading aloud in class, can bring on a temper tantrum (i.e., fight) or refusal to perform (i.e., flight). Learning to adapt to stressful classroom situations can help prepare students for life outside of school. Essentially there are four characteristic stressful conditions that challenge the self-control abilities of students.

1. Coping with Anxiety.   Some students are so ridden with anxiety (i.e., painful apprehension or sense of foreboding) that they are unable to decipher reality-based threats from normal expressions of feeling. Their reaction may be to strike out or verbally assault the perceived protagonist. Many teachers have difficulty understanding that overreaction to routine situations, brought on by a student's inability to cope with anxiety, is a symptom of his or her disability. In the section on the life space interview, we emphasized the value of gathering information on how a youngster perceives events in the classroom. Through the use of LSI and other active listening techniques, it is possible to identify specific stressors that set a youngster off into a fight or flight reaction.

2. Controlling the Floodgates of the Past.   Fortunately most students have the capacity to separate present events from past unpleasant situations. For example, a student will attempt to persevere in a mathematics assignment despite past difficulties with arithmetic. Given this situation, even a well-adjusted youngster will need support and will at times get frustrated. Students with behavioral disorders have life histories replete with failure or trauma. A minor dose of recall is all that is needed sometimes to set off a severe stress reaction.

3. Adapting to New Situations. Learning to adjust to unfamiliar situations or people is an essential adaptive skill. Adaptive responses to stress caused by new situations include questions, verbalization of apprehensions, and caution. When students have not learned these adaptive skills, their reactions can be disturbing. Pretenses of familiarity, avoidant behaviors, and unwarranted hostility are samples of how students overreact to new situations or people.

4. Relaxing. After a hard day at school, a youngster might look forward to going home and playing with friends. On a rainy day, such a child might pick up a favorite book or get back to completing a model. Relaxation reduces stress. Relaxation is an emotional and biochemical state. Numerous body signs indicate an individual is relaxed—pulse rate goes down, skin temperature is warm to the touch, breathing is paced and easy. Chronic stress disables the immune system. Chronic stress can cause sickness and disease. Students with emotional difficulties rarely are able to achieve a prolonged state of relaxation. Even games dissolve into a series of petty disputes. Alone, they have difficulty sustaining solitary activity. Television, alcohol, and drugs are pastimes of youth that are nonadaptive attempts to relax.

Solve Social Problems

Interpersonal problems are difficult to solve. The negotiating of relationships requires the ability to reflect on one's own behavior. One must be able to apply the lessons of the past to present situations. Once a problem is identified, it is necessary to consider various options and eventually choose a course of action. Ultimately, social problem-solving requires evaluation of goals and the means to achieve those goals. A student must be able to apply these skills in both individual and group situations. The final achievement is measured by a student's ability to develop and maintain relationships. When a youngster lacks these skills, interpersonal conflicts are frequent, and a youngster becomes isolated by his own futile social gestures.

1. Recalling Disruptive Actions. Every teacher and parent is familiar with the refrain, "It wasn't my fault." Denial of personal culpability is normal in young children. As students develop better insight into their own behavior, they begin to accept responsibility for their actions. Students with emotional problems sometimes literally "forget" their own behavior. Redl and Wineman (1951) called this forgetfulness—"evaporation of self-contributed links to the causal chain." The youngster is unable to perceive how his or her actions culminated in a classroom disturbance. This lack of recall should not be confused with lying to avoid punishment. Rather the deficiency rests in the inability to perceive personal feelings or behavior clear enough to review a series of events.

2. Learning from Experience. Students should be able to apply past experiences to present situations. Learning from past mistakes is a basic strategy for solving social problems. Natural consequences play a significant role in social maturity and development. Children learn to modify their behavior based on reactions from peers. Teasing is returned in kind. Selfishness keeps others away. Students with behavior or emotional problems may persist in the same social errors regardless of the consequences. Even positive social experiences provide few clues for future behaviors. These students seem unable to learn from their experiences in order to piece together the behavioral steps needed to work out social problems to their advantage.

3. Drawing Inference from Others' Experiences. Some students learn and profit from other students' mistakes or successes. This modeling is a basic style of learning for young people. Adults count on the fact that one youngster may be an example to others. This is the premise behind severe punishment (e.g., expulsions), and it is a premise behind awards and honors. Many youngsters do in fact learn from others and use the experience so gained to guide future actions. A student who cannot learn from the mistakes and successes of others is handicapped by shortsightedness. Adults cringe when they hear a youngster say, "It can't happen to me." The ever increasing rate of teenage pregnancies and drug dependent youngsters are stern reminders that a key social problem-solving skill is drawing inference from what happens to others.

4. Resolving Conflicts. You don't change a lightbulb with a hammer, and you don't solve social problems with aggressive behavior. Many youngsters need to learn conflict resolution, negotiation, and cooperation as social tools. The need for students to be able to appraise social situations and develop peaceful strategies for solving problems has never been greater. Racism and teen violence are commonplace in today's society. Every classroom discipline system should help provide students with the human relations tools needed to function as a productive member in a democratic society.

Why Teach Prosocial Skills?

Students with mild disabilities need to learn adaptive behaviors. It would be unfair to give a student with low frustration-tolerance a check on the blackboard for being restless. Such a practice is tantamount to forcing a student with cerebral palsy to run a fifty-yard dash! Students with emotional problems have not developed their condition due to a lack of sanctions in their lives; in fact, many of their case histories reveal numerous scrapes with authority. Teachers who have students with mild disabilities in their classrooms soon learn the meaning of "disability." It is a lack of ability, a condition that a student can't overcome without help.

Behavioral and emotional difficulties are not visible like physical disabilities, but they are no less debilitating. Limiting behavior is not enough. Students with and without mild disabilities need opportunities to learn socially acceptable behavior. Parents send their children to school because they believe it is a safe and orderly environment. Good classroom management requires a blend of humane practices that combine high expectations for success with a willingness to organize a classroom to maximize the learning of academic and social skills.

Selecting a Prosocial Curriculum

Teachers who practice preventive discipline realize that youngsters need to be taught skills that enhance social adaptability. The Redl-Wineman model identifies specific self-control skills that students need in order to function as mature and responsible members of a classroom community. Other models, such as *Developmental Therapy in the Classroom* (Wood, Combs, Gunn, & Weller, 1986), *Skillstreaming* (McGinnis & Goldstein, 1984), and *Teaching Children Self-Control: Preventing Emotional and Learning Problems in the Elementary Schools* (Fagan, Long, & Stevens, 1975), provide a series of goals, objectives and activities for teaching students prosocial skills.

A sound prosocial curriculum is research-based. It is derived from a theory or model of human development. It substitutes adaptive skills for nonconstructive behavior both in and out of school. A prosocial curriculum begins with general goals and then delineates observable student behaviors matched to goal statements. Specific objectives provide a basis for evaluation of student growth and program accountability.

All prosocial curricula emphasize one key point—scheduling time to teach social skills is a legitimate educational activity. If students are going to change their behavior, they require opportunities to learn new behaviors in an organized and relevant manner. Wood, Combs, Gunn, and Weller state, "A (prosocial) program must have relevance to the student's world beyond the special classroom, and the skills learned in the program must produce satisfying results in personal, real life situations" (Wood, Combs, Gunn, & Weller, 1986, 12).

Schumaker, Pederson, Hazel, and Meyen (1983) pose five questions to serve as a guide in selecting a social skills curriculum:

1. Does the curriculum promote social competence?
2. Does the curriculum accommodate the learning characteristics of the students for whom it is to be applied?
3. Does the curriculum target the social skills deficits of the students for whom it is to be applied?
4. Does the curriculum provide training in situations as well as skills?
5. Does the curriculum include instructional methodologies found to be effective with the population of students for whom it is to be applied? (cited in Walker & Shea, 1991)

Social skills can be taught directly or indirectly. Direct instruction begins with the identification of a specific skill, for example, the social problem solving skill of learning from experience. For an activity, the teacher could select a contemporary problem—increasing drug awareness among schoolchildren. The class is divided into small groups comprised of four students. Each group is given art materials, reference materials, and recent newspaper articles. Each group must brainstorm five ways of increasing drug awareness and present their findings to the entire class.

Social skills also can be taught indirectly. Peer tutoring, cooperative learning, classroom discussions, and role playing are just a sample of ways to teach academic topics while cultivating social abilities. Peer tutoring can be useful for any academic subject. Cooperative learning could produce a single act play. Classroom discussions could highlight the role of different cultures in American history. Role playing such protagonists as Thomas Henry Huxley and Bishop Wilberforce of Oxford in their famous confrontation about evolution could help students gain insight into how discourse shapes science.

Classroom Organization

A well-organized classroom deters discipline problems. Organization includes the total school attitude towards discipline. The principal takes the lead in establishing an atmosphere of trust and respect. Within the classroom, teachers need to manage individual student behavior in group situations. Groups influence individual behavior, and individual behavior shapes group actions. The manner in which a teacher responds to the group dynamics of a classroom can contribute to or prevent discipline problems.

Group Instructional Skills

Effective classroom management requires attention to teacher behaviors that minimize behavior problems. Jacob Kounin (1977) and other researchers have found that teachers prevent discipline problems through their ability to monitor the entire group without becoming distracted by minor incidents that cause the entire class to become diverted. Such teachers demonstrate "withitness" and "overlapping."

"Withitness"
"Withitness" is a constant awareness of what is going on in the classroom (DeLuke & Knoblock, 1987). Two features of "withitness" reduce misbehavior:

1. Select the right student for a desist. When a teacher reprimands the wrong student, the rest of the class assumes she does not know what is going on. Kounin found this "ripple effect" can work to the teacher's disadvantage, as in the above example. Clarity in identifying the correct student and clearly explaining the preferred behavior increases conformity among the rest of the class. Kounin also found that anger, sarcasm or other roughness in the teacher's reproach upset younger children. The "ripple" effect is most pronounced at the beginning of the school year, and it loses its impact as the year goes on.

2. Attend to the more serious infraction when two problems develop at the same time (Charles, 1989). Taking steps to stop a misbehavior before it "sets off" other students is characteristic of "withit" teachers. These teachers have the ability to judge the "contagibility" of student behavior, and they respond accordingly. For example, Eileen is gazing off into space. The "withit" teacher takes note of her inattention but does not disrupt the smooth work flow of the rest of the class. Planned ignoring or proximity control work best. However, when a serious disruption occurs, an immediate verbal desist is warranted.

"Overlapping"

"Overlapping" is closely aligned to "withitness." It refers to the ability to monitor two situations simultaneously. Suppose the teacher is working with a small reading group of seven students, and she lost track of events around the rest of the classroom. This absence of "overlapping" would almost assuredly result in misbehavior. Students with their hands up would be ignored; students who are done with their work would start looking for something else to do; and a mischievous student would have an opportunity to cause a disturbance. The "overlapping" teacher keeps the small group on task while at the same time managing the flow of activity throughout the rest of the classroom.

Maintain a Group Focus

Virtually all of a teacher's day is spent managing students in groups. Kounin reported that the manner in which teachers conduct their group lessons had a significant impact on discipline problems. Teachers maintain a group focus by encouraging cooperation. For example, during a presentation one student demonstrates at the blackboard, and students in their seats offer suggestions and comments. Students are encouraged to listen, help others, share ideas, and work towards group goals. Well-managed groups have a high rate of student work involvement. Student boredom and indifference to work assignments is a main cause of discipline problems. Tasks that are repetitious and require minimal thought invite discipline problems. As Morse observes:

> *If school is not inviting, if the tasks are not clear, interesting, and at an appropriate level, how can we expect students to be on task? Adverse student reactions should be expected when classes are dull, teaching is uninspired, and failure is built in. Their oppositional behavior is a sign of personal growth and integrity. (Morse, 1987, 6)*

Teachers who find ways to relate learning to student interests and lives outside of school help students to see value in their lessons. When students understand the purpose of tasks, they can make a connection between teacher expectations and their personal needs; this increases group harmony and minimizes classroom disruptions.

Autocratic, Permissive, and Democratic Classrooms

Group participation will vary depending on teacher style. Dreikurs classified teachers into three types: autocratic, permissive, and democratic (Charles, 1989). Autocratic teachers rule by will. They believe all power and control should rest with the teacher. Permissive teachers do not provide guidance or leadership. They are unsure of themselves and are easily frustrated with administrators or other teachers who "don't understand." Democratic teachers maintain discipline through student participation. They understand that authority is a natural by-product of their teaching position. Democratic teachers expect students to become disciplined by acquiring inner controls. Autocratic, permissive, and democratic teachers approach their classes in very different ways. Each acts in accordance with a set of attitudes about what students need.

Autocratic teachers believe power is the teacher's best tool for managing student behavior. Such teachers believe students are unable to control themselves. Often students will respond in a manner that supports this Hobbesian view of nature. (Thomas Hobbes, a seventeenth century English philosopher, believed that the natural passions of people ran counter to such virtues as justice and equity. According to Hobbes, only power, exercised by an outside authority, motivates people to behave in a benevolent manner.) Students have an uncanny way of living up to teacher expectations. When teachers expect the worst, that's usually what they get. Negative student behavior confirms the teacher's basic assumptions about the need to control students through power and authority. The result is classroom management by fiat. The teacher makes the rules, rewards the "good," and punishes the "bad." Autocratic discipline strategies are teacher-directed, with minimal student participation.

Permissive teachers are confused. They believe child development theory supports giving children choices, and they naively anticipate that, left to their own devices, students will follow the right course. Permissive teachers want to be democratic, but they are unable to organize classroom practices (e.g., class discussions, cooperative learning) to support democratic procedures. They abdicate their natural authority as adults in the misguided view that they are creating an environment that will allow the natural goodness of children to emerge. This lack of leadership soon leads to chaos. They want their students to like them and will attempt to win students over by favors, shortcutting rules, and making deals. Permissive teachers don't stay in the profession for long. While there is a high tolerance for autocratic classroom practices in public schools, the chaotic classrooms of permissive teachers usually are short-lived. Permissive teachers either burn out quickly or are asked to leave. Ironically, permissive teachers rarely see themselves that way. They consider themselves democratic or "therapeutic."

Democratic teachers believe that students need to share power with the teacher in order to learn how to behave responsibly. Democratic teacher strategies are student-centered. The teacher assumes the role of leader rather than ruler. Democratic teachers know their authority is a natural by-product of being a teacher. It isn't necessary to keep reminding students who is in charge. Democratic teachers combine teacher-directed lessons and student-centered activities. Such classroom practices as cooperative learning, classroom discussions, and peer tutoring are featured in democratic classrooms.

In a democratic classroom, students are asked to help frame rules for the year. This opening gambit establishes the climate for approaching discipline as a cooperative venture. The democratic teacher has two clear goals for her students. First is the development of good interpersonal relationships. Self-esteem is the underpinning of motivation. Students and teacher alike need to be treated with respect and compassion. Such human relations skills as listening, courtesy, and a sense of humor foster student self-esteem and provide a comfortable climate for learning. Second, the democratic teacher wants to see the class evolve into a cohesive group. There is a continual focus on group management. Students work in groups, talk in groups, and play in groups. The democratic teacher strives to create a group identity in the classroom. Students in a democratic classroom share a sense of togetherness not found in autocratic or permissive classrooms.

Rules and Sanctions

One type of teacher response to misbehavior is punishment. Punishment is one of the most misunderstood and attitude-laden reactions to student actions. Punishment stops behavior through force—either physical or psychological. In the attempt to get students to toe the line, punishment communicates the message that might makes right. One of the factors that makes punitive approaches so appealing is that in terms of short-term goals, they appear to work. Such punishments as checks on a blackboard, "timeout," calls to home, or trips to the principal's office may halt disruptions, but too frequently the gains are temporary. Punishment does not change behavior nor does it teach new behaviors (Hyman & D'Allesandro, 1984; Kohn, 1991; Morse, 1991).

In Pell City, Alabama, a mother was sentenced to a reduced penalty of six months in prison for assaulting a school principal. The attack was provoked by the three paddlings the principal had given the woman's seven-year-old son. In sentencing the mother to jail, the judge said, "We have to set an example for others so that they not perform the same act you did. I sentence you to five years" (Smothers, 1987). This bizarre incident serves as a dramatic reminder that in many states corporal punishment is an acceptable means of disciplining students. As the father of two students in Huffman, Alabama, told to a *New York Times* reporter, "If the student needs a paddling, he ought to get a butt busting" (p. A15). Instruments of physical punishment in schools include doubled-over belts, lacrosse sticks, baseball bats, arrows, electrical cords, and wooden drawer dividers. A Chicago principal used a pen knife to drill a hole in a student's fingernail (Hyman & D'Allesandro, 1984, 42).

Sometimes it's difficult to determine where treatment for disruptive behavior ends and violence begins. This is particularly true when punishment is couched in scientific jargon. For example the term "negative aversives" is used in special education to label such tactics as blasts of cold water in the face from an atomizer or pinching to thwart disruptive behavior. Whether or not negative aversives are a euphemism for punishment is a matter of some dispute. In Rhode Island, parents of children attending the Behavioral Research Institute defended the use of negative aversives. The Behavior Research Institute serves diverse types of behavior disorders from juvenile delinquency to autism. "Negative aversives" range from pinches and hot sauces placed in the mouth to blasts of pressurized air on the side of the face, and, ultimately, restraints where a youngster is spread-eagled against a wall face first and held fast by strong cloth bands. While many educators are under the impression that these tactics are directed only at youngsters with severe behavior disorders, the Behavior Research Institute advertises itself as a therapeutic treatment program for students with a variety of disabilities ranging from mild to severe.

When punishment is used, it should be guided by school policy. Bratten, Simpson, Rosell, and Reilly recommend seven procedural elements to guide the use of punishment in schools:

1. Information about the use and abuse of punishment should be provided to teachers.
2. Teachers should be trained in the use of punishment.
3. Punishment procedures should be approved by the school board and be disseminated to teachers, parents, and students.
4. Records of punishment usage should be maintained.
5. Complaint and appeal procedures should be established.
6. Infractions that warrant punishment should be explained to all students and teachers.
7. Procedures for periodic review of punishment procedures should be implemented. (Bratten, Simpson, Rosell, & Riley, 1988, 80)

Punishment is commonplace and controversial. Some teachers use it first; others as the last resort. Punishment is effective when used sparingly. Reserve punishment for events or actions that cause physical or psychological harm to students or teacher. Remember if punishment and its antecedent—threats—are used as a primary discipline tactic, there is nothing left to fall back on when those methods fail to achieve the desired results.

A Problem-Solving Model

Teachers in regular and special classrooms are confronted with a variety of behavior problems. Up to this point, we have emphasized practices that help prevent discipline problems. However, some students, often those with more intense emotional or behavioral problems, require an organized intervention plan. Dealing with chronic disruptive behaviors requires a systematic problem-solving method. The following procedure is a model for responding to persistent classroom disturbances.

1. Describe Student Behavior. Disturbing behavior is described not evaluated. Avoid clinical-sounding terms that interpret behavior. Rather than saying a student is "distractible," describe his behavior; for example, "Steven typically sits still for about five minutes, then he starts sliding books around on his desk, dropping pencils, and talking to other students." Common evaluative comments to be avoided are: hyperactive, immature, aggressive, noncompliant, attention-seeker, and withdrawn. Evaluative terms are too abstract to clearly communicate a problem. A behavior that is "aggressive" to one teacher may be "assertive" to another teacher and "immature" to a third teacher.

Description enhances communication among teacher, parents, and student. It insures that everybody is talking about the same behavior, and it alleviates inevitable misunderstandings that arise when behavior is labeled. Moreover, descriptions of behavior can be counted. Interpretations cannot. You cannot observe "hyperactivity," but you can see and count how many times a youngster gets up from his desk.

2. Count Behavior. Educators use a tool called a behavior frequency chart to count behavior. Disturbing behaviors are listed next to a series of boxes for each day of the week. Each time a student demonstrates a disturbing behavior, the time is written in the appropriate box. This checklist can be located on the teacher's desk or some other convenient spot in the classroom.

The purpose of the behavior frequency chart is to provide a data base for determining the severity of a classroom problem. The more frequent the disturbing behavior, the more likely it is a disturbance in the classroom. The chart gives the teacher an objective way of calculating frequency of the behavior. The data can provide other important information. Perhaps many of the disruptions occur during a specific time of the day; this could provide some insight into cause. Knowing when a disturbing behavior occurs helps the teacher determine antecedents. For example, the student might be most disturbing after transitions from preferred to non-preferred activities. Finally, no program can be properly evaluated without initial baseline data. In a few months, do another count to determine if the intervention program is working.

3. Empathize with the Student. All behavior occurs for a reason. Put yourself in the student's shoes. What does he or she feel? A life space interview would be helpful at this juncture to elicit the student's perspective.

Consider physiological causes first. Is the student getting enough sleep? How about diet? The average American eats a 120 pounds of refined sugar a year. What is your student eating? Is lead poisoning a possible explanation? It is the number one health hazard of youth, particularly children who live near highways, in old homes, and near industrial areas. When was the last time the student's vision and hearing was checked? Some attention problems are traced to hearing impairments.

What about the student's family? Are there problems at home? Does the student have a home? For that matter does the student have a family? Don't forget drug and alcohol abuse. Does the student come to school with frequent bruises? Emotional neglect is more difficult to determine than physical abuse, but no less important. Talking to students provides useful information about his or her family and life after school.

Empathizing means trying to understand the problem from the student's point of view. Disturbing behavior in class, if it's serious enough to require a specific plan, will show up outside of school too. Enlist the aid of family members. Empathy will not alone solve the problem, but it will change your perspective. Judgements of the student might change from a classroom nuisance to a real person with a complicated life. Empathizing helps the teacher to depersonalize the classroom disruptions. Approaching the issue with professional detachment insures an intervention plan is professionally prepared, without anger or resentment.

4. A Twofold Plan: Interventions and Teaching Prosocial Skills.   After describing, charting, and counting the disturbing behavior, the next step is to determine the best intervention to curb the disturbing behavior, and to identify a prosocial skill to replace the disturbing behavior.

Remember Buffy? When we left her at the beginning of this chapter, she was ready to begin her first week teaching. Buffy has completed a behavior frequency chart on a female student, Sylvia (see Figure 8–2). Sylvia is 12 years old. She is verbal, bright, and impulsive. Sylvia's quick tongue is matched by her fast mood changes. Buffy has counted Sylvia's verbal taunts and sarcastic remarks. They are usually directed at Buffy; and when Sylvia launches these verbal missiles, everything in the classroom stops. Watching Buffy and Sylvia match wits has become a great source of entertainment for the rest of the class.

Through her charting, Buffy sees that Sylvia starts her day out well, then around 10:00 A.M., she warms to her task of harassing the teacher. By lunch time, Sylvia has made on average five unprovoked and disturbing remarks aimed at Buffy and other students. Sylvia also moves about the room without permission. Empathizing with Sylvia, Buffy considered the possibility that Sylvia might resent her; but why? A conversation in the teacher's lounge with some of the faculty reveals that Sylvia formed a close attachment to Ms. Collins, her fifth grade teacher. She even asked Ms. Collins to fail her so she could spend another year with her.

Buffy decided to adopt a couple of interventions. First, she would restructure Sylvia's morning. Buffy worked out an arrangement for Sylvia to do peer tutoring each morning in a third grade classroom from 9:45 to 10:15. Sylvia had no problem with academics, and she had a sensitive side that Buffy hoped could be capitalized on to nurture younger children. Second, Buffy determined to bolster her relationship with Sylvia through hypodermic affection and sane messages. She wanted Sylvia to learn that she was a valued classroom member, but at the same time Buffy knew it was important for Sylvia to understand the effect of her taunts.

STUDENT: <u>Sylvia</u>   WEEK: <u>September 7 - 14</u>

DESCRIBE BEHAVIORS	MON.	TUE.	WED.	THU.	FRI.
Verbal taunts directed at teacher	10:00 10:07 10:08 11:15 1:05	9:45 12:57 2:10 2:19	10:12 10:13 10:23 2:19	11:45 11:47 2:29	10:28 10:51 11:12 11:13 11:17
Verbal taunts directed at other students	9:13 12:19 12:20	None	None	11:46 11:51 11:58	None
Moving around the room without per- mission	10:01 10:08 11:17	2:11 2:21	None	11:45 11:47	10:27 10:53

Comments:

FIGURE 8–2   Behavior Frequency Chart

Buffy decided to direct her prosocial activities at helping Sylvia assess social reality. Sylvia needed help specifically in evaluating the effect of her behavior on others. The more she thought about it, Buffy realized that other students could learn more about how their behavior affects people. Buffy determined to develop a unit for the entire class. She would do values clarification, role playing, cooperative learning activities, and more peer tutoring.

5. Evaluate the Plan.   How many times do teachers settle on a system for changing student behavior without ever evaluating the plan? In our experience this happens far too often. W. H. Auden had this to say about changing human behavior,

We would rather be ruined than changed
We would rather live in our dread
Than climb the cross of the moment,
And let our illusions die. (Seldes, 1985, 23)

Changing behavior is a difficult enterprise. A behavior change plan that is elegant on paper can mislead a teacher into overlooking periodic evaluations. Every behavior intervention plan should be evaluated on a regular basis. Three months is a reasonable amount of time to look for some change. Another evaluation requires another behavior frequency count. If there is no decrease in disturbing behaviors, a new plan may be needed. Go back and review the steps outlined in this chapter. Did you miss anything in terms of empathizing with the student? Did you, for instance, fail to talk with family members? Perhaps you need to try some different interventions. If the problem is more serious you might consider life space interviews.

If you are seeing a change in behavior, you hit the mark on your first try. That is a good start. Success in working with a youngster to learn socially adept skills is well worth the effort. Twenty years from now, your students may have forgotten how to multiply mixed numbers; but if they can listen to another person's point of view, you will have left them a valuable legacy.

Summary

Well-managed classrooms facilitate learning. No one can learn in a class that is constantly disrupted by behavior problems. Discipline problems cause stress in both teachers and students. For the novice teacher, classroom management is a major concern. At one time or another all students present discipline problems. While authoritarian discipline tactics hold some appeal, promoting student participation in discipline policies increases their sense of personal responsibility and helps to prevent future behavior problems.

Preventive discipline is based on the premise that many classroom disruptions can be avoided. Teachers who use preventive discipline techniques strive to intervene before a disturbance turns into a full-blown discipline problem. Such teachers are skilled in an array of behavior management tools including behavior modification, nonverbal, and verbal interventions.

Educators are coming to the realization that intervening to eliminate disruptive behavior is not enough. Teaching social skills is a legitimate use of classroom time. Students can learn no more valuable skill than how to get along with others. Values clarification, character education, and self-control programs help students to cope with life both in and out of school. Teachers who exhibit such group management skills as "withitness" and "overlapping" are able to keep classroom activities moving along without constant interruptions. Discipline policies that include punishment require careful scrutiny.

When students present persistent behavior problems in the classroom, effective teachers develop a systematic problem-solving plan. They begin by describing and counting the frequency of disturbing behavior. They try to determine causes. Empathizing with the student helps to provide insight into possible physiological, environmental, or emotional causes for disruptive actions. Problem-solving is a team effort that requires input from other professionals, family, and the student. One of the most effective ways of eliciting the student's point of view is the life space interview. All behavior management programs need to be evaluated on a regular basis. If behavior problems persist, collect new data and implement a different strategy.

Chapter 9

Building Family Partnerships

Advance Organizer

When you complete this chapter, you will be able to:

1. Describe social and economic conditions that threaten children and families in the United States.
2. Discuss factors that enhance teacher-family cooperation.
3. Describe characteritics of model programs that promote family involvement in schools.
4. Explain the impact of having a youngster with special needs on each member of the family.
5. Discuss sources and types of support available to families of students with special needs.
6. Explain how teachers can enhance communication with families.
7. Describe how educators can improve participation of parents in IEP meetings.

Eileen slowly climbed the steps of the rundown, two-family house. She felt apprehensive in this poor neighborhood where every house seemed to need a new coat of paint. As she reached for the doorbell, Eileen reviewed why she was here.

Her student, Alexis, a pretty 12-year-old, seemed to be compensating for her weak academic skills by playing the role of class clown. Every time Eileen gave an assignment,

Alexis had a comment. "You never showed us how to do this," or "This is stupid, why do we have to do it?" were typical of the disturbing remarks Alexis directed at Eileen on a regular basis.

Perhaps this home visit would help. After a moment's hesitation, Eileen knocked on the front door. Within a few seconds the door swung open. Alexis stood in the doorway. She was dressed in her best Sunday dress. "Hi, Mrs. Morrison; my mother is in the living room." Alexis led Eileen into a sunny room with blue muslin curtains. Standing with teapot in hand was Alexis's mother. "I'm Mrs. Taylor; I'm pleased you could visit us; Alexis tells me so many wonderful things about you." Eileen glanced at Alexis whose face had suddenly turned three shades brighter. "Please sit down and have some tea," invited Mrs. Taylor. She turned to Alexis, and said, "Go into the kitchen and get some oatmeal cookies for your teacher." "Yes, momma," was the quick reply, and Alexis breezed into the other room. Eileen watched in astonishment. 'Is this the same child who has been carrying out a single-handed verbal assault on me in class?' she wondered.

Mrs. Taylor smiled, "It's been difficult for Alexis ever since her daddy died, but she tries hard and she's a good girl." "I'm sorry, Mrs. Taylor. I didn't realize your husband had passed away," responded Eileen. Mrs. Taylor's smile slowly melted away. "Alexis needs help with her schoolwork, I know; but trying to raise her and her younger brother and sister on my waitress salary has been difficult for all of us," said Mrs. Taylor. "Tell me, what can I do at home to help Alexis with her reading? I didn't get past 8th grade, and I want Alexis to earn her high school diploma," continued Mrs. Taylor. Eileen sat down and the two women spent the next hour discussing how together they could help Alexis improve her schoolwork.

As Eileen drove home, she reviewed her home visit. Alexis comes home from school and makes dinner for her 7-year-old brother and 9-year-old sister. Her mother is trying to raise three children on a waitress salary. They can't afford a car. And most surprising of all, Alexis is not the disruptive child at home that she appears to be in the classroom. Eileen smiled to herself. She knew that her classroom strategy for handling Alexis would change. The insights she gained from this visit would help her to better manage Alexis's attention-seeking bahavior in school. As she drove towards her condominium in the suburbs, Eileen vowed to make more home visits. An hour in a student's home, she realized, could eliminate countless hours of misunderstanding in school.

Eileen's home visit highlights a little appreciated fact—students' lives do not begin and end at the schoolhouse door. From kindergarten to senior year in high school, students spend only one-eighth of their time in school. Student experiences outside school have a profound influence on student behavior in the classroom. If a student is having difficulty in school, a home visit can provide a teacher with useful insights into how to handle the problem. In today's public schools there are many communication gaps between students and teachers. Language, cultural, and ethnic differences lead to misunderstandings. Communication is a vital link to bridge this gap. Families are the best source of information about a student's likes and dislikes, emotional peaks and valleys, motivation, and activities outside of school.

America's Children—A Threatened Species

Children, James Coleman argued, require "social capital" in order to grow, learn, and prosper. Social capital refers to the social networks and adult relationships which nurture children during their development. Coleman found, for instance, a lower dropout rate among students in Catholic schools (3.4 percent) than among students in public schools (14.3 percent). He explained the discrepancy in terms of social capital in the Catholic schools. The community of school and church helped families keep students in school. Because of the additional adult support outside the family the students attending Catholic schools had a strong incentive to stay in school. Coleman highlighted the bonding together of adults through shared goals and beliefs as a primary source of social capital.

Social capital has steadily eroded since the turn of the century. In early twentieth century agricultural society, children were mentored by extended families, neighbors, and community members. Informal relationships between adults outside the family were commonplace. The transformation to an industrial society disconnected children from the lives of adults. Fathers returned home from factories tired from hours of mindnumbing toil on assembly lines. Soon mothers followed fathers into the workplace. The family unit as a source of social capital began to unravel as the pressure to maintain a decent standard of living increased each year. With more time spent in work, adults had less time to spend in community activities such as PTO and Scouting (Coleman, 1987). The overall effect has been an alienation of children from basic nurturing elements in society that were common throughout history.

As a nation we are almost bankrupt of social capital. Children of the 1990s are more at-risk of physical and psychological harm than any other generation. Grinding poverty, drugs, and violence are features of everyday life for many United States children. In 1989, the U.S. Department of Education estimated that 220,000 school children were homeless (Reed & Sauter, 1990). Every seven minutes a child is arrested for drug abuse (76,986 a year). Ten thousand children a year die from poverty-related conditions (Chidren's Defense Fund, 1990). A study of eight industrialized nations (United States, Switzerland, Sweden, Norway, West Germany, Canada, England, and Australia) revealed that the United States has the highest child poverty rate. The United States ranked 18th among 142 countries in infant mortality. In 1990, an African-American child born in inner-city Boston had less chance for survival than an infant from Uruguay, Panama, or South Korea (Children's Defense Fund, 1990).

A University of Maryland School of Medicine study reported that out of 168 teenagers who visited an inner-city clinic for routine medical care, 24 percent witnessed a murder, and 72 percent knew someone who had been shot. One out of every ten girls who visited the Baltimore clinic had been raped (Zinzmeister, 1990). The violence children are exposed to is impulsive and random. Children have killed other children for sneakers, college jackets, and professional ball team hats (Telander, 1990).

Most parents care deeply about their children. A few parents are ineffective, and, unfortunately, a small minority of parents actually harm their children. Neglect and abuse are a sad reality in some homes. Every 47 seconds, a child is abused or neglected—a total of 675,000 a year (Children's Defense Fund, 1990). Table 9–1 lists the daily state of affairs for children of the United States.

Early medical and educational intervention for youth should be a national priority. As a society, we are at-risk of squandering our most precious national resource—our children. If present poverty trends continue, one out of every four children in the United States will be poor by the year 2000. Without a major shift in our national priorities, many of these youngsters will grow up without hope for success in life. Drugs, crime, violence, and despair will be their legacy to future generations.

TABLE 9–1   One Day in the Lives of American Children

17,051 women get pregnant.
 2,795 of them are teenagers.

1,106 teenagers have abortions.
 372 teenagers miscarry.

1,295 teenagers give birth.

 689 babies are born to women who have had inadequate prenatal care.
 719 babies are born at low birthweight (less than 5 pounds, 8 ounces).
 129 babies are born at very low birthweight (less than 3 pounds, 5 ounces).
  67 babies die before before one month of life.
 105 babies die before their first birthday.

  27 children die from poverty.
  10 children die from guns.
  30 children are wounded by guns.
   6 teenagers commit suicide.

135,000 children bring a gun to school.

 7,742 teens become sexually active.
 623 teenagers get syphilis or gonorrhea.

 211 children are arrested for drug abuse.
 437 children are arrested for drinking or drunken driving.

1,512 teenagers drop out of school.

1,849 children are abused or neglected.
3,288 children run away from home.
1,629 children are in adult jails.

2,556 children are born out of wedlock.
2,989 see their parents divorced.

34,285 people lose jobs.

Source: Children's Defense Fund, Washington, D.C., 1990.

Parents and Teachers: Distant Partners

Home visits, teacher-parent meetings, and school socials were once common aspects of life in the United States. James Comer's memories of his neighborhood recall a time when the authority of parents was transferred to teachers through proximity.

> When I went into the grocery store with my mother and father in the 1940s, it was a rare day that we did not encounter someone from my elementary school— the custodian, the principal, the secretary, or a teacher. There would always be an exchange of pleasantries and sometimes an exchange about my school behavior or achievement. The knowledge that my parents knew and appeared to like and respect the people at my school had a profound impact on my behavior (Comer, 1986, 442).

During the era of the neighborhood school, indirect involvement of parents in school activity was underscored at each chance meeting of teachers and parents at the grocery store, bus stop, park, or library. Trust and mutual respect between school and home was a by-product of close-knit communities. The separation of school and community began in the 1960s with the advent of racial integration through busing. The process of neighborhood-school detachment continued in the 1970s with the middle-class exodus to the suburbs and subsequent regionalization of small town schools. Today, separation of school and family is a pervasive condition in United States education. Sometimes the only time a parent has direct contact with the school is when there is a problem. While such measures as school open houses provide some assurance that teachers and parents get an opportunity for personal meetings, these are usually large group activities that preclude personal conversation between parents and teacher.

A common teacher complaint when parents are missing conferences or open houses is that parents "don't care." There are many explanations for parents not attending school functions. Their own education may have left them with negative feelings about school. Perhaps the parent is illiterate or a school dropout. Parents may not have a phone or transportation. There may be a language barrier or a communication problem (the message doesn't reach the parent). A parent might miss a meeting or school function due to an inability to obtain child care. When schools provide child care, parental attendance increases. Parents may be working when meetings are held. Many IEP meetings, for example, are held during the day without regard for parental work schedules.

In most instances, it is the teacher who makes the initial contact to arrange a meeting. Teachers need adequate administrative support to organize and follow through on parent-teacher contacts. They need time during the school day to make arrangements and adequate space to hold meetings. Teachers need access to a telephone. Providing preparation time for teachers is the best way a principal can enhance parent-teacher communication. Attempts to improve parent-teacher contacts sometimes meets resistance. When teachers in Rochester, New York, were required to make home visits as part of a nationally proclaimed reform model that included higher wages, some reneged on their commitment claiming they did not have the necessary "social worker skills." In some school systems, it is a violation of the union-management contract for teachers to make home visits!

The isolation of school and family continues at the same time that schools and teachers are being asked to take on responsibilities that used to be the sole domain of the family. Fear of AIDS, teenage pregnancies, and drug abuse have reordered curriculum priorities. Sex and drug education have become major concerns in schools. In many urban and suburban school districts, Johnny can't read because he's too "high" to care. When schools find ways to work with parents on problems of youth, the results are impressive.

Benefits of Parent-Teacher Partnerships

The National Committee for Citizens in Education (NCCE) found that when teachers maintain frequent contact with parents, students profit. Parent-teacher partnerships produce measurable gains in student achievement. "Some of the major benefits of parent involvement include higher grades and test scores, better long-term academic achievement, positive attitudes and behavior, more successful programs, and more effective schools" (Henderson, 1988, 149). The greater the degree of parental involvement, the more likely students will succeed in school. In a review of 53 studies that measured the impact of parent-teacher partnerships, the NCCE did not find a single negative report. The evidence also indicated that students who were at-risk of educational failure gained the most from parent-teacher collaboration.

At-risk students include the disadvantaged, the students with mild disabilities, and underachievers. These students are frequently absent from school. Some are behavior problems. Almost all lack the motivation to persevere. By age 16, the at-risk student is a prime dropout candidate. Research on students at-risk indicated that "by the time students are in the third grade we can fairly reliably predict which students will drop out and which will complete their schooling" (Slavin, 1989, 5). The early onset of school failure underscores the need for close school-family partnerships at the beginning of formal schooling. Successful preschool programs, such as Head Start, place a premium on parent involvement. Disadvantaged students who participate in preschool programs with strong parent involvement components outperform their peers through high school. Despite the documented benefits of parent participation in preschools, the carryover of parent participation into general education is at best uneven. Some educators believe the best place for parents is at a bake sale or car wash. Williams (1983) reported that principals and teachers preferred that parent involvement be limited to extracurricular activities. The educators in Williams's study did not view parent involvement in educational decisions as either useful or appropriate.

Leitch and Tangri (1988) investigated barriers to school-family partnerships in two poor, inner-city, Washington, D.C., junior high schools. Twenty-nine teachers and sixty families participated in the study. The researchers found that a parent from single family households was less likely to be involved than two parent households. The larger the family (six members or more), the more likely the involvement. Extended families, both single and two parent, were the most involved. Members of foster families were highly involved. Employment made it difficult for almost half the parents to get to school functions. Among the unemployed, poor health was the most frequent reason for lack of participation. Education did not seem to be a factor; parents who finished and those who did not finish high school were involved on an equal basis.

From the teachers' perspective, their own family responsibilties were factors that impeded setting aside time for parents. Teachers who enjoyed their work tended to value parent involvement more than teachers who were unhappy or disgruntled. Almost half the teachers surveyed blamed parents. Some parental attributes listed by discontented teachers were: unrealistic expectations about the school's role; parental jealousy of teacher's upward mobility; poor parental attitudes about school; large families (although the data showed large families participated more frequently); and lack of parental skills to help with schoolwork. Other teachers listed the following school barriers to parental involvment: absence of school activities; teachers' suspicions of parents; and teacher apathy. All the teachers recognized that changes in society had diminished the parental role. They felt that the schools needed to change to meet the changing social fabric of families and the community.

Leitch and Tangri reported that parents believed teachers looked down on them. "One parent said that teachers have the attitude, 'I got mine, and you got yours to get'" (Leitch and Tangri, 1988, 74). Parents characterized school attempts to get them involved as meager. Parent-teacher organization meetings were the most commonly reported school invitation, although many parents said they never received such notices. The same small group of parents seemed to control most parental activities. Despite the negative attitudes attributed to both teachers and parents, Leitch and Tangri summarized their report by stating that a lack of specific planning about how to organize and utilize parent resources was the major barrier to school-home collaboration.

When administrators and teachers make a commitment to parent involvement, results have followed. In many schools, parents volunteer in classrooms. They sponsor orientation programs, conduct alcohol education classes, welcome new families, arrange for guest speakers, provide library assistance, and much more. The principal is the catalyst in these ventures. The principal allocates resources, persists in parent recruiting efforts, and establishes a school-wide norm that parents are welcome. In order for parent-school partnerships to flourish, parents need to make decisions about school policies. Treating parents as teacher aides and doling out menial tasks works against collaboration. It's not how much time parents spend in school that counts, it's the responsibilities they assume (Sandfort, 1987). A well-planned and comprehensive parent-school partnership can have a positive impact on both individual students and the school (Henderson, 1988).

In 1968, the Yale Child Study Team initiated a pilot program to promote parent participation in the New Haven schools. The first project school initially ranked 32nd out of 33 city public schools on standardized achievement scores. Fourth grade students were 19 months below grade level in reading and 18 months below grade level in mathematics. Behavior problems were rampant. The school climate was permeated with a sense of despair. Staff rivaled students in absences. Working with the Child Study Team and with the principal as director, a group of parents and teachers developed a master plan for school improvement. They formed a School Advisory Committee. The group set goals for academics, staff development, and school spirit.

Parents were soon involved in almost every aspect of educational programming. They worked in classrooms as teacher aides. Their minimum wage salaries for 10 hours a week were funded through Title I (now known as Chapter 1). Parents tutored students in "therapeutic activity groups" that integrated academics with the arts and social skills. A revised social calendar lured parents to school functions. Activities included a Welcome Back to School dinner for orientation and recruitment of new parents. A February "blues" party boosted school spirit. A parent involvement handbook informed mothers and fathers about opportunities for participation in school activities. The handbook outlined parental roles and responsibilities. Each year, new parents were recruited to insure that participation would continue after students graduated. Attendance at school functions increased from twenty to four hundred parents. By 1984, the Yale parent participation model had: raised student achievement scores seven months above grade level; increased student attendance to number one in the city four out of five years; eliminated many discipline problems. The results of the Yale-New Haven project bear testimony to the benefits of school-parental cooperation.

Based on the successes of the Yale Study Team, James Comer continued his work with approximately 100 urban schools throughout the country. His goal was to create school management teams comprised of parents, teachers, and mental health professionals. These schools enhance teachers' knowledge of their students, draw parents into the educational process, especially governance and management, and combine school and community services (Reed & Sauter, 1990). Other such programs throughout the country bear witness to the ability of teachers and parents to work together to improve schools.

In San Francisco and Redwood City, California, Henry Levine's accelerated schools model established specific achievement goals for all elementary school children. Parents as educational decision-makers is a key component in this program. Joyce Epstein developed other parent involvement models, which emphasize reciprocal relationships—the parents within the school and the school within the community. Parent involvement projects share the following values: no child is labeled a potential failure because of social or economic factors; social and physical development of children is as important as academic and cognitive gains; children's development is a shared obligation of school, family, and community. These principles are exemplified in the work of the League of Schools Reaching Out, a confederation of 41 urban schools that span 13 states and Puerto Rico (Davies, 1991).

The League takes an enlarged view on the meaning of parent involvement. The term "parent" is broadened to "family," which may include grandparents, uncles, aunts, and other significant adults in a youngster's life. The League advocates coordinating with social agencies that provide assistance and support to families, for example, agencies that administer housing, mental health, and public health services. Hard-to-reach families are targeted. Included in this group are the non-English speaking, the unemployed, and the indigent. League members recognize that the families that are least responsive are precisely the ones that most need to get involved with educational affairs. The League of Schools Reaching Out is attempting to revitalize Coleman's concept of social capital by abandoning the deficiency view of urban life and identifying strengths in families. Cultural diversity is prized and families are encouraged to establish their own priorities for school-community partnerships (Davies, 1991).

Just as Eileen's home visit deepened her insight into Alexis and her school behavior, educators throughout the country are learning that families are a teacher's best source of information about students. Families can provide information on developmental, social, and academic problems. Student attitudes toward school are shaped in the home. When families value the educational process, students succeed. If teacher and family are at odds, students are left without direction. But when teachers and families cooperate, they are able to help a student focus on productive goals. Each year teachers begin anew the hope of helping their students grow and learn. Building parental partnerships has proven to be one of the most effective means of turning this hope into reality.

The greater the risk of school failure, the more crucial the need for family involvement. When a student has a learning, behavior, or emotional problem, the need for family-teacher cooperation intensifies. An appropriate education for students with mild disabilities is based upon school-family cooperation. According to federal and state laws, parents must participate in decisions regarding their youngster's special education services, educational placement, and individual education plan (IEP). This built-in mechanism for teacher-parent collaboration does not guarantee successful outcomes. Success or failure depends on trust, mutual respect, and cooperation.

Understanding Families of Students with Disabilities

Cooperation begins with understanding. How does it feel to have a child identified as disabled? What is the impact of a child with special needs on the family? What type of support is available to parents of students with mild disabilities? Parenting is complex and difficult. Parents of children with disabilities must deal with all the tensions and pressures familiar to other families, plus the extra stress of raising a child with special needs.

Parent Feelings

A child with a disability demands more of a parent's time and emotional reserves. The daily routine of getting a child with a learning disability ready for school each morning can be a tedious chore. A parent must learn to be patient with a youngster who is disorganized and oblivious to time constraints. For a child with a learning disability, each step of the morning ritual can be filled with frustration. William Cruickshank, a pioneer in the field of learning disabilities, related the following story about a youngster who was staying at his summer home:

> *Ned, who was 12 years old, was always encountering difficulties because of his learning disability. One morning around 9 A.M. my wife and I were serving breakfast and waiting for Ned to join us. Suddenly we heard him yelling from the guest room, "Bill, Bill, come up here." I rushed upstairs. Standing next to the bed was Ned in tears. He was partially dressed with his underwear on over his trousers. "Bill, this is your fault," he said. "You know I need help getting dressed in the morning." I had forgotten that Ned needed each garment laid out for him in the proper sequence for dressing. His ability to order his own actions was so impaired that he became confused and disoriented just by the simple task of dressing himself. (Keynote address, William Cruickshank, Association New York State Educators of the Emotionally Disturbed, 1981).*

Few children with mild disabilities are identified as requiring special services until they enter school and begin to encounter academic or discipline problems. Suddenly, parents are faced with an array of demands as they attempt to cope with the burden imposed by their child's inability to fit into the normal routine of school life. Excerpts from Connie and Ralph Flood's (1989) diary help to convey the feelings experienced by parents whose child became a school "problem."

> *September, 1985. David began school today. The house seemed so quiet when the three left. David was so happy when he got home. Bubbling away about how much fun it is to ride the bus, and have "lots of kids to play with."*

> *October, 1985. David's teacher told us that David has no self control. He has been having a lot of trouble getting along with the kids in his class. We spoke to him, but he says it is all the other kids' fault.*

> *May, 1986. The complaints about David in school never stop. His teacher says she doesn't know what to do with him. Maybe adjustment to school was just difficult. Maybe first grade will be better.*

> *January, 1988. The school called work today and left a message with the switchboard that they need to set up a conference about David's problem behavior. This is just great. Now people at work also know that something is wrong.*

> *November, 1988. We just came from talking with the [school] psychologist. He thinks David would be better off if we let him enter a special class. David seems*

smarter than that, but something has to change. He will be starting in the next few weeks, if some [school] committee says that's what should be done.

December, 1988. The meeting of the Committee on Special Education was like the Inquisition. We got there and had to face seven school people. It seemed like they wanted to know everything. The meeting better be confidential and we hope we don't have to go through that again. David is going to the special class in a couple of days. We hope this is the answer, but what does emotionally disturbed mean? What did we do wrong? How can we tell the family about this?

When dealing with "experts," parents often report feeling overwhelmed with the trappings of authority. Betty Lou Kratoville's description of her meeting with a counselor provides a glimpse into the inner world of one parent's feelings during a meeting with a counselor.

As a parent, my attitude toward all the professional men and women I went to in search of diagnosis and remediation for Mathew was one of absolute humility. In retrospect, my reverence may have, at times, been misplaced. I neglected to remember that counselors are, first and foremost, human beings. That they too laugh and cry and make mistakes and that they are not, really, larger than life. At the time they somehow seemed invincible, ten feet tall, with desks the size of battleships, their offices guarded by iron-spined sentinels who always seemed to be popping in with terse announcements, "Your next appointment is waiting." I, lily livered and abject, would slink from the office, reeling under the impact of cool professionalism and a hundred unanswered questions. (Buscaglia, 1975, 133)

Guilt, denial, anger, and despair are frequently mentioned in professional literature as parental reactions to a child with a disability. The extent that a parent will experience these feelings is contingent on many factors including finances, the severity of the disability, the age of the child, availability of child care, and support from family and professionals.

Miller (1968) reported that parents of students with special needs go through a cycle of disintegration, adjustment, and reintegration. The first stage, after the child is diagnosed as having a disability, is characterized by shock, grief, and guilt. In the second stage, parents alternately accept and deny their child's disability. Finally, parents begin to accommodate to their child's special needs by supporting each other and dealing with issues as they arise. This best case scenario depends on the family's ability, particularly father and mother, to adapt to the stress of managing life when a child has a disability.

Ferguson and Ferguson (1987) stated that guilt has been overemphasized by professionals who studied parental feelings. They said such interpretations as parental "guilt reaction" can lead professionals to conflicting conclusions. Solnit and Stark (1961), for example, viewed parent activism as a method for coping with guilt, while McKeith (1973) reported that parental guilt led to apathy and depression. Analyzing parents' behavior in terms of guilt reactions is based on psychodynamic investigations of the "typical" parent of a child with a disability.

While there is some benefit derived from research that seeks to understand and explain parental reactions to a child's disability, the "typical" parent exists only in normative studies, not in reality. Terms like "typical" and "average" are artifacts of quantitative studies that provide a teacher with limited information about the parent sitting with her at a meeting.

Parents need to be treated as individuals. Each parent has a unique view of his or her child's disability. In order to work effectively, educators need to understand the parent's perspective. This is difficult to do if the parent is pitied or patronized. Trust and respect are essential for communication between parent and teacher. Federal law has made parents key decision-makers in determining the type of educational services that will best suit their youngster.

The Family

The universal role of the family is to nurture the young child. Within the family milieu, the child learns the social and intellectual competencies needed to succeed in society. When a family has a child with a special need, all family members are affected. Mother, father, and siblings must learn to cope with the unique stress of living with their child. A child with a disability imposes demands that strain the family's ability to function. Families must cope with several critical periods in the life of a child with a disability (Gloecker & Simpson, 1988):

1. Birth, when parents, usually of children with moderate to severe disabilities, first realize their child is disabled.
2. When the disability is first diagnosed and treatment begins. For parents of children with mild disabilities, this is usually the beginning school years.
3. When the child is placed in a special education program. Placement in segregated special class, pull-out program, or mainstreamed regular classroom can influence parental perceptions about the severity of their child's disability.
4. When the child reaches adolescence, peer acceptance or rejection becomes a central concern.
5. As the child nears the end of the public school years, parents must make transitional plans for their child's future.
6. If by adulthood the son or daughter has not been able to live independently, parents begin worrying about what will happen when their child outlives them.

The family's ability to manage these stress points depends on the severity of the disability, their emotional resources, and the type of support the family receives.

Sometimes the stress can be too much. For example, studies have found that parents of children with mental retardation have higher suicide and divorce rates than families without disabled children (Price-Bonham & Addison, 1978). It also appears that children with disabilities are at greater risk of child abuse (Embry, 1980). In some instances, child abuse or neglect is the cause of the disability. Other problems encountered by families include increased financial burdens, isolation, chronic fatigue, and emotional problems (Gallagher, Beckman, & Cross, 1983).

Coping with the demands of raising a child with a mild disability begins with the husband-wife relationship. Friedrich (1979) found that marital satisfaction is the single best predictor of a family's ability to rear a child with a disability. When husband and wife share the nurturance and physical care of a son or daughter, their marriage can become stronger.

Rick Bennion's comments about his child with mental retardation highlights the need for fathers and mothers to support each other during difficult times.

> *Finding out you have a retarded child is somewhat analagous to walking through a mine field. You remain in constant shock and fear as you grope along an uncharted course. The next step is always tenuous, and the lack of a clear-cut path adds to an incessant mental fatigue.*
>
> *For us the intial reactions were, I suppose, rather the norm: Why us? How about a second diagnosis? Is there a miracle cure lurking on the horizon?*
>
> *In the midst of continuous anguish, much solace can be derived from a few words of compassion from friends, loved ones, and particularly each other. No matter how trying, an ongoing dialogue between husband and wife is a must to breach the abyss of despair that envelops your being. (Bennion, 1983, 39)*

Gallagher, Cross, and Scharfman (1981) studied families who made a successful adjustment to having a child with a disability. Their data suggested that the quality of the husband-wife relationship was an instrumental factor in helping the family cope with stress. Two personal characteristics that the researchers found associated with adjustment were the mother's self-confidence and a "set of supporting values" (e.g., strong religious beliefs).

Fathers

Osman (1979) observed that parents in her clinic for children with learning disabilities go through emotional stages similar to families that sustain a severe loss or death. She suggests that a learning disability is a family affair. According to some authors, fathers set the pattern for how the rest of the family will adjust to a child with a disability (Peck & Stephans, 1960; Price, Bonham & Addison, 1978).

When fathers see their child as an extension of themselves, the weight of failed expectations can become a burden. Cummings (1976) surveyed the attitudes of a group of fathers of children with mental retardation. He found some fathers depressed, preoccupied with their child's disability, and unhappy with their family relationships. Reed and Reed (1965) reported higher than average desertion rates by fathers of children with disabilities. Higher divorce rates have also been reported among families with children who have special needs (Tew, Lawrence, Payne, & Rawnsley, 1977).

According to Meyer (1986), men deal with several key developmental tasks during their adjustment to fatherhood:

1. *Reconcile Conflicting Conceptions of His Role.* Many men grew up with the idea that child raising is the mother's role. During the 1980s this cultural norm

was reexamined, and fathers began to take on more nurturing responsibilities. Resolving the conflict between the role they grew up with and the role they would like to assume is complicated by a father's attitude towards his child's disability.

2. *Accepting His Share of Responsibilities for the Child.* Beginning with infancy, the more caregiving responsibilities a father shares, the stronger the father-child attachment. During the school years, a close father-child relationship can help the child to cope with frustration. By sharing time with his child, the father helps to offset negative self-perceptions that are inevitable by-products of a child's school problems.

3. *Maintaining Bread Winner Status.* Despite the fact that 45 percent of all mothers of preschool children work, the father's job is the primary source of income in most two parent families. Fathers who desire to spend more time with their child must find ways of balancing the demands of work against the needs of the family. Success and promotion in work usually means longer hours and more time away from the family. This creates a dilemma for the father who wants to provide for both his family's financial and nurturing needs.

4. *Adjusting to Life Style Changes of Parenthood.* A newborn child requires major adjustments in a father's life. New priorities must be established to respond to the demands of being a father. This can mean a major change in life style when independence is replaced by the responsibilities of parenthood.

5. *Encouraging the Child's Full Development.* Fathers and mothers fill different developmental needs for a young child. While mothers often cuddle children, fathers are more likely to engage in physical play. The time spent playing with father helps a child develop spatial concepts, and feelings of control, warmth, and acceptance.

6. *Redefining Himself as Father.* Fatherhood is a time for reappraisal of a man's sense of self. As the demands of family life intensify, priorities and values change. The ability to cope with these changes can enhance self-esteem. A father whose sense of self-worth is tied to his child's successes and failures may have difficulty accepting his child's disability.

There are several factors that can influence a father's perception of his child's disability. If the child is a boy or firstborn, fathers tend to have more difficulty in accepting a disability (Farber, 1972; Tallman, 1965). The severity of a disabling condition and age of the child will affect a father's attitude. Hersh (1970) and Love (1973) found that fathers, more than mothers, are concerned with such future problems as education, life after school, and what the child will do when the parents are no longer around.

One solution to helping fathers adjust is to increase their involvement in school programs. Many parent involvement programs are functionally "mother programs," despite the fact that 75 percent of youngsters with mild disabilities are male. In an exploratory study of father participation in preschool programs, Markowitz (1983) found that fathers were more likely to become involved if: the child had a special meaning to the father, such as namesake; the child was first-born or the first son; the father's work schedule provided flexibility; or the child had an identifiable disability, such as Downs syndrome, rather than an inferred disability, such as a learning disability. Markowitz believes that fathers, more so than mothers, may need visible evidence of a child's disability.

Fathers benefit when they particpate in their child's education. Supporting Extended Family Members (SEFAM) at the University of Washington encouraged fathers to become actively involved in their child's preschool education. The SEFAM program provided fathers with support through father to father linkages and by providing them with information about specific disabilities. According to reports from SEFAM, the fathers in the program experienced less stress, guilt, and depression than nonenrolled fathers of children with disabilities (Vadasy, Fewell, Meyer, & Greenberg, 1985). The success of the SEFAM program highlights the advantages of involving fathers in school activities. The stress of having a child with a disability affects the entire family, and the father plays a crucial role in determining how the family copes with this stress. By encouraging fathers to become actively involved in school programs, educators enhance the ability of fathers to be a strong presence for their family.

Mothers

Even with the more recent trend toward shared child-care responsibilities, mothers still tend to be the primary caregivers. Caring for any young child is taxing—physically, emotionally, and economically. These burdens are compounded when a child has a disability. Behavioral and learning impairments increase a child's dependency and a mother's responsibilities.

Even though a mother may be working at a full-time job, she is usually the first parent contacted when there is a school problem. Mothers comprise the majority of members in parent-teacher organizations. Most of the parent advocacy work in special education organizations, such as the Association for Children with Learning Disabilities, is done by mothers. The female domination of elementary education in general appears to reinforce teacher to mother communication. One study of 30 fathers found that only three took on the major responsibility for communication with the school (Espinoza, 1988).

Because they are the primary caregivers, mothers are more vulnerable to feelings of inadequacy if their child is perceived as different. Mothers frequently compare their children with those of their friends and neighbors. A child with a disability is often a step behind other children in development—slower to share, slower to read, slower to take on responsibility. When a mother notices her youngster is unable to keep pace with other children, feelings of guilt or inadequacy may surface. Margaret Roberts described the distress felt by one mother, Kate, as she attempted to cope with her son's mental retardation.

> *I felt a lot of guilt because I worried about Geoff living at home for the rest of his life. I needed to accept the fact that at some point in time he would live someplace else. He would eventually be someone else's concern. I needed to face that, in*

order to lose that black cloud, that oppressed feeling. But, at the same time, it brought on guilt because, as his mother, I should love him enough to take care of him the rest of his life, right? Another side of my guilt was that I felt, in a way, that because of the nature of Geoff's brain damage, because his placenta had separated early and caused oxygen distress, that I had let my child down—that my body had somehow betrayed him by letting that happen. And if I couldn't "do it all" and be Supermom, I was letting him down. (Roberts, 1986, 204)

Being the primary caregiver of a child with a disability can weigh heavily on a mother. The mother, rather than the father, is generally the one who must forego career plans and aspirations. This is no easy sacrifice for an ambitious woman. When the mother is poor or lacks basic employment skills, the burdens of child rearing can be overwhelming. For mothers from lower socioeconomic backgrounds, who may not have an education to parley into a good paying job, the economic burden is stifling. Daycare alone can eat up a good portion of a minimum wage salary. A mother heading a single parent family has to fend for herself. Glick and Norton (1979) reported that nine out of ten single-parent households are headed by mothers.

The mother of a student with mild disabilities needs support. She is the parent who spends the majority of her time attending to the needs of her child. A youngster's mild disability compounds the difficulties of normal parenting duties. The mother needs the support of her husband, friends, neighbors, and extended family. Because she is tied down with caregiving and home responsibilities, little time is left to cultivate a mother's personal goals.

There are some mothers who attempt to assume the "supermom" role. They are determined that they will care for their children and still pursue life goals and ambitions of their own. Without family support these mothers are likely to experience stress and fatigue because of endless chores, duties, and responsibililties. Respite care, or time away from direct care of a child with a mild disability, is imperative. Mothers who do not work outside the home are sometimes able to get a break when their child is attending school. School personnel who are critical of mothers who do not get involved in their child's special education should be sensitive to the myriad demands such mothers face.

When Winton and Turnbull (1981) interviewed 32 mothers of preschool children with disabilities, 65 percent of the respondents said the professional attention to their children was welcome respite. As one mother stated when queried about her involvement in school activities:

A lot of times I get tired of having to role-God. I don't want to solve that—I'm paying you to take him for three hours and, lady, make it work! Maybe that's a nasty attitude towards teachers but I kind of feel that way sometimes. It's not worth it to me if I have to figure it out—I might as well have him with me at those times. (cited in Turnbull & Turnbull, 1982, 117)

The expectation that parents, particularly mothers, should become active in their child's education may add to parental stress. Not so long ago, educators viewed mild disabilities as a sign of parental failure. Today, educators expect parents to be part of the solution by teaching their children at home and making educational decisions at school. When both mothers and fathers work, they spend an average of eight minutes a day with their children on activities related to learning (Bradley, 1988). Turnbull and Turnbull (1982) suggested that goals of parent involvement programs should be shifted from the child to the needs of the parents. Included would be strategies for reducing stress, a focus on family coping skills, counseling to improve family relationships, and accessible child care. The last item, child care, is an especially vital need, particularly in single parent and disadvantaged families.

Siblings

Brothers and sisters are affected when a sibling is identified as having a mild disability. Older children, particularly daughters, are sometimes expected to take on increased child-care responsibilities. The effect on older children can be both negative and positive. Jealousy, resentment, nurturing, and pride are the mixed feelings expressed by the sister of a child with a hearing impairment.

> *It is hard to sum the feelings I had as a sibling of a handicapped child. A year ago I would have said I felt mainly pride and resentment. I am proud of Jill's accomplishments, for she has done what too few profoundly deaf children will ever do. . .I also mentioned resentment. I'll always remember striving for the attention that was often focused on Jill. . . . Now I am also moved to the point where I feel sadness. I sympathize with my sister, who will always have to struggle to maintain her place in the world. . . .Why didn't I make it easier along the way?. . . . I don't know why. (cited in Crnic & Leconte, 1986, 75)*

Having a brother or sister with a disability can be difficult for younger children when they have to put up with teasing from friends. The following account illustrates the adjustment of one youngster to peer pressure (Dougan, Isbell, & Vyas, 1983).

> *Hi. My name is David Isbell. I have a mentally retarded brother. His name is Walter. He is thirteen years old, and I am ten years old. Even though I'm younger, I'm looked on as the elder brother. One of the problems of living with Walter is being patient with him. Sometimes he wants to play something and I don't, so he gets mad at me and I get mad at him. . . .*
>
> *Most of the time I get teased because I have a mentally retarded brother. People call him names like "retardo" or "mental." They call me the same names.*
>
> *I'm not trying to say that having a retarded brother is misery, but it has its ups and downs. We're a family with a retarded member, and everybody's fine. (p. 126)*

Over the course of a lifetime, siblings play a large role in the life of a person with a disability. Siblings serve as role models through both school and adult years. Sibling relationships become the center of family life after parents die.

Because families are interactional systems, the reaction of a sibling to a brother or sister with a disability can have a profound influence on the entire family.

Research on sibling relationships in families is conflicting. Some studies document such detrimental effects on nondisabled siblings as increased anxiety, lower sociability, or more conflicts with parents (Farber, 1960, 1963; Fowle, 1968; Grossman, 1972). Other studies suggest that a child with a disability in the family does not have a negative effect on brothers and sisters, and in some cases nondisabled children develop a more tolerant attitude than their age-mates towards individuals who are different (Farber, 1963; Grossman, 1972; Cleveland & Miller, 1977). A child with a disability may even influence the career choice of a sibling. Many special educators enter the profession as a result of their experiences with a disabled relative.

The bulk of the evidence suggests that siblings of children with disabilities are vulnerable to various emotional and behavioral problems (Crnic & Leconte, 1986). Crocker (1981) reported six factors that will influence the impact of a child with a disability on siblings.

1. *Family patterns are altered.* Daily routines may be altered to accommodate specific needs of a child with a disability. Family activities such as vacations and trips require careful planning and scheduling.
2. *There is competition for parental attention.* Parents may inadvertently devote more of their time to a special needs child. This can cause resentment among the other children.
3. *Siblings may not understand the nature of their brother's or sister's disability.* Young children may worry that they are somehow responsible. School-mates or friends may ridicule the child with a disability and the non-disabled sibling.
4. *Siblings may have to assume duties of a surrogate parent.* Particularly if both parents work, older sisters or brothers may have to take on child-care responsibilities.
5. *Siblings may feel obligated to overachieve to compensate for a disabled youngster in the family.* Directly or indirectly, parents may show their disappointment about the unmet expectations of a child with special needs. Siblings may push to succeed where their brother or sister failed.
6. *As parents' feelings about their child with a disability change over time, siblings may become confused about their parents' reactions.* Tensions, worries, and stress can wear on all family members. Children in particular may have difficulty coping with feelings of neglect as parents feel the stress of raising a special needs child.

Working Parents

The majority of United States women are now part of the work force. This shift in family dynamics presents problems to husbands and wives in their roles as parents. Among some of the problems facing working parents are day care, after-school care, and job responsibilities. Employer sensitivity to the needs of parents is a key factor in how involved they will become in school activities, conferences, or parent organizations. Keep in mind that some parents work evenings while others may work two jobs. Employers who provide employees with flexible short-term leave help promote school-parent relationships. Without an employee leave arrangement, a parent has to choose between a teacher conference or losing a day or partial day's pay!

Child care is a pressing problem. Particularly difficult is obtaining child care for older youngsters. Espinoza (1988) reported that in a sample of 79 children age eight to thirteen years old, 42 percent were latchkey children. They were left to care for themselves after school. Parents were anxious about their children returning from school to a home with no adult supervision. An additional 20 percent of the youngsters were surpervised by an older sibling, many of whom were just a year or so older. Schools can support working parents by providing after-school child care; arranging evening IEP conferences, and providing an evening telephone service for parent questions regarding homework and other school issues.

Single Parents

Only 13 percent of children lived with a single parent in 1960. By 1986, 22 percent of United States children lived with one parent. From 1970 to 1983, the number of single parent families rose from 3.3 million to 6.8 million, a 107 percent increase (Vadasy, 1986). The majority of single parents are mothers. In 1982, only 2 percent of single parent children lived primarily with their fathers. The most dramatic change in the family structure over the past 20 years is the mother-maintained single parent family.

Kathleen McCoy, author of *Solo Parenting: Your Essential Guide* (1987), calls single parenting the toughest job in the world. The demographics on single parents indicate that it may not only be the toughest job, but the lowest paying as well. The poverty rate for single parent families is higher than for the United States population in general. In 1980, 44 percent of all single parent families headed by mothers lived in poverty. The median income of families headed by women living alone with their children was $7,652 ($14,249 for families headed by men, and $23,930 for married couples). According to the Census Bureau, two-thirds of female headed families with children under eighteen receive some sort of welfare benefits (Zinsmeister, 1990). Some researchers and policymakers have dubbed this phenomenon—the feminization of poverty.

African-Americans have been most affected by this change in the family structure. An estimated three out of four African-American children will spend at least part of their life in a single parent family. The out of wedlock birth of African-American children increased from 38 percent in 1970 to 55 percent in 1979. Bane and Elwood (1984) reported that divorce among white women is the primary cause of single parenthood. Two out of every five American teenagers (of all races) get pregnant, and one in every five gives birth to a child before the age of twenty (Children's Defense Fund, 1990). The overwhelming majority of "kids having kids" are unmarried.

Mothers who care for their children alone struggle to make ends meet. Shelter, food, clothing, medical care, and child care are top priorities. Most single mothers work. Two-thirds of mothers with school-aged children and one-half of mothers of preschool-age children are employed. Wikler (1979) surveyed mothers of children with disabilities and found their greatest need was respite or child care; next was financial assistance; and the third greatest need was moral support. The U.S. Department of Agriculture found that almost 10 percent of the average single mother's income goes for child care. While day care is a necessity for all working mothers, mothers of children with a disability have the combined problem of finding a safe place for their child while they work and locating someone to provide respite care. The more severe a child's disability, the greater the need for respite. Wikler noted that 73 percent of mothers with children who have special needs received some type of social welfare support, but respite care was not included (Vadasy, 1986).

Single mothers experience more stress than married mothers (Beckman, 1983). Daily chores such as shopping and doing laundry are compounded by nonstop parenting duties. Money is almost always a problem. Social isolation, particularly when a child with special needs is involved, increases the loneliness of a single parent. Holroyd (1974) reported that mothers of children with a disability feel their personal development is stifled by the demands of rearing their child alone. McLanahan (1983) found that single parent mothers experience chronic stress due to negative self-image, lack of emotional support, and low income.

Children are affected in many ways by the experience of being raised in a female-headed household. The most obvious impact is financial hardship. Mothers who must work full-time have less time to spend with their children. In addition, many female household heads, particularly minorities, work at low paying jobs. These families are buffeted by the constant strain of paying bills. Older children get recruited as surrogate parents as mothers try to balance impossible schedules. Latchkey children are common in single parent families. Without a husband to provide emotional support, the mother may be less capable of providing nurturance to a difficult-to care-for child. This means that normal developmental milestones, such as "the terrible twos," and adolescent rebelliousness can become the source of severe stress in the single parent family.

Single mothers may cope with their loneliness by relating to their child as an adult friend. Elkind (1982) discovered that single parents are more likely than married couples to treat their children as confidants. Strong emotional bonds can develop between parent and child when children become decision-maker, friend, and helper. Children in single parent families grow up faster than children in two parent families. Weinraub and Wolf (1984) reported that single mothers of preschool children treated their children more maturely than married mothers (cited in Vadasy, 1986).

There are also negative consequences from relating to a child as an adult friend. The child may be unable to cope with the responsibility of providing emotional support. The mother may become possessive of the child and restrict opportunities for independence. Outside support from friends and other family members can lessen a mother's dependence on her child to fulfill the need for companionship.

Many separated or divorced couples continue to share parenting responsibilities. Split child-raising schedules is a common practice that insures a child continues to get parenting from both father and mother. The manner in which each parent is able to make the transition from married to separate lives, while continuing their respective parenting roles, is a key variable in the emotional development of a child.

Support for Families

Help for families who have a child with a disability can be broadly divided into three categories: emotional support, information, and federal government programs. Emotional support for parents of children with mild disabilities begins with the immediate family, branches out to grandparents and other relatives, and continues with friends and neighbors. Professional support agencies complement "grass root" networks by providing information and services that train families to help themselves. The stronger their support system, the more capable the family will be in coping with the daily stresses of raising a child with a disability.

Federal programs are primarily targeted for low income families. Poverty continues to play a significant role in the development of mild disabilities, particularly mild mental retardation and behavior disorders. Children without adequate nutrition and health care are at-risk populations. Environmental threats to normal development include heavy metal poisoning, child abuse, child neglect, community violence, lack of proper educational experiences at home, and drug abuse. Government programs, when funded properly, can prevent and/or remediate medical and environmental conditions that contribute to mild disabilities.

Emotional Support

Parents of children with disabilities often feel alone. Featherstone (1980) reported that "a special loneliness is the most pervasive theme in the stories told by parents of disabled children. This loneliness is nourished from within and without. . . . The two most prominent ingredients of a parent's loneliness are difference—his own and the child's—and isolation" (cited in Stagg & Catron, 283).

Support groups help parents cope with isolation. When parents have an opportunity to discuss their problems with other parents of children with disabilities, they learn they are not alone. Over the years many self-help, support groups for parents have sprung up in local communities. Sometimes leadership for these groups comes from local professionals; more often parents themselves are the organizers.

Support groups provide parents with an emotional lifeline as they discover that others share their experiences. When parents talk to parents, a sense of comradeship supplants feelings of loneliness and isolation. Support groups also help parents learn how to use their influence to get the best educational services for their children. Many school systems have parent advisory councils. These advocacy groups are comprised of parents with disabled children and representatives from the local educational agency. They meet on a regular basis to discuss issues pertaining to delivery of special education services in their community. How much influence a parent advisory council has is largely determined by the political activism of member parents. Some typical activities of a parent advisory council include regular review of special education policy in their school system, dissemination of information to parents of special needs children, and the writing of grants to improve educational services for children with disabilities.

Information

Recent federal legislation has enabled parent-organized groups to develop a national networking system. The Education of the Handicapped Act Amendments of 1983, P.L. 98-199, authorized a grant program to support organized parent efforts to provide information and training through the Technical Assistance for Parents Program (TAPP). The purpose of TAPP, which is a project of the National Network of Parent Centers, is to provide a system of peer support that allows experienced parent centers and new centers to learn from each other and professional experts. The National Network of Parent Centers is an umbrella organization that links parent agencies throughout the country. It is coordinated by the Federation for Children with Special Needs, a parent center in Boston, Massachusetts.

There are four TAPP Regional Centers. Each is listed in Appendix D. More than 50 parent centers located throughout the country are members of TAPP. Each of these parent information centers is committed to improving public perceptions of children with disabling conditions. Their goal is to enhance educational and vocational opportunities for children with special needs. Additionally, there are many informal parent assistance groups located in communities throughout the country. In the West Lyon Community School District, Inwood, Iowa, for instance, resource room teachers and special education support staff organized a support program for parents of students with mild disabilities (Hallenbeck & Beernink, 1989). The program was formed to provide information and emotional support to parents, foster better understanding of mild disabilities among parents, and enhance parent-teacher communication. The organizers utilized a workshop format with panel discussions. They noted that in program evaluations, all 77 participants felt the program was useful.

On a larger scale, the National Information Center for Children and Youth with Handicaps (NICHY) provides educational information and technical assistance to parents, advocates, and professionals. NICHY maintains a collection of resource publications and fact sheets that help parents locate assistance in their local communities.

Since 1922, the Council for Exceptional Children (CEC) has provided both parents and professionals with support services including national and regional conferences, journals, and political activism on behalf of children with disabilities. While CEC provides support activities for all types of disabling conditions, other national organizations provide support services for families of children with specific disabilities. The Association for Children and Adults with Learning Disabilities and The National Association of Retarded Citizens have state and local chapters throughout the country. These organizations provide parents with information on recent developments in research and teaching children with specific impairments. Parents or educators who wish to contact any of these organizations can get the necessary information from state department of education offices.

There are many organizations and agencies eager to help support families. Yet each year countless parents struggle alone, unaware of the support network that is available to help them. By providing parents with a list of local and regional support agencies, teachers can help ensure that their classroom efforts are complemented by help outside of school. Mild disabilities are more than just a school problem. Learning disabilities, mild mental retardation, and behavior disorders are family problems. When families are supported at home, children with special needs have a better opportunity to overcome their impairments in school and in the community.

Government Support

Several federal programs are directed specifically at low income families. These programs provide essential educational, nutritional, and medical services for children who are at risk of acquiring a mild disability.

Chapter 1

Chapter 1 of the Elementary and Secondary Education Act (ESEA, 1965) is the foundation for federal education support for disadvantaged children. The passage of the Hawkins-Stafford School Improvment Amendments of 1988 reaffirmed the commitment of Chapter 1 funds to enable parent-school partnerships. The purpose of this revitalization is to find creative ways to induce parental participation in school affairs. Some novel approaches include a Chapter 1 program in Lima, Ohio, that provides parents with educational packets so they can do learning activities with their children at home. In Buffalo, New York, a Chapter 1 Parent Resource Center was established in the downtown area. Parents were encouraged to borrow educational materials or participate in workshops. In McAllen, Texas, a weekly radio show, "Discusiones Escolares," encouraged Spanish speaking parents to get more involved in their children's education (D'Angelo & Adler, 1991).

Chapter 1 money is used by other school systems to produce tutorial video-tapes for parents, to establish homework telephone hotlines, and to publish newsletters. Chapter 1 is the largest federal education program. It accounts for 22 percent of the entire Department of Education budget. In 1990–91, Chapter 1 provided approximately 5.4 billion dollars for five million school children with learning problems (LeTendre, 1991). The goal of Chapter 1 is to see that students acquire the skills and attitudes necessary for success in school.

First Grants

In 1988, Congress authorized Funding for the Improvement and Reform of Schools and Teaching (FIRST). The purpose of FIRST is to sustain innovative educational programs that improve student achievement. Part of the mission of the FIRST program is to recognize, encourage, and support parental involvement in public schools through the Family/School Partnership. This subsidiary program of FIRST awards federal grants to school systems that strive to train teachers to work more effectively with parents. The program is highly competitive. In 1989, 14 of 414 applicant schools received FIRST grants. In 1990, 31 of 436 applicants were funded.

A sample of FIRST recipients include:

1. *Project MIRROR (Managing Integrating Resources—Reaching Out Remediation).* This West Fresno, California, program uses successful individuals from disadvantaged backgrounds as community role models for disadvantaged students.
2. *Booneville's Family/School Partnership.* School-based management is the foundation of this program that seeks to improve attendance and achievement of students in grades 4 through 9 in Booneville, Kentucky. Parent tutors are utilized in smaller classes. A children's support system provides health, nutrition, and psychological services.
3. *Home/School Partnership.* This Bayonne, New Jersey, program features an adult literacy program, a parent resource center, family workshops, and a tutoring program for students. Each student has an individual learning profile and monthly progress reports are sent to parents.
4. *Family/School Partners in Education: A Model for Rural Schools.* This Greensville County, Virginia, program trains parents as tutors. The business community supplies work-release time to encourage parent participation. A mobile resource center will provide information and materials to rural schools.
5. *Project PACT (Parents—Administrators—Children—Teachers).* This Community School District 2 program in New York City emphasizes trust building between parents and teachers. Parents learn practical approaches for helping their children succeed in school.

The goal of the FIRST grant program is to improve parent-school partnerships. Enhancing the parenting and child-rearing skills of families is a priority.

By reaching out to students' homes, the schools in the FIRST programs are presenting models that other schools can replicate.

WIC

The Special Supplemental Food Program for Women, Infants, and Children (WIC) is a federal program that attempts to reduce infant mortality and numbers of low birthweight babies. WIC provides nutritional help for children from birth to six by providing mothers with vouchers to buy cheese, milk, orange juice, cereal, and infant formula. As of 1989, the WIC program provided food vouchers to 4.5 million expectant and mothers of at-risk babies, yet only 59 percent of eligible women and children received WIC benefits (Children's Defense Fund, 1990).

EPSDT

Medicaid and Early Periodic Screening, Diagnosis and Treatment (EPSDT) services make some health care services available to families who are unable to afford health insurance. Prenatal care, increased birthweight, decreased neonatal deaths, and fewer abnormalities are some of the benefits of EPSDT for poor children. By the end of 1989, only 15 states met federal guidelines for provision of health services to poor families. Childhood immunization programs, which prevent measles, rubella, mumps, polio, diphtheria, tetanus, and pertussis, are successful but underfunded. "American one-year-olds have lower immunization rates against polio than one-year-olds in 14 other countries. Polio immunization rates for nonwhite babies in the United States rank behind 48 other countries, including Botswana, Sri Lanka, Albania, Colombia, and Jamaica" (Children's Defense Fund, 1990, 5).

Head Start

Head Start is a federally funded program that provides preschoolers with a range of crucial services. The Head Start educational programs help youngsters learn school readiness skills, thus increasing their chances for academic success when they enter public school. Nutrition and medical screening, including EPSDT and dental checkups, are components of Head Start. Parent involvement is built into every Head Start program. Parents are encouraged to attend parenting workshops on such topics as nutrition and developmental play at home. Some Head Start programs are home-based. Head Start teachers visit youngsters' homes and demonstrate early childhood activities for parents. Head Start serves over 400,000 children annually.

The most notable accomplishments of preschools were attributed to the Perry Preschool Program in Ypsilanti, Michigan. By age 19, students who had attended the Perry program "were more likely to have finished high school, were dramatically less likely to have committed a crime, were less likely to be on welfare, and were earning more money" when compared to peers who had not attended the Perry program (Stein, Leinhardt, & Bickel, 1989, 149).

Federal programs make significant contributions to strengthening the ability of parents to improve the health and education of their children. Only the federal government has the financial and political leadership required to make children a national priority. In order to provide for the needs of youth, a new vision of community is needed. A community is a network of people working together towards common goals. This new vision would promote community organizations as extended families. Services such as youth clubs, athletic organizations, schools, mental health clinics, and parent resource centers can help parents and children. All of these ventures are woefully underfunded. For approximately 10 billion dollars, the cost of running the Department of Defense for six days, many of these programs could be put on a secure footing.

While we can't turn back the clock to the neighborhood school memories of James Comer, there are many paths to the goal of providing for our nation's children. WIC and EPSDT are based on the premise that children need to be healthy to learn. Head Start integrates health services, parent involvement, and education to help at-risk children succeed in school. Innovative practices of Chapter 1 programs and FIRST grant recipients provide a decision-making role for parents in schools, establish support for parents to assist children learn at home, and enhance parent-teacher communication.

Teacher-Parent Communication

Effective teacher-parent communication is essential in order to provide students with mild disabilities an appropriate education. Good communication with parents serves three useful purposes. First, it provides teachers with information about their students and parental expectations for school. Second, parents get reliable and up-to-date information to help them make decisions about their child's special education. Finally, when parents and teachers communicate and work together, they develop trust and a sense of shared commitment (Catermole & Robinson, 1985). Trust helps the school and family support each other and share expectations for student achievement. This is the type of social capital that can make a significant difference in a youngster's life.

Communication means more than simply relaying information. The medium of exchange tells parents how the school system feels about them. Schools and teachers who seek minimum parent involvement do the least to attract a parent's attention to important issues. For instance, one school system was obligated by state special education regulations to form a special needs parent advisory board. Instead of sending letters of invitation to parents describing the need for parent participation, the superintendent and special education director squeezed the message on the back of the weekly school lunch menu. As expected, there was minimal parent response. Did this mean that the parents in this school system were apathetic? Of course not, but judgments about parent behavior are sometimes based on such transactions.

Each parent is a unique person with his or her own interests, needs, and concerns. Understanding parents of children with mild disabilities requires treating each parent as an individual. Teachers who communicate through words and actions their respect for parents are most successful at forming cooperative parent-teacher partnerships. One strategy to establish a basis for trust and mutual respect is to make telephone calls to parents notifying them of their child's positive classroom contributions. This offsets the parental expectation that the only time they will hear from school is when there is a problem.

The following description of an exceptional teacher by a parent highlights the anxiety and hope that parents harbor when they first meet their child's teacher.

> *I just met a talented and gifted teacher, and I'm still tingling with joy. He invited the parents to a meeting, before the beginning of school, to introduce himself and to discuss the year. I wouldn't have missed it for the world, but I went with fear. What if I didn't like the man? Within half an hour, however, I felt the tension drain from my body to be replaced with excitement. Before me was a talented and gifted teacher. I knew other exceptional teachers before, and this time I could identify the qualities they had in common. (Williams, 1988, 61)*

Linda Williams (1988), parent, goes on to describe a teacher who loves to learn, is not afraid to take risks, believes teaching is helping children to learn, conveys the message that parents are important, and respects children. She might also have added that this teacher was capable of communicating his enthusiasm to parents. Parents need to know what kind of person is teaching their child. A parent's main source of information about a teacher is their child. Face-to-face, telephone, and written communications help parents better understand the teacher as a person.

Parent-Teacher Conferences

When parents and professionals meet to discuss a child, parents need to feel that they are valued participants. Teachers who treat parents with respect, rather than judging their feelings or behavior, create the best climate for a cooperative partnership. It wasn't long ago that professionals placed the majority of the blame for a child's learning problem on inferior parenting skills. Professionals viewed parents as part of the problem rather than part of the solution. The one-sided view that says, "It's all the parents fault," bred a condescending attitude towards parents of children with disabilities (Gallagher, Beckman, & Cross, 1983). In order to avoid barriers to effective communication, teachers should keep in mind the following pointers outlined by Gloecker and Simpson (1988).

1. *Parents of exceptional children are more like parents of nondisabled children than they are different.* There are no generalizations about families of children with

mild disabilities that hold true in all cases. Each situation is unique. The majority of special needs children come from families where other children do not have learning problems.

2. *Parents of children with mild disabilities, in general, are not the cause of their children's disabilities.* The causes of mild disabilities have been traced to many sources including poor instruction, faulty assessment practices, neurological impairments, and poverty. To view parents as the single contributor to a child's disability is misleading and unfair. Teachers may encounter some parents who are inadequate. These individuals need support and help, rather than condemnation.

3. *Parents are interested in their child's welfare and will react positively to those they believe are genuinely interested in their children.* No teacher behavior demonstrates understanding more than listening. Parents need someone to listen more than someone to tell them what to do. Listening indicates concern and interest in each individual situation. Listening helps professionals to problem-solve with parents. When parents feel their point of view is respected, they are more likely to be open and honest in their conversations.

4. *The family is a social unit.* When something happens to one member of a family, all members are affected. When a child is identified as having a learning disability, mild mental retardation, or emotional disturbance, each member of the family—mother, father, siblings, and relatives—will have individual reactions. The interrelationship among family members will have an impact on how a student behaves in school.

5. *Parents have the greatest impact on their own children.* Parents are the most influential adults in a child's life. No matter how many professionals are involved with a youngster, the specialist is still the parent. Parents need accurate and full knowledge of their child's status in school. Explanations of classroom actions, test results, and professional judgments should be honest and direct. Often students behave differently at school than home. Describing student actions in descriptive, nontechnical language helps the parent to understand discrepancies between home and school behavior.

An initial parent-teacher conference is more than a meeting about a child. It sets the tone for all future teacher-parent contacts. In order to prepare for a conference, imagine how the parent feels driving or walking to the conference. What will be on his or her mind? Think about feelings that precede a visit to a doctor, dentist, lawyer, or professor. A common concern is that something is wrong. Some parents, particularly those of children with mild disabilities, approach a conference with apprehension. They might be concerned that they appear to be "bad" parents, or they hope the teacher has some magic up his or her sleeve that is going to turn things around for their child. Their schooling may have been a negative experience, so the simple task of walking into a classroom and sitting down with a teacher can be anxiety provoking.

The first step to a productive parent-teacher conference is preparation. The following are some practical suggestions for parent-teacher meetings.

1. *Physical preparation.* Physical preparation means attending to the accoutrements of the conference. Don't sit behind a desk. If you are an early childhood teacher, provide adult-sized chairs. Have concrete samples of student work available to highlight topics you want to cover. Sit at a table that is wide enough to display student work. Have all your materials ready; it is important for a parent to view you as an organized person.

2. *Mental preparation.* Have a mental or written checklist of specific items you want to review. Avoid using materials, such as test profiles, that require turgid educational jargon to explain. Remember, you want to talk in plain language. If the parent is non-English speaking, make an attempt to communicate in a way that will help set the person at ease. If a translator is necessary, a smile and cheery "Buenas tardes" can go a long way toward helping a Spanish-speaking parent to relax.

3. *Establish a mood.* Always begin a conference with good news. This will set a positive tone and help smooth the waters for any trouble spots that need to be reviewed. Be candid and direct with parents. Honesty helps establish trust. Don't dominate the conference. At least 50 percent of the talk should come from parents. Remember that the purpose of the conference is for both of you to learn about each other. Use active listening skills. Encourage parents to give examples of their concerns by talking about what happens at home. Remember that you are probably the only other adult outside the family that a parent can confide in about his or her child. This is an opportunity for parents, but they need your nonjudgmental support in order to express their concerns. Finally, don't be defensive. If a parent makes what appears to be a negative remark about your teaching or the curriculum, listen to what they have to say. They may have a point. In any case, by listening to them, you demonstrate respect.

4. *Carryover.* Teachers can use a parent conference to assist parents with their children at home. Many parents would like to do more but they need guidance. Table 9–2 offers ideas for parents to improve their children's school performance. Followup is sometimes necessary. For example, you could give a parent a reading list of children's books, or you might refer a parent to another resource such as the WIC program or Head Start. A teacher's credibility rides on followup. After the conference is over, make a careful written record of the conversation. Include suggestions and questions that were discussed, and the type of follow-up you agreed on (Bjorklund & Burger, 1987).

Telephone Communication

School systems that make creative use of telephones can extend educational services to families. For example, the San Diego County Office of Education installed an EdInfo service. It offered 75 prerecorded messages 24 hours a day in English and Spanish. Funded through a grant from the Wells Fargo Bank

TABLE 9–2 Helping Parents Help Their Children

1. You Can Help Your Child Mentally By . . .

—praising your child for work well done and for good effort.

—eliminating comparisons of your child to another child.

—showing confidence in your child's abilities.

—being realistic in your expectations of your child.

—helping your child feel good about himself/herself.

—instilling in your child a sense of self-worth.

2. You Can Help Your Child Physically By . . .

—seeing that your child gets adequate sleep.

—providing a schedule or fixed routine for your child to follow during school days.

—seeing that your child has an appropriate diet with limitations on the amount of "junk food" consumed.

—monitoring medicines perscribed by your doctor.

—providing appropriate dress for existing weather conditions.

—encouraging your child to exercise regularly to keep up good muscle tone and energy level

—seeing that your child visits his/her dentist and doctor on a regular basis.

—showing your child a lot of love.

3. You Can Help Your Child Academically By . . .

—talking with your child. Have your child talk about the day's activities or future plans for the weekend or any other subject of interest.

—listening to your child. Responding to questions encourages curiosity and motivation in a child.

—teaching your child to listen to others. Being able to listen will not only help a child academically, but in social situations as well.

—reading to your child and having your child read to you.

—encouraging your child to read independently. Good reading ability is crucial for academic success in school.

—seeing that your child does assigned homework.

—establishing a regular time and place for your child to study.

—providing materials to use while studying (e.g., pencils, paper, dictionary, etc.).

—allowing your child to do his/her own work, but being available to provide assistance if needed.

—explaining to your child the importance of learning.

—taking your child to the library often.

—playing vocabulary games with your child such as naming common objects around the house and their uses; going to the grocery store and naming fruits and vegetables.

—encouraging your child's understanding of basic concepts such as under, over, bigger, smaller, higher, lower, in, out.

—playing question games with your child. Ask your child questions that begin "What if" or "How will."

—familiarizing your child with coins, clocks and/or watches, and colors.

—having your child memorize some vital pieces of information, such as a family telephone number, his/her address, your place of employment, the police emergency number, and other information needed for your child's safety and well being.

—serving as a positive role model for your child by reading, using appropriate speech, writing notes or letters, watching educational television programs.

—providing your child with as many learning experiences as possible (e.g., local outings, trips).

4. You Can Help Your Child In Test-Taking By . . .

—providing your child with a good supper, but discouraging overeating;

—insuring your child gets a good night of sleep so he/she will be alert during the next day;

—seeing that your child eats breakfast, even if it is only toast and a glass of juice or milk. Taking a test increases anxiety and anxiety uses energy rapidly;

—seeing that your child dresses appropriately for outside weather conditions, and if appropriate, carries a sweater or jacket for inside temperatures;

—getting your child to school on time (so there will be no last minute problems);

—making sure that your child has the following materials: two number 2 lead pencils, already sharpened if possible, and an extra eraser if you think your child will need it;

—encouraging your child to do his/her best on the test, but avoid placing undue pressure on your child;

—demonstrating verbally and non-verbally that you have confidence in your child's abilities to perform well on the test;

—giving your child a big smile and a hug before he/she leaves for school can make a big difference in test performance.

5. You Can Help Your Child In Other Ways By . . .

—encouraging your child to perform to the best of his/her ability.

—seeing that your child turns in assigned homework;

—keeping up-to-date on your child's progress in school;

—getting to know your child's teacher(s);

—volunteering to work in a school classroom or making materials for use in the classroom;

—participating in school sponsored activities;

—reviewing your child's work folder as it is sent home from school;

—supporting the parent-teacher organization of the school that your child attends.

Source: Whiting, J. (Child Service Coordinator), and Aultman, S. L. (Georgia Learning Resources System Center Director). (1990). [Workshop for Parents]. Albany, GA: Southwest Georgia Learning Resources System Center.

Foundation, EdInfo provided families with information on such topics as parents and teachers, tests and testing, drug and alcohol abuse, and special programs (Chrispeels, 1991).

Within the Indianapolis school system, Dial-A-Teacher gives families assistance with homework. This direct access line is staffed by two teams of teacher specialists Mondays through Thursdays from 5 p.m. to 8 p.m. Each five-member team is comprised of teachers with expertise in specific academic subjects. The specialist teams help parents and students solve difficulties with specific homework assignments.

The "Homework Hotline" is a live, call-in television show carried by two Indianapolis cable systems every Tuesday from 5 p.m. to 6 p.m. The purpose of the call-in show is to provide assistance in mathematics for students in grades 1–6. When parents or students make their calls, they talk to teachers who use chalkboards to go over and, if necessary, reteach math concepts.

The Parent Line/Communicator is a computerized telephone message service that provides families with information on approximately 140 different topics such as parenting skills, adult education, and magnet schools. Fifty messages feature information on drug and alcohol abuse. The line is open 24 hours a day. As many as 3,000 calls are made by families each month (Warner, 1991). These innovative programs, sponsored by the Indianapolis School System, illustrate that with a little bit of imagination (and some funding) the telephone can provide families with immediate access to school services.

Recently, a teacher of students with mild disabilities described how he had to confront another teacher about interrupting his classes. The other teacher, who is in an adjacent classroom, would barge into his class two or three times a day to use the telephone affixed to his classroom wall. Her explanation was that she needed to use a phone to contact parents and mentors in her work-study program, and the only telephone that was accessible was in his classroom. While he sympathized with her plight, the special education teacher pointed out that she was constantly disrupting his classes. She apologized, and they both tried to figure out a way to get the school administration to give her a phone line. Unfortunately, this scenario is too common. Teachers need administrative support and the necessary funding to make use of a telephone. As Ron Davies (1991) points out, "A telephone is a low-cost but crucial piece of equipment to encourage school/family/community connections" (p. 379).

Written Communication

Written communication is the most frequent method of school to home communication (Cattermole & Robinson, 1985). Newsletters, parent handbooks, and bulletins provide families with information regarding their rights and obligations under the Individuals with Disabilities Education Act. Teachers and admininstrators usually assume that parents understand this information. Given the importance of parental involvement in special education decisions, it is clearly in the school's best interests to disseminate readable information to parents.

In order to fulfill their obligations, parents need a working knowledge of special education law and regulations. They should understand notification, evaluation, and placement procedures. Parents also must be aware of due process procedures established to protect their rights. Parents should know how to utilize parent advocates. Finally, parents need to understand their role in developing and implementing the individualized education program.

Roit and Pfohl (1984) assessed the readability of written information disseminated to parents regarding their involvement in special education meetings. The readability study was prompted by widespread concern about passive parents. The researchers hypothesized that parents did not clearly understand information presented in school information materials. Their supposition had particular significance for parents of students with mild mental retardation and behavior disorders because a disproportionate percentage of these children come from either non-English speaking or culturally different families. Additonally, Educational Testing Service data on adult literacy indicated that 18–23 million adults cannot read a daily newspaper.

The results of the readability study indicated that large pages filled with small print made reading overwhelming and unappealing. The use of examples, samples, charts, and pictures enhanced readability of printed materials. Additionally, glossaries and questions were found to be helpful aides to parent understanding. The researchers found that bold headings and outlines did not communicate information as effectively as paragraphs that related concepts to specific situations. Such common words as "plan" and "right" needed to be explained when they were used to denote both educational and legal usage. Finally, Roit and Pfohl recommended organizing the content of printed material into five broad categories: (a) handicapping conditions (e.g., what is a learning disability and how does it affect a youngster developmentally, socially, and academically?); (b) normal child development; (c) legal issues and trends in litigation; (d) assessment and placement procedures; (e) the role of parents in the educational process.

While parent-conferences, the telephone, and newsletters represent the traditional approach to school-family communication, educators are beginning to realize that the electronic media has tremendous potential for interconnecting families and teachers, especially in isolated rural areas.

Technology

In Westfield, Massachusetts, the superintendent had a weekly televison show on the local cable public access station. During this show he explained such issues as why school buses ran late and how two new schools would be funded. He interviewed principals and teachers and explained to viewers how public schools compete with other city agencies for shrinking dollars. Television offers educators tremendous opportunities for making contact and educating parents and students alike. Yet television is just one piece in a panoply of electronic devices that present themselves as solutions awaiting someone clever enough to devise the problems. For example, unless someone envisions expert teachers talking with students in far-flung areas, the problem of how they will communicate does not exist and the solution—telecommunications—remains dormant. Or, it takes an appreciation of computer technology to wonder if it would be possible for an expert on student learning styles to design a program to diagnose learning problems of students suspected of having mild disabilities. The technology is available, but it begs for a question to spur the hunt for a solution (Levinson, 1990).

Like the TV show "Jeopardy," technology anticipates our questions. CD-ROM technology is the answer. What is the question? (How can we make the vast information of libraries and museums accessible to the average classroom?) Let's try another. The answer is satellite transmissions. The question is how can an educational institution (school, college, university) make the talents of one gifted teacher available to thousands of students and parents? Such information systems as videodiscs, cassette tapes, satellite TV, interactive computing (i.e., electronic bulletin boards, electronic mail), and teleconferencing are powerful, virtually untapped resources for connecting teachers, schools, and home.

While schools lumber through the electronic information age, home shopping networks, C-Span, public access cable, and CNN news beam immediate and interactive information into millions of United States homes. It appears that the dream of educators—lifelong learning—is about to be fulfilled, but in ways hardly imagined even ten years ago. The classroom has expanded into the living rooms of the United States. Televised college study is available in some areas—and can be validated through supervised examinations offered in regional centers. News of the day, job posters, and recommended stock purchases are all available via home computer access networks. Sears and IBM collaborated to produce PRODIGY, an interactive computer-based information system that, for a monthly fee, provides 750 editorial choices, an encyclopedia and weekly education features.

The tools are available for educators to expand the notion of social captial into social electronic capital. As an illustration, US Vidotel in Houston, Dallas, and Ft. Worth offers terminal users a combination of interactive math games, *Grolier's Encyclopedia*, and a directory that lists information about local school systems and educational services. Electronic communication can provide multiple options for parent involvement. Parents could communciate with teachers and each other via teleconferences. Electronic bulletin boards can provide easy access to school menus, activities, and volunteer schedules. Interactive computer systems can provide tutoring for homework assignments. These information systems are not a substitute for face to face contact, but they do provide a valuable new link between home and school (Grunwald, 1990). While teachers scramble to find an available telephone (see section on telephone communication), the communication industries are scrambling to find new, more profitable ways of bringing electronic communication into United States homes. The use of high tech information systems to facilitate school-home communcation will require a commitment in dollars that does not presently exist within either state or federal budgets. It remains to be seen if educators can turn the present electronic networking possibilities into a future partnership between schools and families.

The Individual Education Program Meeting

One of the remarkable aspects of the Individuals with Disabilities Education Act is that parents are expected to participate with educators to determine the appropriateness of their youngster's individual education program (IEP). The law requires parental involvement in deciding:

1. Type of special services required (e.g., speech therapy, counseling)
2. Educational placement (e.g., full-time regular class with support, resource room, special class).
3. Makeup of the individual education program (IEP) (e.g., annual goals and objectives).

Students with mild disabilities cannot be evaluated or placed in a special education program without parental consent. If parents do not agree with educational decisions about their youngster, they have the due process right to mediation and appeal. Table 9–3 lists parental due process rights. The fact that several parent-school disagreements about special education services have reached the Supreme Court highlights the importance of parent-school cooperation. (The majority of these cases were adjudicated in favor of parents.)

TABLE 9–3 Parents' Due Process Rights

1. The right to examine all your child's school records.
2. The right to request a special education evaluation for your child.
3. The right to refuse the school permission to do a special education evaluation on your child.
4. The right of your child to remain in a regular classroom until you agree to special education services.
5. The right to request an independent educational evaluation paid for by your school system.
6. The right to bring an advocate with you to all meetings about your child.
7. The right to participate in the development of an individual education program (IEP) for your child.
8. The right to disagree with the individual education program (IEP) developed for your child.
9. The right to appeal all decisions made by your school system regarding special education services for your child.
10. The right to expect your child will receive special education services in classrooms alongside nondisabled children.
11. The right to review and amend your child's individual education program each year.
12. The right to expect full cooperation from the school system in all matters concerning your child's special education.

The individual education program (IEP) begins with the initial referral and concludes with the parents agreeing to special education services outlined in the program. The IEP is a management tool designed to insure that special education services match a student's individual needs and that special education services are monitored. It contains annual goals and objectives, a statement about a student's educational strengths and weaknesses, and a description of special education and related services. Table 9–4 lists the basic components of the IEP. The individual education program must be approved by parents before a student can be placed in a special education program.

The purpose of the IEP planning meeting is for educators and parents to discuss their views about a student's special education needs. The participants in the meeting include, but are not limited to, the student's teacher, the student's parents or guardians, a representative of the local education agency (public or private), and a member of the assessment team. Some state guidelines provide for student participation. In Massachusetts, for example, a student fourteen years or older has the right to participate in an IEP meeting. The Individuals with Disabilities Education Act also gives parents the right to bring an advocate with them. There is no stipulation about an advocate's qualifications. An advocate is someone who can help the parent sort through the often bewildering array of decisions they are confronted with during an IEP planning meeting.

In theory, the IEP meeting is democratic and provides for maximum parental input into a child's special education program. Unfortunately, the reality is quite different. Often, parents do not view themselves and are not viewed by educators as colleagues at the meeting. Parent participation at IEP meetings is minimal. A survey of several hundred families (Lynch & Stein, 1987) reported that 50 percent of parents did not feel they were active participants and only 34 percent of parents made suggestions during the meeting. Sometimes, because of time conflicts, transportation problems, child care needs or work commitments, parents are unable to attend the meeting. When parents are absent, the IEP is usually mailed to them for their signature.

TABLE 9–4 Components of an Individual Education Program

An individual education program (IEP) is a written plan for provision of special education services for a student who is disabled.

Each IEP must contain:
(A) A statement of the child's present level of educational performance.
(B) A statement of annual goals, including short-term instructional objectives.
(C) A statement of the specific special educational and related services to be provided the child, and the extent to which the child will be able to participate in regular educational programs.
(D) The projected dates for initiation of services and the anticipated duration of the services; and.
(E) Appropriate objective criteria and evaluation procedures and schedules for determining, on at least an annual basis, whether the short term instructional objectives are being met.

When parents attend the IEP meeting, a variety of group dynamic factors impede participation. Consider the folowing scene. A group of professionals are sitting around a table facing the parents. Each professional takes a turn reporting on the educational failure of their child. The parents are deluged with educational jargon like "subaverage IQ," "deficient adaptive behavior skills," "dyslexic," and "behavior disordered." This "edspeak" places the parents at a serious disadvantage as they try to follow what's being said. Without an advocate to help the parents sort out what is happening, the parents are in jeopardy of consenting to an IEP that is unclear.

All IEP meetings are not as muddled for parents as the one just described. When educators are sensitive to parents' feelings and take the time to explain what they are talking about, parents have an opportunity to be involved. Educators need to remember that it takes a good deal of resolve for a parent to participate in a meeting that is intended to analyze what is wrong with his or her child. One parent expressed her feelings this way.

> *The IEP process was something that was really hard for me to accept and get into, because I'm not by nature an assertive person. In a group I don't speak up that much, but as a parent in an IEP conference, I have to. I have to be totally prepared. I may have a lot of confidence in the staff that's working with him; they're all great people. But I have to know what each is doing with Geoff and where they're headed with him. I need to review my concerns when I go to the conference, to speak up, and really be his advocate. I have to do that. I think the parent is the one who has the best whole concept of the child, with regard to where he's been and where he's going. And the parent has a lot to offer the staff members knowledge and understanding of the child. (Roberts, 1986, 206)*

The IEP planning meeting is an important event in a parent's life. By following a few basic guidelines, educators can insure that the meeting enhances rather than diminishes parent-teacher communication.

1. Before the meeting, give parents basic information on how the meeting will be conducted, who will be attending, and what they can do to be effective participants.
2. Arrange seating so parents are not sitting on one side of a table, "squared off" against the professionals.
3. Avoid general negative statements like "Harry is eight but has a mental age of five." There is enough valid criticism of educational assessment procedures to warrant tempering of professional enthusiasm for the accuracy of test results.
4. Encourage parent questions after each professional makes a contribution.
5. Be conscious of the group dynamics. Is one person dominating? Are there hidden agendas? Are the professionals communicating their views in plain language? Are parents giving off distress signals with body language? Most important, are parents being given ample opportunity to verbally participate?

6. When the meeting is over, summarize the group's conclusions and indicate one professional that the parents can contact to answer questions that may occur to them on the way home.

In order to insure an appropriate education for students with disabilities, Congress mandated parent participation in IEP meetings. By encouraging active parental participation, educators not only fulfill their legal responsibilites, they also provide students with their best opportunity for success.

Summary

Over the years, schools and families have drifted further apart. This is unfortunate because teachers and families share a common vision. Both want our children to develop the social and intellectual skills needed to function as contributing citizens. Homes, schools, and communities are besieged by the ravages of poverty, drugs, and alcohol. Schools and families need each other. When educators reach out to families and seek their involvement, schools improve, students achieve, and communities grow closer together.

As we survey the state of our schools and our youth, it appears that we are losing more student minds than we are gaining. The number of school failures seems to grow steadily each year. The numbers of learning disabled students, for instance, has increased by over 100 percent since incidence figures were first reported in 1976. As poverty grows in this country, so will the numbers of students with mild disabilities. Adolescents with emotional disturbance are the fastest-growing population of students with mild disabilities. Educators cannot stem this tide of school failure without parental help. Congress recognized the need for school-family cooperation by mandating parent participation in special education programming. The Supreme Court has upheld, and in some instances broadened, the role of parents in securing an appopriate education for their children with disabilities. Before the implementation of the Individuals with Disabilities Education Act, educators often perceived parents as the problem. Today, parents are an integral part of the solution.

Parents of children with mild disabilities need support and understanding as they deal with the daily stresses of modern life. When a child is evaluated by the school as having a mild disability, it affects all members of the family. This ripple effect in turn influences the family's ability to cope with the demands of parenting and education. There are many organizations that support families. Yet most families struggle on in isolation, unaware of the network of help that is available to help them. Parents need opportunities to communicate with others who share their problems. Parents need information about their rights and responsibilities as co-determiners of their child's appropriate education. Successful experiences with the schools are needed in order for parents to believe in their ability to promote their child's education. Most of all, parents need teachers who respect them and value their role in shaping the education of their children.

A Chronology

Date	Mental Retardation	Emotional Disturbance	Learning Disabilities	Generic to Education
1790	Jean Itard's attempts to train Victor, the Wild Boy of Aveyron (France). Treatment centered around sensory stimulation exercises coupled with speech formation techniques.			
1802			Franz Joseph Gall speculated that specific regions of the brain control certain mental activities.	
1820s	Almhouses erected in America for destitute, originally designed to provide humane and moral care for the poor; became catchalls for retarded, insane, ill, and other afflicted.			
1828		Horace Mann influenced authorization of funds for state hospitals for the insane in Massachusetts.		

Early information from *A Study of Child Variance: Conceptual Models* (Vols. 1 & 2), by W. C. Rhodes and M. L. Tracy, published by the University of Michigan, Ann Arbor, Michigan.

Date	Mental Retardation	Emotional Disturbance	Learning Disabilities	Generic to Education
1830s & 1840s		Conditions in state hospitals were little better than almhouses. Other forms of treatment included public auctions, selling of chattel slaves, and abandonment.		Horace Mann set economic and legal foundations of American public education. While Secretary of Massachusetts Board of Education (1837-1848), wrote bills which became national standard (e.g., length of school year, tax base for financial support of schools, standardized teacher training, standardized school curriculum, political selection of school superintendent, and so on. Established first state normal (teacher training) school (1839).
1837	Samuel Howe began a class for training retarded children at Perkins Institute in Boston, Massachusetts.			
1842	Edward Sequin was instrumental in founding the first school for care and education of mentally retarded (MR) students in Paris, France.			
1843		Dorthea Dix reported cruel and inhumane treatment to the Massachusetts Legislature (e.g., chains, locks, cages, bloodletting practices). Influenced construction of special asylums—some improvement over prisons and poorhouses. Nonexistent rehabilitation and education programs.		

Date	Mental Retardation	Emotional Disturbance	Learning Disabilities	Generic to Education
1846		First educational facility (Westborough, Massachusetts) for socially maladjusted youth. Established with reformatory and educational goals in mind; thus called a "reform school."		
1848	Massachusetts was the first to support state schools for the mentally retarded in the United States.			
1850s		Overcrowding doubled clientele of reform school. Custodial rather than instructional services rendered.		Depression brought financial strains.
1851	Harvey Willus was the first state-supported school for MR in New York (transferred from Albany to Syracuse in 1855). Other such schools followed in the Northeast U.S. and New England states: Ohio (1857); Connecticut (1858); Pennsylvania (1859); Kentucky (1860); Illinois (1865).			
1850s	Edward Sequin believed retardation to be treatable and curable. Environmental factors (e.g., health, diet) considered important.			
1860s		Prevailing belief that social deviance was inevitable product of	Pierre Paul Broca demonstrated that speech disorders were	

Date	Mental Retardation	Emotional Disturbance	Learning Disabilities	Generic to Education
1860s (cont.)		immigrant population, largely poor and uneducated.	the result of damage to the frontal convolutions of the brain. He proposed that the functions of the brain's left and right hemispheres were different.	
Mid-1860s	Rise of Darwinist thought. Environmental view gave way to emphasis on innate deficiencies. Mood of pessimism became dominant. State institutions became more custodial. Samuel Howe was discouraged with the results of the Perkins Institute.			
1866		Samuel Howe became discouraged by increased size and bureaucratization of mental hospitals and reform schools.		
1870s		Establishment of "ungraded schools" for mischievous and disruptive children in: New Haven, Connecticut (1871); New York City (1874); Cleveland, Ohio (1875).		
Between 1852 and 1918				Compulsory school attendance required in all states of the Union, beginning with Massachusetts (1852) and ending with Mississippi (1918).

Date	Mental Retardation	Emotional Disturbance	Learning Disabilities	Generic to Education
1875-1900		Classes for socially maladjusted children grew rapidly.		
1890s	Increased advocacy efforts for special classes or schools for recalcitrant or mentally deficient children.			More stringent administration of compulsory attendance laws. Educational Commission of the City of Chicago (Harpur Report) urged the establishment of ungraded classes for unmanageable children.
Turn of Century		Establishment of special classes to cope with children who presented problems for regular classrooms.		Anti-immigrant attitude perpetuated Social Darwinism.
1870-1890	Herbert Spencer (Britain) developed a "philosophy of natural selection" (weaker members of society pose threat to future of mankind, thus only the most fit of human species be allowed to survive).			
Late 1800s	First public school programs for the MR in: Providence, Rhode Island (1896); Springfield, Massachusetts (1897); Chicago, Illinois (1898); Boston, Massachusetts (1899); New York City (1900). Called class for "backward" children.			

Date	Mental Retardation	Emotional Disturbance	Learning Disabilities	Generic to Education
1900	Elizabeth Farrell helped to establish classes for MR in New York City.			
Early 1900s	MR children frequently assigned to foreign-speaking "steamer" classes; many normal foreign children placed in classes for the mentally deficient.			
1902	Ungraded classes in New Haven, Connecticut reported to serve three distinct types of children grouped together: Incorrigible boys, mentally defective children, and non-English-speaking youth.			
1908	Henry G. Goddard, while Director of Research at the Training School in Vineland, New Jersey, translated the Binet intelligence scales into English and made adaptations for their use in the United States.			
1909		Elizabeth Farrell helped establish the first psychoeducational clinic.		
1911	Goddard published own version of the Binet-Simon Test. New Jersey was the first state to pass legislation concerning the education of MR children in the public schools. Defined MR as "three or more years retarded in mental development."			
1912	Publication of "The Kallikak Family," which gave fuel to the			

Date	Mental Retardation	Emotional Disturbance	Learning Disabilities	Generic to Education
1912 (cont.)	prevailing eugenics theory. Portrayed the "feebleminded" as a menace to society and to the future of the human race. Proposed that social undesirables (e.g., criminals, paupers, drunkards) arose from the genetic stock of mentally deficient.			
1914	Charles Scott Berry set up the first teacher training program in special education at a residential school for MR in Michigan. St. Louis, Missouri public school system adopted eligibility standards for special schools for the severely MR and ungraded classes for borderline and backward students.			
1915				Connecticut Board of Education hired Arnold Gessell as first official school psychologist to examine slow-learning children, and to devise better methods for their school instruction.
1917			James Hinshelwood, a French physician, defined "word blindness" as a condition in which an individual with normal vision is unable to interpret written or printed language. Hinshelwood theorized that this difficulty is	

Date	Mental Retardation	Emotional Disturbance	Learning Disabilities	Generic to Education
1917 (cont.)			caused by a defect in the left hemisphere of the brain, the portion that stores memories of words and letters.	
1919	St. Louis eligibility standards of 1914 were adopted statewide, and subsequently adopted by other states.			
Years prior to 1920	Relatively small number of teachers trained to work with mentally or socially handicapped. Most facilities were residential with staff members trained on the premises. Technology was not yet developed for assessing individual differences, and special education was not included in curricula at teacher colleges.			
1922	Council for Exceptional Children (CEC) founded with Elizabeth Farrell as first president. Original purposes of establishing the CEC organization included: 1) To emphasize the education of the special child rather than his identification or classification. 2) To establish professional standards for teachers in the field of special education. 3) To unite those interested in the problem of the special child.			
1926			Sir Henry Head theorized that disorders in language could not be dichotomized as sensory or motor.	
1922-1932	MR enrollment in separate facilities within public school systems more than tripled.	Growth of separate facilities within public school systems for deviant children.		
1929		Special classes for socially maladjusted frequently called "disciplinary classes." Employed strong arm rather than education	Samuel T. Orton speculated that one side of the brain dominated the language processes; therefore, he	

Date	Mental Retardation	Emotional Disturbance	Learning Disabilities	Generic to Education
1929 (cont.)		or rehabilitation approach.	concluded that disabled children who had no demonstrable brain injury had failed to establish hemispheric dominance.	
By 1930	Sixteen states passed legislation regarding education of the mentally handicapped.			
Early 1930s			Kurt Goldstein observed meticulosity, perseveration, figure-ground configuration, forced responses to stimuli, and catastrophic reaction in adult, brain-injured patients.	
The 1930s	Decrease in special programs for MR and socially deviant youth due to: 1) Less money for special programs; and 2) Dissatisfaction with the quality of education in special classes. Public schools more likely to provide separate facilities for MR children than for any other exceptionality group, especially the Northeast and north central states. Building principals often experienced difficulty in distinguishing between pupils who were "fit subjects" for disciplinary classes and those who were mentally retarded.	Establishment of disciplinary classes for truant and incorrigible youth in the schools.		
1932				Thirteen states established a state director in charge of administrative special education services.

Date	Mental Retardation	Emotional Disturbance	Learning Disabilities	Generic to Education
1935	New York was the first state to certify school psychologists. Roles consisted largely of evaluating and making recommendations for placement in special services of children viewed as "backward" or MR.			
Late 1930s and Early 1940s			Alfred A. Strauss and Heinz Werner investigated brain-injured, mentally retarded children. Findings led to the identification of the exogenous subgroup of retarded children (externally brain-injured).	
1943			Grace Fernald used the VAKT (visual-auditory-kinesthetic-tactile) approach in the development of remedial reading programs.	
The 1940s-W.W.II years	Use of handicapped (including MR) in many jobs due to able-bodied men being away at war.		Laura Lehtinen collaborated with Strauss to develop teaching procedures. Strauss and Lehtinen co-authored *Psychopathy and Education of the Brain-Injured Child* (1947) in which two interventions were suggested: 1) Manipulating and controlling the environment, and 2) Teaching the child voluntary control.	World War II years necessitated man power.

Date	Mental Retardation	Emotional Disturbance	Learning Disabilities	Generic to Education
1946		Division of Child Welfare in NYC organized "600 schools" for children viewed as emotionally disturbed or socially maladjusted. Despite therapeutic intent, these schools were operated as warehouses for uncontrollable boys, and were custodial in nature.		
Until Early 1950s	Nearly all schools had policies which excluded children with I.Q.s below the mild range. Parents of these children were expected to educate them at home, or place them in state or private residential facilities.			
1948 to 1952 to 1958	Number of children enrolled in special public school programs increased from 87,000 to 113,000 to over 213,000.			
1950	National Association for Retarded Citizens (NARC) first organized in Minneapolis, Minnesota. This organization was considered the primary source of help to families with retarded children, as well as a major information disseminating and legislative lobbying force.			

Date	Mental Retardation	Emotional Disturbance	Learning Disabilities	Generic to Education
The 1950s			William M. Cruikshank facilitated the transfer of brain-injured research from exogenous retarded children to children with normal intelligence.	
1954				Cooperative Research Act of 1954 (P.L. 85-531) authorized support for cooperative research in education; funding was granted for this in 1957.
1955			Helmer R. Mycklebust defined language as symbolic behavior (i.e., using words as symbols for expressing ideas and feelings, and labeling objects). Strauss and Newell C. Kephart co-authored Vol. II of *Psychopathology. . .* in which comparisons were made of research on brain-injured children of normal intelligence with research on mentally-retarded brain-injured children.	
1956			Spaulding presented an approach to written language disability called Unified Phonics Methods. Words are pronounced and component sounds are written in accordance with the rules of English spelling. Jerome Bruner co-authored *A Study*	All 48 states had established legal provisions for some sort of state assistance, advisory and/or financial, to local special education programs. The degree of involvement and support varied from state to state, and the growth of special education services has

Date	Mental Retardation	Emotional Disturbance	Learning Disabilities	Generic to Education
1956 (cont.)			*of Thinking* (Bruner, Goodnow, & Austin) which stressed the importance of studying covert cognitive processes.	not been at the same rate for all types of exceptional programs.
1957				Public attitude toward education for all children was spurred by general concern of the populace for American education after the Russian launching of Sputnik.
1958 & 1959	P.L. 85-926 and P.L. 86-158 authorized fellowship awards for graduate students intent on careers as teacher-trainers or administrators of the mentally retarded.		Noam Chomsky gave support to "inner thinking processes."	
1950s & 1960s	Improved education and training of MR occurred under the Kennedy administration.			
1960s		Edward L. Thorndike, called the "father of reinforcement theory," believed the connection between stimulus and response represented all learning.	J. M. Wepman postulated that the language "transmission" process is divided into receptive and expressive modes. "Integration" provides for the decoding and encoding of previously learned patterns to give meaning to the stimulus. Emphasized role of recall, transmission	

Date	Mental Retardation	Emotional Disturbance	Learning Disabilities	Generic to Education
Early to Mid-1960s		Norris Haring and E. Lakin Phillips combined Cruickshank's structured environment classroom and B. F. Skinner's operant conditioning to develop educational programs for emotionally disturbed children.	(receptive and expressive modes), and integration (the decoding and encoding of previously learned language patterns). Beginnings of educational focus on children with learning difficulties. Ogden R. Lindsley developed a comprehensive set of measuring procedures, called	
1962		The Council for Children with Behavioral Disorders (CCBD) was founded as a division of CEC.	"precision teaching," which includes pinpointing behavior, counting and charting performance, and making instructional decisions based on performance data.	
1963	Passage of P.L. 88-164 increased support for training of personnel and extended support for professional training to severe areas of childhood exceptionality, including mental retardation and emotional disturbance; authorized use of funds for research and demonstration projects in field of handicapped education.		Term "learning disabilities" was introduced by Samuel Kirk at a national conference of parent organizations and subsequently adopted. Association for Children with Learning Disabilities (ACLD) was formed as a parent, teacher, professional interest group.	
Mid-1960s			Department of Health, Education, and Welfare sponsored several task forces to study brain-injured children with learning problems. Term "minimal brain dysfunction" (MBD) was introduced.	Host of domestic legislation was enacted at the federal level, aimed at launching "War on Poverty" and achieving the "Great Society."

Date	Mental Retardation	Emotional Disturbance	Learning Disabilities	Generic to Education
1965	P.L. 89-105, added to P.L. 88-164, permitted the construction and operation of research facilities and related programs, including the training of special personnel.	National Society for Autistic Children (NSAC) was founded. Was one of the first major parent-interest groups devoted to concerns of the emotionally disturbed child. Organization has sought public school involvement for autistic children, and has opposed their placement in private or residential facilities.		Elementary and Secondary Education Act (ESEA) provided assistance to children in "disadvantaged" areas (including handicapped children). Act was called the "Great Society's" legislative package and was considered a significant effort to alleviate poverty through schooling. Eleven colleges and universities received funding by U.S. Office of Education to help support training of personnel in this field. Office of Economic Opportunity (OEO) established to aid the culturally disadvantaged or deprived child. Head Start, an OEO-funded project, along with remedial reading, counseling and tutorial services was begun.
1967	Hobson vs. Hanson litigation resulted in finding the "tracking" system in Washington, D.C. to be unconstitutional. Based on standardized test results, children were placed in honors, general, or special programs. Relying on Brown vs. Board of Education, the court held that assessment measures were culturally biased and sustained an unjustifiable racial separation of students. A dispro-			A separate Bureau for the Education of the Handicapped (BEH) was created within the U.S. Office of Education. Special Education was included in the top policy-making levels for the first time.

Date	Mental Retardation	Emotional Disturbance	Learning Disabilities	Generic to Education
1967 (cont.)	portionate number of African-American children were enrolled in special classes.			
1968			The Division for Children with Learning Disabilities (DCLD)(now Council for Learning Disabilities) was organized as a professional division within the CEC. The National Advisory Committee of Handicapped Children (NACHC) was formed to develop a definition for learning disabilities. *Journal of Learning Disabilities* was published.	
1969			P.L. 91-230, the Specific Learning Disabilities Act of 1969, was passed. The definition developed by the NACHC under Kirk's leadership was used in this act.	
Late 1960s and 1970s		Skinner defined two types of learned behavior: respondent (involuntary) and operant (voluntary). Transferred work with animals in the laboratory (1950s) to observable, measurable events in the educational arena (1960s and 1970s).		"Right to fair classification" cases filed as class action suits. Parents and other interested parties argued that the labeling and placement procedure by which children are processed into special education is culturally discriminatory and a violation of the 14th Amendment's Constitutional guarantee for due process and equal protection under the law.

Date	Mental Retardation	Emotional Disturbance	Learning Disabilities	Generic to Education
Early 1970s				Jean Piaget's developmental theory suggested that instruction should recognize maturational growth and not require students to perform skills for which they are not ready.
The 1970s	NARC organized effective lobbying forces and succeeded in bringing about massive increases in school services for children previously thought to be "unteachable."			
1971	Pennsylvania Association for Retarded Children alleged violations of due process and equal protection under the 14th Amendment of the U.S. Constitution regarding barring of low I.Q. children from public schools in that state. Similar "right-to-education" suits initiated in other states.			
1971	Larry P. vs. Riles was filed as a class action suit in California on behalf of several Black children who had been placed and retained in EMR classes. Plaintiffs alleged use of racially and culturally biased testing procedures which violated the Civil Rights Act of 1871 and the right to equal protection under the California Constitution and the 14th Amendment of the U.S. Constitution.			

Date	Mental Retardation	Emotional Disturbance	Learning Disabilities	Generic to Education
1972	A preliminary injunction was issued by the court halting the use of I.Q. tests in the state of California for placing Black children in classes for the EMR.			
1975				Public Law 94-142 (Education for All Handicapped Children Act) (EHA) provided for a free, appropriate public education for all handicapped children, and defined special education and related services.
1978			Formation of the National Joint Commission for Learning Disabilities (NJCLD).	
Late 1970s				The Reagan Administration attempted to deregulate and decentralize all phases of public education; however, most categorical services and mandates regulating special education survived this initiative. Department of Education established by Congress.
1982			The DCLD membership voted to withdraw from CEC and form an independent organization, the Council for Learning Disabilities (CLD). A cadre of former DCLD members began a new CEC division called the Division for Learning Disabilities (DLD).	

Date	Mental Retardation	Emotional Disturbance	Learning Disabilities	Generic to Education
1983				Office of Special Education and Rehabilitative Services (OSERS) created under the newly established Department of Education.
				Public Law 98-199 (EHA Amendments) passed. Reaffirmed the federal role in special education by expanding P.L. 94-142 with supported preschool, secondary, and post secondary programs for the handicapped, and support for special education teacher preparation, early childhood education, parent training, and information dissemination.
				Public Law 101–336 (Americans with Disabilities Act) (ADA) gives civil rights protection to individuals with disabilities in private sector employment, all public services, public accommodations, transportation, and telecommunications. Patterned after section 504 of the Rehabilitation Act of 1973.
1986				Public Law 99-457 (EHA Amendments) reauthorized existing EHA, amended PL 94-142 to include financial incentives for states to educate children ages 3 to 5 by the 1990-91

Date	Mental Retardation	Emotional Disturbance	Learning Disabilities	Generic to Education
1986 (Cont.)				school year, and established incentive grants to promote programs serving handicapped infants (birth to age 2).
1990 to 1991			The U.S. House of Representatives opened for citizen comment the issue of a separate exceptionality category for students with attention deficit disorders. The issue died without legislative action.	Public Law 101-476 (Individuals with Disabilities Education Act)(IDEA) reauthorized and renamed existing EHA. This amendment to EHA changed the term "handicap" to "disability," expanded related services, and required individual education programs (IEPs) to contain transitional goals and objectives for adolescents (ages 16 and above, special situations age 14).

Appendix *B*

Commonly Used Psychoactive Medications

Stimulants

Dextroamphetamine sulfate (Dexedrine) is usually administered in 5 milligram dosages (daily at 8 am and 12 noon). Less classroom restlessness, increased attention span, and improvements in social and emotional behavior patterns are the expected effects. Most common side effects are loss of appetite and loss of sleep; less common are headaches with blurred vision, apathy, stupor, tiredness, dry mouth, and drug tolerance over long periods of use.

Methylphenidate hydrochloride (Ritalin) is usually administered in a single 20 milligram dose in the morning or in two 10 milligram doses in the morning and afternoon; it is generally taken before a meal. Less classroom restlessness, increased attention span, and improvements in social and emotional behavior patterns are the expected effects. Most common side effects are loss of sleep; less common are headaches with blurred vision, apathy, stupor, tiredness, dry mouth, and drug tolerance over long periods of use. Ritalin does not suppress appetite as much as Dexedrine.

Magnesium pemoline (Cylert) is usually administered once a day in a 37.5 milligram dosage and is considered slower acting than other stimulants. Less classroom restlessness, increased attention span, and improvements in social and emotional behavior patterns are the expected effects. Most common side effects are loss of appetite and loss of sleep; less common are headaches with blurred

Source: B. Algozzine (1990). Behavior Problem Management: Educator's Resource Service. Rockville, MD: Aspen Publishers.

vision, apathy, stupor, tiredness, dry mouth, and drug tolerance over long periods of use. Cylert is preferred over Dexedrine because it does not suppress most children's appetites as much.

Minor tranquilizers

Deanol acetamid obenzoate (Deaner) is usually administered in one 100 milligram dose in the morning. Improved emotional and social patterns result in children tending to be immature or anxious. Most common side effects are headaches, constipation, insomnia, and skin rashes.

Imapramine hydrochloride (Tofranil) is usually administered in one 10-25 milligram dose an hour before bed to control enuresis or 75 milligrams once a day for more serious problem behaviors. It is the most widely recognized and recommended antidepressant for children under 12 years of age; there can be as much as a three week lag before effects are noticed. Controlled bed-wetting and improved emotional and social patterns result in children tending to be depressed or overly anxious. Most common side effects are dry mouth, urinary retention, blurred vision, tremors, drowsiness, sweating, and some postural rigidity.

Chlordiazepoxide hydrochloride (Librium) is usually administered in divided doses up to 30 milligrams a day; it is not recommended for children under six. Expected effects include reduction in anxiety, general relaxation, sense of well-being, and general drowsiness. Most common side effects are confusion, skin eruptions, edema, gastrointestinal symptoms, unwanted drowsiness, jaundice, and some changes in electroencephalogram patterns.

Hydroxine hydrochloride (Atarax) is usually administered in doses that vary with the level of the individual's problems. Expected effects include reduction in anxiety, aggressiveness and hyperactivity. Most common side effects are tolerance, dependence and dry mouth.

Meprobamate (Equanil) is usually administered 2 or 3 times a day in 100-200 milligram dosages. Expected effects include reduction in anxiety; it is used for its sedative effects. Most common side effects are unwanted drowsiness, dependency, and hematologic disorders.

Oxazepam (Serax) does not have a prescribed dosage for children; it is not recommended for children under six. Expected effects include reduction in hostility and muscle relaxation. Most common side effects are ataxia, skin rashes, nausea, and dependence.

Major Tranquilizers

Haloperidol (Haldol) is usually administered in 1 milligram dosages several times a day; it is not recommended for children. Haldol is used to treat mania, paranoia, social withdrawal, and aggressive problems associated and schizophrenia. Most common side effects are skin reactions, jaundice, and impaired vision.

Chlorpromazine hydrochloride (Thorazine) is usually administered in 10-24 milligram dosages two or three times a day; it can be increased to 50 milligrams for adolescents. Expected effects include reduction in activity and general reduction in aggressive, negative symptoms commonly seen in seriously disturbed individuals. Most common side effects are skin reactions, impaired vision, and weight gain.

Thioridiazine hydrochloride (Mellaril) is usually administered in 10 milligram dosages three or four times a day for preschoolers and in 25 milligram dosages three or four times a day for older children. Expected effects include antidepressive symptoms, reduced anxiety, aggression reduction, and less overall activity. Most common side effects are sexual dysfunction in males, disturbed color vision, and weight gain.

Anticonvulsants

Phenobarbitol (Luminal) is usually administered in 100 milligram dosages and may require as long as 15 minutes to take effect. Expected effects include control of grand mal seizures. Most common side effects are sedation, rashes, slurred speech.

Diphenylhydantoin (Dilantin) is usually administered in varying milligram dosages dependent on age of individual, ranging from 50 milligrams for 1-2 year olds to 300-400 milligrams for adolescents. Expected effects include control of grand mal seizures; generally considered drug of choice for most forms of epilepsy (except petit mal seizures). Most common side effects are ataxia, nystagamus, vertigo, blurred vision, confusion, hallucinations, nausea, and urinary incontinence.

Ethosuximide (Zarontin) is usually administered in 0.5-1.0 milligram dosages two or three times a day. Expected effects include control of petit mal seizures; generally considered drug of choice for this form of seizures. Most common side effects are gastric distress, nausea, vomiting, anorexia, headaches, fatigue, dizziness, and blood disorders.

Appendix C

Genetic, Pre-, Peri-, and Postnatal Disorders

A. GENETIC DISORDERS occur at the time of conception within the fetus's genetic code. Some common genetic disorders are:

1. Cystic fibrosis: severe health impairment of the lungs, causing ill health and eventual death.
2. Muscular dystrophy: a wasting disease of the muscles, causing gradual weakness and inability to walk.
3. Diabetes: caused by lack of insulin output by the pancreas; usually controllable.
4. Asthma: a breathing disorder which frequently limits physical activity; often controllable.
5. Inherited personality characteristics and abilities: sometimes precipitate behavior disorders or learning disabilities.
6. Phenylketonuria (PKU): can result in retardation if not controlled at birth with diet; defect in metabolism of proteins.
7. Galactosemia: can result in retardation if not controlled at birth with diet; defect in metabolism of carbohydrates.
8. Tay-Sachs Disease: a defect in metabolism of fats; most prevalent in Jewish families; usually causes paralysis, blindness, convulsions, and death by the age of 3.
9. Arthogryphosis: characterized by stiff joints and weak muscles, and missing or smaller than normal limbs; crippling but not progressive.

SOURCE: Eyes on the Special Education: Professional Knowledge Teachers Competency Test by R. S. Ramsey, M. J. Dixon, and G. G. B. Smith, with publication assistance from S. L. Aultman (Director), Southwest Georgia Learning Resources System Center, Albany, Georgia, 1986.

10. Osteogenesis imperfecta: Brittle Bone Disease; bones break very easily; causes crippling and deafness or hearing impairment.

11. Spinal muscular atrophy: progressive degeneration of motor nerve cells; results in clumsiness to paralysis, depending on degree of severity.

12. Congenital blindness.

13. Congenital deafness

14. Tuberous sclerosis: a biochemical disorder causing the growth of tumors on the brain, face, eyes, and internal organs; can result in retardation, blindness, disfigurement, and death.

15. Down's Syndrome: an abnormal number of chromosomes; more common in children of mothers over 40; often results in retardation and is accompanied by physical problems, particularly heart problems.

16. Cretinism: lack of the thyroid hormone; almost always causes retardation.

B. PRENATAL DISORDERS occur during the time of intrauterine development before birth. The most frequently encountered prenatal disorders are:

1. Clubfoot: one foot turned down or turned in; results in physical impairment.

2. Spina Bifida: a congenital defect resulting when the bones of the spine fail to grow together; occurs during the first 30 days of pregnancy; can result in paralysis, mental retardation, and early death, depending on the degree of involvement, but does not necessarily cause retardation or death.

3. Scoliosis (curvature of the spine), lordosis (swayback), and kyphosis (humpback): can cause physical deformities and difficulty in ambulation.

4. Phocomelia (missing or stunted limbs): affect motor activities and-or ambulation, depending on affected limbs; caused by maternal infection, such as Rubella, early in pregnancy, or by the taking of medications such as Thalidomide or other drugs.

5. Deafness or blindness: can result from maternal illnesses such as Rubella early in pregnancy.

6. Hydrocephalus: an excess of cerebrospinal fluid, causing enlargement of the skull and increased pressure on the brain, resulting in retardation.

7. Fetal alcohol syndrome: results in microcephaly, retardation, and stunted growth and other physical abnormalities, including curved spine caused by excessive consumption of alcohol by the mother during pregnancy.

8. Drug dependency at birth: results from the mother using drugs during pregnancy, which also often causes retardation.

9. Cleft lip and palate: incomplete fusion of the upper lip and/or palate, which even if surgically repaired can result in nasality and other speech problems.

10. Rh incompatibility: caused by an incompatibility in the Rh factors in the blood of an Rh- mother and an Rh+ fetus; can result in tissue damage and retardation.

11. Prematurity and/or low birthweight: caused by cigarette smoking or drug usage during pregnancy, or resulting from teenage pregnancy.

C. PERINATAL DISORDERS occur during or at the time of birth. The most common causes of perinatal disorders are:

1. Anoxia, or oxygen deprivation: can cause brain damage (with resulting paralysis, blindness, and learning or behavior disorders); epilepsy (seizures); and cerebral palsy (resulting in gross- and fine-motor impairment and speech defects).
2. Maternal infections, such as syphilis and herpes simplex, which can infect the child before or during birth, resulting in brain damage and retardation.

D. POSTNATAL DISORDERS occur after birth. They include:

1. Encephalitis and meningitis: can result in mental retardation, behavior disorders, or attention disorders.
2. Measles, whooping cough: can result in visual impairment, deafness, hyperactivity, disorders of attention, mental retardation, and behavior disorders.
3. Stroke or brain injury: can result in aphasia and paralysis.
4. Spinal cord injuries; paralysis.
5. Polio: paralysis or muscle weakness.
6. Amputation: due to injury or disease, the effect depends on the limb involved.
7. Retrolental fibroplasia: blindness resulting from excessive oxygen being given to premature infants in incubators.
8. Lead poisoning: can result in retardation; other learning and behavior disorders.
9. Brain tumors: can cause blindness, deafness, gross or fine motor impairment, or retardation.
10. Extreme malnutrition: can stunt growth, cause cretinism, or cause retardation.
11. Immune disorders: (a) Rheumatoid arthritis: causes joint pain and impairs gross and fine motor ability; (b) AIDS (Acquired Immune Deficiency Syndrome): destroys the body's immune system and results in gradually increasing weakness and susceptibility to disease.
12. Leukemia and other childhood cancers: affects the child's general health; treatments often produce weakness and nausea.

Appendix *D*

Tapp Project Regional Centers and Areas of Responsibilities

Northeast Regional Center

Parent Information Center
155 Manchester Street
P.O. Box 1422
Concord, NH 03301
Linda Klausmeyer, TA Coordinator
Judith Raskin, Director

Area Served

Connecticut
Delaware
Maine
Maryland
Massachusetts
New Hampshire
New Jersey
New York
Pennsylvania
Puerto Rico
Rhode Island
Vermont
Washington

Midwest Regional Center

Pacer Center, Inc.
4826 Chicage Avenue
Minneapolis, MN 55417
Paula Goldberg, Co-Director
Polly Edmunds, TA Coordinator
(612) 827-2966

Area Served

Colorado
Illinois
Indiana
Iowa
Kansas
Kentucky
Michigan
Minnesota
Missouri
Nebraska
North Dakota
Ohio
South Dakota
Wisconsin

Provided by Federation for Children, Boston, MA

West Regional Center

Washington State PAVE
6316 South 12th Street
Tacoma, WA 98465
(206) 565-2266
Martha Gentili, Director
Jo Butts, TA Coordinator

Area Served

Alaska
American Territories
Arizona
California
Department of Defense
   Dependent's Schools (DODDS)
Hawaii
Idaho
Montana
Nevada
New Mexico
Oregon
Texas
Utah
Washington
Wyoming

South Regional Center

Parents Educating Parents
Georgia Association for
Retarded Citizens
1851 Ram Runway, #104
College Park, GA 30337
(404) 761-2745
Mildred Hill, Director
Carla Putnam, TA Coordinator

Area Served

Alabama
Arkansas
Florida
Georgia
Louisiana
Mississippi
North Carolina
Oklahoma
South Carolina
Tennessee
Virginia
West Virginia

References

Abeson, A., & Weintraub, F. (1973). The law and that other minority. In N. Kreinberg and S. H. L. Chow (Ed.), *Configurations of change: The integration of mildly handicapped children into the regular classroom.* California: National Institute of Education, 12–44.

Achenbach, T. M., & Edelbrook, C. S. (1981). Behavioral problems and competencies reported by parents of normal and disturbed children aged 4 through 16. *Monographs of the Society for Research in Child Development, 46,* (Serial No. 188).

Adelman, H. S. (1989). Beyond the learning mystique: An interactional perspective on learning disabilities. *Journal of Learning Disabilities, 22*(5), 301–304, 328.

Ager, C. L., & Cole, C. L. (1991). A review of cognitive-behavioral interventions for children and adolescents with behavioral disorders. *Behavioral Disorders, 16*(4). 260–275.

Ainsworth, M. D. S. (1978). *Patterns of attachment.* Hillside, N.J.: Lawrence Erlbaum Associates.

Alberto, P. A., & Troutman, A. C. (1982). *Applied behavior analysis for teachers.* Columbus; OH: Merrill Publishing.

Algozzine, B. (1977). The emotionally disturbed child: Disturbed or disturbing? *Journal of Abnormal Child Psychology, 5,* 205–211.

Algozzine, B. (1990). *Behavior problem management. Educator's resource service.* Gaithersburg, MD: Aspen Publishers.

Algozzine, B., Christenson, S., & Ysseldyke, J. E. (1982). Probabilities associated with the referral to placement process. *Teacher Education and Special Education, 5* 19–23.

Algozzine, B., & Korinek, L. (1985). Where is special education for students with high prevalence handicaps going? *Exceptional Children, 51,* 388–394.

Algozzine, B., & Maheady, L. (1986). When all else fails, teach. *Exceptional Children, 52*(6), 487–300.

Algozzine, B. Morsink, C. V., & Algozzine, K. M. (1988). What's happening in self-contained special eduction classrooms? *Exceptional Children, 55,* 259–265.

Algozzine, B., Ruhl, K., & Ramsey, R. (1991). *Behaviorally disordered? Assessment for identification and instruction* CEC Mini-library. Reston, VA: The Council for Exceptional Children.

Algozzine, B., Schmid, R. E., & Connors, R. (1978). Toward an acceptable definition of emotional disturbance *Behavioral Disorders, 4,* 48–52.

Algozzine, B. R., Schmid, R., & Mercer, C. D. (1981). *Childhood behavior disorders: Applied research and education practice.* Rockville, MD: Aspen.

Algozzine, B., & Ysseldyke. J. E. (1983). Learning disabilities as a subset of school failure: The oversophistication of a concept. *Exceptional Children, 50,* 242–246.

Algozzine, B., & Ysseldyke, J. E. (1986). The future of the LD field: Screening and diagnosis. *Journal of Learning Disabilities, 19,* 394–398.

Algozzine, B., & Ysseldyke, J. E. (1987). Questioning discrepancies: Retaking the first step 20 years later. *Learning Disabilities Quarterly, 10*, 301–312.

Allen, D. (1989). Evaluating solutions, monitoring progress, and revising intervention plans. In M. R. Shinn (Ed.), *Curriculum based measurement: Assessing special students.* New York: Guilford Press.

Allen, L. D., Gottselig, M., & Boylan, S. (1982). A practical mechanism for using free time as a reinforcer in the classroom. *Education and Treatment of Children, 5*(4). 245–253.

Alley, G., & Deshler, D. (1979). *Teaching the learning disabled adolescent: Strategies and methods.* Denver, CO: Love Publishing.

American Psychiatric Association. (1968). *Diagnostic and Statistical Manual of Mental Disorders* (2nd ed.) Washington, D.C.: Author.

Apter, S. J. (1982). *Troubled children, troubled systems.* New York: Pergamon.

Armor, D., Conry-Oseguera, P., Cox, M., King, N., McDonnell, L., Pascal, A., Pauly, E., & Zellman, G. (1976). Analysis of the school preferred reading program in selected Los Angeles minority schools. (Report No. R–2007–LAUSFD). Santa Monica, CA: The Rand Corporation. ERIC Document Reproduction No. ED 130–243).

Baca, L., & Harris, K. C. (1988). Teaching migrant exceptional students. *Teaching Exceptional Children, 20*(4). 32–35.

Baker, K. (1985). Research evidence of a school discipline problem. *Phi Delta Kappan, 66*(7), 482–488.

Bane, M. J., & Ellwood, D. T. (1984a). *The dynamics of children's living arrangements.* Cambridge, MA: Harvard University. (Contract No. HHS–S2A–82). Washington, DC: U.S. Department of Health and Human Services.

Bane, M. J., & Ellwood, D. T. (1984b). *Single mothers and their living arrangements.* Cambridge, MA: Harvard University. (Contract No. HHS–100–82–0038). Washington DC: U.S. Department of Health and Human Services.

Barnes, E., & Knoblock, P. (1973). Openness and advocacy: Teacher attributes for mainstreaming children with special needs. In N. Kienberg, & S. L. Chow (Eds.), *Configurations of change.* San Francisco, CA: Far West Laboratory for Educational Research and Development.

Barrisi, J. (1984). Interstate migrant council. National policy workshop on special education needs of migrant handicapped students. *Proceedings Report.* Denver, CO: Education Commission of the States.

Barsch, R. H. (1968). Perspectives on learning disabilities: The vectors of a new convergence.

Bartoli, J. S. (1989). An ecological response to Cole's interactivity alternative. *Journal of Learning Disabilities, 22*(5), 292–297.

Bateman, B. D. (1974). Educational implications of minimal brain dysfunction. *Reading Teacher, 27*, 662–668.

Bauer, A. M., & Shea, T. M. (1989). *Teaching exceptional students in your classroom.* Boston: Allyn and Bacon.

Beckman, P. J. (1983). Influence of selected child characteristics on stress in the family of handicapped infants. *American Journal of Medical Deficiency, 88*, 150–156.

Belch, P. (1975). The question of teachers' questions. *Teaching Exceptional Children, 1*, 46–47.

Bender, L. (1968). Neuropsychiatric disturbances. In A. H. Keeney & V. T. Keeney. (Eds.), *Dyslexia*, St. Louis, MO: Mosby.

Bender, W. N., & Golden, L. B. (1988). Adaptive behavior of learning disabled and nonlearning disabled children. *Learning Disability Quarterly, 11*, 55–61.

Benniga, J. S. (1988). An emerging synthesis in moral education. *Phi Delta Kappan, 69*(6), 415–418.

Bennion, R. (1983). Why us? In Dougan, Isbell and Vayas Associates (Ed.), *We Have Been There.* Nashville, TN: Abington, 32–40.

Benson, D., Edwards, L., Rosell, J., & White, M. (1986). Inclusion of socially maladjusted children and youth in the legal definition of the behaviorally disordered population: A debate. *Behavioral Disorders, 11*(3), 213–222.

Bereiter, C., & Englemann, S. (1966). *Teaching disadvantaged children in the Preschool.* Englewood Cliffs, NJ: Prentice-Hall.

Berliner, D. C. (1979). Tempus Educare. In P. L. Peterson & H. J. Walberg (Eds.), *Research on teaching: Concepts findings and implications.* Berkeley, CA: McCutchan Publishing.

Berliner, D. C. (1988). The half-full glass: A review of research on teaching. In E. L. Meyen, G. A. Vergason, & R. J. Whelan (Eds.), *Effective instructional strategies for exceptional children.* Denver, CO: Love Publishing.

Berman, P., McLaughlin, M., Bass, G., Pauly, E., & Zelman, G. (1977). Federal programs supporting educational change. Vol. 7: Factors affecting the implementation and continuation. Santa Monica, CA: The Rand Corporation. (ERIC Document Reproduction Service No. ED 140 432)

Bernstein, B. (1961). Social class and linguistic development: A theory of social learning. In A. H. Halsey, J. Flored, & C. A. Anderson (Eds.), *Education, economy and society.* New York: Free Press.

Berres, & Knoblock, P. (Eds.). (1987). *Program models for mainstreaming: Integrating students with moderate to severe disabilities.* Rockville, MD: Aspen Systems.

Bickel, W. E., & Bickel, D. P. (1986). Effective schools, classrooms, and instruction: Implications for special education. *Exceptional Children, 52*(6), 489–499.

Biklen, D., & Zollers, N. (1986). The focus of advocacy in the LD field. *Journal of Learning Disabilities, 19*, 579–586.

Bjorklund, G., & Burger, C. (January, 1987). Making conferences work for parents, teachers and children. *Young Children,* 26–31.

Blackman, H. P. (1989). Special education placement: Is it what you know or where you live? *Exceptional Children, 55*, 459–462.

Blakenship, C. (1985). Using curriculum based assessment data to make instructional decisions. *Exceptional Children, 52*(3), 233–238.

Bly, R. (1990). *Iron John: A book about men.* Reading, MA: Addison Wesley Publishing.

Boder, E., & Jarrico, S. (1982). *The Boder Test of Reading-Spelling Patterns.* New York: Grune & Stratton.

Boeckx, R. L., Postl, B., & Coodin, F. J. (1977). Gasoline sniffing and tetraethyl lead poisoning in children. *Pediatrics, 60*, 140–145.

Bohline, D. S. (1985). Intellectual and affective characteristics of attention deficit disordered children. *Journal of Learning Disabilities, 18,* (10), 604–608.

Bower, E. M. (1969). *Early identification of emotionally handicapped children* (2nd ed.). Springfield, IL: Charles C. Thomas.

Braaten, S., Simpson, R., Rosell, J., & Reilly, T. (1988). Using punishment with exceptional children. *Teaching Exceptional Children, 20*(2), 79–81.

Bracey, G. W. (1991). Why can't they be like we were? *Phi Delta Kappan. 73*(3), 104–117.

Bradley, B. (March, 1988). School: The parent factor. *Parents, 88*, 111–114.

Brady, P. M., Manni, J. L. Winikur. D. W. (1983). Implications of ethnic disproportion in programs for the educable mentally retarded. *The Journal of Special Education, 3*, 295–302.

Brandt, R. (1989). On parents and schools: A conversation with Joyce Epstein. *Educational Leadership, 47*(2), 24–27.

Brandt, R. (1990). Overview: Making connections. *Exceptional Leadership, 47*(5), 3.

Brantlinger, E. A., & Guskin, S. L. (1988). Implications of social and cultural differences for special education. In Meyen, E. L., Vergason, G. A., & Whelan, R. J. *Effective instructional strategies for exceptional children.* Denver, CO: Love Publishing.

Brickland, M. (1976). *Natural healing.* Emmas, PA: Rodale Press.

Brown, A. (1978). Knowing when, where, and how to remember: A problem of meta-cognition. In R. Glasser (Ed.). *Advances in instructional Psychology.* Hillsdale, NJ: Lawrence Erlbaum Associates.

Bruininks, V. L. (1978). Actual and perceived peer status of disabled students in mainstream programs. *The Journal of Special Education, 12,* 51–58.

Bruner, J., Cole, M., Lloyd, B. (1978). *The developing child series.* In S. Farnham-Diggory. (1978). *Learning disabilities: A Psychological Perspective.* Cambridge: Harvard University Press.

Bryan, T. H. (1974). Peer popularity of learning disabled children. *Journal of Learning Disabilities, 7,* 621–625.

Bryan, T. H. (1978). Social relationships and verbal interactions of learning disabled children. *Journal of Learning Disabilities, 11,* 107–115.

Bryan, T., Bay, M., & Donahue, M. (1988). Implications of the learning disabilities definition for the regular education initiative. *Journal of Learning Disabilities, 21*(1), 23–28.

Bryan, T., Donahue, M., & Pearl, R. (1981). Studies of learning disabled children's pragmatic competence. *Topics in Learning and Learning Disabilities. 1,* 29–39.

Bryan, T., Werner, M., & Pearl, R. (1982). Learning disabled students conformity responses to prosocial and antisocial situations. *Learning Disability Quarterly, 5.* 344–352.

Bryen, D. N. (1982). *Injuries into child language.* Boston, MA: Allyn and Bacon.

Buber, M. (1965). *Between man and man.* New York: MacMillan.

Burgan, T. S. (1974). Peer popularity of learning disabled children. *Journal of Learning Disabilities, 7*(7). 621–625.

Buscaglia, L. (1875). *The disabled and their parents: A Counseling Challenge.* Thorofare, N.J., Leo F. Buscaglia.

Bush, W. I., & Waugh, K. W. (1982). *Diagnosing learning problems* (3rd ed.). Columbus, OH: Charles E. Merrill.

Canter, L. (1976). *Assertive discipline: A take charge approach for today's educator.* Seal Beach, CA: Canter and Associates.

Canter, L. (1978). Be an assertive teacher. *Instructor, 88,* 60.

Canter, L. (1989). Assertive discipline: More than names on the board and marbles in a jar. *Phi Delta Kappan, 71*(1), 57–60.

Carbo, M. (1987a). Matching reading styles: Correcting ineffective instruction. *Educational Leadership, 45,* 55–62.

Carbo, M. (1987b). Reading styles research: What works isn't always phonics. *Phi Delta Kappan, 68*(6), 431–435.

Carbo, M., Dunn, R., & Dunn, K. (1986). *Teaching students to read through their individual learning styles.* Englewood Cliffs, NJ: Prentice-Hall.

Carlson, C. I. (1987). Social interaction goals and strategies of children with learning disabilities. *Journal of Learning Disabilities, 20*(5). 306–311.

Carpenter, D. (1985). Grading handicapped pupils: Review and position statement. *Remedial and Special Education, 6*(4), 54–59.

Casey, A., Skiba, R. & Algozzine, B. (1988). Developing effective behavioral interventions. In J. L. Graden, J. E. Zins, & M. J. Curtis (Eds.), *Alternative educational delivery systems: Enhancing instructional options for all students.* Washington, D.C.: National Association of School Psychologists.

Castro, G. & Mastropieri, M. (1986). The efficacy of early intervention programs: A meta-analysis. *Exceptional Children, 5,* 417–424.

Cattermole, J., & Robinson, N. (1985). Effective home school communication—from the parents perspective. *Phi Delta Kappan, 67*(1), 48–50.

Cawley, J. F., Fitzmaurice, A. M., Shaw, R. Kahn, H., Bates, H., III. (1979). LD youth and mathematics: A review of characteristics. *Learning Disability Quarterly,* 29–44.

Cegelka, P., Lewis, R., & Rodriguez, A. (1987). Status of educational services to handicapped students with limited English proficiency: Report of a statewide study in California. *Exceptional Children, 54*(3). 220–227.

Chalfant, J. C. (1985). Identifying learning disabled students: A summary of the National Task Force Report. *Learning Disabilities Focus, 1, 9–20.*

Chalfant, J. C., Pysh, M. V. D., Moultrie, R. (1979). Teacher assistance teams: A model for within—building problem solving. *Learning Disability Quarterly, 2, 85–96.*

Chalfant, J. C., & Scheffelin, M. A. (1969). *Central Processing dysfunction in children: A review of the research.* National Institute of Neurological Diseases and Stroke, Monograph #9. Bethesda, MD: U.S. Department of Health, Education, and Welfare.

Charles, C. M. (1976). *Individualizing instruction.* St. Louis: C. V. Mosby.

Charles, C. M. (1983). *Elementary Classroom management.* New York: Longman.

Charles, C. M. (1989). *Building classroom discipline: From models to practice* (3rd ed.). New York: Longman.

Cheek, E. H., & Cheek, M. C. (1983). *Reading instruction through content teaching.* Columbus, OH: Merrill Publishing.

Children's Defense Fund (1971). *The way we go to school: The exclusion in Boston.* Boston: Beacon Press.

Children's Defense Fund (1990). *Children 1990: A report card, briefing book and action primer.* Washington DC: U.S. Government Printing Office.

Chmelynski. C. (1990). All-Black, all-male classes. *The Educator, 12*(10), 16–18.

Chrispeels, J. H. (1991). District leadership in parent involvement—Policies and actions in San Diego. *Phi Delta Kappan., 72, 367–371.*

Cicci, R. (1983). Disorders of written language. In H. R. Myklebust (Ed.) *Progress in learning disabilities.* New York: Grune & Stratton.

Classroom discipline and lessons in social values. (1990, January 31). *New York Times,* P. 87.

Cleveland, D. W., & Miller, N. B. (1977). Attitudes and life commitments of older siblings of mentally retarded adults: An exploratory study. *Mental Retardation, 15,* 38–41.

Cloward, R. D. (1967). Teenagers as tutors of low achieving children: Impact on tutors and tutees. In V. Allen (Ed.), *Children as teachers: Theory and research in tutoring.* New York: Academic Press.

Coleman, J. M. (1985). Achievement level, social class, and the self-concepts of mildly handicapped children. *Journal of Learning Disabilities. 18*(1), 26–30.

Coleman, M. (1986). *Behavior disorders: Theory and practice.* Englewood Cliffs: Prentice-Hall.

Coleman, J. (1987). Families and schools. *Educational Researcher,* August–September, 31–38.

Coles, G. S. (1989). Excerpts from *The learning mystique: A critical look at "Learning Disabilities".* *Journal of Learning Disabilities, 22*(5). 267–273, 277–278.

Comer, J. P. (1986). Parent participation in the schools. *Phi Delta Kappan, 67*(6), 442–446.

Cooper, H. M. (1989a). *Homework.* White Plains, NY: Longman.

Cooper, H. M. (Nov. 1989b). Synthesis of research on homework. *Educational Leadership, 47*(3), 85–91.

Cooper, J. O., Heron, T. E., & Heward, W. L. (1987). *Applied behavior analysis.* Columbus, OH: Merrill Publishing.

Coles, G. S. (1989). Excerpts from *The Learning Mystique: A critical look at "Learning Disabilities."* *Journal of Learning Disabilities, 22*(5), 267–273, 277.

Cordin, F. S. (1977). Lasting effects of early learners and education: A report from the consortium for longitudinal studies. In Heller, Holtzman, and Messick (Eds.). (1982). *What research and experience say to the teacher of exceptional children: The reasoning ability of mildly retarded learners.* Reston, VA: The Council for Exceptional Children.

Cornett, C. E. (1983). *What you should know about teaching and learning styles.* Bloomington: Phi Delta Kappa. (Phi Delta Kappa Fastback Series #191).

Cott, A. (1972). Megavitamins: The orthomolecular approach to behavioral disorders and learning disabilities. *Academic Therapy, 7,* 245–257.

Cox, R. D., & Gunn, W. B. (1980). Interpersonal skills in the schools: Assessment and curriculum development. In D. P. Rathjier & J. P. Foreyt (Eds.). *Social competence: Interventions for children and adults.* New York: Pergamon Press.

Cremin, L. (1961). *The transformation of the school.* New York: Vintage Books.

Crnic, K. A., & Leconte, J. M. (1986). Understanding sibling needs and influences. In R. Fewell & P. Vadasy (Eds.), *Families of handicapped children: Needs and supports across the life span.* Austin, TX: Pro-Ed., 75–90.

Crocker, A. C. (1981). The involvement of siblings of children with handicaps. In A. Milunsky (Ed.), *Coping with crisis and handicap.* New York: Plenum

Crook, W. G. (1980). Can what a child eats make him dull, stupid, or hyperactive? *Journal of Learning Disabilities, 13,* 53–58.

Crook, W. G. (1989). Dr. Crook discusses hypoglycemia. *Complex carbohydrates promote good health.* Jackson, TN: Professional Books.

Cruickshank, W. M. (1967). *The brain injured child in home, school, and community.* Syracuse: Syracuse University Press.

Cruickshank, W. M. (Spring, 1986). The learning disabled hyperactive child. *Perceptions, 1,* 7–9.

Cruickshank, W. (1981). *Learning disabled children and neurological impairment.* Keynote address to the Association of the New York State Educators of the Emotionally Disturbed, Syracuse, NY.

Cruickshank, W. M., Bentzen, F. A., Ratzelburg, F. H., & Tannhouser, M. T. (1961). A teaching method for brain injured and hyperactive children: A demonstration-pilot study. In W. M. Cruickshank (Ed.), *Syracuse University special education and rehabilitation.* (Monograph Series 6). Syracuse, NY: Syracuse University Press.

Cuenin, L. H., & Harris, K. R. (1986). Planning, implementing, and evaluating time out interventions with exceptional students. *Teaching Exceptional Children, 18*(4), 272–276.

Cummings, S. T. (1976). The impact of the child's deficiency on the father: A study of the mentally retarded and the chronically ill children. *American Journal of Orthopsychiatry, 46,* 246–255.

D'Angelo, D., & Adler, R. C. (1991). Chapter 1. A catalyst for improving parent involvement. *Phi Delta Kappan, 72,* 350–354.

Danielson, L. C., & Bellamy, T. C. (1989). State variations in placement of children with handicaps in segregated environments. *Exceptional Children, 55*(5), 448–455.

Davies, R. (1991). Schools reaching out. *Phi Delta Kappan, 72*(5), 376–382.

Debor, M. (1975). What is to become of Katherine? *Exceptional Children, 41.* 517–518.

Decker, T. W., & Polloway, E. A. (1989). Written language. In G. A. Robinson, J. R. Patton, E. A. Polloway. & L. R. Sargent (Eds.). *Best Practices in Mild Mental Retardation.* Reston, VA: The Division of Mental Retardation Council for Exceptional Children.

de Hirsch, K. (1965). Plasticity and learning disabilities. In J. Hellmuth (Ed.), *Learning disorders* (Vol. I). Seattle, WA: Special Child Publications.

DeLuke, S. V., & Knoblock, P. (1987). Teacher behavior as preventive discipline. *Teaching Exceptional Children, 19,* 18–24.

Dennison, G. (1969). *The lives of children: The Story of the first street school.* New York: Random House.

Deno, E. (1970). Special Education an Developmental Capital. *Exceptional Children, 37,* 229–237.

Deno, S. L. (1985). Curriculum-based measurement: The emerging alternative. *Exceptional Children, 52* (3), 219–232.

Deno, S. L. (1986). Formative evaluation of individual student programs: A new role for school psychologists. *School Psychology Review, 15*(3), 358–374.

Deno, S. (1989). Curriculum-based measurement and special education services: A fundamental and direct relationship. In M. Shinn (Ed.). *Curriculum-based Measurement: Assessing special children.* New York: Guilford Press.

Deno, S. L., & Mirkin. P. K. (1977). *Data-based program modification: A manual.* Reston, VA: Council for Exceptional Children.

Deno, S. Maruyama, G. Espin, C., & Cohen, C. (1990). Educating students with mild disabilities in general education classrooms: Minnesota alternatives. *Exceptional Children. 57*(2). 157–161.

Derr, A. M. (1986). How learning disabled adolescent boys make moral judgments. *Journal 19*(3), 160–164.

Desanctis, S. (1906). On varieties of dementia praecox. *Rivista Sperimentale diFrenlatria, 32,* 141–165.

Deshler, D. D. (1978). Psychoeducational aspects of learning disabled adolescents. In L. Mann, L. Goodman, & J. L. Wiederholt (Eds.), *Teaching the learning disabled adolescent.* Boston, MA: Houghton Mifflin.

Deshler, D. D., Schumaker, J. B. (1983). Social skills of learning disabled adolescents: Characteristics and intervention. *Topics in Learning Disabilities, 3,* 15–23.

Deshler, D. D., Schumaker, J. B., & Lenz, B. K. (1984). Academic and cognitive interventions for LD adolescents: Part I. *Journal of Learning Disabilities. 17*(2), 108–117.

Deshler, D. D., Warner, M. M., Schumaker, J. B., & Alley, G. R. (1983). Learning strategies intervention model: Key components and current status. In J. D. McKinney & L. Feagans (Eds.), *Current topics in learning disabilities.* Norwood, NJ: Ablex.

Dewey, J. (1909). *Moral principles in education.* Boston: Houghton Mifflin.

Diagnostic and statistical manual of mental disorders (3rd ed. rev.) (1987) Washington, DC: American Psychiatric Association.

Diana vs. State Board of Education, Civil No. 70–37 R.F.P. (N. D. Cal, January, 1970).

DiGangi, S. A., Perryman, P., & Rutherford, R. B., Jr. (1990). Juvenile offenders in the 90's: A descriptive analysis. *Perceptions, 25*(4), 5–8.

Dobbins, D. A., & Rarick, G. L. (1977). The performance of intellectually normal and educable mentally retarded boys on throwing accuracy. *Journal of Motor Behavior, 9,* 23–28.

Dougan, T., Isbell, L., & Vegas, P. (Eds.). (1983). *We have been there.* Nashville: Abingdon Press.

Dreikurs, R., Grunwald, B., & Pepper, F. (1982). *Maintaining sanity in the classroom.* New York: Harper & Row.

Dunn, L. (1968). Special education for the mildly retarded—is much of it justifiable? *Exceptional Children, 35,* 5–22.

Dupont, H. (1978). *Counseling and Human Development.* Denver, CO: Love Publishing.

Edgar, E. (1987). Secondary programs in special education: Are many of them justifiable? *Exceptional Children. 53,* 555–561.

Edge, D., & Burton, G. (1986). Helping learning disabled middle school students learn about money. *Journal of Learning Disabilities, 19*(1), 46–51.

Edgerton, R. B. (1979). *Mental retardation.* Harvard, CN: Harvard University Press.

Edmonds, R. (September, 1979). Effective schools for the urban poor. *Educational Leadership. 37,* 15–27.

Edwards, J. (1991). To teach responsibility, bring back the Dalton Plan. *Phi Delta Kappan, 72*(5). 398–401.

Elkind, D. (1982). Parental stresses: Their detrimental effects on the emotional well-being of children. *International Journal of Sociology of the Family, 12,* 275–283.

Elkind, D. (1986). Formal education and early childhood education: An essential difference. *Phi Delta Kappan, 67*(9), 631–637.

Ellis, N. R. (1963). The stimulus trace and behavioral inadequacy. In N. Ellis (Ed.), *Handbook of Mental Deficiency.* New York: McGraw-Hill. England, D. A., &

Embry, L. H. (1980). Family support for handicapped preschool children at risk for abuse. *New Directions for Exceptional Children, 4,* 29–57.

England, D. A., & Flatley, J. K. (1985). *Homework—And why.* Bloomington, IN: Phi Delta Kappa Educational Foundation (Monograph, Fastback 218).

Epstein, M. H., Cullinan, D., & Polloway, E. A. (1986). Patterns of maladjustment among mentally retarded children and youth. *American Journal of Mental Deficiency, 2*(2). 127–134.

Epstein, M. H., Patton, J. R., Polloway, E. A., & Foley, R. (1989). Mild retardation: Student characteristics and services. *Education and Training of the Mentally Retarded, 24,* 7–16.

Erikson, E. (1963). *Childhood and society* (2nd ed.). New York: W. W. Norton.

Espinoza, R. (1988). Working parents, employees, and schools. *Educational Horizons.* Winter, 62–65.

Executive Committee of the Council for Children with Behavior Disorders (1987). Position paper on definition and identification of students with behavioral disorders. *Behavioral Disorders. 13*(1), 9–18.

Fagen, S. (Winter, 1886). Conducting an LSI: A process model. *Perceptions.* 4–5.

Fagen, S. A., Hill, J. M. (1987). Teaching acceptance of frustration. *Teaching Exceptional Children, 19*(4). 49–51.

Fagen, S. A., & Long. N. J. (1975). Teaching children self-control: A new responsibility for teachers. *Focus on Exceptional Children, 7*(8). 1–10.

Fagen, S. A., Long, N. J., & Stevens, D. J. (1975). *Teaching children self-control: Preventing emotional and learning problems in the elementary school.* Columbus, OH: Merrill Publishing.

Fancher, R. E. (1985). *The intelligence men: Makers of the IQ controversy.* New York: W. W. Norton.

Farbe, B. (1963). Interaction with retarded siblings and life goals of children. *Marriage and Family Living, 25,* 96–98.

Farber, B. (1960). Family organization and crisis: Maintenance of integration in families with a severely mentally retarded child. *Monographs of the Society for Research in Child Development, 25* (Serial No. 75).

Farber, B. (1972). Effects of a severely retarded child on the family. In E. P. Trapp & B. P. Himelstein. (Eds.), *Readings on the exceptional child.* New York: Appleton—Century—Crofts. 225–245.

Farley, J. W. (1986). An analysis of written dialogue of educable mentally retarded writers. *Education and Training of the Mentally Retarded, 21*(3), 181–191.

Farnham-Diggory, S. (1978). *Learning disabilities: A Psychological Perspective.* Cambridge: Harvard University Press.

Farrell, E. E. (1908–1909). Special classes in the New York city schools. *Journal of Psycho-Asthenics, 13* (1–4), 91–96.

Featherstone, H. (1980). *A difference in the family.* New York: Basic Books.

Feingold, B. (1975). *Why your child is hyperactive.* New York: Random House.

Feiter, F., & Tokar, E. (1982). Getting a handle on teacher stress—*Educational Leadership. 39*(6) 456–457.

Ferguson, P. M., & Ferguson, D. L. (1987). Parents and professionals. In P. Knoblock (Ed.), *Understanding exceptional children and youth* (pp. 346–388). Boston: Little, Brown.

Fine, E. (1987). Are we preparing adolescents with learning disabilities to cope with social issues? *Journal of Learning Disabilities, 20*(10), 633–635.

Fisher, C. W., Filby, N. N., Marliave, R. S., Cahen, L. S., Dishaw, M. M., Moore, J. E., & Berliner, D. C. (1978). *Teaching behaviors, academic learning time and student achievement.* Final Report of Phase III–B, Beginning Teacher Evaluation Study. (Technical Report V–1). San Francisco, CA: Far West Laboratory for Educational Research and Development.

Fiske, E. B. (1988, February 12). Standardized test scores: Voodoo statistics? *New York Times.*

Flatley, J. K. (1985). *Homework—and Why.* Bloomington, IN: Phi Delta Kappa Educational Foundation. (Phi Delta Kappa Fastback Series #218).

Flood, C. R. (1989). Living with David: Excerpts from the parents diary. *Perceptions, 24*(4). 18–21.

Forness, S. R. (1985). Effects of public policy at the state level: California's impact on MR, LD and ED categories. *Remedial and Special Education. 6.* 36–43.

Forness, S. R., & Kavale, K. A. (1984). A Meta-analysis of the validity of Wechsler scale profiles and recategorizations: Patterns or parodies? *Learning Disability Quarterly, 7,* 136–156.

Forness, S. & Polloway, E. (1987). Physical and psychiatric diagnoses of pupils with mild mental retardation currently being referred for related services. *Education and Training in Mental Retardation, 22*(4), 221–228.

Fowle, C. (1968). The effect of the severely mentally retarded child on his family. *American Journal of Mental Deficiency, 73,* 468–473.

Frankenberger, W. (1984). A survey of state guidelines for identification of mental retardation. *Mental Retardation, 22,* 17–20:

Friedrich, W. N. (1979). Predictors of the coping behavior of the mothers of handicapped children. *Journal of Consulting and Clinical Psychology, 47,* 1140–1141.

Frymier, J., & Gansneder, B. (1989). The Phi Delta Kappa study of students at risk. *Phi Delta Kappan, 71*(2). 142–146.

Fuchs, L. S., & Deno, S. L. (1992). Effects of curriculum within curriculum-based measurement. *Exceptional Children, 58*(3), 232–242.

Fuchs, L., & Fuchs, D. (1986). Effects of systematic formative evaluation: A Meta-analysis. *Exceptional Children. 53*(3). 199–208.

Fuchs, D., & Fuchs, L. S. (1988a). Evaluation of the adaptive learning environments model. *Exceptional Children, 55*(2), 115–127.

Fuchs, D., & Fuchs, L. S. (1988b). Response to Wang and Walberg. *Exceptional Children, 55*(2). 138–146.

Fuchs, D., & Fuchs, L. S. (1989). Effects of examiner familiarity on Black, Caucasian and Hispanic children: A Meta-analysis. *Exceptional Children, 55,* 303–308.

Fuchs, L. S., & Shinn, M. R. (1989). Writing CBM IEP objectives. In M. R. Shinn, *Curriculum-based measurement: Assessing special students.* New York: Guilford Press.

Gage, N. L. (1990). Dealing with the dropout problem? *Phi Delta Kappan, 72*(4). 280–285.

Gallagher, J. J. (1972). The special education contract for mildly handicapped children, *Exceptional Children, 28*(7), 527–535.

Gallagher, P. A. (1988). *Teaching students with behavior disorders: Techniques and activities for classroom instruction* (2nd ed.). Denver, CO: Love Publishing.

Gallagher, J. J., Beckman, P., a Cross, A. H. (1983). Families of handicapped children: Sources of stresses and its amelioration. *Exceptional Children, 50*(1), 10–19.

Gallagher, J. J., Cross, A., & Scharfman, W. (1981). Parental adaptation to a young handicapped child: The father's role. *Journal to the Division for Early Childhood, 3,* 3–14.

Garmen, N. B., & Hazi, H. M. (1988). Teachers ask: Is there life after Madeline Hunter? *Phi Delta Kappan, 69*(9). 669–672.

Gartner, A., & Lipsky, D. K. (1987). Beyond special education: Toward a quality system for all students. *Harvard Educational Review, 57*(4), 367–395.

Garrett, J. E., & Brazil, N. M. (1989). *Categories of exceptionality: A ten-year follow up.* Manuscript submitted for publication.

Gazaway, R. (1969). *The longest mile.* Garden City, NY: Doubleday.

Georgia Department of Education, Program for Exceptional Children. (1986). *Mild mentally handicapped* (Vol. II). Atlanta, GA: Office of Instructional Services, Division of Special Programs, Program for Exceptional Children. Resource manuals for Program for Exceptional Children. Georgia Department of Education (1989). Revised flow chart. (Correspondence from Dr. Joan Jordan, State Director of Special Education.)

Gersten, R., Walker, H., & Darch, C. (1988). Relationship Between teachers' effectiveness and their tolerance for handicapped students. *Exceptional Children, 54*(5). 433–438.

Gickling, E., & Havertape, J. (1981). *Curriculum-based assessment (CBA).* Minneapolis, MN: National school Psychology Inservice Training Network.

Gillie, O. (1980). Burt: The scandel and the coverup. *Supplement to the Bulletin of the he British Psychological Society, 33,* 9–16.

Ginott, H. (1971). *Teacher and child.* New York: Macmillan.

Ginott, H. (1973). Driving children sane. *Today's Education 62*, 20–25.

Ginsburg, H. (1972). *The myth of the deprived child: Poor children's intellect and education.* Englewood, NJ: Prentice-Hall.

Glasser, W. (1985). *Control theory in the classroom.* New York: Perennial Library.

Glavin, J., Quay, H., Annesley, F., & Werry, J. (1971). An experimental resource room for behavior problem children. *Exceptional Children, 38,* 131–138.

Glick, & Norton. (1973). Perspectives on the recent upturn in divorce and remarriage. *Demography. 10,* 301–304.

Glickman, C. D. (1987). Good and/or effective schools: What do we want? *Phi Delta Kappan, 68*(8), 622–624.

Glidewell, J., & Swallow, C. (1968). *The Prevalence of maladjustment in elementary schools.* Chicago, IL: University of Chicago Press.

Gloeckler, T., & Simpson, C. (1988). *Exceptional students in regular classrooms: Challenges, services, and methods.* Mountain View, CA: Mayfield Publishing.

Goldberg, M. F. (1990). Portrait of Madeline Hunter. *Educational Leadership, 47*(5). 41–43.

Goldstein, H. (1974). *Social learning curriculum.* Columbus, OH: Charles E. Merrill.

Goldstein, K. (1942). *After effects of brain injuries in war.* New York: Grune & Stratton.

Goldstein, H. Mischio, G. S., & Minskoff. E. (1969). A demonstration-research project in curriculum and methods of instruction for elementary level mentally retarded children. *Final Report.* Eric Document: ED058–696.

Good, T. L., & Brophy, J. E. (1986). School effects. In M. C. Wittrock (Ed.), *Handbook of research on teaching* (3rd ed.). New York: Macmillan.

Good, R. H., & Salvia, J. (1987). Curriculum bias in published, norm-referenced reading tests: Demonstrable effects. *School Psychology Review, 17,* 51–60.

Goodlad, J. I. (1984). *A place called school.* New York: McGraw-Hill.

Gorham, K. A. (1975). A lost generation of parents. *Exceptional Children, 41,* 521–525.

Gorham, K. A., Des Jardins, C., Page, R., Pettis, E., & Scherber, B. (1976). Effect on parents. In N. Hobbs (Ed.), *Issues in the classification of children* (Vol. 2). San Francisco: Jossey-Bass.

Gough, P. B. (1987). The key to improving schools: An interview with William Glasser. *Phi Delta Kappan, 68* (9), 656–662.

Gould. S. J. (1981). *The mismeasure of man.* New York. NY: W. W. Norton.

Grady, M. P., & Luecke, E. A. (1978). Education and the brain. (Phi Delta Kappan Series #108). Bloomington: Phi Delta Kappa.

Gresham, F. M. (1983). Social validity in the assessment of children's social skills: Establishing standards for social competency. *Journal of Psychoeducational Assessment,* 297–307.

Gresham, F. M. (1989). Utility of cognitive-behavioral procedures for social skills training with children: A critical review. *Journal of Abnormal Child Psychology. 13,* 411–423.

Gresham, F. M. & Reschly, D. J. (1986). Social skill deficits and low peer acceptance of mainstreamed learning disabled children. *Learning Disabilities Quarterly,* (9). 23–32.

Grosenick, J. K., & Huntze, S. L. (1979). *National needs analysis in behavior disorders.* Columbia, MO: University of Missouri, Department of Special Education.

Grossman, F. K. (1972). *Brothers and sisters of retarded children: An exploratory study.* Syracuse, NY: Syracuse University Press.

Grossman, H. J. (1973). *Manual on terminology and classification in mental retardation.* Baltimore: Garamond/Pridemark Press.

Grossman, H. J. (1983). *Classification in mental retardation.* Washington, D.C.: American Association on Mental Deficiency.

Grunwald, P. (1990). The new generation of information systems. *Phi Delta Kappan, 72*(2). 113–114.

Guetzloe, E. (Summer, 1988). Suicide and depression: special education's responsibility. *Teaching Exceptional Children.* 20(4). 25–28.

Guralnick, M. J., & Groom, J. M. (1988). Peer interactions in mainstreamed and specialized classrooms: A comparative analysis, *Exceptional Children, 54*(5). 415–425.

Guskey, T. R. (1990). Integrating innovations. *Educational Leadership, 47*(5), 11–15.

Guttman, B., & Henderson, A. (1987). *A summary of state Chapter 1 participation and achievement information for 1984–85.* Washington, DC: Decision Resources Corporation.

Hagerty, G. J., Abramson, M. (1987). Impediments to implementing a national policy change for mildly handicapped students. *Exceptional Children, 53,* 315–323.

Hahn, A. (1987). Reaching out to America's dropouts: What to do? *Phi Delta Kappan, 69*(4). 256–263.

Hallahan, D., & Cruickshank, W. (1973). *Psychoeducational foundations of learning disabilities.* Englewood Cliffs, NJ: Prentice-Hall.

Hallahan, D. P., & Kauffman, J. M. (1977). Categories, labels, behavioral characteristics: ED, LD, and ENR reconsidered. *Journal of Special Education 11,* 139–149.

Hallahan, D. P., & Kauffman, J. M. (1978). Categories, labels, behavioral characteristics: ED, LD, and ENR reconsidered. *Journal of Special Education, 11,* 139–147.

Hallahan, D. P., & Kauffman, J. M. (1982). *Exceptional children: Introduction to special education* (3rd ed.). Englewood Cliffs, N.J.: Prentice-Hall.

Hallahan, D. P., & Kauffman, J. (1986). *Exceptional Children.* Englewood Cliffs, NJ: Prentice-Hall.

Hallenbeck, M., & Beernink, M. (1989). A support program for parents of students with mild handicaps. *Teaching Exceptional Children, 21*(4), 44–47.

Hammill, D. D., Leigh, E., McNutt, G., & Larsen, S. E. (1981). A new definition of learning disabilities. *Learning, Disability Quarterly, 4*(Fall).

Hammill, D. D., & Bartel, N. R. (1986). *Teaching students with learning and behavior problems* (4th ed.). Boston, MA: Allyn and Bacon.

Hammill, D. D., Brown, L., & Bryant, B. (1989). *A Consumer's guide to tests in print.* Austin, TX: Pro-Ed.

Hardman, M. L., Drew, C. J., Egan, M. W., & Wolf, B. (1990). *Human Exceptionality* (3rd ed.). Boston, MA: Allyn and Bacon.

Haring, N. G., & Phillips, E. L. (1362). *Educating emotionally disturbed children.* New York: McGraw-Hill.

Harris, K. R., & Pressley, M. (1991). The nature of cognitive strategy instruction: Interactive strategy instruction. *Exceptional Children, 57,* 392–401.

Hearne, J. D., Cowles, R. V. DeKeyzer, J. O. (1987). Spelling: A brief study of three instructional approaches with learning disabled students. *Reading Improvement, 24*(3), 198–201.

Hebb, D. O. (1966). *A textbook on psychology* (2nd ed.). Philadelphia, PA: W. B. Saunders.

Heller, K., Holtman, N., & Messick, S. (Eds.). (1982) *Placing children in special education: A strategy for equity?* Washington, DC: National Academy Press.

Heller, K., & Monahan, J. (1977). *Psychology and community change.* Homewood, IL: Dorsey Press.

Heller, T. (1930). About dementia infantalis. Reprinted in J. G. Howells (Ed.). (1969). *Modern perspectives in international child psychiatry.* New York: Bruner/Mazel.

Henderson, A. (1987). *The evidence continues to grow: Parent involvement improves student achievement.* Columbia, MD: National Committee for Citizens in Education.

Henderson, A. T. (1988). Parents are a school's best friend. *Phi Delta Kappan. 70*(2), 148–153.

Hendrick, I. G., & MacMillan, D. L. (1987). Coping with diversity in city school systems: The role of mental testing in shaping special classes for MR children in Los Angeles, 1900–1930. *Education and Training in Mental Retardation. 22,* 10–17.

Henley, J. (1987). Discipline, process or product? *The Pointer, 3*(4), 36–39.

Henley, M. (1985). *Teaching mildly retarded children in the regular classroom.* (Phi Delta Kappan Fastback series #220). Bloomington, IN: *Phi Delta Kappan.*

Henley, M. (1986, 1990). Unpublished interviews with parents, Westfield, MA.

Henley, M. (1986). Training teachers to manage the feelings and behavior of emotionally disturbed students. Paper presented at the National Adolescent Conference, Minneapolis, MN.

Henley, M. (1987). Ego function and dysfunction: A guide to understanding discipline problems. *The Pointer, 31*(4), 24–30.

Henley, M. (January, 1991). Unpublished interview with special education teacher, Westfield, Massachusetts.

Hersh, A. (1970). Changes in family functioning following placement of a retarded child. *Social Work, 15,* 93–102.

Hewett, F. M., & Taylor, F. D. (1980). *The emotionally disturbed child in the classroom: The orchestration of success.* Boston, MA: Allyn and Bacon.

Hobbs, N. (1966). Helping disturbed children: Ecological psychological strategies. *American Psychologist, 21,* 1105–1115.

Hobbs, N. (Ed.). (1975). *Issues in the classification of children* (Vol. II). San Francisco: Jossey-Bass.

Hobbs, N. (1978). Perspectives on re-education. *Behavioral Disorders, 2,* 65–66.

Holland, B. V. (1987). Fundamental motor skill performance of non-handicapped and educable mentally impaired students. *Education and Training in Mental Retardation, 22*(3). 197–203.

Holroyd, J. (1974). The questionnaire on resources and stress: An instrument to measure family responses to a handicapped family member. *Journal of Community Psychology, 2,* 92–94.

Holt, J. (1989, November). Learning all of the time. *Parents,* pp. 231–233.

Hops, H. (1983). Children's social competence and skill: Research practices and future directions. *Behavior Therapy, 14,* 3–18.

Horn, J. L. (1924). *The education of exceptional children: A consideration of public school problems and policies in the field of differentiated education.* New York: Century.

Horn, J. L., O'Donnell, J. P., & Leicht, D. J. (1988). Phonetically inaccurate spelling among learning-disabled, head-injured, and nondisabled young adults. *Brain and Language, 33*(1), 55–64.

Houts, P. L. (1977). *The myth of measurability.* New York: Hart Publishing.

Howell, K. W., & Lorson-Howell, K. A. (1990). Fluency in the classroom. *Teaching Exceptional Children, 22*(3), 20–23.

Hresko, W. P., & Reid, D. K. (1980). Five faces of cognition: Theoretical influences on approaches to learning disabilities. *The Forum.* Summer, 14–23.

Hyman, I., & D'Alessandro, J. (1984). Good old fashioned discipline: The politics of punitiveness. *Phi Delta Kappan, 66*(1), 39–45.

Hynd, G. W., & Hynd, C. R. (1984). Dyslexia: Neuroanatomical/nourolinguistic perspectives. *Reading Research Quarterly, 19*(4), 482–498.

Idol, L., Paolucci-Whitcomb, P., & Nevin, A. (1981). *Collaborative Consultation,* Aspen Publishers.

Inhelder, B. (1968). *The diagnosis of reasoning in the mentally retarded.* New York: John Day.

An interview with B. F. Skinner. (1987, August 25). *New York Times,* p. A1.

Jackson, P. W. (1968). *Life in classrooms.* New York: Holt, Rinehart, & Winston.

Jacobs, L. (1984). Cognition and learning disabilities. *Teaching Exceptional Children. 16*(3). 213–216.

Jenkins, J. R. & Heinen, A. (1989). Students' preferences for service delivery: Pullout, in class or integrated model. *Exceptional Children. 55*(6). 516–523.

Jenkins, J. R., & Jenkins, L. M: (1981). *Cross age and peer tutoring: Help for children with learning problems.* Reston, VA: The Council for Exceptional Children.

Jenkins, J. R., Pany, D. (1978). Standardized achievement tests: How useful for special education. *Exceptional Children, 44,* 448–453.

Jenkins, J. R., Pious, C. G., & Peterson D. L. (1988). Categorical programs for remedial and handicapped students: Issues of validity. *Exceptional Children, 55*(2). 147–158.

Jensen, A. R. (1969). How much can we boost IQ and scholastic achievement? Environment, heredity, and Intelligence. *Harvard Medical Review, 39*, 1–123.

Johnson, D. W. (1972). *Reaching out: interpersonal effectiveness and self-actualization.* Englewood Cliffs, NJ: Prentice-Hall.

Johnson, D. W., & Johnson, R. T. (1886). Mainstreaming and cooperative learning strategies. *Exceptional Children. 52*(6). 553–561.

Johnson, D. W., & Johnson, R. T. (1990). Social skills for successful group work. *Educational Leadership, 47*(4). 29–33.

Johnstone, E. R. (1908). The functions of the special class. National Education Association Journal of Proceedings and Address of the 46th Annual Meeting, 114–118.

Jones, F. (1987). *Positive classroom discipline.* New York: McGraw-Hill.

Jones, V. F., & Jones, L. S. (1981). *Responsible classroom discipline: Creating positive learning environments and solving problems.* Boston: Allyn and Bacon.

Jones, V. F., & Jones. L. S. (1986). *Comprehensive classroom management: Creating Positive learning environments* (2nd ed.). Boston: Allyn and Bacon.

Jordan, J. B. (1989). *1988 Special Education Yearbook.* Reston, VA: Council for Exceptional Children. *Journal of Special Education* (1989).

Kamin, L. J. (1977). The polities of IQ. In P. L. Houts (Ed.). *The myth of measurability.* New York: Hart Publishing.

Kanner, L. (1943). Autistic disturbances of affective contact. *Nervous Child, 2.* 217–250.

Kauffman, J. M. (1885). *Characteristics of children's behavior disorders* (3rd ed.). Columbus, OH: Charles E. Merrill.

Kaufmann, J. M., Gerber, M. M., & Semmel, M. I. (1988). Arguable assumptions underlying the regular education initiative. *Journal of Learning Disabilities, 21*(1). 6–11.

Kelly, T., Bullock, L. Dykes, M. K. (1974). *Teacher perceptions of behavioral disorders in children.* Gainesville, FL: Florida Educational Research and Development Council.

Keogh, B. K. (1977). Working together: A new direction. *Journal of Learning Disabilities, 10,* 478–482.

Kephart, N. C. (1971). Foreward. In T. S. Ball (Ed.). *Itard, Sequin,, and Kephart: Sensory education, a learning interpretation.* Columbus, OH: Charles E. Merrill.

Kinsbourne, M., & Caplan, P. J. (1979). *Children's learning and attentional Problems.* Boston, MA: Little, Brown.

Kirk, S. A. (1962). *Educating exceptional children.* Boston, MA: Houghton Mifflin.

Kirk, S. A. (1976). In J. K. Kauffman & D. P. Hallahan, *Teaching children with learning disabilities: Personal perspectives.* Columbus, OH: Charles E. Merrill.

Kirk, S. A., & Kirk, W. D. (1983). On defining learning disabilities. *Journal of Learning Disabilities, 16*(1), 20–21.

Knapp, M. S., Turnbull, B. J., & Shields, P. M. (1990). New directions for educating the children of poverty. *Educational Leadership. 48*(1), 4–8.

Knoblock, P. (1983). Teaching emotionally disturbed children. Dallas, TX: Houghton Mifflin.

Knoblock, P. (1987). *Understanding exceptional children and youth.* Boston: Little, Brown.

Knopf, I. J. (1979). *Childhood Psychopathology.* Englewood Cliffs, NJ: Prentice-Hall.

Kohl, H. (1967). *36 children.* New York: New American Express.

Kohlberg, L. (1973). The claim to moral adequacy of a highest stage of moral judgement. *Journal of Philosophy, 70,* 630–636.

Kohn, A. (1988, November). Suffer the restless children, *The Atlantic Monthly*, pp. 90–100.

Kohn, A. (1991). Caring kids: The role of schools. Phi *Delta Kappan. 72*(7). 496–506.

Koppitz, E. M. (1972–1973). Special class pupils with learning disabilities: A five year follow-up study. *Academic Therapy, 8,* 133–138.

Kounin, J. (1971, 1977). *Discipline and group management in classrooms.* New York: Holt, Rinehart and Winston.

Kraeplin, E. (1923). *Textbook of Psychiatry* (8th ed.). New York: Macmillan.

Kronick, D. (1988). *New approaches to learning disabilities: Cognitive, metacognitive, and holistic.* Philadelphia, PA: Grune & Stratton.

Kuveke. S. (1983). School behaviors of educable mentally retarded children. *Education and Training of the Mentally Retarded. 14*(2). 134–137.

Lambert, N. M. (1988). Perspective on eligibility for and placement in special education programs. *Exceptional Children. 54*(4), 287–304.

Langdon, H. (1983). Assessment and intervention strategies for the bilingual language-disordered student. *Exceptional Children, 50*(1), 37–46.

Lapointe, A. (1986). The state of instruction in reading and writing in U.S. elementary schools. *Phi Delta Kappan, 68* (2). 135–138.

Larivee, B. (1988). Effective strategies for academically handicapped students in the regular classroom. In R. E. Slavin, N. L. Karweit, & N. E. Madden (Eds.), *Effective Programs for students at risk.* Boston: Allyn and Bacon.

Larson, K. A. Gerber, M. M. (1987). Effects of social metacognitive training for enhancing overt behavior in learning disabled and low achieving delinquents. *Exceptional Children, 54*(3), 201–211.

Lasley, T. J. (1989). A teacher development model for classroom management. *Phi Delta Kappan, 7*(1), 36–38.

Lazar, I., & Darlington, R. (1982). Lasting effects of early education: A report from the consortium for longitudinal Studies. *Monograph of the Society for Research in child Development. 47*, (Serial No. 175).

Leitch, L. M., & Tangri, S. S. (1988). Barriers to home-school collaboration. *Educational Horizons*, Winter, 70–74.

Lemeshow, S. (1982). *Handbook of clinical types in mental retardation.* Boston, MA: Allyn and Bacon.

Lerner, J. (1985). *Learning disabilities: Theories, diagnosis, and teaching strategies* (4th ed.). Boston: Houghton Mifflin.

Lerner, J. (1988). *Learning disabled: Theories, diagnosis, and teaching strategies* (5th ed.). Boston, MA: Houghton Mifflin.

LeTendre, M. J. (1391). Improving Chapter 1 programs: We can do better. *Phi Delta Kappan, 72*(8), 577–585.

Levereault, A. H. (1990). Preventive discipline in the secondary school. Unpublished research paper.

Levinson, E. (1990). Will technology transform education or will schools co-opt technology? *Phi Delta Kappan, 72*(2), 121–126.

Lewis, A. C. (1990). Tracking the national goals. *Phi Delta Kappan, 72*(7), 496–506.

Lewis, R. B., a Doorlag. D. H. (1987). *Teaching special students in the mainstream* (2nd ed.). Columbus, OH: Merrill Publishing.

Lickona, T. (1988). Four strategies for fostering character development in children. *Phi Delta Kappan, 69*(6). 419–423.

Lilly, M. S. (Ed.). (1879). *Children with exceptional needs: A survey of special education.* New York: Holt.

Lindsley, O. R. (1964). Direct measurement and prothesis of retarded behavior. *Journal of Education. 147.* 62–81.

Lindsley, O. R. (1990). Precision teaching: By teachers for children. *Teaching Exceptional Children, 22*(3). 10–15.

Lipsky, D., & Gartner, A. (1989). *Beyond separate education: Quality education for all.* Baltimore, MD: Brookes.

Lloyd, J. (1980). Academic instruction and cognitive behavior modification: The need for attack strategy training. *Exceptional Education Quarterly, 1*(1), 53–63.

Lobav, W. Cohens, C., & Lewis, J. (1968). *A study of the non-standard English of Negro and Puerto Rican speakers in New York City.* New York: Columbia University (Research Project No. 3288).

London, P. (1987). Character education and clinical intervention: A paradigm shift for U.S. schools. *Phi Delta Kappan, 68*(9). 667–673.

Long, N. L. (1986). The nine psychoeducational stages of helping emotionally disturbed students through the reeducation process. *The Pointer, 30*(3). 5–20.

Long, N. (1990). Life space interviewing. *Beyond 2*(1), 10–15.

Long, N. J., & Newman. R. G. (1965). Managing surface behavior of children in school. In N. J. Long, W. Morse, & R. G. Newman (Eds.), *Conflict in the classroom*. Belmont, CA: Wadsworth Publishing.

Love, H. (1973). *The mentally retarded child and his family.* Springfield, IL: Charles C. Thomas.

Lovitt, T. C. (1989). *Introduction to learning disabilities.* Boston, MA: Allyn and Bacon.

Lovitt, T. C., Fister, S., Freston, J. L., Kemp, K., Moore, R. C., Schroeder, B., Bauernschmidt. M. (1980). Using precision teaching techniques: Translating research. *Teaching Exceptional Children, 22*(3), 16–18.

Lund, N. J., & Duchan. J. F. (1988). *Assessing children's language in naturalistic contexts.* Englewood Cliffs, NJ: Prentice-Hall.

Lynch, E. W., & Stein, R. C. (1987). Parent participation by ethnicity: A comparison of hispanic, black, and anglo families. *Exceptional Children. 54*(2), 105–111.

Mack, J. H. (1980). An analysis of state definitions of severely emotionally disturbed. Reston, VA: Council for Exceptional Children. (ERIC Document Reproduction Service No. ED 201 135).

MacMillan, D. L. (1989). Incorporating adaptive behavior deficits into instructional programs. In G. A. Robinson, J. R. Patton, E. A. Polloway, & L. R. Sargent (Eds. *Best Practices in mild mental retardation*. Reston, VA: The Division of Mental Retardation Council for Exceptional Children.

MacMillan, D. L., & Bothwick, S. (1880). The new educable mentally retarded population: Can they be Mainstreamed? *Mental Retardation, 18*, 155–158.

Mackeith, R. (1973). Parental reactions and responses to a handicapped child. In F. Richardson (Ed.). *Brian and intelligence* (pp. 131–141). Hyattsville, MD: National Education Consultants.

Maeroff. G. I. (1988). Withered hopes, stillborn dreams: The dismal panorama of urban schools. *Phi Delta Kappan, 69* (9), 632–638.

Maheady, L., Sacca, K. M., & Harper, G. F. (1988). Classwide peer tutoring with mildly handicapped high school students. *Exceptional Children, 55*(1). 52–59.

Mallery, D. (1971). High school students speak—An excerpt. In M. L. Silberman (Ed.). *The experience of schooling.* New York: Holt, Rinehart, and Winston.

Mandelbaum, L. H. (1989). Reading. In G. A. Robinson, J. R. Patton, E. A. Polloway, & L. R. Sargent (Eds. *Best practices in mild mental retardation.* Reston, VA: The Division of Mental Retardation Council for Exceptional Children.

Mandell, & Gold. (1984). Teaching handicapped students. St. Paul, MI: West Publishing.

Mann, L., & Sabatino. D. (1985). *Foundations of cognitive process in remedial and special education.* Rockville, MD: Aspen Systems.

Mannix. J. B. (1960). The number concepts of a group of ESN children. *British Journal of Educational Psychology, 30*, 180–181.

Marchi, J. U. (1971). Comparison of selected Piagetian tasks with the Weschler Intelligence Scale for children as measure of mental retardation. *Dissertation Abstracts International, 31*, 6442A.

Margalit, M., & Shulman, S. S. (1986). Autonomy perceptions and anxiety expressions of learning disabled adolescents. Journal of Learning Disabilities, *19*(5). 291–293.

Margolis, R. J. (1988). *Out of harm's way: The emancipation of juvenile justice.* New York: Edna McConnel Clark Foundation.

Markowitz, J. (1983). *Participation of fathers in early childhood special education programs: An exploratory study of factors and issues.* Washington, DC: George Washington University.

Marshall et al. vs. Georgia. U.S. District Court for the Southern District of Georgia. C.V. 482–233. June 28, 1984.

Marston, D. (1987). Does categorical teacher certification benefit the mildly handicapped child? *Exceptional Children, 53*(5), 423–431.

Marston, D. (1988). The effectiveness of special education: A time series analysis of reading performance in regular and special education settings. *Journal of Education, 21,* 13–26.

Marston, D. B. (1989). A curriculum-based measurement approach to assessing academic performance: What it is and why do it. In M. Shinn (Ed.). *Curriculum-based measurement: Assessing special children.* New York: Guilford Press.

Marston, D., & Magnusson, D. (1985). Implementing curriculum-based assessment in special and regular education settings. *Exceptional Children, 52*(3). 266–277.

Maslow, A. (1966). *The psychology of science.* New York: Harper & Row.

Massachusetts Department of Education (1991). Tracking: It's bad practice to identify ability groups, educators told. *Massachusetts Education Today. 6*(5). 1;7.

Mayron (1979). *Correlates of success in transition of mentally retarded to regular class* (Vols. I and II). Final Report, Pamona, California. Los Angeles, CA: New Psychiatric Institute, Pacific State Hospital. (ERIC Document Nos. EC 081–038 and EC 081–039).

McConaughy, S. H. (1986). Social competence and behavioral problems of learning disabled adolescents. *Journal of Learning Disabilities, 19*(2). 101–106.

McCoy, K. (1987). *Solo Parenting: Your essential guide.* New York: Signet.

McCoy, K. M. & Prehm. H. J. (1887). *Teaching mainstreamed students: Methods and techniques.* Denver, CO: Love Publishing.

McDaniel, T. R. (1986). A primer on classroom discipline: Principles old and new. *Phi Delta Kappan, 68*(1), 63–67.

McDaniel, E. A., & Dibella-McCarthy (1989). Enhancing teacher efficacy in special education. *Teaching Exceptional Children. 21*(4), 34–38.

McFall, R. M. (1982). A review and reformulation of the concepts of social skills. *Behavioral Assessment, 4,* 1–33.

McGinnis, E., & Goldstein, P. (1984). *Skillstreaming the elementary school child: A guide for teaching pro-social skills.* Champaign, IL: Research Press.

McGinnis, E., Goldstein, A. P. (1990). *Skillstreaming in early childhood:. Teaching prosocial skills to the preschool and kindergarten child.* Champaign, IL: Research Press.

McGuffey's Fourth Eclectic Reader (1920). New York: H. H. Vail, 38–39.

McKey, R., Condelli, L., Ganson, H., Barret, B., McConkey, C. Plantz, M. (1985). *The impact of Head Start on children, families, and communities.* Washington, D.C.: DHHHS. Publication #85–31193 (OHDS).

McKinney, J. D., McClure, S., & Feagans, L. (1882). Classroom behavior of learning disabled children. *Learning Quarterly, 5*(1), 45–52.

McLanahan, S. (1983). Family structure and stress: A longitudinal comparison of two-patient and female-headed families. *Journal of Marriage and the Family, 45,* 347–357.

McLoughlin, J. A., & Lewis, R. B. (1986). *Assessing special students* (3rd ed.). Columbus, OH: Charles E. Merrill.

McManis, D. (1970). Seriation and transitivity performance by retarded and average individuals. *American Journal of Mental Deficiency, 74*(6), 384–392.

McWhirter, J. J., McWhirter, R. J., & McWhirter, M. C. (1985). The learning disabled child: A retrospective review. *Journal of Learning Disabilities. 18*(6). 315–318.

Meichenbaum, D. (1977). *Cognitive behavior modification: An integrative approach.* New York: Plenum.

Meichenbaum, D. (1985). Teaching thinking: A cognitive-behavioral perspective. In S. F. Chipman & J. W. Segal (Eds.), *Thinking and learning skills: Research and open questions* (Vol. 2). Hillsdale, N.J.: Lawrence Erlbaum Associates.

Meichenbaum, D., & Goodman, J. (1971). Training impulsive children to talk to themselves: A means of developing self-control. *Journal of Abnormal Psychology. 77,* 115–126.

Menacker, J., Weldon, W., & Hurwitz. E. (1889). School order and safety as community issues. *Phi Delta Kappan. 71*(1), 39–40, 55–56.

Mercer, J. (1973). The pluralistic assessment project. *School Psychology Digest, 2,* 10–18.

Mercer, C. D., & Mercer, A. R. (1985). *Teaching students with learning problems* (2nd ed.). Columbus; OH: Merrill Publishing.

Meyen, E. L., Vergason, G. A., & Whelan, R. J. (Eds. (1988). *Effective instructional strategies for exceptional children.* Denver, CO: Love Publishing.

Meyer, D. J. (1986). Fathers of handicapped children. In R. Fewell and P. Vadasy (Eds.). *Families of handicapped children: Needs and supports across the life span* (pp. 121–148). Austin, TX: Pro-Ed.

Meyers, C. E., MacMillian, D. L., & Yoshida, R. K. (1975). *Correlates of success in transition of mentally retarded to regular class. Volume I and II: Final report.* Los Angeles, CA: New Psychiatric Institute Pacific State Hospital (ERIC documents EC 081–038 & EC 081–039).

Miller, L. G. (1968). Toward a greater understanding of the parents of the mentally retarded. *Journal of Pediatrics, 73,* 699–705.

Miller, T. L., & Davis, E. E. (1982). The mildly handicapped: A rationale. In T. L. Miller and E. E. Davis (Eds.), *The mildly handicapped student.* New York: Grune and Stratton.

Mills v. the Board of Education of the District of Columbia, 348F. Supp. 866 (D.C. 1972).

Mitchell, P. B. (1988). Tower of Babel or shared vision. *Teaching Exceptional Children, 21*(1), 49–50.

Moore, B. C., & Moore, S. M. (1977). *Mental retardation: Causes and prevention.* Columbus, OH: Charles E. Merrill Publishing.

Moores, D. F. (1982). *Educating the deaf: Psychology, principles. and practices* (2nd ed.). Boston: Houghton Mifflin.

Morse, W. C. (1985). *Pursuit of excellence for educating the behavior disordered.* Paper presented at the Midwest Symposium for Leadership in Behavioral Disorders. Kansas City, MO.

Morse, W. (1987). Introduction. *Teaching Exceptional Children, 19*(4), 4–6.

Morsink, C. V. (1984). *Teaching special needs students in regular classrooms.* Boston: Little Brown.

Morsink, C. V., Thomas, C. C., & Correa, V. I. (1991). Interactive teaming, consultation and collaboration in special programs. New York: MacMillan Publishing.

Moskowitz, F. C. (1988, July/August). Success strategies: Help for struggling students. *Learning,* 46–47.

Myers, P. I., & Hammill, D. D. (1982). *Learning disabilities: Basic concepts, assessment practices, and instructional strategies.* Austin, TX: Pro-Ed.

Myklebust, H. R. (1964). Learning disorders: Psychoneurological disturbances in childhood. *Rehabilitation Literature. 25,* 354–359.

National Assessment of Reading Progress (1985). *The reading report card: Progress towards excellence in our schools: trends in reading over four national assessments. 1971–1984.* Princeton, NJ: NAEP.

National Committee on Excellence in Education. (1983). *A nation at risk: The imperative for educational reform.* Washington, D.C.: U.S. Government Printing Office.

Neill, M. D., & Medina, N. J. (1989). Standardized testing: Harmful to educational health. *Phi Delta Kappan, 70*(9), 668–697.

Neisworth, J. T., & Greer, J. G. (1975). Functional similarities of learning disability and mild retardation. *Exceptional Children, 42,* 17–21.

Nelson, C. M. (1988). Social skills training for handicapped students. *Teaching Exceptional Children, 20*(4), 19–22

Nelson, M. C., Rutherford, R. B., Jr., & Wolford, B. I. (Eds.) (1987). Special education in the criminal justice system. Columbus, OH: Merrill.

Norwacek, J. E., McKinney, J. D., & Hallahan, D. P. (1990). Instructional behaviors of more and less effective beginning regular and special educators. *Exceptional Children, 57*(2). 140–149.

Noyes, K. G., & McAndrew, G. L. (1971). Is this what schools are for? In M. L. Silberman (Ed.), *The experience of schooling.* New York: Holt, Rinehart, & Winston.

Ohanian, S. (1991). P. L. 94–142: Mainstream or quicksand? *Phi Delta Kappan, 72*(3), 217–222.

Orlich, D. C. (1984). Education reforms: Mistakes, misconceptions, miscues. *Phi Delta Kappan, 70*(7), 512–517.

Ornstein, R. (May, 1978). The split and the whole brain. *Human Nature,* 76–83.

Osman, B. B. (1979). *Learning disabilities: A family affair.* New York: Warner .

Palinesar, A. S. (1982). *Improving the reading comprehension of junior high students through reciprocal teaching of comprehension-monitoring strategies.* Unpublished doctoral dissertation, University of Illinois, Urbana-Champaign.

Pasamanick, B., & Knoblock, H. (1973). The epidemiology of reproductive casualty. In S. Sapir & A. Nitzburg (Eds.), *Children with learning problems.* New York: Brunner/Mazel.

Pate, J. (1963). Emotionally disturbed and socially maladjusted children. In L. Dunn (Ed.). *Exceptional children in the schools.* New York: Holt, Rinehart, & Winston.

Patton, J. R., Cronin, M. E., Polloway, E. A., Hutchinson, D., & Robinson, G. (1989). Curricular considerations: A life skills orientation. In G. A. Robinson, J. R. Patton, E. A. Polloway, & L. R. Sargent (Eds.), *Best practices in mild mental retardation.* Reston, VA: The Division of Mental Retardation Council for Exceptional Children.

Patton, J. R., Kauffman, J. M., Blackbourn, J. M., & Brown. B. G. (1991). *Exceptional children in focus* (5th ed.). New York: Macmillan.

Paul, J. L., & Epanchin, B. C. (1991). *Educating emotionally disturbed children and youth: Theories and Practices for teachers* (2nd ed.). New York: Merrill Publishing.

Peck, J. R., & Stephens, W. B. (1960). A study of the relationship between behavior of parents and that of their mentally defective child. *American Journal of Mental Deficiency, 64,* 839–844.

Pennsylvania Association for Retarded Children vs. Commonwealth of Pennsylvania, 334 F. Supp. 1257 (E.D. Pa., 1971), 343 F. Supp. 279 (L. D. Pa., 1972).

Perry, J. (1984, August 17). Migrant children may miss special education services. *San Antonio Light.*

Peterson, N. L. (1987). *Early intervention for handicapped and at–risk children.* Denver, CO: Love Publishing.

Phi Delta Kappa Commission on Discipline. (1982). *Handbook for developing schools with mood discipline.* Bloomington, IN: Phi Delta Kappa.

Phillips, V., & McCullough, L. (1990). Consultation based programming: Instituting the collaborative work ethic. *Exceptional Children, 56*(4), 291–304.

Piaget, J. (1950). *The psychology of intelligence.* New York: International Universities Press.

Piaget, J. (1977). *The development of thought: Equilibration of cognitive structures.* New York: Viking Press.

Polloway, E. A., & Epstein, M. H. (1985). Current issues in mild mental retardation: A survey of the field. *Education and Training of the Mentally Retarded, 20,* 171–174.

Polloway, E. A., & Smith, J. D. (1983). Changes in mild mental retardation: Population, programs and perspectives. *Exceptional Children, 50,* 142–157.

Polloway, E. A., Epstein, M. H., Patton, J. R., Cullinan, D., & Luebke, J. (1986). Demographic, social and behavioral characteristics of students with educable mental retardation. *Education and Training of the Mentally Retarded, 21*(1), 27–34.

Polloway, E. A., Patton, J. R., Epstein, M. H., Cullinan, D., & Luebke, J. (1986). Demographic, social, and behavioral characteristics of students with educable mental retardation. *Education and Training of the Mentally Retarded, 21*(1). 27–34.

Polloway, E. A., Patton, J. R., Payne, J. S. Payne, R. A. (1989). *Strategies for teaching learners with special needs* (4th ed.). Columbus, OH: Merrill Publishing.

Polloway, E. A., & Smith, J. D. (1983, October). Changes in mild mental retardation: Population, Programs, and Perspectives. *Exceptional Children, 50*(2). 149–159.

Poplin, M. S. (1989). The reductionistic fallacy in learning disabilities: Replicating the past by reducing the present. *Journal of Learning Disabilities,* 21(7), 389–400.

Prasse, D. P., & Reschly, D. J. (1986). Larry P. A case of segregation, testing, or program efficacy? *Exceptional Children, 52,* 333–346.

Pressley, M., & Harris, K. R. (1890). What we really know about strategy instruction. *Educational Leadership, 48*(1), 31–33.

Price-Bonham, S., & Addison, S. (1978). Families and mentally retarded children: Emphasis on the father. *The family coordinator, 3,* 221–230.

Przychodin, J. (1981). Improving classroom discipline. *Clearing House.* 55(1), 16.

Pugach, M. C., & Johnson, L. J. (1989a). The challenge of implementing collaboration between general and special education. *Exceptional Children, 56*(3), 232–235.

Pugach. M. C., & Johnson, L. J. (1989b). Prereferral interventions: Progress, problems, and challenges. *Exceptional Children.* 56(3). 217–226.

Putnam, J. W., Rynders, J. E., Johnson, R. T., & Johnson, D. W. (1989). Collaborative skill instruction for promoting positive interactions between mentally handicapped and non-handicapped children. *Exceptional Children, 55*(6), 550–558.

Quay, H. C., & Peterson, D. R. (1967). *Manual for the Behavior Problem Checklist.* Unpublished manuscript.

Quay, H., & Peterson, D. (1977). *Manual for Quay-Peterson-Revised.* Unpublished manuscript: Author.

Ralph, J. (1989). Improving education for the disadvantaged: Do we know whom to help? *Phi Delta Kappan.* 70, 395–401.

Ramirez, B. A. (1988). Culturally and linguistically diverse children. *Teaching Exceptional Children, 29*(4), 45–46.

Ramsey, R. S. (1981). *Perceptions of disturbed and disturbing behavioral characteristics by school personnel.* Unpublished doctoral dissertation, University of Florida, Gainesville.

Ramsey, R. S. (1988). *Preparatory guide for special education teacher competency tests.* Boston, MA: Allyn and Bacon.

Ramsey, R. S., Dixon, M. J., & Smith, G. G. B. (1986). *Eyes on the special education: Professional knowledge teacher competency test.* Albany, GA: Southwest Georgia Learning Resources System Center.

Ratekin, N. (March, 1979). Reading achievement of disabled learners. *Exceptional Children,* 45(16), 454–458.

Redl, F. (1971). The concept of the life space interview. In N. Long. W. Morse, & R. Newman (Eds.), *Conflict in the classroom.* Belmont, CA: Wadsworth Publishing.

Redl, F., & Wineman, D. (1951). *Children who hate.* Glencoe, IL: The Free Press.

Redl, F., & Wineman, D. (1957). *The aggressive child.* Glencoe, IL: Free Press.

Reed, E. W., & Reed, S. C. (1965). *Mental retardation: A family study.* Philadelphia: Saunders.

Reed, S., & Sautter, C. R. (1990). Children of poverty, the status of 12 million young children. *Phi Delta Kappa,* K1–K12.

Reid, D. (1978). *Toward the application of development epistemology to the education of exceptional children.* Proceedings of The Eighth Annual Conference on Piagetian Theory and the Helping Professions (8th). Los Angeles, California.

Reid, D. K., & Hresko, W. P. (1980). Thinking about it in that way: Test data and instruction. *Exceptional Education Quarterly, 1*(3), 47–57.

Reid, D. K., & Hresko, W. P. (1981). *A cognitive approach to learning disabilities.* New York: McGraw-Hill.

Reinert, H. (1976). *Children in conflict.* St. Louis, MO: C. V. Mosby.

Renzuilli, J. S., Reis, S. M., & Smith, L. H. (1981). *The revolving door identification model.* Mamsfield Center, CN: Creative Learning.

Research Brief for Teachers (1988). *Curriculum based assessment*. (ERIC/OSEP Special Project). Reston, VA: The Council for Exceptional Children.

Reschly, D. J. (1988). Minority overrepresentation and special education reform. *Exceptional Children, 54*(4), 316–323.

Reschly, D. J. (1989). Incorporating adaptive behavior deficits into instructional programs. In G. A. Robinson, J. R. Patton, E. A. Polloway, & L. R. Sargent (Eds.), *Best practices in mild mental retardation*. Reston, VA: The Division of Mental Retardation Council for Exceptional Children.

Restak, R. M. (1984). *The brain*. New York: Bantam Books.

Reynolds, M. C., & Balow, B. (1971). Categories and variables in special education. *Exceptional Children, 38*(4), 357–366.

Reynolds, W. M. Miller, K. L. (1985). Depression and learned helplessness in mentally retarded and non-mentally retarded adolescents: An initial investigation. *Applied Research in Mental Retardation. 6*(3), 295–306.

Rezmierski, V. E. (1987). Discipline: Neither the steel nor the velvet, but the maturity inside the glove, that makes the difference. *The Pointer, 31*(4), 5–13.

Rhodes, W. C. (1967). The disturbing child: A problem of ecological management. *Exceptional Children. 33*, 449–455.

Rhodes, W. C. (1970). A community participation analysis of emotional disturbance. *Exceptional Children, 37*, 309–314.

Rhodes, W. C., & Tracy, M. L. (1972a). *A study of child variance: Conceptual models* (Vol. 1). Ann Arbor, MI: University of Michigan.

Rhodes, W. C., & Tracy, M. L. (1972b). *A study of child variance: Interventions* (Vol. 2). Ann Arbor, MI: University of Michigan.

Rich, H. L., & Ross, S. M. (1983). Students' time on learning tasks in special education. *Exceptional Children, 55* (6), 508–515.

Ritschl, C. Mongrella, A. J., & Presbie, R. L. (1972). Group time out from rock and roll music and out of seat behavior of handicapped children while riding a school bus. *Psychological Reports, 31*, 967–873.

Ritter, D. (1989). Teachers perceptions of problem behavior in general and special education. *Exceptional Children, 58*(6), 558–564.

Rivers, W. L. (1977). *The disruptive student and the teacher*. Washington, DC: National Education Association.

Roberts, M. (1986). Three mothers: Life span experiences. In R. Fewell & P. Vadasy (Ed.), *Families of handicapped children: Needs and supports across the life span* (pp. 193–218). Texas: Pro-Ed.

Robinson, S. M. (1989). Oral language: Developing pragmatic skills and communicational competence. In G. A. Robinson, J. R. Patton, E. A. Polloway, & L. R. Sargent (Eds.), *Best practices in mild mental retardation*. Reston, VA: The Division of Mental Retardation Council for Exceptional Children.

Robinson, W. A. (1965). The elaborated code in working class language. *Language and Speech, 8*, 243–252.

Robinson, N., & Robinson, H. (1976). *The mentally retarded child*. New York: McGraw-Hill.

Robinson, N., & Robinson, H. (1982). *The mentally retarded child* (2nd ed.). New York: McGraw-Hill.

Roit, M. L., & Pfohl, W. (1984). The readability of P.L. 94–142. Parent materials: Are parents truly informed? *Exceptional Children, 50*(6), 496–504.

Rosenshine, B. V. (1979). Content, time, and direct instruction. In P. L. Peterson & H. J. Walberg (Eds.), *Research on teaching: Concepts, findings, and implications*. Berkeley, CA: McCutchan Publishing.

Rosenshine, B., & Stevens, R. (1984). *Classroom instruction in a reading research*. New York: Longman.

Rourke, B. P. (1989). Cole's learning mystique: The good, the bad, and the irrelevant. *Journal of Learning Disabilities, 22*(5), 274–277.

Rubin, R., & Balow. B. (1871). Learning and behavior disorders: A longitudinal study. *Exceptional Children, 38.* 293–299.

Ryan, E. B., Short, E. J., & Weed, K. A. (1986). The role of cognitive strategy training in improving the academic performance of learning disabled children. *Journal of Learning possibilities, 18.* 521–529.

Sabornie, E. J., & Kauffman, J. K. (1987). Assigned, received, and reciprocal social status of adolescents with and without mild mental retardation. *Education and Training in Mental Retardation, 22*(3), 139–149.

Salend, S. J. (1987). Contingency management systems. *Academic Therapy, 22*(3), 245–253.

Salend, S. J., & Lutz, J. G. (1984). Mainstreaming or mainlining: A competency based approach to mainstreaming. *Journal of Learning Disabilities, 17,* 27–29.

Salvia, J., & Ysseldyke, J. E. (1981). *Assessment in special and remedial education* (2nd ed.). Boston: Houghton Mifflin.

Salvia, J., & Ysseldyke, J. E. (1985). *Assessment in special and remedial education* (3rd ed.). Boston: Houghton Mifflin.

Salvia, J., & Ysseldyke, J. E. (1988). *Assessment in Special and Remedial Education* (4th ed.). Boston: Houghton Mifflin.

Salvia, J., & Ysseldyke, J. E. (1991). *Assessment* (5th ed.). Boston: Houghton Mifflin.

Samuels, S. J., & Miller, N. L. (1985). Failure to find attention differences between learning disabled and normal children on classroom and laboratory tasks. *Exceptional Children. 51,* 358–375.

Sandford, J. A. (1987). Putting parents in their place in public schools. NASSP *Bulletin. 47.* 99–103.

Sarason, S. B., & Doris, J. (1979). *Educational handicap, public policy, and social history.* New York: Free Press.

Schloss, P. J., & Sedlak, R. A. (1986). *Instructional methods for students with learning and behavior problems.* Boston, MA: Allyn and Bacon.

Schroeder, C. S., & Riddle, D. B. (1991). Behavior theory and practice. In J. L. Paul & B. C. Epanchin (Eds.). *Educating emotionally disturbed children and youth: Theories and practices for teachers* (2nd ed.). New York: Merrill Publishing.

Schulte, A. C., Osborne, S. S., & McKinney, J. D. (1990). Academic outcomes for students with learning disabilities in consulting and resource programs. *Exceptional Children, 57*(2), 162–172.

Schultz, E. W., & Heuchen, C. M. (1983). *Child stress and the school experience.* New York: Human Sciences Press.

Schulz, J. B., Carpenter, C. D., & Turnbull, A. P. (1991). *Mainstreaming exceptional students: A guide for classroom teachers.* Boston, MA: Allyn and Bacon.

Schumaker, J. B., & Hazel, J. S. (1984). Social skills assessment and training for the learning disabled: What's on second? Part I. *Journal of Learning Disabilities, 17*(7), 422–431.

Schumaker, J. B., Pederson, C. J., Hazel, J. S., & Meyen, E. L. (1983). Social skills curricula for mildly handicapped adolescents: A review. *Focus on Exceptional Children, 16*(4), 1–16.

Schwartz, L. W. (1979). *Psychopathology of Childhood.* New York, NY: Holt, Rinehart & Winston.

Scott, M. E. (1988). Learning strategies can help. *Teaching Exceptional Children, 20*(3), 30–34.

Scott, J., Wolking, B., Stoutimore, J., & Harris, C. (1990). Challenging reading for students with mild handicaps. *Teaching Exceptional Children, 22*(3), 32–35.

Scruggs, T. E., & Laufenberg, R. (1986). Transformational mnemonic strategies for retarded learners. *Education and Training of the Mentally Retarded, 21*(3). 165–173.

Scruggs, T. E., & Mastropieri, M. A. (1986). Improving the test-taking skills of behaviorally disordered and learning disabled children. *Exceptional Children, 53*(1), 63–68.

Seldes, C. (1985). *The great thoughts.* New York: Ballantine.

Selman, R. L. (1980). *The growth of interpersonal understanding: Developmental and clinical analysis.* New York: Academic Press.

Semmel, M. I., Abernathy, T. V., Butera, G., & Lesar, S. (1991) Teacher perception of the regular education initiative. *Exceptional Children, 58*(1), 3–23.

Senf, G. M. (1978). Implications of the final procedures for evaluating learning disabilities. *Journal of Learning Disabilities, 11,* 124–126.

Seyle, H. (1975). *Stress without distress.* New York: Signet.

Shanker, A. (1988). Joe Clark's school days: Teaching to the tune of a bullhorn. *The New York Times.*

Sheinker, A., Sheinker, J. M., & Stevens, L. J. (1988). Cognitive strategies for teaching the mildly handicapped. In Meyen, E. L., Vergason, G. A., & Whelan, R. J. (Eds.), *Effective instructional strategies for exceptional children.* Denver, CO: Love Publishing.

Sherry, L. (1982). Non-task oriented behaviors of educable mentally retarded, emotionally handicapped, and learning disabled students. *Educational Research Quarterly, 4,* 19–29.

Shinn, M. R. (1986). Does anyone care what happens after the refer-test-place sequence: The systematic evaluation of special program effectiveness. *School Psychology Review. 15,* 49–58.

Shinn, M. (1989a). *Curriculum-based measurement.* New York: Guilford Press.

Shinn, M. R. (1989b). Identifying and defining academic problems: CBM screening and eligibility procedures. In M. Shinn (Ed.), *Curriculum-based measurement: Assessing special children.* New York: Guilford Press.

Shinn, M. R., Ysseldyke, J. E., Deno, S., & Tindal, G. (1986). A comparison of differences between students labeled learning disabled and low-achieving on measures of classroom behavior. *Journal of Learning Disabilities, 19,* 545–552.

Shumaker, J. B., & Deschler, D. D. (1988). Implementing the regular education initiative in secondary schools: A different ball game. *Journal of Learning Disabilities, 21*(1), 36–42.

Sigmon, S. B. (1989). Reaction to excerpts from *The Learning Mystique:* A rational appeal for change. *Journal of Learning Disabilities, 22*(5), 298–300, 327.

Silver, L. B. (1975). Acceptable and controversial approaches to treating the child with learning disabilities. *Pediatrics, 55*(3). 406–415.

Silver, L. B. (1989). Frequency of adoption of children and adolescents with learning disabilities. *Journal of Learning-Disabilities. 22*(5), 325–327.

Silverman, R., Zigmond, N., & Sansome, J. (1981). Teaching coping skills to adolescents with learning problems. *Focus on Exceptional Children, 13*(6), 1–20.

Siperstein, G. N., & Goding, M. J. (1985). Teachers' behavior toward LD and non-LD children: A strategy for change. *Journal of Learning Disabilities, 18* (3), 139–144.

Slate, N. M. (1983). Nonbiased assessment of adaptive behavior; Comparison of three instruments. *Exceptional Children, 50,* 67–70.

Slavin, R. E. (1989a). PET and the pendulum: Faddism in education and how to stop it. *Phi Delta Kappan. 70*(10), 752–758.

Slavin, R. E. (1989b). Students at risk of school failure: The problem and its dimensions. In Slavin, R. E., Karweit, N. L., & Madden, N. A. (Eds.), *Effective programs for students at risk* (P. 319). Boston: Allyn and Bacon.

Slavin, R. E., Karweit, N. C., & Madden, N. A. (1989). *Effective programs for students at risk.* Needham Heights, MA: Allyn and Bacon.

Slavin, R. E., Madden, N. A., & Leavey, M. (1984). Effects of cooperative learning and individualized instruction on mainstreamed students. *Exceptional Children, 50*(5), 434–443.

Smith, C. R. (1991). *Learning disabilities: The interaction of learner, task, and setting.* Boston: Allyn and Bacon.

Smith, C. R. (1983). *Learning disabilities: The interaction of learner, task, and setting.* Boston, MA: Little Brown.

Smith, G. R. (1984). Desegregation and assignment of children to classes for the mildly retarded and learning disabled. *Integrated Education, 28,* 208–211.

Smith, R. A. (1987). A teacher's views on cooperative learning. *Phi Delta Kappan, 68*(9), 663–666.

Smith, S. (1980). *No easy answers: The learning disabled child at school and home.* New York: Bantam Books.

Smith, J. E., & Patton. J. M. (1989). *A resource module on adverse causes of mild mental retardation.* (Prepared for the President's Committee on Mental Retardation).

Smith, T. E. C., Price, B. J., & Marsh, G. E., II. (1986). *Mildly handicapped children and adults.* St. Paul, MN: West Publishing.

Smith-Davis, J. (1989a, April). *A national perspective on special education.* Keynote presentation at the GLRS/ College/University Forum, Macon, Georgia.

Smith-Davis, J. (1989b). Exceptional children in tomorrow's schools. In E. L. Meyen (Ed.), *Exceptional children in today's schools.* Denver, CO: Love Publishing.

Smothers, R. (1987, November 13). Jailed for paddling the paddler. *The New York Times.* P. A1.

Solnit, A. J., & Stark, M. H. (1961). Mourning and the birth of a defective child. *Psychoanalytic study of the child, 16*, 523–537.

Speece, S. L., McKinney, J. D., & Appelbaum, M. I. (1986). Longitudinal development of conservation skills in learning disabled children. *Journal of Learning Disabilities, 19*(5), 302–307.

Sperry, R. W. (1968). Hemisphere deconnection and unity in conscious awareness. *American Psychologist, 23*, 723–733.

Stafford, P., & Klein, N. (1977). Application of Piaget's theory to the study of thinking of the mentally retarded: A review of the research. *The Journal of Special Education. 11*(2).

Stagg, V., & Catron, T. (1986). Networks of social supports for parents of handicapped children. In R. R. Fewell, P. F. Vadsay (Eds.), *Families of handicapped children:, Needs and supports across the life span.* Austin, TX: Pro-Ed.

Stainback, W., & Stainback, S. (1984). A rationale for the merger of special and regular education. *Exceptional Children, 51*(2), 102–111.

Stainback, D., Stainback, W., & Forest, M. (1989). *Educating all students in the mainstream of regular education.* Baltimore, MD: Brookes.

Stainback, W., & Stainback, S. (1984). A rationale for the merger of special and regular education. *Exceptional Children, 51*(2), 102–111.

Stein, K. S., Leinhardt, B., & Bickel, W. (1989). Instructional issues for teaching students at risk. In R. E. Slavin, N. L. Karweit, & N. A. Madden (Eds.)., Boston: Allyn and Bacon.

Stephens, T. (1977). *Teaching skills to children with learning and behavior disorders.* Columbus, OH: Charles E. Merrill Publishing.

Stephens, R. J., & Slavin, R. E. (1991). When cooperative learning improves the achievement of students with mild disabilities: A response to Tateyama-Sniezek. *Exceptional Children, 57*(1), 9–23.

Stephens, T. M., Blackhurst, A. E., & Magliocca, L. A. (1988). *Teaching mainstreamed students* (2nd ed.). New York, NY: Pergamon Press.

Sternberg, R. J. (1990). Thinking styles: Key to understanding performance. *Phi Delta Kappan, 71*(5), 366–371.

Stevens, G. D., & Birch, J. W. (1957). A proposal for clarification of the terminology used to describe brain-injured children. *Exceptional Children, 23*, 346–349.

Stevens, R. J., & Slavin, R. E. (1991). When cooperative learning improves the achievement of students with mild disabilities: A response to Tateyama-Sniezek. *Exceptional Children, 57*(3). 276–280.

Strauss, A., & Lehtinen, L. S. (1947). Psychopathology and education of the brain injured child. New York: Grune & Stratton.

Strawser, S., & Weller, C. (1985). Use of adaptive behavior and discrepancy criteria to determine learning disabilities severity subtypes. *Journal of Learning Disabilities, 18*(4), 205–211.

Strong, R. W., Silver, H. F., Hanson, J. R., Marzano, R. J., Wolfe, P., Dewing, T., & Brock, W. (1990). Thoughtful education: Staff development for the 1990's. *Educational Leadership, 47*(5), 25–29.

Strother, D. B. (1985). Practical applications of research: Classroom management. *Phi Delta Kappan, 66*(10), 725–728.

Swanson, H. L. (1988). Toward a metatheory of learning disabilities. *Journal Learning Disabilities, 21*(4), 196–209.

Talley, R. C. (1979). Evaluating the effects of implementing the system of multicultural pluralistic assessment: A qualitative perspective. *School Psychology Digest, 8,* 71–78.

Tallman, I. (1965). Spousal role differentiation and the socialization of severely retarded children. *Journal of Marriage. and the Family, 27,* 37–42.

Tarver, S. G. (1986). Cognitive behavior modification, direct instruction and holistic approaches to the education of students with learning disabilities. *Journal of Learning Disabilities, 19*(6), 368–375.

Tateyama-Sniezek, K. M. (1990). Cooperative learning: Does it improve the academic achievement of students with handicaps? *Exceptional Children, 57*(2), 426–427.

Taylor, S. J., & Searle, S. J. (1987). The disabled in America: History, policy and trends. In P. Knoblock (Ed.), *Understanding Exceptional Children and Youth.* Boston: Little, Brown.

Telander, R. (1990). Senseless. *Sports Illustrated, 72*(20). pp. 36–49.

Tew, B. J., Lawrence, K. M., Payne, H., & Rawnsley, K. (1977). Marital stability following the birth of a child with spinal bifida. *British Journal of Psychiatry, 131,* 79–82.

The Executive Committee of the Council for Children with Behavioral Disorders (1987). Position on definition and identification of students with behavioral disorders. *Behavioral Disorders, 13*(1), 9–19.

The National Institute of Education (1987).

Thomas, A., & Chess, S. (1977). Temperament and development. New York: Bruner/Mazel.

Thomas, A. M. (1960). Strategies for problem solving: A conversation with Herbert Goldstein about mildly retarded learners. *Education & Training of the Mentally Retarded, 15*(3), 216–223.

Tindal, G. (1385). Investigating the effectiveness of special education: An analysis of methodology. *Journal of Learning Disabilities, 18,* 101–112.

Torgesen, J. K. (1977). Memorization processes in reading disabled children. *Journal of Educational Psychology, 69,* 571–578.

Tucker, J. (1985). Curriculum-based assessment: An introduction. *Exceptional Children, 52,* 199–204.

Turnbull, A. P., & Turnbull, R. H. (1982). Parent involvement in the education of handicapped children: A critique. *Mental Retardation. 20*(3), 115–122.

Umbreit, J., & Ostrow, L. S. (1980). The fetal alcohol syndrome. *Mental Retardation, 18*(3), 109–111.

U. S. Department of Education. (1985). *Tenth Annual Report to Congress on the Implementation of The Education of the Handicapped Act.* Washington, DC: Author.

U.S. Department of Education. (1990). *To assure the free appropriate public education of all handicapped children: Twelfth annual report to Congress on the implementation of The Education of the Handicapped Act.* Washington, DC: Office of Special Education Programs.

Utley, C. A., Lowitzer, A. C., & Baumeister, A. A. (1987). A comparison for the AAMD's definition eligibility criteria and classification schemes with state departments of education. *Education and Training in Mental Retardation, 22*(1), 35–43.

Uzgiris, I. C., & Hunt, J. M. (1966). *Assessment in infancy: Ordinal scales of psychologies development.* Urbana, IL: University of Illinois Press.

Vadasy, P. F. (1986). Single mothers: A social phenomenon and population in need. In R. Fewell and P. Vadasy (Eds.), *Families of handicapped children: Needs and Supports across the life span* (pp. 221–249). Austin, TX: Pro-Ed

Vadasy, P. F., Fewell, R., Meyer, D. J., & Greenberg, M. T. (1985). Supporting the future of handicapped children: Preliminary findings of program young effects. *Analysis and intervention in Developmental Disabilities, 5,* 125–137.

Van Sickle, J. H. (1908–1909). Provision for exceptional children in the public schools. *Psychological Clinic*, 2. 102–111.

Vaughn, S., Bos, C. S., & Lund, K. A. (1986). But they can do it in my room: Strategies for promoting generalization. *Teaching Exceptional Children*, 18(3), 176–180.

Vergason, G. A., & Anderegg, M. L. (1989). Save the baby! A response to 'Integrating the children of the second system.' *Phi Delta Kappan*. 71(1), 61–63.

Villa, R. A., & Thousand, J. S. (1988). Enhancing success in heterogenous classrooms and schools: The powers of partnerships. *Teacher Education and Special Education*, 11(4), 144–154.

Wagschal, P. H. (1984). A last chance for computers in the school. *Phi Delta Kappan*. 66(4), 251–254.

Walker, H., & Rankin, R. (1983). Assessing the behavior expectations and demands of less restrictive settings. *School Psychology Review*, 12, 274–284.

Walker, J. E., & Shea, T. M. (1991). *Behavior management: A practical approach for educators.* New York: MacMillan.

Walker, D. K., Singer, J. D., Palfrey, J. S., Prza, M., Wenger, M., & Butler, J. A. (1988). Who leaves and who stays in special education? *Exceptional Children*. 54(5), 393–402.

Wallace, H. (1972, October). The epidemiology of developmental disabilities. Paper delivered to the Annual Meeting of United Cerebral Palsy, Kentucky.

Wallace, G., & Kauffman, J. M. (1986). *Teaching students with learning and behavior problems* (3rd ed.). Columbus, OH: Merrill Publishing.

Walls, R. T., Werner, T. J., Bacon, F., & Zane, T. (1977). Behavior checklists. In J. D. Cone & R. P. Hawkins (Eds.), *Behavioral Assessment: New directions in clinical psychology*. New York: Brunner/Mazel.

Wang, M. C., & Baker, E. T. (1986). Mainstreaming programs: Design features and effects. *The Journal of Special Education*, 19(4), 503–520.

Wang, M. R., & Birch, J. W. (1984a). Effective special education in regular classes. *Exceptional Children*, 50(5). 391–398.

Wang, M. R., & Birch, J. W. (1984b). Comparison of a full time mainstreaming program and a resource room approach. *Exceptional Children*. 51(1), 33–40.

Wang, M. C., Reynolds, M. C., & Walberg, H. J. (1986). Rethinking special education. *Educational Leadership*, 44(1), 26–31.

Wang, M. C., & Walberg, H. J. (1988). Four fallacies of segregationism. *Exceptional Children*. 55(2), 128–137.

Warner, I. (1991). Parents in touch—District leadership for parent involvement. *Phi Delta Kappan*, 72(5), 372–375.

Weikert, D. P. (1984). *Changed lives: The effect of the Perry preschool project on youths through age 19*. Ypsilanti, MI: High/Scope Educational Research Foundation.

Weinstein, S., & Roschwalb. S. A. (1990). Is there a role for educators in telecommunications policy? *Phi Delta Kappan*, 72(2), 115–117.

Weintraub, M., & Wolf, B. M. (1983). Effects of stress and social supports on mother child interactions in single and two parent families. *Child Development*, 54, 1297–1311.

Weller, C., Strawser, S., & Buchanan, M. (1985). Adaptive behavior: Designator of a continuum of severity of learning disabled individuals. *Journal of Learning Disabilities*, 18(4), 200–203.

Werner, H. (1944). Development of visuo-motor performance on the marble board test in mentally retarded children. *Journal of Genetic Psychology*, 64, 269–279.

Werry, J. S., & Quay, H. C. (1971). The prevalence of behavior symptoms in younger elementary school children. *American Journal of Orthopsychiatry*, 41, 136–143.

Wesson, C. L. (1991). Curriculum-based measurement and two models of follow-up consultation. *Exceptional Children*. 57(3), 246–256.

West, R. P., Young, K. R., & Spooner, F. (1990). Precision teaching: An introduction. *Teaching Exceptional Children*. 22(3), 4–9.

Whelan, R. J., de Saman, L. M., & Fortmeyer, D. J. (1988). The relationship between pupil affect and achievement. In E. L. Meyen, G. A. Vergason, & R. J. Whelan (Eds.), *Effective instructional strategies for exceptional children.* Denver, CO: Love Publishing.

White, O. R. (1986). Precision teaching—precision learning. *Exceptional Children, 52,* 522–534.

White, M. A. (1971). The view from the pupil's desk. In M. L. Silberman (Ed.), *The experience of schooling.* New York: Holt, Rinehart, and Winston.

Whiting, J., & Aultman, L. (1990). *Workshop for Parents* (Workshop materials). Albany, GA: Southwest Georgia Learning Resources System Center.

Wickman, E. K. (1929). *Children's behavior and teachers' attitudes.* New York: The Commonwealth Fund.

Wiederholt, J. (1974). Historical perspectives in the eduction of the learning disabled. In L. Mann & D. Sabatino (Eds.), *The second view of special education.* Philadelphia: Journal of Special Education Press.

Wiggins, G. (1989). A true test: Toward more authentic and equitable assessment. *Phi Delta Kappan. 70*(9), 7.

Wikler, L. (1979). *Single parents of mentally retarded children: A neglected population.* Paper presented at the American Association of Mental Deficiency, Miami, Florida.

Will, M. (1986). *Educating students with learning problems: A shared responsibility.* Washington, DC: U.S. Department of Education.

William T. Grant Foundation Commission on Work, Family and Citizenship (1988). The forgotten half: Non-college bound youth in America. *Phi Delta Kappan, 69*(6), 409–414.

Williams, L. D. (1988). A parent's opinion: Exceptional teachers. *Teaching K–8, 9–10,* 88.

Wilson, C. R. (1983). Teaching reading comprehension by connecting the known to the new. *The Reading Teacher, 36,* 382–390.

Winick, M. (1976). *Malnutrition and brain development.* New York: Exford Press.

Winton, P. J., & Turnbull, A. P. (1981). Parent involvement as viewed by parents of preschool handicapped children. *Topics in Early Childhood Special Education, 1,* 11–19.

Witcher, D. (1988, November). Perspective. *CCBD Newsletter.,* 1.

Wojnilower, D. A., & Gross, A. M. (1988). Knowledge, perception, and performance of assertive behavior in children with learning disabilities. *Journal of Learning Disabilities, 21*(2), 109–117.

Wolford, J. N. (1991, August 11). Discovering Columbus. *The New York Times Magazine,* pp. 25–29; 45–46; 48–49; 55.

Wolking, B. (1991). Personal correspondence.

Wolking, B. (1992). Precision Teaching Graph.

Wong, B. Y. L. (1979). Increasing retention of main ideas through questioning strategies. *Learning Disability Quarterly, 2,* 42–47.

Wong, B. Y. L. (1985). Potential means of enhancing content skills acquisition in learning disabled adolescents. *Focus on Exceptional Children, 17*(5), 1–8.

Wood, M. (1986). *Developmental therapy* (2nd ed.). Austin, TX: Pro-Ed.

Woodward, M. (1959). The behavior of idiots interpreted by Piaget's theory of sensorimotor development. *British Journal of Educational Psychology, 29,* 60–71.

Wyne, M. D., & O'Connor, P. D. (1979). *Exceptional children: A developmental view.* Lexington, MA: D. C. Heath.

Ysseldyke, J. E., & Algozzine, B. (1982). *Critical issues in special and remedial education.* Boston: Houghton Mifflin.

Ysseldyke, J. E., & Algozzine, B. (1984). *Introduction to special education.* Boston: Houghton Mifflin.

Ysseldyke, J. E., & Algozzine, B. (1990). *Introduction to special education* (2nd ed.). Boston, MA: Houghton Mifflin.

Ysseldyke, J. E., Algozzine, B., & Epps, S. (1983). A logical and empirical analysis of current practice in classifying students as handicapped. *Exceptional Children, 50,* 160–166.

Ysseldyke, J. E., Algozzine, B., Shinn, M. R., a McGue, M. (1882). Similarities and differences between low achievers and students classified learning disabled. *The Journal of Special Education, 16*(1), 73–85.

Ysseldyke, J., Algozzine, B., & Thurlow, M. (1983). On interpreting institute research: A response to McKinney. *Exceptional Education Quarterly, 4*(1), 145–147.

Ysseldyke, J. E., Thurlow, M. L., Wotruba, J. W., Nania, P. A. (1990). Instructional arrangements: Perceptions from general education. *Teaching Exceptional Children, 22*(4), 4–8.

Zargona, N. Vaughn, S., & McIntosh, R. (1991). Social skills interventions and children with behavior problems: A review. *Behavior Disorders, 16*(4), 260–275.

Zigler, E. (1978). National crises in mental retardation research. *American Journal of Mental Deficiency, 83*, 1–8.

Zigmond, N., & Baker, J. (1990). Mainstream experiences for learning disabled students (Project Meld): Preliminary report. *Exceptional Children, 57*(2), 176–185.

Zigmond, N., & Miller. S. E. (1986). Assessment for instructional planning. *Exceptional Children. 52*(3). 501–509.

Zigmond, N., Levin, E., & Laurie, T. (1985). Managing the mainstream: An analysis of teacher attitudes and student performance in mainstream high school programs. *Journal of Learning Disabilities, 18*, 505–568.

Zinsmeister, K. (1990). Growing up scared. *The Atlantic, 265*(6). 49–66.

Zucker, S. H., & Polloway, E. A. (1987). Issues in identification and assessment in mental retardation. *Education and Training in Mental Retardation, 22*(2), 69–76.

Index